STUDIES IN INTERNATIONAL INVESTMENT

By the same author

American Investment in British
Manufacturing Industry
(*Allen & Unwin*)

with C. J. Thomas
British Industry
(*Hutchinson*)

Economic Planning and Town Expansion
A Case Study of Basingstoke
(*W.E.A.*)

STUDIES IN INTERNATIONAL INVESTMENT

BY

JOHN H. DUNNING

Professor of Economics
University of Reading

London

GEORGE ALLEN & UNWIN LTD

RUSKIN HOUSE MUSEUM STREET

FIRST PUBLISHED IN 1970

SBN 04 332038 4

PRINTED IN GREAT BRITAIN
in 10 *on* 11*pt Times type*
AT THE PITMAN PRESS
BATH

CONTENTS

FOREWORD

Most of the contributions to this book were originally published in one form or another between Spring 1962 and Autumn 1969. Apart from Chapters 8 and 9, each of the studies has been updated and revised, and Chapter 5 has been substantially enlarged. Two essays – Chapters 2 and 4 – have not been previously published.

I am indebted to the editors of the various journals and reviews in which these studies first appeared for permission to republish them in this volume, and also to Messrs. Weidenfeld and Nicholson for allowing me to use a contribution of mine which first appeared in *Economic Integration in Europe* (ed. G. R. Denton), published by them in June 1969.

Two of the studies of this book were originally co-authored. Mr Max Steuer contributed a major part of Chapter 8 and Professor D. C. Rowan wrote much of the earlier sections of Chapter 9 and Appendix A to Chapter 2. I much appreciate their share in this volume. At one time or another, Mr M. J. Barron, Mr T. C. Coram, Mr R. D. Pearce and Mr F. J. B. Stilwell have provided valuable research assistance.

I wish to thank Mrs P. Powell of the University of Southampton, Miss C. M. Brown of the University of Reading, and the secretarial staff of the University of Western Ontario, Canada, for their most competent typing services. Miss Brown has also been of considerable help to me in preparing this work for the publishers.

Much of the final writing of this book was undertaken at the University of Western Ontario between September 1968 and June 1969. My final word of appreciation is to Professor G. Reuber and the members of the Department of Economics for their kind hospitality during this period, and to the University of Reading – and particularly my friends and colleagues of the Department of Economics – for allowing me the necessary leave of absence.

READING J.H.D.
September, 1969

INTRODUCTION

THE STUDY OF INTERNATIONAL DIRECT INVESTMENT

As a world economic phenomenon of any importance, international direct investment is of comparatively recent origin. In 1950, the value of the stock of direct foreign investment held by US companies was \$11·8 billions, compared with \$7·2 billions in 1935, \$7·6 billions in 1929 and \$3·9 billions in 1914.[1] In the following decade, these investments increased by \$22·4 billions, and at the end of 1967 their total value stood at \$59 billions. World international investment is now rising at twice the rate of world trade, while the value of manufacturing sales produced by US foreign subsidiaries and branches in 1967 was more than five times the exports of US manufacturers. The National Industrial Conference Board has predicted that, by 1975, these same branches and subsidiaries will account for 25 per cent of the total free world gross national product outside the US,[2] while another 10 per cent is likely to be supplied by European and Japanese affilitates. The first chapter in this book traces some of the reasons for the growth of the multi-national company and for other types of capital movement in the twentieth century;[3] it also introduces the reader to a number of topics dealt with, in more detail, in later chapters.

This remarkable expansion in foreign direct investment is having a very substantial impact both on patterns of economic growth of individual business enterprises and on the national economies of investing and recipient countries. Many large US and European companies now derive more than one-half of their profits from their foreign operations,[4] while, of recipient economies, Canada, Australia

[1] C. Lewis, *America's Stake in International Investment*, The Brookings Institution, Washington, 1938.

[2] *U.S. Production Abroad and the Balance of Payments*. NICB, New York, 1966.

[3] For further details see J. W. Vaupel and J. P. Curham, *The Making of Multinational Enterprise*, Harvard University Press, Cambridge (US), 1969, and Economist Intelligence Unit, *The Growth and Pattern of the Multinational Company*, E.I.U., London, 1969.

[4] S. Rose, 'The rewarding strategies of multi-nationalism,' *Fortune*, September 1968.

and a number of less developed countries are substantially dependent on inward investment for their prosperity. The studies in this book touch on a number of the more important aspects, but in no way pretend to be a complete examination of the economics of foreign investment or the multi-national company. As, however, the subject is only now commanding serious attention by economists, it might be helpful to try and identify its main characteristics and briefly describe the lines of research now being pursued. This is the task of this introduction.

The history of direct investment

In 1914, 90 per cent of all international capital movements took the form of portfolio investment – i.e. the acquisition of securities by individuals or institutions issued by foreign institutions, without any associated control over, or participation in their management. It is true that several American and European companies – i.e. Lever, Singer, General Electric, Courtaulds, Nestlés – already owned sizeable foreign manufacturing ventures,[1] but these were the exceptions rather than the rule, and they rarely accounted for a major part of the enterprises' total activities. In a world operating under the gold standard, capital normally moved across national boundaries in response to interest rate differentials. The classical theory of international investment, as propounded by Ricardo, Hume, Mill, Bastable and others, was largely concerned with explaining the transfer process of these capital movements, and their effects on the money supply and level of economic activity of the lending and borrowing countries.[2]

Later, the Keynesian revolution and the economic circumstances of the inter-war period changed the complexion, though not the principles underlying the earlier theories. New approaches were introduced to deal with capital movements under a paper standard, fixed exchange rates, and controls on the trade of both goods and capital; and new ideas – e.g. that the purchasing power generated by the transfer process might be greater or less than the amount of capital actually involved – advanced. But economists still sought to answer basically similar questions as they did in the past, and the theme of Carl Iversen's comprehensive study published in 1936

[1] H. Martyn, *International Business*, The Free Press, New York, 1964, pp. 27 ff.

[2] See C. Iversen, *International Capital Movements*, Oxford University Press, London, 1936.

was little different from that of the classicists nearly a century earlier. Even J. M. Keynes, in his very derogatory remarks about foreign investment, confined his remarks largely to movements in portfolio capital.[1]

Gradually, however, the centre of interest was shifting. The collapse of the world monetary system in 1930 caused a profound change in both attitudes and thinking towards international investment.[2] The immediate consequence of the depression was to curtail the flow of capital movements to a trickle and substantially to reduce the real value of those still outstanding. Compared to a substantial net outflow of capital from the leading capital exporters between 1905 and 1914, and 1919 and 1929, there was a net repatriation of between 1929 and 1939. At the same time, direct investments came through the depression reasonably well and even increased in value:[3] by 1939, most of today's leading multi-national manufacturing corporations had already established – albeit, in a small way – foreign branches and/or subsidiaries.

Since 1930 there has never been a free international capital market, nor have interest rates been solely the outcome of market forces. In consequence, and for political reasons too, investors have remained considerably more cautious in their attitudes to foreign securities than once they were. As Chapter 1 shows, the greater part of private foreign investment today takes the form of the foreign activities of multi-national corporations, while public or semi-public institutions have replaced private investors in supplying funds for those types of projects which previously accounted for the bulk of capital exports in the early nineteenth century.

In recent years, there has been a noticeable recovery in the international bond market: between 1958 and 1968 foreign bond issues in Europe and America recorded a four-fold increase.[4] In addition new markets, e.g. the Eurodollar and Eurobond market, have increased, while existing markets have become more closely integrated

[1] 'Foreign investment and the national advantage,' *The Nation and the Athenaeum*, August 1924.

[2] United Nations, *International Capital Movements during the Inter-war Period*, Lake Success, 1949.

[3] Cleona Lewis, *America's Stake in International Investment*, The Brookings Institution, Washington, 1938.

[4] R. N. Cooper, 'Toward an international capital market?' Paper presented to Conference on *The Mutual Repercussions of North American and Western European Economic Policies*, organized by the International Economic Association Algarve, August/September 1969.

as capital mobility has increased.[1] Nevertheless, private portfolio investment still accounts for less than one-fifth of all international investment. Its movements – both short and long term – can still be explained essentially by use of the tools of international economics. Flows in direct investment are differently determined; it is now recognized that an explanation for these movements lies more in the theory of (the growth) of the firm than in international economics.

Direct and portfolio investment

Let us now illustrate the main distinguishing features of direct foreign investment. First, unlike portfolio investment, direct investment implies the investing unit (usually a business enterprise) purchases the power to exert some kind of control over the decision-taking process of the invested-in unit (again, usually, a business enterprise). This immediately suggests that something other than money capital is (or may be) involved in international direct investment. This might simply be informal managerial or technical guidance; on the other hand it could incorporate the dissemination of valuable knowledge and/or entrepreneurship, in the form of research and development, production technology, marketing skills, managerial expertise, and so on; none of which usually accompanies investment. Where such knowledge is not separately obtainable (e.g. by licensing agreements) and is an important determinant of a company's competitiveness, this may be as crucial a component of direct investment to the host company and country as the capital *per se*, as it will initiate not only an income-generating effect but a 'technological generating' effect which reflects directly in the superior knowledge of the investing country.[2] (Compare, for example, a US investment in the French computer industry with that in the UK cotton textiles industry.) One interesting implication of this difference is that while portfolio capital will normally move to those sectors within the recipient economy which, as revealed by their profitability, have a comparative advantage over their counterparts in the investing country, in the case of much direct investment, capital will flow to those industries in which the investing country (initially) has the comparative advantage but which it is possible

[1] One result of this is a convergence of international interest rates. See Cooper *op. cit.*

[2] This idea is more fully explored in Chapter 8.

for the recipient country to gain. The character of this process, which has recently engaged the attention of trade theorists, is explored in further detail in Chapter 7.

The special features of direct investment, then, are first that it buys, for the investing company, a *power* of control over decision-taking in a foreign enterprise – the extent of which will vary according to its equity participation – particularly in relation to that of other investors.[1] Secondly, it is usually accompanied by the transference of other factor inputs, or the output of such inputs, in the form of knowledge and ideas. In some ways, the multi-national corporation is better conceived as a vehicle for the dissemination of other factor inputs and/or services than a provider of finance. From the viewpoint of the investing country, while portfolio capital is mainly supplied by individuals and institutions to different foreign individuals and institutions through the mechanism of the capital market, direct investment, except where the purchase or part-purchase of an existing enterprise is involved, may be accomplished without any change in ownership at all. Essentially, it represents the vertical or horizontal geographical extension of a firm's activities (see Chapter 1), and must thus be viewed in the light of its overall objectives, of which the expected profit rate of the new offshoots may be only one.

In general, direct investment – particularly direct manufacturing investment – is more likely to promote world economic growth than portfolio investment. This is because it tends to be concentrated in the dynamic and technologically advanced sectors where the knowledge content of the investing firm is superior to that of local competitors. The *distribution* of the gains resulting from the investment between the host and investing country will depend *inter alia* on the extent of competition and Government policy in the host country.[2] Britain, in the nineteenth century, largely invested overseas in those outlets which yielded a safe return, but little capital growth. Outside trade and distribution and certain resource industries, US firms today invest either to exploit certain economic advantages not possessed by competitors (or potential competitors) in host countries, or where the pattern of market growth is likely to follow

[1] A 30 per cent ownership with no other individual shareholder holding more than 10 per cent of the total shareholding is likely to afford a more significant element of control than a 49 per cent shareholding where the remaining shares are held by one enterprise.

[2] For further details see Chapter 7.

that of the US. Not only have these investments, in general, yielded high profits, but a considerable capital appreciation.[1]

Motives and determinants

Since foreign direct investment represents the territorial expansion of business activities, it may be assumed that, in principle at least, it is undertaken to advance the interests of the investing institution – whatever these interests may be. It is true that most firms are influenced in their behaviour by more than one objective, and, sometimes, different values are placed on the same objectives. Moreover, not all firms view their overseas investments in the same light as their domestic investments. For example, one of the earliest theories of foreign direct investment suggested that businessmen were prepared to gamble more with their foreign investments than those at home simply because the former constituted such a small part of their total operations. This is no longer true; in 1967, for example, one-fifth of all plant and equipment expenditure by US manufacturing companies was undertaken by their foreign subsidiaries. It would, then, seem reasonable to argue that behaviour of firms in respect of overseas activities will be broadly influenced by similar objectives as domestic operations and that no specific theory of motivation is required.

There are, however, two qualifications to this statement. The first is that the decision-takers in the foreign subsidiaries may not be the same people as those in the parent companies or subject to the same economic pressures. An obvious example of a possible difference in objectives is where the foreign enterprise is partly owned by local interests, whose motives may not be the same as the foreign shareholders.[2] The second qualification concerns the precise combination of the 'mix' of objectives which make up a firm's utility function, which may vary *inter alia* to the type of investment being made and economic (and other) circumstances. Thus, at certain times, a firm may value security and a low profit relative to uncertain growth and at other times the reverse. Income earned by a sales or distribution venture may be discounted at quite a different rate from that earned by a mining subsidiary. Since the environment facing the firm in different countries will be different it may well follow that its

[1] For details of the return on US and UK investment see Appendix to Chapter 6.
[2] E. Kolde, *International Business Enterprise*, Prentice Hall, 1968.

objectives will not be identical. The behaviour of a subsidiary of a US chemical company in Ghana may not be quite the same as its counterpart in Holland, purely because of the difference in political and/or exchange risks in the two countries.

Most of the literature dealing with the theory of direct foreign investment has, however, been more concerned with the *determinants* of such investment than its objectives. Again, many of these determinants are common to domestic investment, although their value will differ according to economic circumstances. The principles influencing whether a New York based pharmaceutical company sets up a branch plant in California will be much the same as those which it takes into account in deciding whether or not to set up a similar subsidiary in France. There will, however, be certain considerations which apply in the French case and not in the Californian case (and sometimes *vice versa*). For example, free trade exists within the United States but a tariff is imposed on American pharmaceutical imports into France; there is always the possibility of an alteration in the exchange rate between the franc and the dollar; and there are additional political-cum-environmental factors involved in investing in a foreign country which do not apply at a domestic level. In a number of cases too, domestic and foreign investments are complementary to, rather than competitive with, each other, and factors influencing investment abroad may not have any counterpart at home.

Studies so far undertaken on the determinants of foreign direct investment fall into three categories. First, there are those which try to evaluate – mainly from data supplied by individual businesses, the main factors influencing the decision to invest in a particular country and/or industry. The work of Behrman, Basi, Robinson, and the NIBC fall into this group.[1] Though the authors usually attempt to rank the various influences according to their importance, none has quantified their significance in any systematic way, and in some cases, the variables considered (either by the researchers or the enterprises in question) are not only loosely defined but are inter-dependent of each other.[2] It is difficult to summarize the findings of this kind of approach. Investments vary in type; they are under-taken for different reasons, and economic conditions in one country

[1] See sources quoted at end of Chapter 7.

[2] 'Increased profits,' 'expanded foreign demand or market,' 'diversification,' quoted by Behrman in his study published in R. Mikesell (ed.) *U.S. Government and Private Investment Abroad*, University of Oregon Books, Eugene, 1962, are examples of three closely related variables.

are often so different from those in another. Sometimes, too, an investment is made to protect existing markets or avoid losses rather than to make profits;[1] in other cases, it is more aggressively oriented. The determinants of a vertically integrated investment by a manufacturing company in a resource industry may be prompted by completely different factors than an investment by the same company in a subsidiary overseas to produce a similar line of products to those produced at home. The decision-taking process behind any foreign investment is often very complex and time-consuming and involves many different personalities.[2]

The second type of approach is more macro-oriented. This takes, as its starting point, such published data as are available on direct investment by one country either in various countries abroad or in particular industries, and seeks to establish some kind of functional relationship between this and possible determinants. Bandera and White, for example, related US investment in Europe to profitability and growth in real output. Their results are described in some detail in Chapter 7. On similar lines a more econometric examination has been undertaken by Guy von Stevens of the Brookings Institution.[3] Both groups of studies seem to support the 'accelerator principle' of investing overseas, which US economists have found to be dominant with respect to domestic investments,[4] but, at present, data are not sufficiently disaggregated for conclusions of any pragmatic value to be drawn. Other economists have attempted to evaluate the importance of particular variables affecting foreign investment. The work of Balassa, Kreinin and d'Arge on the effects of tariffs and customs unions fall into this category.[5]

The third approach – which runs parallel to the two just described – is perhaps the most interesting intellectually. Essentially, it seeks to explain why foreign direct investment is preferred to other forms of resource allocation. For example, assuming overseas investment is considered worth while, why should it take the form of direct

[1] A. Lamfalussy, *Investment and growth in mature economies*, Basil Blackwell, Oxford, 1961.

[2] Y. Aharoni, *The Foreign Investment Decision Process*, Harvard University Press, Boston, 1966.

[3] 'Fixed investment expenditures of foreign manufacturing affiliates of U.S. firms: theoretical models and empirical evidence,' *Yale Economic Essays*, Vol. 9, No. 1, Spring 1969.

[4] D. W. Jorgenson and C. D. Siebert, 'A comparison of alternative theories of corporate investment behaviour,' *American Economic Review*, Vol. LXIII, September 1968.

[5] Again, see references at end of Chapter 7.

rather than portfolio investment? Second, why should direct investment be preferable to other ways of exploiting a foreign market, e.g. by exports or licensing agreements? Third, what is the cost of foreign investment in terms of forgone investment opportunities at home?

To answer these (and similar) questions let us first assume that a firm has a certain amount of capital available for investment, and that it wishes to secure the highest rate of return on that investment. Then, it follows that it will choose to invest abroad by extending its own operations, rather than investing in a domestic company (or companies) operating in the country in which it is interested, as long as the income it expects to earn will be greater. This will occur whenever the investing company possesses some advantages over its foreign competitor which are not readily available to it and are sufficient to compensate for the disadvantage of operating a subsidiary at a distance. These advantages, as described by Professor Charles Kindleberger in his book *American Business Abroad*[1] may take various forms and include superior technology, access to markets, entrepreneural expertise and experience, economies of integration and so on. A firm will wish fully to exploit these benefits rather than share them with potential competitors, and this encourages them to undertake direct rather than portfolio investment. The more significant the advantages, the greater the likelihood of monopoly profits being earned, and the more a firm is encouraged to engage in direct rather than portfolio investment. Since, over the years, not only have technological advances become the key determinant of most countries' economic progress, but the gap in knowledge between both countries and firms within particular industries has widened, the incentive for direct, *vis-à-vis* portfolio, investment has become increasingly pronounced.

The above hypothesis does not, however, explain why enterprises should exploit their economic and technological advantages *in this particular way*. Why, for example, should direct investment be preferable to *other* means of international involvement, e.g. exports? The traditional theory suggests that where the (additional) cost of producing a certain quantity of output for export (to a particular country), plus distribution and marketing costs, is greater than the cost of producing this same product in the country concerned, it will pay the exporting company to set up local production facilities.[2] This tendency will be accentuated whenever there are external

[1] Yale University Press, New Haven, 1969.

[2] R. Vernon, *Manager in the International Economy*, Prentice Hall, 1968, p. 201.

economies, or spillover effects, of producing abroad, which accrue to the benefit of the investing company. In recent years, too, it has become increasingly difficult for many business enterprises to maintain, let alone advance, their export markets due, partly, to the tariff policy or other forms of import control imposed by host Governments (and/or regional customs unions) and, partly, the ease with which technology and managerial expertise can be obtained by other means than direct investment. This point is elaborated upon in various chapters of this book, and is most frequently cited by businessmen as one of the key determinants of overseas investment.

International direct investment is, then, only likely to occur where there is an imperfect market in the dissemination of knowledge, and where it is not profitable to exploit the foreign markets in question by alternative means.[1] There is, however, a third type of opportunity cost of foreign investment which still needs to be considered, viz. the return which could have been made had the capital been utilized domestically. Chapters 3 and 4 deal, in some detail, with this issue in so far as British experience is concerned. From the viewpoint of the individual enterprise, both foreign and domestic investment will be profitable as long as the expected income from each exceeds the borrowing costs involved. Assuming that there is complete mobility of capital, this implies that, in equilibrium, subject to a discount for risk, the marginal return on foreign investment should be equal to that of home investment. Where, however, there are constraints on the outlets for investment within the investing country, businessmen may invest more overseas than they might otherwise do if such restrictions were removed. The ease of capital mobility and Government policy are, perhaps, the two most important factors influencing the level and structure of domestic investment and, thus, indirectly the level and direction of investment overseas. Most certainly, there is powerful evidence to suggest that domestic economic conditions do influence the rate of investment abroad. In the mid-1950s, for example, the share of new manufacturing investment (undertaken by US companies at home and abroad) accounted

[1] For an interesting discussion of the comparative advantages of direct investment and licensing agreements and an explanation of why businessmen in host countries might discount future income streams from an investment differently from non-resident investors, see R. Z. Aliber, *The Theory of Direct Foreign Investment and the International Capital Market*, paper given to C. K. Kindleberger's seminar on the International Corporation at the Sloane School of Management, Boston, Spring 1969.

for by the European subsidiaries of such companies rapidly expanding, as profit rates and growth prospects in Europe were so much more favourable than those in the US. More recently, improved domestic economic conditions and restrictive Government measures towards foreign investment have caused a deflection of new investment from Europe to domestic outlets. (See Chapter 7.)

To conclude our brief discussion of the *determinants* of foreign investment, mention should be made of the work now being undertaken on the relationship between international trade and international investment. One approach, pioneered by Raymond Vernon and his colleagues at Harvard, suggests that US direct investment in manufacturing industry is part and parcel of a cycle in the goods it trades, and a means of ensuring the US's competitive position in the products it innovates;[1] and that – over time – investment is both influenced by and influences the structure of world trade. We discuss this and related theories in Chapter 7, although, at this point, we would observe that these theories are less explanations of *why* foreign direct investment takes place and more an attempt to explain the role of direct investment in the international operations of enterprises, and the relationship between the various strands of these activities.

The subject of international investment today

The study of international direct investment today, then, embraces both international economics and the theory of the business enterprise. As part of the wider discipline of international business, it stands in the same relationship as the economics of the firm does to business administration. Up to this point, indeed, most of the writings on the multi-national company have been the work of business economists or business administrators – notably Kolde, Fayerweather, Farmer and Richman, and Martyn.[2] These, in general, have been more concerned with *functional* questions of finance, ownership, organization, performance management and marketing, and, less with the economics of overseas activities and the broader *environ-*

[1] See particularly R. Vernon, 'International investment and international trade in the product cycle,' *Quarterly Journal of Economics*, Vol. LXXIV, May 1966.

[2] The major texts on the subject include: E. Kolde, *International Business Enterprise*, Prentice Hall, New Jersey, 1968; J. Fayerweather, *Management of International Operations*, McGraw-Hill, New York, 1960; R. N. Farmer and B. M. Richman, *International Business: an Operational Theory*, R. Irwin, Illinois, 1966; H. Martyn, *International Business: Principles and Problems*, The Free Press, New York, 1964.

mental issues.[1] As Professor Kolde points out in his book, international direct investment is – at a micro-level at least – a narrower concept than the study of the multi-national corporation. The former is concerned essentially with the economics of operating overseas activities which involve the transfer of capital, but is only incidentally concerned with organizational or administrative aspects. By contrast, a study of the multi-national corporation is multi-disciplined, and is more interested in the factors – political, legal and sociological as well as economic – influencing the process of decision-taking as such.

It is, however, the macro-economic implications of international direct investment which are currently attracting the most attention today of economists and policy makers. This is sometimes classified as the *environmental* approach, which is concerned with the cost and benefits of the operations of multi-national companies on the national economies of which they are part – be they host or recipient countries. The macro-theory of foreign direct investment has been explored by several economists, notably MacDougall, Simpson, Frankel, Jasay, M. C. Kemp, and Pearce and Rowan[2] – both from the angle of the host and investing countries. Usually these models involve either highly simplified assumptions or, in the case of the more complex models, cannot be tested at the moment because of the absence of appropriate data.

From a more pragmatic viewpoint, there have been a number of issues in recent years, which have focused attention on the macro-economic significance of international direct investment. We give three illustrations. First, in the 1960s, both the United States and the United Kingdom have been concerned about their balance-of-payments position and, in particular, about the impact of capital exports on that position. Governments of both countries have

[1] Two recent exceptions are R. Blough, *International Business Environment and Adaptation*, McGraw-Hill, New York, 1966; R. Vernon, *Manager in the International Economy*, *op. cit*.

[2] G. D. A. MacDougall, 'The benefits and costs of private investment from abroad,' *Economic Record*, Vol. XXXVI, 1960; P. B. Simpson, 'Foreign investment and the national economic advantages: a theoretical analysis,' in *US Government and private investment abroad*, ed. R. Mikesell, University of Oregon Books, Eugene, 1962; M. Frankel, 'Home versus foreign investment: a case against capital exports,' *Kylos*, Vol. XVIII, 1965; A. E. Jasay, 'The social choice between home and foreign investment,' *Economic Journal*, Vol. LXX, March 1960; M. C. Kemp, 'Foreign investment and the national advantage,' *Economic Record*, Vol. XXXVIII, March 1962; I. Pearce and D. C. Rowan, 'A framework for research into the real effects of international capital movements,' *Essays in honour of Marco Fanno*, ed. T. Bagiotti, Padova, 1966.

adopted policies to reduce outward investment as a means of improving the balance of payments in the short run – much to the criticism of business enterprise, which has directed its arguments more to the long-term gains of such investment. Until very recently, little substantive evidence was available to support either (or both) views, but, in 1968, two reports – one British and the other American – were published which systematically attempted to evaluate the balance-of-payments implications both of investing and not investing overseas. These models are discussed in some detail in Chapter 2.[1]

Second, since investment – particularly innovatory investment – is a key component of economic development, and (for different reasons) both industrially advanced and less developed countries are currently seeking means to accelerate their development, the importation of such knowledge capital, via the medium of multi-national corporations, is of considerable interest to host countries. Various studies have already shown that the contribution of foreign subsidiaries to the technological advancement of host countries can be, and often is, an important one;[2] but less desirable effects may also be generated. The role of the multi-national company as a disseminator of knowledge is only now being seriously investigated by the economists. Some of the issues under review are summarized in a British context in Chapter 8.

Thirdly, there is the whole question of the impact of the multinational company on the sovereignty of the nation-states in which its investments are made.[3] This issue is becoming increasingly important with the growing contribution of multi-national enterprises to the output of various economies, and the tendency of such enterprises to become geocentric and more closely integrated in their activities. Moreover, the economic power of such companies is sometimes sufficient to thwart or interfere with Government policy in the host countries whenever the objectives of the multi-national companies conflict with those of the host countries. The welfare

[1] Host Governments are no less concerned with the impact of inward investment of their balance of payments. See, e.g. G. C. Moffatt, 'The foreign ownership and balance-of-payments effects of direct investment from abroad,' *Australian Economic Papers*, June 1967.

[2] See, for example, those of Dunning, Brash and Safarian cited in footnotes to Chapter 7.

[3] An especially good summary of the main issues are discussed in R. Vernon, 'Multinational enterprise and national sovereignty,' *Harvard Business Review*, March/April 1967, and R. Vernon, 'Economic sovereignty at bay,' *Foreign Affairs*, October 1968.

implications of the multi-national companies have recently been analysed by Professor Harry Johnson[1] and is currently the subject of a detailed investigation by Professor Jack Behrman. The issue is not only that the forces controlling decisions taken by subsidiaries of an international enterprise (including Government policies of the investing country) may not always coincide with the economic strategy of the host country, but that these latter can be sidestepped. This might show itself in various ways – e.g. manipulation of intra-group prices, anti-trust legislation, intra-group capital transfers, export-sharing agreements and so on. Some of the issues involved are touched upon in Chapter 7. A more detailed examination is contained in some of the studies of the impact of foreign investment on individual host economies which have appeared in recent years.

There are other fascinating areas of research into the effects of international investment now being pursued. This is a rapidly growing field of study. Indeed, probably more than half the words written on the subject are less than five years old. In so far as some of the contributions in this book were initially written in 1962, the reader will appreciate that they lack a certain amount of refinement and sophistication. The studies are also highly selective in their coverage.

Chapter 1 broadly surveys the role of international capital movements in the twentieth century. The second and third studies look specifically at the costs and benefits of foreign direct investment from the viewpoint of the investing country, taking the UK as a case study. Chapter 4 is an historical essay which, like Chapter 2, has not been published before. *Inter alia* it attempts to construct a series of British exports to the US of capital in the fifty years before the First World War. The following chapter presents the results of some original research by the author into British direct investment in Canada in the years since the last World War, viewed particularly from the aspect of the investing enterprises and country. Chapter 6 is an analysis of the profitability of British enterprise in North America. An Appendix to the chapter makes some comparisons between the character and profitability of UK and US foreign investment.

The final three chapters are concerned with some of the effects of inward investment. Chapter 7 summarizes the impact of UK and US multi-national companies on European economic growth, while the

[1] H. Johnson, *The efficiency and welfare implications of the international corporation*, paper given to the Seminar on The International Corporation for the Sloane School of Management, M.I.T. Boston, Spring 1969.

following study concentrates upon the repercussions of US investment on British technological development. The last chapter has a somewhat different purpose than those preceding it. It attempts to see how far one can get in making comparisons between the profitability and productivity of foreign-owned companies and their domestic competitors. This study is based upon some research undertaken by Professor D. C. Rowan and the author for the National Economic Development Office in the early 1960s. In our opinion, it throws up a number of interesting issues surrounding the performance of US companies in Britain, and indirectly, the causes of some of the UK's industrial difficulties in the last decade or so.[1]

[1] See also R. E. Caves, 'Industrial Efficiency' in R. E. Caves and associates, *Britain's economic prospects*, The Brookings Institution, Washington, 1968.

1
CAPITAL MOVEMENTS IN THE TWENTIETH CENTURY[1]

The half-century prior to the First World War was a period uniquely favourable to the free movement of international capital. There were several reasons for this. In the first place, the world was sharply divided into capital-exporting and capital-importing countries whose needs and opportunities ideally complemented each other; a rapidly increasing demand for loanable funds by a group of nations at or around the 'take-off stage' in their development was matched by a no less remarkable expansion of savings available for foreign investment by the mature industrial nations. Second, during these years there were virtually no impediments to the international mobility of productive factors; indeed, both lending and borrowing countries actively encouraged the migration of capital and people between them. Third, due to the secure anchoring of the world's currencies to gold, there were few foreign exchange problems and no transfer difficulties; at the same time, the institutional machinery through which international investments were arranged was more highly developed and better equipped than its counterpart for financing domestic enterprise. Fourth, the movement of capital was paralleled, on the one hand, by a no less spectacular migration of population and, on the other, by a striking expansion of trade between debtor and creditor countries. While the former gave added stimulus to foreign investment, the latter helped to ensure the ready servicing of its debt. Lastly, these were years of unrivalled political stability, coupled with revolutionary developments in ocean-going transport.

The years to 1914

It was within such a setting as this that the value of world foreign long-term investment rose from under $4 billions in 1864 to $44

[1] First published in *Lloyds Bank Review*, April 1964; since then, amended and updated.

billions in 1913 and that some 60 million people migrated from Europe to the so-called 'regions of recent settlement' (Nurkse 1954). Of the creditor countries, the UK was much the most important, accounting for about three-quarters of all international capital movements up to 1900. Thereafter, her share of new investment fell as the US and Continental Europe became important lenders, but, in 1913, she still accounted for $18 billions of the total stake. At this date, France and Germany held foreign assets worth $9 billions and $5·8 billions respectively. Belgium, the Netherlands and Switzerland had a combined foreign investment of $5·5 billions and the US (though on balance a debtor country) owned credits valued at $3·5 billions (United Nations 1949).[1]

In the main, capital moved abroad for economic reasons, although substantial loans were made by both France and Germany for political and military purposes. Such investments were, however, largely confined to Continental Europe, whereas most other capital exports were much more widely dispersed. In 1913, for example, some two-thirds of British overseas assets were located in the richer primary-producing areas of North and South America and Australasia; 28 per cent was in the older and more densely populated countries of the Middle and Far East and only 6 per cent in Continental Europe. The corresponding ratios for France were 18 per cent, 21 per cent and 61 per cent, and for Germany 32 per cent, 18 per cent and 52 per cent, respectively (Feis 1930).

Of the total long-term international debt outstanding in 1913, the main borrowers were Europe, chiefly Russia and Central Southern Europe ($12 billions), North America ($10·5 billions), Latin America ($8·5 billions), Asia ($6 billions), Africa ($4·7 billions) and Oceania ($2·3 billions).

In a few cases – notably Canada, New Zealand, Denmark and Sweden – foreign investment made a significant contribution to the take-off in development. For the most part, however, it had only a marginal impact, either because it represented a small proportion of domestic savings, or because counteracting influences, such as a rise in population, outweighed any income-raising effects which it might otherwise have generated. Qualitatively, foreign capital was much more important, partly because it was often accompanied by new ideas, technology and entrepreneurship, and partly because, in the

[1] All value figures in this chapter are stated in terms of dollars. Except where otherwise mentioned, other currencies have been converted at the rates of exchange prevailing at the time.

main, it was absorbed by the growth or pre-growth sectors of the recipient country. In 1913, 40 per cent of the British foreign investment portfolio was in railways, one of the most powerful initiators of growth, and 30 per cent in Government or municipal securities (most of which was spent on internal improvements and social overhead capital items). Of the balance, 5 per cent was invested in public utilities and 15 per cent in industry, finance and commerce (Feis 1930). Only 10 per cent took the form of the traditional or 'colonial' type of investment – i.e. mineral or raw material exploitation – which has, perhaps, the least beneficial effects on the development of the host countries apart from that of the export enclaves which it creates (Royal Institute of International Affairs 1937).

Foreign investment was of no less significance to the economy of the creditor countries. The United Kingdom for example, invested overseas the equivalent of 4 per cent of her national income and 40 per cent of her gross capital formation between 1870 and 1913. Indeed, in the last ten years of this period, she exported capital worth 7 per cent of her national income and 75–80 per cent of her capital formation. As mentioned earlier, the financial environment for foreign investment was particularly favourable, as there were no adequate outlets for debt capital at home. This also helps to explain why 85 per cent of the UK investment overseas in 1913 took the form of fixed-interest-bearing securities and was channelled through a chain of specialist banking and issuing houses.

Neither equity portfolio nor direct entrepreneurial capital played an important part in financing overseas enterprises at this time, except in India, where the managing agency system flourished and nearly half of all UK investments were business investments. Probably this pattern of capital exports was typical of the other European lenders as well. By contrast, three-quarters of the $3·5 billions of US foreign assets in 1913 represented direct entrepreneurial investments, and of this amount nearly half was directed to resource exploitation of one kind or another (Lewis 1937).[1]

After the First World War

Even before 1914, certain changes were taking place in the character and industrial distibution of international capital movements.

[1] *The Problem of International Investment*, Royal Institute of International Affairs, 1937. For further details of the nineteenth-century capital movements see Cairncross (1953), Ford (1965), Hobson (1914), Imlah (1958), North (1962), Brinley Thomas (1967), White (1933).

The war not only accelerated this process by dramatically altering the position of the leading participants, but heralded an era which eventually had a fundamental effect on the whole climate of international capital movements. In the 'twenties, however, there were few signs of the upheaval to come, and, by 1929, the total international debt was of the same order as that in 1913. On the face of it, the main change which had occurred was the emergence of the US as the prime lender and the transformation of continental Europe from a substantial creditor into a substantial debtor. Even by 1919, the US had invested $6·5 billions abroad, excluding the large war loans to the Allies. In the following decade, her foreign investments rose by $8·3 billions – about two-thirds of the world total of new investment – raising America's total capital stake in 1930 to $15·7 billions. By contrast, most European countries were forced to relinquish large quantities of their foreign assets during the war; the UK gave up 15 per cent of hers, France over half of hers, and Germany nearly the whole. Germany, in fact, was by far the largest borrower in the 'twenties, and by the end of the decade owed $7·5 billions, mostly to the US. The UK recovered her international status in the late 'twenties, and in 1930 her long-term investments were only fractionally less in value than those in 1913. France was then the third largest international creditor, with investments worth $2·5 billions, while the Netherlands, Switzerland, Belgium and Sweden were also net lenders.

The character of foreign investment of the 1920s differed from that of the earlier period in two other major respects. First, a somewhat larger share, about a quarter, took the form of 'direct' investment, i.e. investment by companies in overseas subsidiaries and branches. But this was about equalled by the proportion of new capital going to finance relief, reconstruction and stabilization programmes in Europe. While the former, with the portfolio investment in primary-producing countries, was largely devoted to income-creating activities and thus helped service its own debt out of increased exports (or reduced imports), this was not the case with the European loans, which were often allocated to 'non-productive' projects.

Investment of the latter kind was no less a feature of loans made to some South American States, for the US had neither the machinery nor the discriminating experience accumulated by the UK in this field, and there was a good deal of extravagant and imprudent lending (Mikesell 1962). Moreover, the US proved an extremely poor market for some of the countries to which she lent capital, such as Germany, whose exports were competitive with, rather than complementary to, the American home economy. This, together with the collapse in raw material and foodstuff prices in the 'twenties, not only reduced the ability of borrowing countries to service their debts but seriously undermined the stability of the international capital market as a whole. A climate of investment so radically different from that of pre-war days, combined with substantial short-term capital movements, powerfully contributed to the world economic collapse of 1931 and its aftermath.[1]

The depression: a dividing line

With this collapse, the whole edifice of the international capital market tumbled and the depression which followed constituted a dividing line in the history of foreign investment. Not only were its immediate effects far more serious than anything which had occurred before – as shown by the wholesale defaults of debtor countries and sales of assets by creditor countries. The crisis itself was but a prelude to a series of events which were cumulatively disastrous for the international savings/investment process as it was then organized. The gold standard and free convertibility of currencies were replaced by exchange controls, and free trade gave way to import restrictions and bilateral trading. Trade in goods fell and the flow of foreign investment was virtually halted; when it was resumed after the Second World War its character was completely different.

As the US was the main supplier of non-resident capital in the 1920s, so it suffered most from the retrenchment which followed. In 1938 America's (gross) overseas investments were worth $3·8 billions less than in 1930; nearly 90 per cent of this fall in value was due to the liquidation or depreciation of portfolio investments. Direct investments proved more resilient and indeed recovered slightly in the later 'thirties. The UK suffered to a lesser degree, due to the wider and better placing of her loans, but with other creditors she, too, was adversely affected by the declining fortunes of the primary countries as they sought to reduce the burden of their debts in various ways.

Unfortunately, such a loss of income only aggravated the position of the creditor countries and forced them to cut back imports from the debtor countries even more. The ultimate effect was to destroy the marketability of portfolio capital, as lenders became suspicious of the credit standing of borrowers who, in turn, were reluctant to

[1] For acomprehensive review of Britain's capital exports in the 1920s see Atkin (1968).

borrow in case they could not service their debts. Indeed, the conditions for international investment in 1939, in a world riddled with tariffs, exchange controls and bilateral trading, were as different from these prevailing in 1914 as it is possible to imagine.

Nevertheless, an estimate of the international investment position in 1938 reveals that aggregate world indebtedness on long-term account at that date amounted to $55 billions. Though this estimate is not directly comparable with earlier ones, it is interesting to relate the position of the main creditor and debtor countries in that year with that in 1913. Table 1 shows the dominating role of the UK in both years, the growing significance of the US and the decline of France and Germany as leading creditor nations. Of the debtor countries (or areas), Canada, Asia and Oceania are seen to have increased their dependence on foreign capital relative to Europe and Africa. Of the *net* creditors, the importance of the UK is even more marked, while Latin America, Asia and Canada are seen to be the major net importers of capital.

Changes during the last war

The war which followed had much the same effect on the foreign investments of the belligerents as did the First World War, save that losses suffered by the leading creditor nations (including the US) were much more devastating. Indeed, in 1945, neither of the two leading lenders of 1938 were net creditors. While there was a slight increase in the long-term assets of the US during the war years, this was more than offset by the increase in American short-term obligations, due both to the expenditure of her Government and armed services abroad and to the accumulation of trade credits by foreigners.

The UK, from being a net creditor of $21·6 billions, emerged from the war owing about as much as she was owed, but within two years had become a net debtor to the tune of $2·6 billions. This dramatic change in Britain's position was due to three main factors: (*a*) the sale of $6·5 billions' worth of long-term investments, (*b*) an increase in long-term obligations (mostly to the US and Canada) of $7·1 billions, and (*c*) an enormous increase in short-term liabilities (almost entirely sterling balances) of $14·1 billions. On long-term account alone, the UK was a *gross* creditor of $20·1 billions and a *net* creditor of $10·8 billions (Lewis 1948). The Netherlands, Belgium, Switzerland, Sweden and Portugal each retained their creditor status in spite of war losses.

On the other side of the balance sheet, there was a marked fall in

TABLE 1

International Investment Position 1913 and 1938

(*a*) Leading Creditor Countries

	Gross Credits				Net Credits	
	1913		1938		1938	
	$000m.	%	$000m.	%	$000m.	%
United Kingdom	18·0	40·9	22·9	43·3	21·6	64·9
France	9·0	20·4	3·9	7·4	3·3	10·0
Germany	5·8	13·2	0·7	1·3	−2·0	−6·0
United States	3·5	8·0	11·5	21·8	4·5	13·5
Belgium, Netherlands and Switzerland	5·5	12·5	7·7	14·6	7·5	22·5
Other countries	2·2	5·0	6·1	11·6	−1·6	−4·8
	44·0	100·0	52·8[1]	100·0	33·3	100·0

(*b*) Leading Debtor Countries

	Gross Debts				Net Debts	
	1913		1938		1938	
	$000m.	%	$000m.	%	$000m.	%
Europe	12·0	27·3	10·3	18·8	—	—
Latin America	8·5	19·3	11·4	20·8	11·3	33·9
United States	6·8	15·5	7·0	12·8	—	—
Canada	3·7	8·4	6·6	12·0	4·7	14·1
Asia	6·0	13·6	11·2	20·4	9·3	27·9
Africa	4·7	10·7	4·0	7·3	3·9	11·7
Oceania	2·3	5·2	4·4	8·0	4·1	12·3
	44·0	100·0	54·9[1]	100·0	33·3	100·0

[1] The discrepancy between the total figures is due to certain inconsistencies in the data reported by investing and recipient countries.

Sources: United Nations, *International Capital Movements during the Inter-War Period*, Lake Success, 1949. C. Lewis, *The United States and Foreign Investment Problems*, Washington, 1948.

the obligations of the debtor nations. The countries of the British Commonwealth reduced their debts by about $12·5 billions, mainly the result of an accumulation of sterling balances arising out of Britain's large war-time expenditures. The Latin American countries similarly benefited from an increased demand for strategic and essential materials by the US. Since their imports rose much less quickly, these latter countries were able to reduce their total foreign indebtedness from $11 billions to $5 billions.

As a result of the war, then, aggregate *net* international obligations (long- and short-term) fell from $25 billions to well under $10 billions. The *gross* value of long-term investments declined rather less, from $55 billions to between $35 and $40 billions.

Expansion since 1945

Since the war, a remarkable resurgence has taken place in international capital movements, the volume of which has risen much faster than that of world trade and industrial production during the last fifteen years. The most comprehensive source of material available is, perhaps, the various United Nations publications on international capital flows, from which the statistics contained in the next few paragraphs have been derived.[1]

In the period 1946 to 1950 the *net* flow of *private long-term capital* from the traditional *capital-exporting* countries averaged $1·8 billions per annum (equal to one-half the average for the 1920s). In the following decade it rose to $2·9 billions per annum, reaching a peak of $3·6 billions in 1958; since then it has fallen somewhat to less than $2 billion in the early 1960s. To these figures must be added the value of *official donations and long-term capital*. While no estimate of the total of these is available for the period 1946/50, in the following ten years such exports averaged $3·4 billions a year, and by 1961/64 were running at the rate of $5·8 billions per annum. This gives a total *net* international investment for the period 1951/60 of $63 billions, or $6·3 billions a year, and for 1961/64 of $31 billions or $7·7 billions a year (United Nations, 1966).

As can be seen from Table 2, the trend of international capital movements moved steadily upwards until 1960, but after that fell

[1] *The International Flow of Private Capital*, 1946/52 (1953), . . . 1953/55 (1956) and . . . 1956/58 (1959); *International Flow of Long-term Capital and Official Donations* 1951/59 (1961), . . . 1959/61 (1963) and . . . 1961/65 (1966), all published by United Nations Department of Economic and Social Affairs, New York.

back to its level in the mid 1950s. Nevertheless, in the two years 1963 and 1964, the average annual flow amounted to $7·6 billion, an amount considerably greater, in real terms, than the corresponding average in the 1920s.

The figures so far quoted refer to the value of *net* capital movements of the *capital-exporting* countries. But a better guide to the role of international investment in world economic development is, perhaps, provided by the value of *gross* capital flows for *all* countries. Unfortunately, data on such flows are available only for the period between 1958 and 1960, and for a group of selected developed countries (which, however, includes all but France and Switzerland

TABLE 2

Net Flow of Long-term Capital and Official Donations from Capital Exporting Countries 1946–64

	Private		*Official (Donations and Capital)*		*Private and Official together*	
	Total	*Per Annum*	*Total*	*Per Annum*	*Total*	*Per Annum*
	$m.	$m.	$m.	$m.	$m.	$m.
1946–50	9,145	1,829	n.a.	n.a.	n.a.	n.a.
1951–55	9,675	1,935	12,970	2,594	22,645	4,529
1956–59	14,760	3,690	16,416	4,104	31,176	7,794
1960–61	6,213	3,106	11,174	5,582	17,377	8,689
1961–64	5,310	1,770	17,427	5,809	22,737	7,579
1946–64	45,103	2,374	n.a.	n.a.	n.a.	n.a.
1951–64	35,958	2,568	57,977	4,141	93,935	6,710

among the important capital importers and exporters). Over the years in question, their *gross* outflow of capital averaged $5·4 billions a year, compared with a *net* outflow of $3·3 billions. At the same time, the 'gap' between *gross* and *net* capital outflows appears to be widening. This reflects the growing importance of capital transactions *between* the main capital exporters – a trend which we shall discuss in more detail later.

Adding the flow of official capital and donations to the *gross* export of private long-term capital, we obtain an aggregate long-term international investment of the order of $12–$13 billions per annum and increasing steadily each year. Finally, with the restoration of full or partial convertibility of many European currencies, the movement of short-term capital has also risen markedly in recent years. In 1960, it amounted to $2·4 billions (gross) between the main developed countries.

Taking all these factors into account, there seems little doubt that the value of external capital movements each year is now running at three to four times that of fifteen years ago and in 1964 was about 10 per cent of the value of world trade. Private and official capital together (net) in 1964 was estimated at around 9·5 per cent of world trade.

No estimate of the current value of *total* international indebtedness is available. We do know, however, that the US and UK between them owned long-term foreign assets with a book value of $125 billions at the end of 1966. Since these countries accounted for three-quarters of world investment, income receipts in 1964 (Committee on Invisible Exports, 1967) and in 1964/65 were responsible for four-fifths of all private capital exports (IMF, 1968), it might reasonably be assumed that world international indebtedness was around $160 billions in 1966 and is probably now (1969) close on the $200 billion mark. Book values of US and UK assets 1965 were approximately $130 billion (US $100 billion and UK $30 billion). This estimate excludes, of course, the official and private *donations* which between 1951 and 1965 alone totalled over $40 millions (*net*). Moreover, it considerably underestimates the *market* value of the investments.

To appreciate further the reasons for the trends described above and their implications for world economic development, we shall discuss the main features of post-war international capital movements under four headings:

(*a*) the changing media or forms of international lending, with particular reference to the growing significance of official donations and capital.

(*b*) the growing multilateralism of foreign investment transactions, as shown by the trade in capital *between* developed industrial nations;

(*c*) the emergence of the international business venture as the dominant form of private overseas investment and its expanding contribution to economic growth;

(*d*) the attitudes adopted by lending and borrowing countries to foreign investment, viewed in the light of private and social costs and benefits of such investment.

The changing media of capital transactions

Like domestic investment, international capital transactions may involve three types of participants: lenders, financial intermediaries and borrowers. Any one, or all, of these may be (*a*) private individuals or business enterprises, or (*b*) public bodies. Up to 1914, both savers and intermediaries in the international capital market were almost entirely private persons or companies, while the borrowers were either public bodies or private corporations such as railways and public utility undertakings.

In the 1920s, there were a number of bilateral government transactions – e.g. between the US and Germany – and in the following decade, the Export-Import Bank of Washington was formed to lend to both foreign governments and private enterprise. Only in the last two decades have public agencies, both national and international, become of dominating importance as lenders and intermediaries. Today, within a variety of lender/intermediary/borrower relationships, three broad groups may be distinguished, differing from each other in kind, purpose and effect. They are:

(i) private *direct* and *portfolio* investment, in which lender, intermediary and borrower are either business enterprises or individuals;
(ii) bilateral inter-government loans and donations transacted directly between lending and borrowing countries;
(iii) private and official loans channelled through international financial agencies.

In the period 1951/64, about 38 per cent of the *net* capital exports of the developed countries were private, about 51 per cent bilateral government transfers and about 11 per cent made through international financial agencies. In the last decade, the role of inter-government loans has steadily increased relative to that of the other two sources. Of the private investment, at least four-fifths took the form of business capital for the establishment and operation of overseas enterprises and branch plants. Donations accounted for two-thirds and loans for one-third of the inter-governmental transfers. Just under two-fifths of official long-term capital and one-tenth of private capital was channelled through such bodies as the International Bank and its affiliates (the International Finance Corporation and International Development Association), the International Monetary Fund, the Export-Import Bank, the EEC Development Fund and the EEC Investment Bank. While virtually all these loans and inter-government donations were absorbed by the under-developed areas, such areas attracted less than one-third of private capital in 1966.

Figures of *net* capital outflow, however, understate the role of private foreign investments, where offsetting movements of capital in opposite directions are greater than in the case of official capital. It is also worth noting that only about one-twentieth of international investment today is of the kind which predominated a half-century ago: namely, the purchase of foreign government, municipal or corporate securities by individual investors, usually through the medium of the stock market or specialist issuing houses. Security investment has been replaced as the main type of lending by entrepreneurial capital exports and official loans, either direct or through international agencies. Both, and particularly the former, are, in general, more income-stimulating than their nineteenth century counterpart, in that they usually comprise a 'package' deal of finance, entrepreneurship, management and technical knowledge – four of the essential ingredients of economic growth.

These changes in investment media reflect, partly, the structural developments which have taken place in both capital-exporting and importing countries, and, partly, the growing recognition by governments of the wealthier nations of their responsibilities towards the less developed nations.

The growth of direct investment essentially represents the *horizontal* or *vertical* extension of business enterprise across national boundaries, motivated by purely commercial considerations. Such capital exports (including reinvested profits) are directed mainly towards industrially advanced countries or (like their nineteenth century equivalent) to countries rich in natural resources. Public or official investment is influenced by different reasons. Initially, such institutions as the Export-Import Bank were intended to fill part of the vacuum left by the break-up of the international capital market in the 'thirties. In 1944, the World Bank (IBRD) was established as part of the Bretton Woods agreement to help the reconstruction of war-ravaged countries and to promote long-term development. In the last few years, attention has been directed mainly to this latter end, particularly in respect of the under-developed nations whose capital needs have been growing all the time.

With the private capital market in both Europe and the US largely closed to such countries, and with international business finding more profitable outlets elsewhere, it is only loans and grants from governments and the growth of multi-national financial intermediaries that have made such development possible. Capital exports of this kind have been directed largely to 'basic development' or infrastructure projects which often have no inherent earning capacity, but which are an essential prerequisite to private investment. Official grants and loans are thus not only helping to finance projects which the private international capital market is unable or unwilling to finance; they also act as a catalyst for entrepreneurial investment by providing the necessary basic services and economic framework for growth.

International agencies

International and regional financial agencies have mushroomed in recent years: there are now, at least, a dozen of these, either publicly or privately sponsored, of which the World Bank (IBRD) is by far the largest. It is financed both from private and public sources and makes untied loans on the guarantee of the borrowing state, to both governments and private enterprise. Two-thirds of its 552 disbursements, which up to June 1968 had totalled $11·2 billions, have so far been in the field of communications, power and agriculture.

The International Finance Corporation (IFC) is a complementary body, set up in 1956 to help finance industrial and commercial ventures in developing areas. The unique feature of this intermediary is that it provides equity capital rather than fixed-interest loans and participates only in projects for which private enterprise subscribes at least one-half of the capital. In the last twelve years, the IFC has made commitments of $272 millions in thirty-nine countries. A third World Bank affiliate – The International Development Association (IDA) – was established in 1960, to meet the needs of a growing number of developing countries whose balance of payments position made it difficult for them to service conventional loans. The IDA issues long-term credits at very low or zero rates of interest; amortization begins after a 10-year period of grace and all loans are repayable in local currencies. It has so far made 127 commitments with a combined value of $1·8 billions.

Supplementing these international intermediaries is the United Nations Special Fund – formed in 1959 to provide technical assistance and funds for basic development projects such as roads, harbours, schools and hospitals in the under-developed areas – and several regional agencies such as the Inter-American Development Bank, which provides socio-economic development funds for Latin American States, and the European Development Fund (which makes grants to the associated states overseas of the EEC). Finally, in recognition of the need for a more systematic co-ordination of aid efforts, several consultative bodies have been established, the best known of which is perhaps the Development Assistance Committee set up in 1960 to represent member countries of OECD.

The changing pattern of capital exporters and importers

The lenders

For most of the post-war period, the US and UK have supplied between them 80 to 90 per cent of the world's international capital. More recently, other nations have become sizeable foreign investors.

Table 3 indicates the average annual net flow of long-term capital and official donations from the main capital-exporting countries between 1951 and 1964. For the period as a whole, the US supplied 68 per cent of all net exports and the UK 10 per cent, but their shares of the total have been falling: for the US from 78 per cent in the first five years (1951/55) to 59 per cent in 1962/64; for the UK, from 10 per cent to about 8 per cent. Indeed, in 1960/61 France and Germany replaced the UK as the second and third largest net overseas investors. However, most of the new strength of these countries appears to have been in the field of official capital exports: in 1961, for example, both imported more *private* capital than they exported. Here the US is by far the most important creditor; between 1964 and 1966 it accounted for 92·0 per cent of the net private foreign investment of creditor countries. The only other net exporters were the UK (6·0 per cent of the total), Switzerland na[1] and Japan (2·0 per cent) (IMF 1968).

Again, it is important to note that these figures refer to *net* capital exports. But one of the features of the last decade has been the increasing number of countries which have emerged as *both* exporters and importers of capital, i.e. where the traffic in investment is essentially 'two-way' in character. In 1966, for example, there were at least nine countries which exported (gross) $100 millions or more of private capital.[2]

Two examples of this 'two-way' traffic in capital are set out in Table 4. At the end of 1966, the US owned long-term private foreign assets worth over $75 billions; but, at the same time, foreigners owned similar assets in the US worth $27 billions. The Bank of England has estimated that the value of direct and portfolio assets held overseas came to close on £10 billions in 1966; comparable

[1] Excluded from total.

[2] US, UK, Germany, Netherlands, Canada, Italy, France, Switzerland and Japan.

TABLE 3

Developed Countries: Average Net Exports of Long-term Capital and Official Donations
(millions of dollars per annum)

	US	*UK*	*Belgium/ Lux.*	*France*	*West Germany*	*Japan*	*Netherlands*	*Switzerland*	*Total*
				Private					
1951/55	1,280	477	70	−59	30	−18	−38	160	1,902
1956/59	2,924	595	113	−277	74	−8	−47	243	3,617
1960/61	2,958	70	−17	−15	−167	59	−14	182	3,056
1962/64	878	182	46	289	129	95	42	81[1]	1,742
1951/61	2,183	446	70	−130	10	—	−37	194	2,736
1951/64	1,903	389	65	−40	36	20	−20	170	2,523
				Official					
1951/55	2,244	−6	−38	171	68	22	45	23	2,529
1956/59	2,326	375	36	520	708	115	78	33	4,191
1960/61	2,974	468	47	1,043	839	62	98	68	5,599
1962/64	3,302	415	88	900	395	154	70	3	5,327
1951/61	2,406	228	4	456	441	63	67	35	3,700
1951/64	2,598	268	22	551	431	83	68	28	4,049
				Total					
1951/55	3,524	471	32	112	98	4	7	183	4,431
1956/59	5,250	970	149	243	782	107	31	276	7,808
1960/61	5,932	538	30	1,028	672	121	84	250	8,655
1962/64	4,180	597	134	1,189	524	249	112	84	7,069
1951/61	4,589	674	74	326	451	63	30	229	6,436
1951/64	4,501	657	87	511	467	103	48	198	6,572

[1] 1962–63 average only.

TABLE 4

International Investment Position of the UK and US, 1962 and 1966

	Assets						Liabilities					
	1962		1966		1962–1966		1962		1966		1962–1966	
	UK £m.	*US* $m.	*UK* £m.	*US* $m.	*UK* *Percentage Increase*	*US*	*UK* £m.	*US* $m.	*UK* £m.	*US* $m.	*UK* *Percentage Increase*	*US*
Private investments												
Short term[a]	(2,479)	7,293	(5,057)	10,670	103·9	46·3	2,833	13,344	5,164	20,796	89·1	55·8
Long term:												
Direct	(4,855)	37,226	(6,400)	54,562	31·8	46·6	(2,170)	7,612	(3,185)	9,054	46·3	18·9
Portfolio	(3,000)	15,506	(3,200)	21,003	6·7	35·5	(1,050)	12,604	(1,025)	17,946	−2·4	42·4
Total long term	(7,855)	52,732	(9,600)	75,565	22·2	43·3	(3,220)	20,216	(4,210)	27,000	30·7	33·6
Total private	(10,334)	60,025	(14,657)	86,235	41·8	43·7	(6,053)	33,560	(9,374)	47,796	57·5	42·4
Official investments												
Short term[b]	2,056	20,333	2,158	17,692	5·0	−29·9	3,044	12,720 (short and long term)	4,485	12,593 (short and long term)	47·3	−0·1 (short and long term)
Long term	709	16,042	983	21,182	38·6	32·0	(2,650)		(2,536)		−4·3	
Total official	2,765	36,375	3,141	38,874	13·6	6·9	(5,694)	12,720	(7,021)	12,593	23·3	−0·1
All investments	(13,099)	96,400	(17,798)	125,109	35·9	29·8	(11·747)	46,280	(16,395)	60,389	40·8	30·5

[a] Banking and other external claims in domestic and foreign currencies and trade credits.

[b] Gold and convertible currency reserves; monetary authorities' holdings of convertible currencies; short-term claims and IMF gold tranche position.

N.B. Figures in brackets are precarious estimates and/or known to be incomplete.

Source: Bank of England and US Department of Commerce.

investments by foreigners in the UK in that year amounted to just over £4·2 billions.

Likewise with other countries. Between 1962 and 1966, the estimated gross outflow of direct investment from Germany was $1,134 millions and the gross inflow $2,825 millions. Italy was similarly placed, with an outflow of $794 millions and an inflow of $1,800 millions. By contrast, the Netherlands invested $652 millions abroad and received $393 millions from foreigners: the corresponding figures for Japan were $438 millions and $356 millions (IMF 1968). The proportion of capital transactions *between* developed countries is increasing. In 1965, excluding oil investments, some two-thirds of the direct foreign assets of the main capital-exporting countries were located in the developed countries. This proportion has slightly risen during the 1960s.

Apart from the liberalization of capital movements and the widening territorial horizons of many enterprises, the main reason for this trend seems to lie in the heterogeneity of the 'package deal' so often involved in international business investment. Capital exports are no longer homogeneous or near-homogeneous, as in the last century; more often than not they are accompanied by specialized knowledge and techniques which, like the exports of goods, reflect the particular economic structure of the investing country. Just as it pays a country to specialize in the production of goods with the lowest comparative costs and exchange these for others which it is less suited to supply, so, similarly, it often pays to trade factors of production. Indeed, it is only by an unrestricted flow of capital and knowledge across national boundaries that the world's resources can be most effectively utilized.[1]

Thus it is quite consistent that the UK should wish to invest in oil wells in the Middle East, while welcoming US capital and expertise in its own motor-vehicles and pharmaceutical industries; that the Canadians should encourage British capital to exploit their iron-ore mining and wood-pulp industries, while they themselves set up foreign subsidiaries to manufacture agricultural machinery in France and Germany; that Latin American republics should seek long-term capital from the US and Europe, while exporting large sums of flight capital to North America. Although the *net* flow of long-term funds from the main capital-exporting countries is now substantial in absolute terms, it amounted to a little less than 1 per cent of their combined gross domestic product and to just under 6 per cent of their combined gross domestic savings in 1960/64.

[1] This point is enlarged upon in later chapters.

The borrowers

The capital-importing countries may be classified into four main groups:

(*a*) Advanced industrial countries, such as the US and most of Western Europe, which offer large and developed markets and good opportunities both for business and portfolio capital. Such countries attract the great proportion of entrepreneurial investment in manufacturing industry, and a large proportion of portfolio investment. They are mainly *net exporters of capital* and currently receive very little aid from foreign government or international agencies.

(*b*) Rapidly expanding countries rich in natural resources, with a high income per head and a substantial industrial sector. Australia, New Zealand, Italy and Canada fall within this category, each of which is a *net importer of capital* and attracts business investment in both manufacturing and in resource exploitation. Such countries also receive a limited amount of portfolio investment and official capital and donations.

(*c*) Low-income countries, well endowed with a specialized range of raw materials such as oil and non-ferrous metals, which attract direct investment by the large international business in resource exploitation, and also some official capital and donations for basic development projects. Venezuela, Brazil, Argentina, Mexico and the Middle East oil states come within this group.

(*d*) Low-income countries, in general unattractive to entrepreneurial investment as they have neither large domestic markets nor important natural resources to offer. These include densely populated and under-developed areas such as India, and it is here that aid from official sources is most concentrated.

Groups (*a*) and (*b*) may be broadly defined as the *developed countries* and groups (*c*) and (*d*)) as the *less developed* countries.

So far as the *gross* outflow of private capital from the developed countries is concerned, between 1958 and 1960 group (*a*) countries received 40 per cent, group (*b*) countries 36 per cent, and groups (*c*) and (*d*) 24 per cent between them. For direct investment alone, as has already been pointed out, the developed countries absorbed a considerably larger share.

As regards official donations and loans, the situation is quite different. Of the total donations of nearly $18 billions made between 1951 and 1959, five-sixths went to the less developed countries as did more than two-thirds of the official loans and the net disbursements of the World Bank and IFC. As far as all net capital exports are concerned, the proportion absorbed by the less developed areas, either directly or through financial intermediaries, has increased from 68 per cent in 1951/55 to 70 per cent in 1956/59 and 77 per cent in 1960/61. Put another way, the net flow of funds from capital-exporting countries to the less developed countries more than trebled over this period, whereas the flow to other regions (and to international agencies) rose by a little over 150 per cent.

Looking at the matter from the recipient countries' viewpoint, the developed capital-importing countries received all their capital from private sources in the last decade; in fact, they were net exporters of official capital while being net importers of private capital. For the less developed countries, the relative significance of private and official capital largely depends on their stage of development and income levels. In 1959/64, those countries with a *per capita* national income of $350 or more in 1962 received equal proportions of their foreign capital from private and official sources; those with a *per capita* national income of $150 or less received 91 per cent of their receipts from official loans and donations (United Nations, 1966).

Capital flows to less developed countries

Indeed, over the years, the poorer developing countries have come to rely upon official aid even more, while those slightly better off have been financed increasingly by private capital. Thus Latin America, with only one-sixth of the population of all less developed countries, received half of the *private* long-term capital in 1961/64, the same proportion as 10 years earlier. Africa and South East Asia, in contrast, with two-thirds of the population, received only 26 per cent and 6 per cent respectively. Of the total capital imports absorbed in 1965 by the less developed countries, 49 per cent originated from the US, 25 per cent from Western Europe, 6 per cent from international institutions and 3 per cent from the Sino-Soviet bloc.

While the impact of foreign investment on the level of individual incomes in less developed countries is, as yet, insignificant – most of the countries in question have not reached the take-off stage in their development and their populations are increasingly rapidly – the contribution of non-resident capital to economic resources has steadily increased over recent years. The inflow of long-term capital and donations has risen three times as fast as the export earnings of the recipient countries, with the result that such capital contributed one-sixth of the total foreign exchange receipts of the less developed countries in the early 1960s.

When related to *size of population*, the average flow of capital into less developed countries in the period 1959/64 was \$3·3 per head; in South America it was as high as \$3·9; in South East Asia – the most densely populated area of all – \$2·8. Expressed as a proportion of *gross domestic product* the contribution of foreign capital averaged nearly 3·3 per cent, although there were very wide variations between countries; from over 23 per cent in Puerto Rico to ½ per cent in Morocco. As a percentage of *gross domestic capital formation* the differences were even more noticeable. The average was 21 per cent over the period 1958/64, but the foreign contribution was well above this figure in some cases (e.g. South East Asia 60 per cent, and Latin America 7·9 per cent). Of particular significance is the fact that whereas the proportion of *domestic* savings to gross domestic product has fallen for most less developed countries since 1950, that of *foreign* savings has generally risen. Indeed, it is mainly due to the enlarged flow of foreign capital that these countries have been able to raise or maintain their total supply of savings for economic development.

No less significant, and, in some cases, more easily discernible in its impact on income and growth, has been the contribution of foreign capital to the economies of some of the developed countries. It has been estimated that for the period 1949/64 the inflow of overseas capital to Australia (nine-tenths of which was direct investment) contributed about a tenth of total savings (Commonwealth of Australia, 1965). In Canada, *net* capital imports financed 15 per cent of total imports between 1955 and 1960 – a higher proportion than at any time since before 1930.[1] Foreign-owned enterprises in Norway account for 32 per cent of the net income of all corporations (Stonehill 1965). In the UK, foreign firms accounted for a quarter of all British exports in 1966 and, on present trends, will be responsible for about the same proportion of UK manufacturing output by 1980 (Dunning 1969). Over these same years, the accumulated US capital stake, as a proportion of Europe's gross national product, rose from 1·2 per cent to 3 per cent. Whatever measure is used, there is no doubt that the contribution of foreign capital in the economic growth of many developed economies has risen markedly in the last decade. We now turn to consider reasons for this.

[1] See Chapter 5.

The role of international business investment

We have seen that, in recent years, over a third of the *net* outflow of capital from capital-exporting countries has comprised private long-term capital investment; when calculated in terms of *gross* capital exports, the proportion rises to about three-fifths. At least three-quarters of *net* private exports, and more than four-fifths of *gross* private exports, took the form of entrepreneurial or business investment. Like donations and loans from the public sector, this has risen markedly in the last decade. Partly, at least, this reflects the built-in growth component of reinvested profits. The value of US (direct) business assets abroad in 1965 amounted to $45 billions, compared with under $12 billions in 1950; those of British overseas companies (excluding oil and insurance) increased by 42 per cent between 1960 and 1965.

The multi-national company is a new force in the world economy. It has been estimated that the total foreign sales of such enterprises (both exports and local output) in 1966 were second in value only to the gross national product of the United States and the USSR, and that, if present trends continue, at least one-third of the output of the free world will be supplied by subsidiaries and associates of non-resident companies by the mid 1970s (Fortune 1968).

The great majority of multi-national enterprises are American or British in origin. In 1966, some 56 per cent of the total foreign capital stake of such businesses and 52 per cent of their foreign income was accounted for by American corporations; the respective figures for British companies were 19 per cent and 18 per cent. In the last five years, other countries, notably Japan and Germany, have become quite important overseas investors. Of the 200 largest corporations in 1967, other than those incorporated in the US, forty-three were Japanese (Dunning and Pearce 1969). Most of these engage in international operations.

The majority of international investments are still owned by a comparatively few firms. Probably three-quarters of the total stake of $85 billion (Fortune 1968) is owned by the leading 500 companies and as much as half by the largest 100. Some of these enterprises derive more of their income from foreign than domestic operations. Of the 109 manufacturing and mining companies with world-wide sales of $1,000 million or more in 1966, fifty-five had at least one-quarter of either their assets or sales[1] outside their country of

[1] Including direct exports.

origin (*Management Today* 1968). Some twenty-three of these companies were European and, in a number of cases, the significance of their foreign operations is overwhelming.[1]

The extent to which European companies have been, for many years now, dependent on external markets for their growth and prosperity is not always appreciated as it might be. Too often, one is dazzled by the magnitude of US interests abroad to appreciate that the foreign business operations of other countries are, relatively speaking, even more important to their economies. Table 5 ranks countries

TABLE 5

Income Earned on Foreign Direct Investment as a Percentage of Gross National Product, 1966
(Selected Countries)

		%
1.	Switzerland	2·54
2.	Netherlands	1·55
3.	United Kingdom	1·10
4.	Belgium	0·81
5.	Unites States	0·76
6.	South Africa	0·58
7.	Norway	0·24
8.	Canada	0·23
9.	Sweden	0·22
10.	Australia	0·19
11.	Italy	0·16
12.	France	0·15
13.	Denmark	0·10
14.	Austria	0·08

Source: *I.M.F. Balance of Payments Year Book* and *U.N. Statistical Year Book.*

according to the income earned from direct overseas investment, expressed as a proportion of their gross national product. This shows that, in 1966, apart from the UK and the US, the five countries which were most dependent on their foreign business ventures were all quite small European economies. In most cases, these interests date back well beyond those of American companies, whose major contribution has been only since 1950 or thereabouts. They reflect one thing: the recognition that, due to the limitations of domestic

[1] Nestlés, for example, sells less than 3 per cent of its total output in Switzerland and the sales of Philips Eindhoven outside Holland are ten times greater than those within (Sampson 1969).

markets, the best way to create companies of any size is to engage in international operations, either by export or the establishment of foreign producing facilities (Economists Advisory Group 1969).

Why firms invest abroad

The forces making for direct investment abroad are many and varied.[1] Basically, the investing firm is interested in the contribution which such a capital outlay will make to the prosperity of the *whole organization*. In general, it would seem reasonable to assume that the firm will invest abroad as long as the marginal rate of return is greater than could be earned elsewhere (allowing for any differences in risk). It is, however, increasingly unusual for this to be the case, as there are so many ways in which the establishment of a foreign enterprise can and does affect the profitability of the investing company. Exports may be increased or raw materials procured more easily and cheaply; there may be a valuable feed-back of technical knowledge; markets may be preserved against competitors, and so on.

The fact that the international business venture has become such a potent force in recent years may be due as much to the growing importance of these factors, as to the profits earned on the capital invested. Thus, in 1965, about two-fifths of the total US capital invested abroad was concentrated in resource industries – e.g. petroleum and mineral extraction – compared with a third before the war. No less than one-quarter of American imports are currently derived from US productive facilities overseas (30 per cent in the case of imports from Canada and Latin America). As the US exhausts more of her indigenous raw materials, the urgency of the need to develop new supplies abroad increases (Lary 1968). This form of 'international backward integration' also explains many Western European investments in the Middle and Far East and is the modern counterpart of the 'colonial-type' investments of the nineteenth century.

A no less important reason for the migration of business operations abroad has been the desire to expand horizontally or laterally, either to overcome import restrictions of one kind or another or to open up new markets. Not only may it be cheaper for a firm to manufacture in a foreign country than to export to it; fear of competition has also been a powerful inducement. In 1965, manufacturing investments (including petroleum refining) accounted for 39 per cent of all US investments abroad (in advanced industrial

[1] For a summary of the more important of these, see Chapter 7, pp. 277 ff.

nations 48 per cent). Sometimes such investments will lead to an increase in the exports of the investing company and/or country (a quarter of American exports of machinery are currently bought by US subsidiaries abroad); sometimes they lead to a decrease.

Empirical evidence on this subject is mostly impressionistic. According to one survey, over four-fifths of US firms with manufacturing subsidiaries in Canada claimed that their exports had been either raised or unaffected as a result of local production.[1] There is reasonable, though by no means conclusive, evidence that US direct investment abroad has stimulated rather than curtailed exports of US goods and services. Whatever the truth, the desire to penetrate new markets or to protect existing ones is one of the most commonly stated factors influencing foreign investment. Opportunities for this latter type of overseas investment have been very favourable in recent years – particularly in the case of the US, where between 1950 and 1965 the rate of return earned on manufacturing capital at home and the rate of growth in manufacturing output was generally well below that in most other developed industrial countries.

This prospect of higher profits and market growth has also prompted British investment overseas, and latterly German and French as well. Looking at the geographical *distribution* of UK direct overseas investment since the war, we see that between 1952 and 1956 Canada was the main attraction. Then, when the Canadian boom burst, attention was switched to Australia, and since the formation of the EEC the continent of Europe has been the most favoured. Most of this investment has been undertaken for both defensive and aggressive reasons. Unlike US overseas investment, however, it has rarely been productive of higher returns, e.g. for the period 1960/64 the net profits to net assets ratio of UK firms in the major industrial areas worked out at 8·0 per cent, compared with 7·2 per cent at home. Nevertheless, it has often led to very valuable indirect benefits, such as a feed-back of technical knowledge (particularly so in the case of US and German investments), and to increased exports.

The increasingly significant role of the multi-national enterprise is strikingly illustrated by the fact that, between 1946 and 1967, the investments of US companies in foreign subsidiaries and affiliates increased at twice the rate of the domestic assets of US corporations.[2]

[1] See Chapter 5.

[2] In 1966, these same foreign companies produced abroad goods worth four times the value of US exports and earned an income equal to 19·6 per cent of these same exports – compared with 17·2 per cent in 1960.

The income of UK companies abroad as a proportion of income earned at home rose from under a third in 1950 to over two-fifths in 1966. To the extent that direct investment finances its own growth out of re-invested profits, and the more advanced less developed countries develop their own economies and markets with the aid of official capital, private investment will gradually assume the predominant role, as it is doing in many South American states.

Modern economic conditions favour the growth of the multinational company, and today most European companies of any size have to look beyond their national boundaries for growth. This has been accelerated by changing international demand and supply conditions. On the demand side, as incomes have expanded and communications have improved, international tastes have become more and more standardized. On the supply side, developments in capital intensive technology and the increasing cost of research and development programmes have reinforced the need for companies to seek new markets to spread costs economically. In part, these needs have been met by exports, but, increasingly, conditions have favoured the replacement of these by the establishment of local producing facilities. Besides transport costs, these include tariff barriers and the formation of regional economic blocs, the importance of adapting to local markets, after-sales servicing and so on. There has been a growing impetus of companies to invest abroad and this has been enhanced by the concentrated structure of competition which exists between international firms. At a national level, no country can afford to adopt an entirely isolationist policy. Small countries invest abroad to secure the markets to enable them to compete with large countries. Large innovating countries, e.g. US, invest to protect existing markets and as a way of promoting new outlets (Economists Advisory Group 1969).

As might be expected, the *form* of entrepreneurial investment varies according to the local situation and policy of the parent company. In some cases complete ownership is considered desirable; in others, joint participation with local firms. In almost every instance, however, technical and managerial expertise is exported with capital, and disseminated into the economy of the host country. The influence of the international corporation as a pioneer of new products, new techniques and new skills is now spreading across national boundaries with a vengeance. Sometimes knowledge is transmitted by licensing arrangements, which usually involve no financial investment but, where management is important, an equity control is often required. Local manufacturing is preferred to exports, partly on the basis of costs, partly on the basis of offering servicing facilities and adaptations to local market needs.

Attitude of lending countries

In recent years, the international flow of capital has been restricted by both lending and borrowing countries. Up to 1960, the US actively encouraged overseas investment, but since that date, balance-of-payments difficulties have forced a reappraisal of the effects of such investment and there has been some pressure to reduce the outflow of capital. For similar reasons, the UK has controlled overseas investments for most of the post-war period, although the scope and intensity of control have varied with the balance-of-payments position.

In addition, there are other longer-term considerations which have led some countries to question the desirability of foreign investment. It has been argued, for example, that even if the private rate of return on overseas investment is higher than that at home, the loss of tax revenue, the possible deterioration of the terms of trade, the retardation of growth at home due to a deflection of capital overseas – these and other drawbacks may outweigh any benefits in the form of higher profits and external economies arising from investment.

To what extent this is true it is difficult to say, although recent empirical studies on the costs and benefits of foreign investment would seem to suggest there has been little or no misallocation of resources – except perhaps when viewed from the short-term external position. (Reddaway 1968, Hufbauer/Adler 1968.) Nevertheless, both the US and most European countries have treated foreign investment – particularly security investment – as somewhat of a luxury in the post-war period, the quantity allowed having varied very closely with the balance-of-payments and the likely effects of such investment on the investing country's economic growth and stability (Kindleberger 1969).

Views of borrowing countries

Borrowing countries have also regarded the inflow of foreign capital with mixed feelings. Increasing attention is now being given to analysing the repercussions of such investment and, through a variety of policy measures, to align its magnitude and composition to national resource allocation and growth. In the past, the most substantial benefit of foreign investment has been its stimulus to economic development. Direct investment is particularly welcomed as it brings to the recipient country all the elements necessary to create new production units: improved technology, new products and marketing methods, patents and trade-mark rights, managerial expertise and entrepreneurial initiative. By example, and contact with other firms, these benefits percolate to the rest of the economy.

Capital also brings with it access to research activities of the parent company: some years ago, it was estimated that more than a quarter of US research and development was made available to the UK economy through the media of American subsidiaries (Dunning 1958). Clearly, the impact of such investment will depend on the *direction* of investment and its industrial spread; usually, however, the package-deal type of investment is attracted to growth industries. There are other benefits to the host country, such as the additional supply of capital provided and the taxation levied on the income it creates.

Set against the benefits are the costs of foreign investment – particularly direct investment. These fall broadly into two groups: (*a*) the servicing of the debt, and (*b*) the fear that national economic, strategic or cultural objectives may in some way be interfered with or thwarted.[1] The latter applies particularly where foreign enterprise controls key sectors of an economy (Kindleberger 1969). As with the investing country, the balance of advantage will depend on many factors, such as the type and ownership of capital invested, its character and its industrial distribution. Thus, investment by foreign firms in the exploitation of natural resources for export to the investing country may prove less beneficial to the host country than would investment, if forthcoming, in public works or manufacturing industry. Since, too, the indirect benefits of entrepreneurial investment tend to lessen with the passing of time, while the cost of its servicing tends to increase, a minimum foreign equity stake consistent with the acquisition of these benefits may be thought preferable to a 100 per cent control. In certain circumstances, also, foreign investment may adversely affect domestic savings and cause a deterioration in the host country's terms of trade.

To maximize the benefits and minimize the costs of foreign investment, it may well be that the host country will consider it desirable to integrate and regulate the capital flow not only into a particular project but in the light of its expected contribution to the national development programme as a whole (Meier 1963). This may require a discriminatory policy designed to attract capital into

[1] These are explored in more depth in Chapters 7 and 8.

particular sectors of the economy where it will have the maximum catalytic effect of mobilizing national resources, while restricting the inflow elsewhere, e.g. into luxury industries. To minimize and stabilize the cost of foreign borrowing, while obtaining the maximum technological advantages, thus implies the drawing of distinctions between various types and forms of foreign capital.

Extent of foreign control

More recently, other causes for concern have been voiced and have led to a more cautious attitude being adopted to foreign investment. This is shown particularly among the advanced industrial nations, where a growing proportion of domestic capital is owned by foreigners, and such capital is concentrated in a number of key growth sectors. In Canada, in 1965, non-resident investors owned over half the capital in manufacturing industry and nearly two-thirds of the capital in all industry. In Australia, about one-quarter of all company assets are currently owned by foreign firms, who occupy an important role in thirteen of the twenty-five industrial groups listed as 'large and highly concentrated'. In the UK, where profits of overseas companies account for 12 per cent of all company profits, nine-tenths of the investment is concentrated in the fast expanding trades of motor-cars, oil refining and petro-chemicals, industrial instruments, office machinery, pharmaceuticals, rubber tyres and electrical equipment. In France, the fastest growing industries (telecommunications, petroleum, chemicals and vehicles) are also dominated by foreign firms.

Foreign investment in manufacturing industry is usually directed either to the mass production of consumer goods or to producer goods trades which are highly capitalized and/or usually dependent on research and development for their prosperity. These latter industries are also those which are vital in the implementation of government planning. Hence, the fears which are currently being voiced by many advanced countries that investment planning at a national level is in danger of being jeopardized by industries under foreign control which will not be so amenable to planning and control. Not only this, it is argued that such industries may well operate to the detriment of the economy: that decisions taken by foreign firms may not be in the best interests of the host country.

Several examples of this might be cited. The Canadians for several years have been concerned that the purchasing policy of US parent companies has meant that Canadian subsidiaries have had to buy their parts and components from the US rather than in Canada. Often too, the parent companies control the allocation of markets of their subsidiaries and, in some cases, by refusing to grant export franchises, deprive them of opportunities of seeking new outlets. Indigenous research may be stifled where foreign capital monopolizes the research-based industries. Little effort is made to develop local technical and scientific talent when easy access to the parent company's research facilities is available.[1]

These arguments and others have also been put forward by the less-developed countries, although the policies adopted have usually been more specific than in the advanced countries (Vernon 1968). Various devices have been adopted to channel investment in the 'right' direction. The Philippines control the remittances of foreign companies according to their 'social productivity' rating; Indonesia levies a special tax on the transfer of dividends; Burma prohibits capital repatriation altogether. In some countries, such as India, efforts are made to limit the foreign participation in domestic businesses to not more than 50 per cent of the equity capital, while others insist that overseas-controlled enterprises employ a certain minimum proportion of local workers (Wells 1962). Such restrictions as these are understandable and, up to a point, reasonable. But, all too often, the price of political expediency is carelessly paid – and the cost in terms of economic progress is unnecessarily high (Stikker 1968).

Conclusion

From what has been written in this chapter, it is clear that the world is entering a new era of international capital movements. These movements are of two distinct, yet complementary, types. First, there is the export of official capital and donations, either transacted directly between countries or through the medium of international lending agencies. Such capital is mainly used to finance the infrastructure of developing economies, preparatory to private investment. Because of this, the capital is absorbed very largely by the underdeveloped areas, and though there are signs that its significance is growing, it still has a long way to go to fulfil the tasks required of it.

The other main kind of capital outflow is entrepreneurial invest-

[1] In fact, this latter assertion is not true by any means; several US subsidiaries in this country operate sizeable research units.

ment. This takes a variety of forms[1] and is motivated primarily by the prospect of private gain. It is in this field, in particular, that both capital-importing and capital-exporting countries are attempting to evaluate the costs and benefits. It is becoming increasingly recognized that the package-deal type of direct investment is not the only (nor always the most desirable) form of business capital import. It is, as has been said, a short cut to development, in that the ingredients for production are 'prefabricated'; but it can also be very expensive.[2]

In the nineteenth century, portfolio investment and export of labour and knowledge proceeded concurrently but independently of each other. It is possible that, quite apart from the introduction of new kinds of licensing or technical assistance agreements (Behrman 1962), something in between direct and security assistance agreements could evolve in the future. Thus, a country may find it cheaper to borrow capital from one source and obtain managerial and technical skill from another. Indeed, as an alternative to direct investment the *Economic Commission for Latin America* has suggested that new industries in less developed countries should be financed by official loans or grants and that their organization, management and operation be contracted out to foreign firms for the first few years. Under this arrangement, the developing country would borrow its capital at a fixed rate of interest and receive the benefits of foreign technical and managerial skills for a once-and-for-all payment. Other possibilities being explored include the formation of a consortia of business investors, in which foreign private capital is associated with local private capital or public official capital; the co-production agreement, under which an entity is owned and managed by a public authority in the host country but receives technical assistance from foreign enterprises (Benoit 1967), and joint ventures between a foreign company and the Government of the developing country (or a development corporation set up by it) in which the former invests up to 49 per cent of the capital for a pre-arranged period, after which time its interests are bought out by the host Government (Streeten 1967, Singer 1950). Some examples of the kinds of arrangements

[1] These are very succinctly outlined by Vernon (1968). For an evaluation of joint ventures by potential investors, see National Industrial Conference Board (1966).

[2] For example, the average rate of return on direct investment in South America in fields other than public institutions averages 20 per cent. Since the cost of local capital is only 7 per cent, Latin America is in effect paying 13 per cent for knowledge and entrepreneurial services.

so far negotiated between non-resident enterprises and Governments of less developed countries in resource industries are given in Mikesell (1967).

These are undoubtedly years of experiment in finding new combinations of the international savings/investment process and new means of transmitting skills and knowledge across national boundaries (Rosenstein-Rodan 1966, Gabriel 1967). Whatever the *form* of investment, one feels that some selective control of foreign investment will continue to be necessary, both by investing and recipient countries. For the recipient country, this may require a discriminatory tax structure and other devices to promote investment considered most in keeping with national objectives. As far as the investing country is concerned, more research is necessary into the cost/benefit balance of foreign investment – both inwards and outwards. From a private investor's viewpoint, the improvement of investment guarantees and insurance facilities, more fiscal incentives (OECD 1965, Lent 1967), and the removal of foreign exchange obstacles would do much to help (Stikker 1966). Nevertheless, it seems reasonable to suppose that the volume of private investment will continue to rise and that the next ten years will show a greater volume of capital exports than at any time since the decade before the First World War.

REFERENCES

J. H. Adler. (ed.) *Capital Movements and Economic Development*, Macmillan, 1967.

J. M. Atkin. *British overseas investment* 1918/31, Ph.D. thesis, University of London, 1968.

J. N. Behrman. 'Foreign investment and the transfer of knowledge and skills' in R. Mikesell (ed.), *U.S. Government and Private Investment Abroad*, Oregon University Press, 1962.

E. Benoit. 'East–West Business Co-operation,' *New Republic*, Vol. CLVI, February 1967.

A. K. Cairncross. *Home and Foreign Investment* 1870–1913, Cambridge University Press, 1953.

Committee on Invisible Exports. *Britian's Invisible Earnings*, British National Export Council, 1967.

Commonwealth of Australia. *Private Overseas Investment in Australia*, Supplement to the *Treasury Information Bulletin*, May 1965.

J. H. Dunning. *American Investment in British Manufacturing Industry*, Allen & Unwin, 1958.

Economists Advisory Group. *The Location of International Offices*, Committee on Invisible Exports, 1969.

H. Feis. *Europe: the World's Banker*, 1870/1914, Yale University Press, 1930.

A. G. Ford. 'Overseas lending and international fluctuations 1870/1914,' *Yorkshire Bulletin*, Vol. 17, No. 1, 1965.

P. P. Gabriel. *The International Transfer of Corporate Skills*, Harvard Graduate School of Business Administration, 1967.

G. C. Hufbauer and F. Adler. *Overseas Manufacturing Investment and the Balance of Payments*, Tax Policy Research Study No. 1, U.S. Treasury Department, Washington, 1968.

C. K. Hobson. *The Export of Capital*, Constable, 1914.

International Monetary Fund. *World Summary of International Transactions*, 1961/66 (unpublished paper), 1968.

A. Imlah. *Economic Elements in the Pax Britannica*, Cambridge University Press, 1958.

A. Kafka. 'Economic effects of capital imports,' in J. H. Adler, *Capital Movements and Economic Development*, Macmillan, 1967.

C. Kindleberger. *American Business Abroad*, Yale University Press, 1969.

H. B. Lary. *Imports of Manufactures from the Less Developed Countries*, National Bureau of Economic Research, Columbia University Press, 1968.

G. E. Lent. 'Tax incentives for investment in developing countries,' *I.M.F. Staff Papers*, July 1967.

C. Lewis. *The United States and Foreign Investment Problems*, Washington, 1948.

Management Today. 'The march of the multi-nationals,' *Management Today*, March 1968.

G. Meier. *International Trade and Development*, Harper & Row, New York, 1963.

R. Mikesell (1962). 'U.S. post-war investment abroad: a statistical analysis,' in R. Mikesell (ed.), *U.S. Government and Private Investment Abroad*, Oregon University Press, 1962.

R. Mikesell (1967). 'Healing the breach over foreign resource exploitation,' *Columbia Journal of World Business*, Vol. II, No. 2, March/April 1967.

National Industrial Conference Board. *Joint ventures with Foreign Partners*, New York, 1966

D. North. 'International capital movements in historical perspective,' in R. Mikesell (ed.), *U.S. Government and Private Investment Abroad*, Oregon University Press, 1962.

R. Nurkse. 'The problem of international investment today in the light of nineteenth-century experience,' *Economic Journal*, Vol. LXIV, December, 1954.

OECD. *Fiscal Incentives for Private Investment in Developing Areas*, Paris, 1965.

F. Pazos. 'The role of international movements of private capital in promoting development,' in J. H. Adler, *Capital Movements and Economic Development*, Macmillan, 1967.

W. B. Reddaway, S. J. Potter and C. T. Taylor. *The Effects of UK Direct Investment Overseas*, Cambridge 1967 and 1968.

S. Rose. 'The rewarding strategies of multi-nationalism,' *Fortune*, 15/9/68.

P. Rosenstein Rodan. 'Philosophy of international investment in the second half of the twentieth century,' in J. H. Adler, *Capital Movements and Economic Development*, Macmillan, 1967.

Royal Institute of International Affairs, *The Problem of International Investment*, Cass, London, 1937.

A. Sampson. *The New Europeans*, Hodder & Stoughton, London, 1968.

H. W. Singer. 'The distribution of gains between investing and borrowing countries,' *American Economic Review*, Vol. XL, May, 1950.

D. Stikker. *The Role of Private Enterprise in Investment and Promotion of Exports in Developing Countries*, United Nations, New York, 1968.

A. Stonehill. *Foreign Ownership in Norwegian Enterprises*, Oslo, Central Bureau of Statistics, 1965.

P. Streeten. 'New approaches to private overseas investment for development,' *Institute of Development Studies*, 1967.

Brinley Thomas. 'The historical record of International Capital Movements to 1913,' in J. H. Adler (ed.), *Capital Movements and Economic Development*, Macmillan, 1967.

United Nations (1949). *International Capital Movements during the Inter-war Period*, Lake Success, 1949.

United Nations (1953/59). *International Flow of Private Capital* 1946/52 (1953), 1953/55 (1956), 1956/58 (1959), U.N. Department of Economic and Social Affairs.

United Nations (1961/66). *International Flow of Long-Term Capital and Official Donations* 1951/59 (1961), 1959/61 (1963), 1961/65 (1966), U.N. Department of Economic and Social Affairs.

R. Vernon. 'Conflict and resolution between foreign direct investors and less developed countries,' *Public Policy*, Vol. XVII, Fall 1968.

D. Wells. 'Economic analysis of attitudes to host countries toward direct private investment,' in *U.S. Private and Government Investment Abroad*, R. Mikesell, Oregon University Press, 1962.

H. D. White. *The French International Accounts* 1880/1913, Cambridge (Mass.), 1933.

2

THE COSTS AND BENEFITS OF FOREIGN DIRECT INVESTMENT TO THE INVESTING COUNTRY

THE UK EXPERIENCE

Introduction

This chapter summarizes the main economic implications of foreign direct investment from the viewpoint of the investing country – in this case, the United Kingdom. No attempt is made to develop particular points of argument in detail; this has been done or is being done elsewhere.[1] We have drawn our data from various sources but mostly from the reports of W. B. Reddaway and his colleagues published in March 1967 and November 1968,[2] and a comprehensive article 'Book values of overseas investment' which appeared in the *Board of Trade Journal* in January 1968.

The scope and structure of UK foreign direct investment

The average annual amount of UK outward private direct investment in the period 1960/66 was £300m.[3] This was the equivalent of just over one-fifth of the net domestic investment by UK companies and 9·5 per cent of all net investment in the UK; it was also about one-fifth greater than the combined (average annual) deficit on current and long-term capital account in these years.

In December 1966, the UK share of the net foreign assets controlled by UK companies overseas was between £5,750m. and £6,250m., of which investments by the oil companies accounted for £1,500m., insurance and financial investments, £850m. and manufacturing,

[1] See particularly the selected bibliography at the conclusion of this chapter.

[2] W. B. Reddaway *et al.*, *The Effects of U.K. Direct Investment Overseas*, Cambridge 1967 and 1968.

[3] Board of Trade, 'Book values of overseas investment,' *Board of Trade Journal* 26/1/68.

mining and other non-manufacturing investments, the balance.[1] The growth of these assets, excluding oil, since 1960, compared with the growth of assets of foreign companies in the UK is given in Table 1.

Including oil investments, the geographical distribution of UK foreign-owned assets was fairly evenly divided between the developed and less developed countries at the end of 1965. Excluding oil investments, the share of the developed countries was 67 per cent, and their share of the new investment undertaken between 1960 and 1965, 76 per cent. Table 2, which gives the relevant details, also reveals that UK investment is growing fastest in Western Europe, particularly in Switzerland, the Netherlands and West Germany. Table 3 presents a broad industrial breakdown of UK interests overseas. It shows the major and growing importance of most kinds of manufacturing and distribution investments. The traditional activities of agriculture and mining have become steadily less attractive with the passing of years.

Of the 5,162 large investing companies (excluding oil companies) giving data to the Board of Trade in 1965, 929 were branches of UK enterprises and 4,233 subsidiary or associate companies. Some 2,220 of the latter concerns, with assets of £1,477m. (34·6 per cent of the total) were fully owned subsidiaries. Of the rest, 1,260, with assets of £356m. (8·8 per cent of the total), owned minority interests in foreign companies.

Just over a third of UK overseas enterprises (1,757) were first established before 1946, but two-fifths (2,045) have been operating for less than a decade. But, while the UK share of the net assets of these latter firms was worth only £720m. in 1965 (17·7 per cent of the value of all large investments), pre-war-originated investments were worth £2,575m. (63·6 per cent). Of the investments worth more than £5m. in 1965, just under four-fifths originated before 1946. Most recent investments have been in small to medium-size plants. There is also a trend away from the setting up of branch plants and fully owned subsidiaries towards jointly financed companies – particularly in the mining and transport industries.

No complete information is available on the size structure of UK outward investment but, of the 3,667 companies giving details of *both* investment and earnings in 1965,[2] 131 with assets of more than £5m. accounted for 45·8 per cent of all net assets, while nearly one-

[1] Balance sheet values.

[2] See Table 16, p. XVII, *Board of Trade Journal*, 26/1/68.

TABLE 1

Book Values of UK Direct Capital Stake Abroad and Foreign Capital Stake in UK[1]

£m.

	1960	1961	1962	1963	1964	1965	1966	1900/66 Percentage Increase
UK capital stake abroad	2,950	3,190	3,410	3,640	3,910	4,215	4,500	52·5
Foreign capital stake in UK	1,040	1,290	1,430	1,610	1,780	1,980	2,200	111·5

[1] Excluding investments in the oil industry and in banking and insurance.
Source: *Board of Trade Journal*, 26/1/68.

TABLE 2

Growth of UK Direct Capital Stake Abroad 1960/65 by Area and Country[1]

£m.

	Net assets 1960	Net assets 1965	Change in Net assets 1960–1965	Rate of growth of Net assets 1960–1965 (per cent)	Per cent of total change in Net assets
North America	719·1	919·0	199·9	27·8	15·8
USA	268·4	387·6	119·2	44·4	9·4
Canada	450·7	531·4	80·7	17·9	6·4
Western Europe	298·6	548·9	250·3	83·8	19·8
EEC	217·8	392·2	174·4	80·0	13·8
Belgium and Luxembourg	51·2	67·7	16·5	32·2	1·3
France	67·9	117·6	49·7	73·2	3·9
Italy	35·9	39·8	3·9	10·9	0·3
Netherlands	20·7	56·3	35·6	172·0	2·8
W. Germany	42·1	110·8	68·7	163·2	5·4
EFTA	55·4	114·5	59·1	106·7	4·7
Denmark	8·2	17·0	8·8	107·3	0·7
Switzerland	4·8	26·8	22·0	458·3	1·7
Other Countries	25·4	42·2	16·8	66·1	1·3
South and Central America	144·1	212·8	68·7	47·7	5·4
Argentina	34·0	64·0	30·6	90·0	2·4
Brazil	30·0	45·1	15·1	50·3	1·2
Mexico	24·2	41·0	16·8	69·4	1·3
Commonwealth	1,787·8	2,429·8	642·0	35·9	50·8
Australia	431·8	712·9	281·1	65·1	22·2
New Zealand	93·3	137·1	43·8	46·9	3·5
S. Africa	258·3	391·7	133·4	51·6	10·5
India	227·5	304·0	76·5	33·6	6·0
Malaysia	110·5	144·0	33·5	30·3	2·6
Jamaica	14·8	20·4	5·6	37·8	0·4
Ghana	47·8	53·4	5·6	11·7	0·4
Nigeria	88·0	96·7	8·7	9·9	0·7
Developing Countries	1,087·0	1,395·0	308·0	28·3	24·3
Developed Countries	1,863·0	2,820·0	957·0	51·4	75·7
All Countries	2,950·0	4,215·0	1,265·0	42·9	100·0

[1] Including investments in the oil industry and in banking and insurance.
Source: *Board of Trade Journal*, 26/1/68.

TABLE 3

Industrial Composition and Growth of UK Direct Capital Stake Abroad, 1960/65

	Net Assets 1960 £m.	Percentage of Net Assets 1960	Net Assets 1965 £m.	Percentage of Net Assets 1965	Change in Net Assets 1960 to 1965 £m.	Rate of Growth of Net Assets 1960 to 1965	Percentage of Total Change in Net Assets
Agriculture (including plantations)	294·5	10·0	365·0	8·7	70·5	23·9	5·6
Mining	197·2	6·7	271·1	6·4	73·9	37·5	5·8
Electrical and mechanical engineering	214·4	7·3	296·7	7·0	82·3	38·4	6·5
Vehicles, shipbuilding and marine engineering	102·5	3·5	97·3	2·3	−5·2	−5·1	−0·4
Other manufacturing	1,133·3	38·4	1,709·4	40·6	576·1	50·8	45·5
Total manufacturing	1,450·2	49·2	2,103·4	49·9	653·2	48·4	51·6
Construction	26·4	0·9	49·6	1·2	23·2	87·9	1·8
Distribution	430·6	14·6	671·1	15·9	240·5	55·9	19·0
Transport and communications	97·3	3·3	139·5	3·3	42·2	43·4	3·3
Other activities	453·8	15·4	615·3	14·6	161·5	35·6	12·8
Total all industries	2,950·0	100·0	4,215·0	100·0	1,265·0	42·9	100·0
Petroleum	922·6	—	1,275·3[1]	—		38·2[2]	

[1] 1964, [2] 1960/65.

Source: *Board of Trade Journal*, 26/1/68; Reddaway, *Interim Report*, p. 41.

half of all companies (1,913) has assets worth less than £¼ million. Industries with larger than average investment include mining, vehicles and other manufacturing; the smaller investments were in construction and distribution.

About 45 per cent of the new outward investment by British companies in the period 1960/65 was financed by reinvested profits, and, the balance, capital exported from the UK or changes in branch indebtedness. The proportion of self-financing was slightly more important in the developed than in the developing countries. Little data are available on the extent to which UK companies borrow locally. We do know, however, that at the end of 1965, UK companies, with total net assets of £3,384·6m., had long-term loans outstanding to overseas residents of £603·3m., mostly in the US, Canada, Australia and Western Europe. In addition short-term liabilities held locally were valued at £1,603 million.[1]

Measuring the 'return' or payback on investment

Let it be said straight away that there are very considerable problems in evaluating the return or payback to a particular foreign direct investment. These are basically of two kinds, viz. (*a*) conceptual, and (*b*) practical.

The conceptual difficulties arise at a *micro-level*, through trying to identify the income stream arising from a particular increment of capital stock or investment. The Discounted Cash Flow (DCF) formula implies that one can isolate the stream of receipts accruing to an investment by an individual firm from that accruing to the rest of the capital owned. In practice, this is only possible when the two streams of receipts are independent of each other. At a *macro-level*, there is the no less intractable problem of assessing both the direct and indirect effects of foreign investment by a particular company on the investing community as a whole, i.e. its social costs and benefits.

The practical difficulties arise mainly through data limitations; notwithstanding the work of Reddaway and the Board of Trade in the UK, and the US Department of Commerce, these remain considerable. It is also important to be quite clear about the context in which the foreign investment issue is debated and the underlying assumptions involved, e.g. with respect to substitution possibilities and remissions behaviour. These will differ (and hence one's interpretation of the worthwhileness of foreign investment will differ)

[1] Table 5, p. xi, *Board of Trade Journal*, 26/1/68.

according, *inter alia*, from whose viewpoint we are considering the problem; with which particular aims in view; and under what economic constraints? For the moment, however, we are interested in assessing the *actual* returns associated with foreign investment; we leave until later a discussion of whether such returns are higher or lower then those which could have been earned with alternative patterns of resource allocation.[1]

Evaluating the return on investment at a micro-economic level

(*a*) *Average returns*

Let us suppose that we are interested in evaluating the average annual private rate of return on capital invested abroad by a UK company ($\bar{r}_{fpg}$) over a given period of time (in years). Let $Y_{fpg}n$ represent the total income (less all taxes and depreciation) accruing to the investing company in a particular year as a direct consequence of the capital invested overseas, and $K_{fp}n-1$ the foreign capital invested at the end of the previous year. Then:

$$\bar{r}_{fpg} = \frac{1}{n}\left(\frac{Y_{fpg}1}{K_{fp}0} + \frac{Y_{fpg}2}{K_{fp}1} + \cdots \frac{Y_{fpg}n}{K_{fp}n-1}\right).$$

Now normally Y_{fpg} (and hence $\bar{r}_{fpg}$) will be made up of two components:

1. The income earned directly by the foreign subsidiary, or charges made by the investing company on it, which can be either reinvested or remitted to the investing company (Y_{fp}). This consists of:

   (i) interest and profits ($Y_{fp(i)}$); and
   (ii) royalties and fees ($Y_{fp(ii)}$).

In addition, allowance should also be made for changes in the market value of the capital stock of the subsidiary or associate ($Y_{fp(iii)}$). Expressed as a percentage of K_{fp}, we then have four relevant rates of return, viz. $\bar{r}_{fp}$, $\bar{r}_{fp(i),\ (ii)\ \text{and}\ (iii)}$.

2. The indirect costs and benefits accruing to the rest of investing firm's organization, as a consequence of such foreign investment ($Y_{d'p}$). $Y_{d'p}$ consists of a number of components, not all of which can be easily identified. The most important of these are:

[1] See pp. 84ff; also G. C. Hufbauer and F. M. Adler, *Overseas Manufacturing and the Balance of Payments*, US Treasury Department, 1968, pp. 6ff.

(i) the costs incurred, by the investing company, of providing research and development and various kinds of services to the foreign subsidiary.

(ii) the value of the additional (or reduced) output produced and sold by the investing company, less the cost of supplying that output;

(iii) the change in the prices of factor inputs (including imports) and finished products (including exports) due to the foreign investment (i.e. the terms-of-trade effect).

(iv) the value of the managerial, technological and marketing expertise gained and passed back from the subsidiary to the investing company *less* any payments made for such expertise.

(v) the tax paid (or rebate received) by the investing company on direct or indirect earnings (losses) of the foreign subsidiary.

(vi) the effect on the stability of demand for output (particularly exports) of the investing company or the supply of its inputs;

(vii) the effect on the international competitive position of the investing company and its access to new managerial and marketing philosophies, etc.

It should also be remembered that the evaluation of:

$$Y_{fpg}(= Y_{fpg} + Y_{d'p})$$

is a function of (i) accounting procedures, and (ii) intra-group pricing policies (with respect to both services and goods) of the investing company, both of which are likely to be geared to the minimization of its international tax burden (for any given (world) level of gross profits).[1] The size of $\bar{r}_{fpg}$ (and its components) is further affected by the valuation of K_{fp}. For the purposes of this analysis, we shall take K_{fp} to mean book values of capital (however calculated) and K_{fpr} capital valued at replacement cost (however calculated).

The Board of Trade has published some data on K_{fp} and certain components of Y_{fp} for particular areas and industries for the period 1960/65. In addition, the Reddaway enquiry calculated average rates of return for the firms in its sample for the period 1955/64, valuing capital at replacement cost (K_{fpr}) and, treating as income, appreciation in the market value of the UK stake ($Y_{fp(iii)}$).

Tables 4 and 5 give details of the crude profitability ratios ($Y_{fp(1)}/K_{fp}$)[2] for each year from 1960 to 1965 (Board of Trade data)

1 These points are illustrated in more detail in Chapter 10.

2 More particularly $Y_{fp(1)}n/K_{fp}n$ (end year).

TABLE 4

Average Rates of Return on UK Direct Capital Stake by Area and Country, 1960/65

$Y_{fp(i)}/K_{fp} = \bar{r}_{fp(i)}$[1]

	1960	1961	1962	1963	1964	1965 $r_{fp(i)}$	1965 $r_{fp(ii)}$[2]	1960/65 $\bar{r}_{fp(i)}$
North America	5·2	5·0	5·6	7·3	8·0	8·5	0·7	6·6
USA	6·8	6·6	7·2	10·6	10·8	11·5	1·4	8·9
Canada	4·3	4·0	4·6	5·1	6·1	6·4	0·2	5·1
Western Europe	7·3	8·0	6·9	6·6	5·0	5·1	0·8	6·5
EEC	6·8	8·0	7·1	6·7	3·9	4·6	0·8	6·2
Belgium and Luxembourg	1·2	2·4	5·3	4·4	−4·0	1·3	0·6	1·8
France	3·3	4·1	2·4	5·5	3·8	2·6	0·6	3·6
Italy	0·6	3·6	−1·2	−2·8	−3·7	2·5	1·2	−0·1
Netherlands	7·7	9·9	7·5	5·1	2·1	5·0	0·8	6·2
West Germany	19·0	22·3	19·2	15·2	12·0	9·5	0·9	16·2
EFTA	9·9	8·5	5·1	6·0	8·8	6·6	0·8	7·4
Denmark	4·9	4·3	2·7	0·8	2·8	−0·6	1·2	2·5
Switzerland	20·8	15·9	5·3	7·7	9·9	11·9	0·4	11·9
Other Countries	6·3	6·9	9·7	6·9	6·1	5·2	0·8	6·8
South and Central America	9·6	6·9	7·5	8·4	9·1	8·3	0·7	7·7
Argentina	12·4	5·3	4·5	6·0	10·4	7·7	0·1	7·7
Brazil	17·3	12·2	9·9	10·3	7·9	8·9		12·9
Commonwealth	8·1	6·9	7·2	7·3	8·1	8·0	0·3	7·6
Australia	7·3	5·0	6·1	6·6	7·0	7·7	0·2	6·6
New Zealand	7·4	4·2	6·3	4·8	8·1	7·5	0·3	6·4
South Africa	10·3	10·4	12·1	12·9	14·8	12·1	0·2	12·1
India	8·4	8·3	8·4	6·7	6·9	7·6	0·5	7·7
Malaysia	17·8	17·1	14·8	15·3	15·8	14·5	n.a.	15·9
Jamaica	6·8	5·9	−1·3	11·2	9·7	4·9	n.a.	6·2
Ghana	15·5	15·3	11·1	8·0	14·4	9·4	n.a.	12·3
Nigeria	6·9	4·1	1·5	5·0	6·8	6·3	n.a.	4·3
Developing Countries	10·2	8·9	8·5	8·7	8·9	8·8	0·3	9·0
Developed Countries	7·0	6·5	7·1	7·8	8·2	8·1	0·5	7·1
All Countries	8·4	7·4	7·6	8·1	8·5	8·4	0·4	8·0

[1] Excluding investments in the oil industry and in banking and insurance.

[2] Defined for this purpose as royalties received by the UK firms from 'related firms' abroad. See *Board of Trade Journal*, 21/1/67.

Source: *Board of Trade Journal*, 26/1/68.

TABLE 5

Average Rates of Return on UK Direct Investment by Industry Group [$Y_{fp(i)}/K_{fp} = \bar{r}_{fp(i)}$], 1960/65

	1960	1961	1962	1963	1964	1965	1960/65 (Average)
Agriculture (including plantations)	9·4	8·1	9·6	7·8	7·6	6·8	8·2
Mining	19·8	18·1	17·2	19·2	12·6	13·4	16·7
Electrical and mechanical engineering	2·6	4·6	4·5	3·4	5·0	5·4	4·2
Vehicles, shipbuilding and marine engineering	2·4	0·1	2·1	2·6	−2·3	0·9	1·0
Other manufacturing industries	9·5	8·5	9·3	9·5	10·8	10·1	9·6
Construction	6·4	10·4	5·8	7·5	9·1	10·3	8·1
Distribution	7·2	5·9	5·0	5·7	8·0	7·8	6·6
Transport and communications	12·8	11·5	7·1	9·0	8·0	8·5	9·5
Other activities	3·2	2·7	3·1	4·8	5·0	5·4	4·0
All industries	8·2	7·4	7·6	8·1	8·5	8·4	8·0

Source: *Board of Trade Journal*, 26/1/68.

and Tables 6 and 7 the more realistic income/asset ratios (Y_{fp}/K_{fp}), averaged for the period 1956/64 (Y_{fp}) and end 1955/63 (K_{fp}) (Reddaway data). It can be seen that in some instances, e.g. mining and chemical investments, and investments in Ghana, Italy and Denmark, the inclusion of the $Y_{fp(\text{ii}) \text{ and } (\text{iii})}$ components of Y_{fp} makes a considerable difference both to the aggregate rate of return earned and its ranking between countries and industries.

It should be noted that each set of profitability ratios is considerably influenced by the size distribution of UK firms. Since, according to the Board of Trade, only 9·3 per cent of the firms with overseas interests of £1m. and above (which accounted for four-fifths of all assets in 1965) earned a rate of return of 20 per cent or more, compared with 20·7 per cent of firms with interests of below £1m., the figures of Tables 4 to 7 almost certainly underestimate the *median* or *modal* rate of return.

Both Tables 4 and 5 reveal wide divergencies in the crude profitability ratios ($Y_{fp(\text{i})}/K_{fp}$) recorded by the Board of Trade. The coefficient of variation around the mean of 8·4 per cent for the year 1965 was 0·453 for the geographical distribution and 0·417 for the industrial distribution. The Reddaway data for Y_{fp}/K_{fp} show (rather surprisingly) an even wider dispersion, the respective coefficient of variations being 0·912 for the geographical distribution (around a mean of 13·6) and 0·523 for the industrial distribution (around a mean of 13·0). There is, however, some evidence to suggest that the dispersion of both the geographical and industrial (crude) rate of return has lessened between 1960 and 1965.[1] A quick glance at the distributions in each of the tables also shows that they are moderately positively skewed.

In general, UK firms appear to do better in the less developed countries than in the developed countries. Mining and the production of building materials show up as the most profitable of activities; the engineering, paper and metal industries the least profitable. There appears to be no correlation between $\bar{r}_{fp(\text{i})}$ and $\bar{r}_{fp(\text{ii})}$, but (as one would expect) a good correlation between $\bar{r}_{fp(\text{i})}$ and $\bar{r}_{fp(\text{iii})}$.

We have only piecemeal data on the indirect costs and benefits associated with foreign investment ($Y_{d'p}$), which are hidden in the earnings recorded by the investing company (or other parts of its organization), although we do know that, in certain cases, these may be very high in relation to Y_{fp}. The Reddaway enquiry has shed some

[1] The coefficient of variations for $Y_{fp(\text{i})}/K_{fp}$ for 1960 being 0·621 and 0·623 around a mean of 8·2 per cent.

light on the value of the feedback of technical knowledge from foreign manufacturing activities ($Y_{d'p(iv)}$) and the costs involved to the investing company ($Y_{d'p(i)}$).[1] It also suggests that except in the motor vehicles and non-electrical engineering industries, such activities (unlike those in sales and marketing) have little effect on the exports (and, hence, output) of the investing enterprises ($Y_{d'p(ii)}$)[2] and that, apart from oil imports, UK parent companies (in contrast to their US counterparts) purchase very little from their overseas offshoots. None of the output of the plantation subsidiaries, dealt with by the Cambridge study, was exported *directly* to UK parent companies[3] and only 1½ per cent of that of manufacturing and mining subsidiaries.[4] On the basis of these data, we might conclude that the impact of foreign direct investment on the stability and prices of UK imports ($Y_{d'p(iii)}$ and $Y_{d'p)iv)}$) is negligible, although this evidence is not entirely conclusive as it ignores both the exports of UK subsidiaries to *other* UK firms, and the fact that open-market prices might be higher or lower in the absence of UK investment. It is also possible to make a rough calculation of the UK tax levied on profits remitted by foreign businesses, where the tax rate in the host country is less that that in the UK ($Y_{d'p(v)}$).

The benefits of technical feedback are clearly most likely to arise from investments in 'knowledge' productive industries, especially those concentrated in technologically advanced countries. In 1964, 89 per cent of the UK capital in US manufacturing industry was in subsidiaries which were reckoned to yield a significant feedback of knowledge;[5] the corresponding percentage for Western Germany was 74 per cent, for Australia 68 per cent, for Canada 48 per cent and for the world as a whole 41 per cent.[6] In an attempt to put a monetary figure on the net gain in knowledge acquistion and that resulting from knowledge transmission which would be lost to the investing company if overseas investment ceased to exist, the Cambridge economists considered three types of income:

(i) payments made by subsidiaries to the investing company for knowledge transmitted (part of $Y_{fp(ii)}$) less the cost of pro-

[1] W. B. Reddaway, *Final Report*, *op. cit.*, pp. 309ff.
[2] W. B. Reddaway, *Interim Report*, *op. cit.*, p. 78.
[3] W. B. Reddaway, *Final Report*, *op. cit.*, p. 381.
[4] W. B. Reddaway, *Interim Report*, *op. cit.*, p. 78.
[5] W. B. Reddaway, *Final Report*, *op. cit.*, p. 322.
[6] This includes eight of the fifteen countries covered in the enquiry which reported no feedback.

ducing this knowledge where otherwise it would not need to be produced ($Y_{d'p(i)}$);

(ii) the value of research and development undertaken by foreign subsidiaries (this is regarded as a proxy for research output) less that part which is of local interest only, less any payment made by the investing company (or the rest of its organization) for this knowledge);

(iii) an estimate of the value of informal knowledge or general expertise gained as a result of foreign investment, i.e. which would not have been obtained in the absence of the investment.

An estimate was also made of the likely income that the investing company would have derived from licensing agreements concluded in the absence of its overseas activities. This represented one of the costs of foreign investment and, like the benefits, was expressed as a proportion of the net operating assets of the investing companies. The data are incorporated in Tables 6a and 7, which reveal that, for all manufacturing industries and countries, the gain was about 1·0 per cent of net operating assets in 1964, with the greatest gains being recorded by the chemicals and non-electrical engineering industries and by subsidiaries operating in West Germany, the United States and Canada. The value of formal research and/or informal knowhow originating in the host country was particularly marked in the chemical, food, drink and tobacco and metal products industries.

It is difficult from the data available to make allowance for the UK taxes paid on profits remitted by subsidiaries, as the method of dealing with these taxes differs. Sometimes they are charged against the profits of subsidiaries and sometimes against those of the investing companies. On the whole ($Y_{d'p(v)}$) would not seem to be very important. In only four of the fifteen countries covered in the Reddaway enquiry did the overseas tax rate on profits in 1964 work out less than 40 per cent and the average rate was 45·3 per cent.[1] In general, the tax rates were rather less in the less developed than in the developed countries. To give some idea of the possible value of the (UK) tax differential, if one assumes (*a*) that 50 per cent of the profits earned by subsidiaries in 1955/64 (after overseas tax) were remitted and that these are taxed at the difference between the overseas tax rate and the average UK tax rate (41·5 per cent), then

[1] W. B. Reddaway, *Final Report*, p. 219. The profits data for Argentina and Brazil have been adjusted to record the actual profits earned. See *Interim Report*, p. 180.

TABLE 6

Combined Rate of Return on UK Direct Investment by Industry Groups $\bar{Y}_{fp}/\bar{K}_{fp} = \bar{r}_{fp}$ 1955/64

	(1) UK Groups Stake (Annual Average 1955/63)	(2) Post-tax Profits Attributable to UK Group (Annual Average 1956/64)		(3) Royalties and Management Fees after Overseas Tax (Annual Average 1956/64)		(4) Capital Appreciation[1] (end 1955 to end 1964 Expressed as 9-yr. Annual Average)		(5) Combined Rate of Return (Percent per Annum 1956/64) $\frac{(2)+(3)+(4)}{(1)}$	
	$\bar{K}_{fp}$ (£m.)	$\bar{Y}_{fp(i)}$ (£m.)	$\bar{r}_{fp(i)}$	$\bar{Y}_{fp(ii)}$ (£m.)	$\bar{r}_{fp(ii)}$	$\bar{Y}_{fp(iii)}$ (£m.)	$\bar{r}_{fp(iii)}$	$\bar{Y}_{fp}$ (£m.)	$\bar{r}_{fp}$
Building materials, etc.	57·2	7·8	13·7	0·0	0·1	3·3	5·7	11·1	19·4
Chemicals	128·1	10·7	8·4	1·0	0·8	12·3	9·6	24·0	18·7
Textiles	77·6	6·0	7·7	0·8	1·0	3·3	4·2	10·1	13·0
Food, drink, tobacco, and household products	447·2	39·2	8·8	4·8	1·1	8·4	1·8	52·4	11·7
Vehicles and components	90·1	4·5	5·0	1·0	1·1	3·1	3·5	8·6	9·5
Metals and metal products	96·5	7·1	7·4	0·2	0·2	1·2	1·2	8·5	8·8
Paper	69·2	5·3	7·7	0·1	0·1	−0·2	−0·2	5·2	7·5
Electrical engineering	48·7	2·6	5·4	0·8	1·6	1·0	2·0	4·4	9·0
Non-electrical engineering	18·0	0·8	4·5	0·1	0·5	−0·1	−0·4	0·8	4·5
Total manufacturing	1,032·8	84·1	8·1	8·9	0·9	32·3	+3·2	125·3	24·3
Mining	89·3	12·8	12·8	1·3	1·5	10·8	12·1	24·9	26·4
Plantations	92·7	8·9	9·6	0·3	0·4	−1·5	−1·7	7·7	8·3
Total (excluding oil)	1,214·8	105·9	8·7	10·6	0·9	41·6	3·4	158·1	13·1

[1] 'Capital appreciation' – 'Growth in Market Value' (end 1955 to end 1964) less 'additional capital invested' during same period. 'Additional capital invested' increments of share and loan capital supplied to subsidiaries, sub-subsidiaries and branches by the UK [illegible] including all forms of loan and credit on long- and short-term account, plus retained profits of subsidiaries, etc.

TABLE 6a

Return from Profits, Capital Appreciation and Knowledge-sharing – UK Overseas Manufacturing Subsidiaries

Return on UK share of net operating assets

	(1) Post-tax Profits	(2) Capital Apprecia-tion	(3) Net Gain from Knowledge-sharing	(4) (1), (2) and (3) com-bined
Building materials, etc.	13·7	5·7	0·4	19·8
Food, drink, tobacco, etc.	8·8	4·2	0·9	13·9
Textiles	7·7	1·8	0	9·5
Chemicals	8·4	9·6	3·0	21·0
Metals and metal products	7·4	1·2	0·4	9·0
Paper	7·7	−0·2	0·1	7·6
Electrical engineering	5·4	2·0	1·0	8·4
Vehicles and components	5·0	3·5	0·9	9·4
Non-electrical engineering	4·5	−0·4	1·7	5·8
Total	8·1	3·2	1·0	12·3†
Total (adjusted)*	5·5	—	0·9	6·4

Notes: Columns (1) and (2) are 9-year averages for the period 1956/64; (3) was calculated by dividing the gain from research, etc. in 1964 by assets at end-1963.

* Calculated on replacement cost basis, with stock appreciation eliminated.

† 12·2 per cent after allowing for estimated UK taxation of remitted profits.

Source: Derived from Tables XI.1 and XXV.3 of *Reddaway reports.*

the overall profit rate is reduced by only 0·1 per cent – from 8·7 per cent to 8·6 per cent. In certain countries, however, as Table 7 shows, the differences are rather more pronounced, viz. South Africa, 0·5 per cent, Malaysia 0·7 per cent, Jamaica 0·2 per cent, and Denmark 0·4 per cent.

(*b*) *Marginal returns*

An additional problem arises when one tries to calculate the return on incremental investment = $\Delta Y_{fp}/\Delta K_p$ or r'_{fpg}. Much depends here on the market conditions assumed to be facing the investing firm. Under a competitive static situation, average and marginal returns will normally be the same. Under a monopolistic static situation,

TABLE 7

Combined Rate of Return on UK Direct Investment by Country[1] (%)

	(1) UK Stake (Annual Average 1955/63) £m. $\bar{K}_{fp}$	(2) Post-tax Profitability of UK Stake (Annual Average 1956/64) $\bar{r}_{fp(i)}$	(3) Royalties and Management Fees (Annual Average 1956/64) $\bar{r}_{fp(ii)}$	(4) Capital Appreciation[2] (Annual Average 1955 to 1964) $\bar{r}_{fp(iii)}$	(5) Combined Rate of Return (Items 2+3+4) $\bar{r}_{fp}$	(6) Net Gain from Knowledge-Sharing (1964) $\bar{r}_{d'p(i)}$	(7) Differential Tax on Remitted Profits (Annual Average 1956/64) $\bar{r}_{d'p(v)}$	(8) Combined Rate of Return (Items 5+6+7) $\bar{r}_{fp}$
Germany	27·8	22·8	1·4	11·7	35·9	2·5	—	37·4
Malaysia	50·8	19·8	1·0	8·1	28·9	neg.	−0·7	28·2
Italy	6·0	12·3	1·9	4·9	19·1	neg.	—	19·1
India	132·4	7·7	0·3	0·0	8·0	0·4	—	8·4
Ghana	24·1	13·4	4·1	−0·6	16·9	neg.	—	16·9
Brazil	24·0	5·3	1·2	4·5	11·0	neg.	—	11·0
South Africa	97·0	10·5	0·5	9·0	20·0	0·1	−0·5	19·6
Australia	156·4	8·0	0·8	7·5	16·3	0·7	—	17·0
USA	211·8	8·6	1·0	2·6	12·2	1·5	−0·2	13·7
Jamaica	5·2	8·4	0·1	−1·7	6·8	neg.	—	6·6
Canada	171·4	5·5	0·2	−0·6	6·3	0·8	—	7·1
Nigeria	49·5	4·7	1·9	1·1	7·7	neg.	—	7·7
Argentina	14·0	1·6	0·4	4·2	6·2	neg.	—	6·2
France	14·5	1·9	1·2	−1·7	1·4	0·7	—	2·1
Denmark	4·4	5·3	2·6	−0·3	7·6	neg.	−0·4	7·2
Total 15 countries	989·3	8·7	0·8	3·0	12·5	0·7	−0·1	13·1
World	1,214·8	8·7	0·9	3·0	12·6	0·7	−0·1	13·2

[1] Excluding investments in oil industry, plantations, banking and insurance. For further details see *Reddaway Report*, Appendix B, p. 138.

[2] Data here refer to appreciation of operating assets *controlled* by UK firms at end of each year. See Table XVI.1 of *Final Report*. Source: Derived from *Reddaway Report*, Tables IV.5, IV.10, XVI.1, XVI.2 and XXV.5.

marginal returns will normally be less than average returns.[1] Under an oligopolistic dynamic situation, where firms may invest not to exploit new markets, innovations or products, but to protect *existing* profits, r'_{fpg} may be greater than $\bar{r}_{fpg}$. This is the *organic* theory of investment put forward in 1966 by the US National Industrial Conference Board.[2] In its extreme form, this theory suggests that all new investment should be regarded as a necessary support to the earning capacity of the existing capital employed, and that any attempts to curtail such investment will weaken this capacity.

Let us define $r'_{fpg}{}^*$ as the difference between the earnings on present capital ($K_{fp}n$), and the income that *would have been earned* on past capital ($K_{fp}n - 1$) *had not the new investment been made.* This is only equal to r'_{fpg} where $\bar{r}_{fpg}$ (the average rate of return) is constant.

Tables 8 and 9 present the Board of Trade data, which show, first that the world marginal rate of return ($r'_{fp(i)}$) exceeded the average rate of return ($\bar{r}_{fp(i)}$) for the period 1960/65 and second that the variation in $r'_{fp(i)}$ between countries and industries is very wide indeed. In some countries, notably the USA, Canada, Italy and South Africa, the profitability of UK firms has noticeably improved; in others, e.g. West Germany, Jamaica and Ghana, it has considerably fallen. Over the longer period (1955/64) the marginal rate of return worked out at 8·1 per cent – slightly below the average return of 8·7 per cent. Most industries maintained a fairly steady profitability in these years: the exceptions are building materials, which has steadily become less profitable, and electrical engineering and vehicles, which have increased their profitability.[3]

For reasons stated earlier, both $\bar{r}_{fp}$ and $\bar{r}'_{fp}$ are likely to be considerably greater than the published figures of $\bar{r}_{fp(i)}$ and $r'_{fp(i)}$, but as some of the external benefits to foreign investment, i.e. those accruing to the investing company, are essentially once-for-all benefits r'_{fp} may well be slightly less than $\bar{r}_{fp}$. No data at all are available on $r'_{fp}{}^*$.

If one accepts the organic theory of investment (and it is certainly upheld by businessmen both in this country and in the US) and assumes that the minimum proportion of UK profits reinvested in any one year between 1960 and 1965 is a fair measure of this 'dynamic-replacement' type investment, then about 30 per cent

[1] M. Frankel, 'Home versus foreign investment; a case against capital exports,' *Kyklos*, Vol. XVIII, 1965.

[2] National Industrial Conference Board, *US production abroad and the US balance of payments*, New York, 1966.

[3] See particularly Table G.2, p. 192, of W. B. Reddaway, *op. cit.*

TABLE 8

Marginal Rate of Return on UK Direct Investment Abroad 1960/65

(*a*) By Country

	(1) Change in Net Assets 1960/65 £m. ΔK_{fp}	(2) Change in Net Earnings 1960/65 £m. $\Delta Y_{fp(1)}$	(3) Marginal Rate of Return $\frac{(2)}{(1)}$ $r'_{fp(1)}$
North America	199·9	46·5	23·3
USA	119·2	29·5	24·7
Canada	80·7	17·0	21·1
Western Europe	250·3	7·5	3·0
EEC	174·4	4·0	2·3
Belgium and Luxembourg	16·5	0·4	3·8
France	49·7	1·2	2·4
Italy	3·9	0·8	20·5
Netherlands	35·6	1·2	3·4
West Germany	68·7	0·6	0·9
EFTA	59·1	2·7	4·6
Denmark	8·8	−0·5	−5·7
Switzerland	22·0	2·4	10·9
Other Countries	16·8	0·9	5·3
South and Central America	68·7	5·3	7·7
Argentina	30·6	1·1	3·6
Brazil	15·1	−1·1	−7·3
Commonwealth			
Australia	281·1	28·0	10·0
New Zealand	43·8	4·5	10·3
South Africa	133·4	27·9	20·9
India	76·5	5·4	7·1
Malaysia	33·5	2·3	6·9
Jamaica	5·6	0·0	0·0
Ghana	5·6	−1·7	−32·9
Nigeria	8·7	1·7	19·5
Developing Countries	308·0	22·0	7·1
Developed Countries	957·0	121·0	12·6
All Countries	1,265·0	143·0	11·3

Source: *Board of Trade Journals*, 26/1/68 and 30/6/67.

TABLE 9

Marginal Rate of Return on UK Direct Investment Abroad 1960/65

(*b*) **By Industry**

	(1) Change in Net Assets 1960/65 £m. ΔK_{fp}	(2) Change in Net Earnings 1960/65 £m. $\Delta Y_{fp(1)}$	(3) Marginal Rate of Return $\frac{(2)}{(1)}$ $r'_{fp(1)}$
Agriculture (including plantations)	70·5	−2·7	−3·8
Mining	73·9	−2·8	−3·8
Electrical and mechanical engineering	82·3	10·5	12·8
Vehicles, shipbuilding and marine engineering	−5·2	−1·6	30·8
Other manufacturing	576·1	65·3	11·3
Construction	23·2	3·4	14·7
Distribution	240·5	21·1	8·8
Transport and communications	42·2	2·3	5·5
Other activities	161·5	51·9	32·1
Total all industries	1,265·0	143·0	11·3

Source: *Board of Trade Journals*, 26/1/68 and 30/6/67.

of new investment – including direct capital flows from the UK – by British firms over this period was of this kind. This implies that any attempt to reduce UK (direct) foreign investment by more than around £90m. a year (on the basis of the 1963/65 figures) might well bring about a fall in the *average* rate of profit earned on the existing capital stake overseas. Unfortunately, we do not have the data to put this hypothesis to the test, and, in any event, it could be argued (i) that it does not follow that all new investment controlled by UK firms overseas must be financed from the UK (once again, it is important to distinguish between the capital *controlled* by UK foreign enterprises and the amount actually *owned* by them), and (ii) part of domestic investment might equally be regarded as of the dynamic-replacement type.[1]

The organic theory of investment has also been put forward to explain the impetus for the establishment of a completely new foreign

[1] In the period 1960/65 the average ratio of reinvested to total profits by UK firms in the UK was only slightly less than that of UK firms operating overseas.

enterprise. Here, it is suggested that much of UK outward investment is undertaken purely for defensive reasons, e.g. to counteract falling export markets and international competition, and that, if the UK manufacturers did not set up an operating unit in particular countries, native or third-country firms would do so, and this would be not only to the detriment of the competitive position of the UK manufacturers in question but of the UK economy in general.[1]

Viewed in its wider context, this particular approach to investment behaviour helps us to understand the changing role of the international company in the world economy. So often one observes that yesterday's leading exporters of goods are today's leading exporters of capital, and that an increasing proportion of the profits of such companies are derived from their overseas operations. In 1965, income earned abroad by UK companies was just two-fifths of the profits earned by all companies at home, and the trend is steadily upwards. Expressed as a percentage of visible exports, income from interests, profits and dividends increased from 7·0 per cent in 1952 to 11·5 per cent in 1960 and 13·1 per cent in 1965.

In the US, the growing contribution of the international company to the invisible account is even more dramatically revealed. Between 1950 and 1964, while US visible exports of manufactured and semi-manufactured goods rose by 87·8 per cent, the income earned by foreign manufacturing subsidiaries and associate companies increased by 185·1 per cent. Sales of American affiliates abroad have grown twice to three times as fast as US exports of similar commodities. Whereas, at one time, the international exchange of goods compensated for the international immobility of capital and labour, nowadays, due *inter alia* to the trend towards economic nationalism and the formation of regional trading blocs, international investment is often the only way by which advanced industrial nations can protect export markets and advances their foreign exchange earnings.

Evaluating the return on foreign investment at a macro-economic level

Here, it is important to distinguish between the alternative aims of the community with respect to its foreign investment. Basically, UK economic policy in recent years seems to have been oriented towards two objectives:

[1] A. Maddison, 'How fast can Britain grow,' *Lloyds Bank Review*, January 1966; B. Balassa, 'American direct investment in the common market,' *Banca Nazionale del Lavoro Quarterly Review*, June 1966.

(*a*) the maximization of the social product (or rate of growth of social product) independently of its composition.
(*b*) the maximization of (net) foreign exchange earnings.

Sometimes these objectives are complementary to each other – sometimes they compete with each other. In practice (*b*) has been the main constraint on the rate which (*a*) has been achieved. In addition, foreign investment may be undertaken for various non-economic objectives, e.g. as a form of aid to developing countries, to protect military bases or the security of the investing country, etc., but we shall not attempt to evaluate these in this chapter.

There are a number of differences between appraising the *private* and *social* return to overseas investment ($\bar{r}_{fpg}$ and $\bar{r}_{fsg}$).[1] First, the impact of private foreign investment on the welfare of the rest of the community may be positive or negative in terms of both (*a*) the quantity and composition of output produced and/or (*b*) the price of that output. Much will depend on the type of foreign investment involved. Obviously the macro-economic effects of setting up a sales enterprise overseas, the purpose of which is to advance the exports of the investing company, are likely to be quite different from those following an investment in oil drilling or mineral exploitation. Here, there is little firm empirical evidence but plenty of impressions. Secondly, there is the question of interpreting the returns from overseas investment. To the investing enterprise, the returns represent the money income (net of *all* taxes) earned directly or indirectly, from foreign operations (Y_{fp}) and accruing to the investing company. To the community, it is the *social* product, i.e. the (real) income, derived by the investing country – irrespective of how it is distributed – from overseas investment, *gross* of UK taxation *less* UK subsidies (Y_{fs}). Y_{fp} and Y_{fs} will tend always to be different as long as the UK Exchequer taxes any part of overseas income earned.

Thirdly, the private investor is not, in general, concerned with the macro-economic objective (*b*) listed on the previous page.

We now examine the social return to overseas investment in respect of (*a*) resource allocation and (*b*) the balance of payments.

(*a*) *The social product 'return' to foreign investment*
The impressions we have on the various components of

$$\bar{r}_{fsg} = \frac{Y_{fs} + Y_{d's}}{K_{fp}}$$

[1] These are examined in detail in Chapter 4.

are as follows:

1. $\bar{r}_{fs}$ is likely to exceed $\bar{r}_{fp}$ by the amount of tax paid to the UK Government on income earned on overseas operations. In recent years this difference has averaged between 0·1 per cent and 0·2 per cent in the case of the leading UK companies overseas.[1]

2. We have no real evidence on the relationship between $\frac{Y_{d's}}{K_{fp}}$ and $\frac{Y_{d'p}}{K_{fp}}$. However of the social (i.e. non-private) *costs* of overseas investment, the most important are:

C (i) Costs borne by the UK Exchequer in support or protection of UK investments overseas, e.g. in the trouble spots of the world such as Malaysia and Nigeria.

C (ii) Any reduction in the real output produced in UK by other than the investing firms.

C (iii) Any movement in the terms of trade *against* the UK apart from changes in import and/or export prices affecting the investing firms.

The social *benefits* of overseas investment include:

B (i) Any increase in the real output produced in the UK by other than the investing firms.

B (ii) Any movement in the terms of trade in favour of the UK apart from changes in import and/or export prices affecting the investing firms.

B (iii) The value of the feedback of managerial technology or marketing knowhow accruing to the UK economy apart from the investing firms.

B (iv) The value of the competitive stimulus of (iii) and more dynamic managerial and marketing philosophies imported from overseas and accruing to the UK economy apart from the investing firms.

Nowhere, to our knowledge, have these costs and benefits been systematically evaluated, though a framework of research for doing this has been suggested by Professors Pearce and Rowan of Southampton University.[2] We cannot say at the moment if $Y_{d's}$ is greater

[1] See p. 64.

[2] I. F. Pearce and D. C. Rowan, 'A framework of research into the real effects of international capital movements,' in T. Bagiotti, Padova (ed.), *Essays in honour of Marco Fanno*, 1966.

or less than $Y_{d'p}$ mainly because of the very considerable problems of assessing the terms-of-trade effect and, as is shown as an Appendix to this essay, it takes only a very small movement in the terms of trade to influence the social return on capital markedly. As regards C (ii) and B (ii) most researchers have evaded the question by assuming a permanent situation of full employment at home existed. Whatever the justification of this assumption for policy reasons it ignores the impact of foreign investment on the *efficiency* of resource utilization and allocation – both from a static and dynamic standpoint.

Our impressions, gained largely from the Reddaway enquiry and our own researches[1], are that *apart* from the terms-of-trade effect (C (iii) and B (ii)) $Y_{d's}$ will normally be slightly higher than $Y_{d'p}$ and that in 1965, $\bar{r}_{fs(1)}$ was probably between 0·5 per cent and 1·0 per cent higher than $\bar{r}_{fp(1)}$. There is likely to be less difference between $r'_{fs(1)}$ and $r'_{fp(1)}$: our 'guesstimate' is that it was between 0·2 per cent and 0·5 per cent in 1965 – mainly because some of the (net) benefits contained in $\bar{r}_{fs}$ are once-for-all benefits and largely independent of the flow of new investment.

(b) The balance-of-payments 'return' to foreign investment

To estimate the balance-of-payments return of foreign investment involves the same sort of problems as estimating the profitability of foreign investment.[2] Formally, the return is represented by the following equation:

$$I_f(1 - \alpha) = \sum_{i=1}^{i=n} \frac{Y_{fs}(1 - t) + \Delta Ei}{(1 + r)^i}$$

where I_f = the initial foreign investment;
α = the percentage of this investment financed by the export of capital goods from the investing country;
t = the tax levied by the host country;
Y_{fs} = the (social) income earned on I_f;
ΔEi = the change in national exports minus the change in national imports of the investing country associated with I_f.

[1] In his *Final Report*, Reddaway attempts to evaluate certain of the social costs and benefits of foreign investment (see, e.g., Table XII. 4, p. 373, in which he presents estimates on certain 'invisible' receipts associated with foreign investment) but serious gaps in our knowledge still remain.

[2] For further details see Appendix A to this chapter.

This formula, however, takes no account of the balance-of-payments *opportunity cost* of foreign investment, i.e. the exports (less imports) that would have been earned had not the investment been made. This involves assessing the impact of *not* investing on the economies of both the investing and host countries. At this stage in our argument, we shall assume that the opportunity cost of investing overseas, from the viewpoint of the *investing* country, is zero, and concern ourselves only with the substitution possibilities facing the *host* country. The Reddaway report postulates that UK investment abroad substitutes for investment by native or third-country firms; it makes no net addition to plant capacity in the host country over and above that which would have otherwise existed. This, as Hufbauer and Adler point out in their analysis of US direct manufacturing investments and the balance of payments,[1] broadly follows the form of the *reverse classical* substitution model, in which direct investment is assumed to substitute freely for foreign investment but does not affect home outlays.

Before proceeding to review the Reddaway findings in some detail, it might be helpful to outline the two other models used by Hufbauer and Adler in their study. These are first, the *classical* substitution model, which hypothesizes that direct foreign investment completely supplements investment in the host country but completely replaces home investment; in this model, plant capacity is created in the host country which would not otherwise exist, while in the investing country there is a corresponding decline in plant capacity. By contrast, the *anti-classical* substitution model postulates that foreign investment increases plant capacity abroad but does not decrease capacity at home, i.e. it has a zero domestic opportunity cost. This model is the only one of the three that implies that world capital formation will increase as a result of international investment.

Each of these models has a number of variants, but all three appear to assume that a state of full employment exists in the host country, and that total market activity can only increase by a rise in autonomous expenditure, e.g. net exports. The Hufbauer/Adler *anti-classical* model is essentially an import substitution model in that it assumes that any addition in output of local firms caused by direct foreign investment will require the host country to reduce its imports by the same amount. The Reddaway model, by contrast, assumes that other firms in the host country – competitive with the

[1] G. C. Hufbauer and F. M. Adler, *Overseas Manufacturing Investment and the Balance of Payments*, US Treasury Department, 1968.

potential British investors – will exploit any investment opportunities forgone by them. None of the approaches appears to consider the type of situation where inward investment leads to an increase in market activity in the host country equal to the net output of the investing firms, which in the absence of such investment would not have occurred. This is a variant of the *anti-classical* model (which we shall call the *income-generating* model) and is most likely to be appropriate wherever (*a*) there is less than full employment in the host country, and (*b*) the potential investors are able to exploit particular opportunities not available to or not appreciated by native or third-country firms.[1]

Three other differences between the Reddaway and Hufbauer/Adler studies should be mentioned at this point. First, the former enquiry was based on information supplied by sixty of the largest UK foreign investors about their foreign manufacturing and mining operations, including estimates of the differential impact of British ownership, *vis-à-vis* third-country or native ownership. The US investigators, on the other hand, had to rely exclusively on the published statistics available, classified only by broad industrial and country groupings. Second, while the Hufbauer/Adler exercise attempted a very general evaluation of the macro-economic effects of US foreign investment on the balance of payments, the Reddaway enquiry tended to confine its attention to the direct transactions between the subsidiaries of UK companies and enterprises in the UK. No direct estimate was made, for example, of how the exports of firms competitive to those investing overseas might have been affected as a consequence. Third, as we have already seen, the Reddaway report included both market appreciation of UK assets and reinvested profits as part of the earnings of foreign investment.

[1] Let us illustrate the three situations by a hypothetical example. Suppose that the Ford Motor Company (US) invests £10m. in building a new factory in Britain and produces from this factory an output of cars of £15m. each year. The *reverse classical* model assumes that, in consequence, investment and output by other firms, e.g. B.M.C., will fall (or not increase) and there will be no change in capital stock and output of the host country. The *anti-classical* model assumes that investment and output by other firms will not be affected by Ford's actions, but that since the total demand for all goods and services is autonomously determined this increase in domestic output is achieved at the expense of a fall in imports of an equivalent amount. The income-generating model assumes that at the same time that Ford increases its output there is also an increase in autonomous demand of the same amount; in this situation, neither the output of competitive firms nor imports need *necessarily* be affected though normally this will be the case.

The US writers excluded capital appreciation. In an Appendix to their report, they claim that the Reddaway approach involves double counting as the investing country cannot simultaneously repatriate both the reinvested earnings and the current value of the going enterprise.[1]

We now turn to consider the results of the Reddaway report. Where possible we shall compare these with those obtained from the *reverse classical* model of the American study. Unfortunately the data available permit few observations to be made of the UK balance-of-payments returns of either of the *anti-classical* or the *income-generating* models, but we shall do our best to suggest, at least, orders of magnitude of the main variables in each case.[2]

1. AVERAGE RETURNS

Let E_{fs} represent the actual purchases from the UK made by UK foreign subsidiaries and associates in a given year, and $\bar{e}_{fs}$ these purchases expressed as a percentage of the total capital invested (i.e., E_{fs}/K_{fp}) averaged over a period of years. Let E_{fs}^* represent the difference between the *actual* purchases of these subsidiaries and associates and those which might have occurred had their assets been owned by native or third-country firms. Let $\bar{e}_{fs}^*$ be these earnings (which might, of course, be negative) expressed as a percentage of the total capital invested by the controlled firms.

[1] This argument would be correct if, over the period in question (1955/64) that part of the increase in total assets financed by reinvested profits were excluded and profits were expressed as a percentage of the net figure. In the Reddaway report, however, corresponding to total profits and capital appreciation as a credit item on the balance of payments, there is an outflow of capital which includes the reinvested profits. An example may help to illustrate this point. Assume a UK firm invests £1m. in a new enterprise overseas at the beginning of Year 1 and at the beginning of each subsequent year up to Year 10, invests £100,000, which is financed entirely by profits earned in the preceding year. Suppose profits of £200,000 are earned each year, £100,000 of which is remitted to the parent company. Assume finally that the market value of the enterprise at the end of ten years is £2·5m., £500,000 more than the book value, and the enterprise is sold for this sum. The balance-of-payments return over the ten-year period to the investing firm can be thought of in two ways, both of which give the same result.

(i) the total earnings of the firm (£2m.) plus capital appreciation (0·5m.) divided by the initial investment (£1m.) plus growth of investment (£1m.) = 1·25.

(ii) the remitted profits of the firm (£1m.) plus its capital appreciation (0·5m.) divided by the initial investment (£1m.) = 1·25.

[2] For a more detailed criticism of the Reddaway and Hufbauer/Adler models see Appendix B to this chapter.

There are two components of E_{fs} (and $\bar{e}_{fs}$). The first of these $E_{fs(i)}$ (and $\bar{e}_{fs(i)}$) comprises the initial or once-for-all effects of an export of new capital. This is the α part of the equation on p. 71. Since it is non-recurrent and has little to do with the existing *stock* of capital invested it is better treated as an offsetting credit to the initial investment. Table 10 presents the Reddaway estimates for $E_{fs(i)}$ and $E_{fs(i)}{}^*$ for the period 1955/64, and the relationship between these and the increases in capital assets ΔK_{fp} over this time, i.e. $E_{fs(i)}/\Delta K_{fp}$ and $E_{fs(i)}{}^*/\Delta K_{fp}$. On average, for every increase of £100 of net assets, UK exports actually rose by nearly £14. Under the *classical* and *anti-classical* models this would also register the *effects* of foreign investment since, in its absence, no additional domestic expenditure would have occurred. Under the *reverse classical* model, Reddaway calculates that the UK ownership effect works out at just over 10 per cent. The corresponding percentages for the Hufbauer/Adler exercise were 27 per cent and 3 per cent.[1]

Table 10 also reveals significant industrial differences both in the actual export contribution and the effect of the ownership of foreign assets. The exports of vehicles and components, textiles, building materials and chemicals show up well; those of paper and electrical engineering products poorly. Geographically, the less developed countries are Britain's best customers. Nigeria spent £39 of every £100 invested in 1955/64 on the capital equipment imported from the UK, Malaysia £35, Jamaica £27, South Africa £27 and India £21. By contrast the corresponding figure for the US was £1 and that for Germany, Canada and France, £2, £4, £1 respectively.

The second component of $E_{fs}(E_{fs(ii)})$ is made up of the various recurrent export earnings associated with foreign investment. There are four of these:

(*a*) profits, interests and dividends ($E_{fs(ii)a}$);
(*b*) net payments for services rendered by the investing companies (royalties and fees) ($E_{fs(ii)b}$ and $E_{fs(ii)b}{}^*$);
(*c*) 'input' items, e.g. raw materials, components, semi-manufactured goods, imported from the UK by UK subsidiaries and associates ($E_{fs(ii)c}$ and $E_{fs(ii)c}{}^*$).
(*d*) finished goods imported from the UK for resale by UK subsidiaries and associates ($E_{fs(ii)d}$ and $E_{fs(ii)d}{}^*$).

Table 11 sets out the Reddaway data on each of these items, expressed as a percentage of the net operating assets of UK

[1] For further details, see Table XVI. 1, p. 216 in the Reddaway *Final Report*.

TABLE 10

Estimated Initial Effect on UK Exports by Operations by UK Overseas Subsidiaries Classified by Industry 1955/64

	Vehicles and Components	Textiles	Building Materials	Chemicals	Metals and Metal Products	Non-electrical Engineering	Food, Drink, Tobacco and Household Products	Mining	Electrical Engineering	Paper	Plantations	Total
1. Actual purchases of capital goods from UK by overseas subsidiaries in 10 years 1955/64 £m. ($E_{fs(1)}$)	18·9	7·8	6·1	23·7	21·3	1·6	21·1	10·6	2·2	4·0	6·0	123·3
2. Actual purchases of capital goods less those which might have been experienced had subsidiaries been in non-UK ownership £m. ($E_{fs^*(1)}$)	13·8	5·7	5·0	19·0	18·9	1·1	11·8	9·2	1·2	1·8	4·4	92·1

3. Increase in net operating assets of subsidiaries, etc. in 9 years 1956/64 £m. (ΔK_{pf})	60·5	26·4	28·8	110·9	165·9	9·3	157·5	147·6	41·6	121·7	22·1	892·3
4. Actual purchases of capital goods from UK per £100 of increase in net operating assets, i.e. (1)/(3)($\bar{e}_{fs(1)}$)	31·2	29·5	21·2	21·4	12·8	17·2	13·4	7·2	5·3	3·3	27·1	13·8
5. 'Effect of UK ownership' per £100 of increase in net operating assets, i.e. (2)/(3) on basis of annual rates ($\bar{e}*_{fs(1)}$)	21·0	20·0	16·0	15·0	10·0	11·0	7·0	6·0	3·0	1·0	18·0	9·0

Source: *Reddaway Report*, Table X.1.

TABLE 11

Estimated Recurrent Effects on UK Exports of Operations by UK Overseas Subsidiaries Expressed as a Percentage of Their Net Operating Assets. (Annual Averages 1955/64)

(*a*) Industrial Distribution

	(1) Profits after Overseas Tax[a]	(2) Effect of UK Ownership on Royalties' Management Fees, Freights, etc.[b]	(3) Actual Purchases of Input Items by UK Subsidiaries Overseas[c]	(4) Effect of UK Ownership on Purchases of Input Items[c,d]	(5) Actual Purchases of Finished Goods for Resale by UK Subsidiaries Overseas[c]	(6) Effect of UK Ownership of Purchases of Finished Goods for Resale[c]	(7) Total Additional Balance-of-Payments Earnings from UK due to UK Ownership of Subsidiaries[c]
	$\bar{e}_{fs(11a)}^*$	$\bar{e}_{fs(11b)}^*$	$\bar{e}_{fs(11c)}$	$\bar{e}_{fs(11c)}^*$	$\bar{e}_{fs(11d)}$	$\bar{e}_{s(11d)}^*$	$\bar{e}_{fs(11a/d)}^*$
Building materials, etc.	13·8	0·1	8·4	6·9	3·1	−7·2	13·6
Chemicals	7·7	0·0	2·8	2·4	16·2	−4·3	5·8
Textiles	8·0	0·6	4·5	3·7	6·8	−4·9	7·4

Food, drink, tobacco and household products	8·5	0·8	1·9	1·4	8·3	−1·2	9·5
Vehicles and components	5·3	0·2	18·5	13·5	29·7	−3·2	15·8
Metals and metal products	6·8	−0·1	3·9	3·2	4·4	−3·4	6·5
Electrical engineering	5·6	0·1	7·6	6·9	20·2	−3·6	9·0
Paper	6·2	−0·1	0·1	0·1	2·1	−0·1	6·1
Non-electrical engineering	5·3	0·8	17·2	13·0	6·7	4·2	29·4
Total manufacturing	7·7	0·3	4·7	3·7	10·3	−2·5	9·2
Mining	12·3	1·4	0·1	0·1	0·0	0·0	13·8
Plantations	9·3	0·3	0·1	0·0	0·0	0·0	9·6
Total (excluding oil)	8·2	0·4	4·1	3·1	8·6	−2·1	9·6

Notes:

[a] Profits after overseas taxation and depreciation, but before deduction of interest on non-current liabilities, as a percentage of net operating assets (book value) at the beginning of the year. (Derived from data relating to subsidiaries, etc. in all overseas countries.)

[b] Data relates to all overseas countries.

[c] Data relates to fifteen countries only. Data in Column 2 include estimates of effects of UK foreign investment on certain invisible exports, e.g. freights. (See Table XII.4.)

[d] This is measured by the reduction in purchases from the UK that might have been experienced if the subsidiaries had not been in UK ownership; where an increase would have been likely the figure for UK ownership is negative. The figures are the Reddaway team's best guesses.

Source: *Reddaway Report*, Tables X.1, XII.4, and XIV.

subsidiaries and associates. It reveals several interesting facts, the most striking of which, as shown in Column 7, is the very small proportion of UK exports to foreign subsidiaries and associates which is due specifically to their UK ownership. Only in the case of the non-electrical engineering and vehicles industries was there a recurrent exports/net assets ratio ($\bar{e}_{fs(ii)c}$* and $_a$*) of any significance. This is particularly noticeable in the case of finished goods for resale ($\bar{e}_{fs(ii)d}$*), where firms in all but the non-electrical engineering and mining industries estimated that the net impact of UK ownership was to *reduce* the exports of UK goods between 1955 and 1964. On the other hand, it was reckoned that nearly four-fifths of the purchases of inputs actually made by foreign subsidiaries and associates from the UK were a direct result of their UK ownership.

Adding together the various components of $\bar{e}_{fs(ii)}$* – all averaged for the period 1955/64 – we arrive at a recurrent foreign exchange receipts/net operating assets ratio of 9·6 per cent. If capital appreciation is included as part of $E_{fs(ii)}$ (let us call this $E_{fs(iia)}$ and fixed assets are revalued at replacement cost (K_{fpr}) the appropriate ratio of $\bar{e}_{fsr(iia)}$* works out at 9·0 per cent.[1] It is interesting to compare the data in Table 11 with those in Table 6a. In general, the industries which are the least profitable make the more substantial contribution to the UK balance of payments, while those which are the most profitable make the least contribution.

The geographical distribution of $\bar{e}_{fs(ii)}$* and some of its components is given in Table 12. Clearly in the period 1955/64, UK investments in less developed countries benefited the UK balance of payments more than those in the developed countries, with the exception of those in Germany. In general, those countries which contribute most to the UK balance of payments also yield the best rate of return. The rank coefficient of correlation between Column 4 of Table 12 and Column 8 of Table 7 works out at +0·66 (excluding Jamaica, +0·82).

Under the *classical* and *anti-classical* models, in the absence of UK investment $\bar{e}_{fs(iia\text{ and }c)}$* would have a zero value, but there would be some royalties and fees $\bar{e}_{fs(iib)}$* resulting from foreign companies concluding agreements with UK firms. Reddaway estimates these at about one-half those actually received from UK subsidiaries.[2]

Unfortunately, we do not have the data to calculate the export displacement effect $\bar{e}_{fs(iid)}$* under these other models, but it would

[1] For further details see W. B. Reddaway, *op. cit.*, p. 374.
[2] £5·2m. cf. £10·6m. See Tables IV. 9 and XXV. 2.

probably be in the range of −20 per cent to −30 per cent for every additional £100 of investment. Hufbauer and Adler estimate that, where US manufacturing investment overseas leads to an increase in the capital formation in the host country, but does not affect

TABLE 12

Estimated Recurrent Effects of UK Exports of Operations by UK Subsidiaries[a] – Expressed as a Percentage of Their Net Operating Assets (Annual Averages 1955–64)

	(1) Profits on Net Operating Assets Less Overseas Tax $\bar{e}_{fs(11a)}$*	(2) Additional Exports of Goods and Services from UK $\bar{e}_{fs(11bcd)}$*	(3) Total $\bar{e}_{fs(11)}$*
Jamaica	7·9	9½	17
Ghana	12·9	8½	21
South Africa	10·0	7	17
Nigeria	4·5	5	9½
Malaysia	18·8	4	23
Denmark	4·8	3½	8
India	7·9	3½	11
Germany	22·6	3	26
Argentina	2·0	1	3
Australia	8·5	1	9½
Canada	5·3	½	6
USA	9·0	−1	8
Brazil	6·1	−1	5
France	3·0	−4½	−1½
Italy	15·1	−9	6
Total 15 Countries	8·4	1½	10

[a] Excluding investments in oil industry, plantations, insurance and banking. For details of exact coverage see *Reddaway Report*, Appendix B, p. 138.
Source: *Reddaway Report*, Table XVI. 1.

the rate of domestic investment, that US exports will fall by $51 for every additional $100 invested abroad.[1]

Neither the Cambridge nor the American economists made any estimate of the export-displacement effect using the income-generating

[1] Estimate the UK displacement effect will be considerably less, as the percentage of total imports purchased from the UK of countries in which UK investment is concentrated is considerably lower than its US counterpart.

model. The main difficulty here is to isolate the effect of a change in the volume and structure of activities of foreign subsidiaries in host countries from the activities of other firms. One such measure might be the *actual* value of imports, or change in the value of imports, purchased by subsidiaries from the investing country. This, of course, would completely ignore (or, at least, assume as neutral) the impact of the activities of these firms on other imports from the investing country. Alternatively, using the Hufbauer/Adler procedure, one might postulate that the ratio between the imports from the investing country and output of native and third-country firms in the host country remains unchanged (or its trend remains unchanged) as total output rises, and assume that the difference between changes in these imports and changes in *total* imports from the investing country are due to the activities of the foreign subsidiaries.[1] However, these balance-of-payments effects omit from consideration the impact of foreign direct investment on:

(i) The imports (of the investing country) which arise from foreign investment overseas. In the *classical*, *anti-classical* and *income-generating* models these may be taken as the actual imports from foreign subsidiaries. The Hufbauer/Adler *reverse classical* model takes as its import parameter the difference in the imports of the US from its foreign subsidiaries and those from other firms in the host country. The Reddaway study gives details only of the actual imports of UK firms from UK foreign subsidiaries.[2]

(ii) The secondary repercussions of an increase in net capital formation in the host country. These, the American economists estimate by multiplying the changes in investment in both investing and host countries by the reciprocal of the appropriate savings and import parameters. Hufbauer and Adler attempt to estimate both an *immediate* multiplier effect and sustained and multiplier effect in respect of trade flows between the US and both host and third countries. The *classical* and *anti-classical* models reveal higher parameters than those of *reverse classical* models. This is because in the latter model, US income receives more, and host countries less, stimulus,

[1] We tried this out using US investment in Canada as our case study, and in place of Hufbauer/Adler's export replacement parameter of −0·69, assuming the *anti-classical* model, we got a figure of +0·10.

[2] See pp. 74–78 and 115–20.

when US firms displace native (or third-country) firms. Since the *anti-classical* model assumes that overseas investment does not depress home spending, the trade balance of the US is not as favourably affected as under the *classical* model. After the first year, sustained multiplier effects occur under the framework of all three assumptions. Since no calculations of this kind have been made for the UK we have not included these effects in our summary.[1]

(iii) The effects of foreign investment on the terms of trade of the *investing* country. Under the *reverse classical* model used by Reddaway, these effects would not appear to be important and probably cancel themselves out. On rather different assumptions, they may be quite important. For example, though the exports of the investing company might increase following foreign investment, this might only be achieved at the expense of exports of competitors in the same industry. This is a field for further research.

2. MARGINAL RETURNS

The marginal balance-of-payments return of foreign investment, i.e. $\Delta E_{fs}(\Delta E_{fs}^*)\Delta K_{fp}$ or $e'_{fs'}(e'_{fs}{}^*)$ between 1955 and 1964, was probably slightly lower than the average rate of return. Unfortunately, we have virtually no data on any of its components except changes in capital and changes in profits and interest; and even here, there is no way of distinguishing between the profitability of a completely new investment and that of an increase in the capital stock of an established subsidiary.[2] Once again, however, it is likely that there are marked variations in the marginal export contributions between industries and probably between firms in the same industry.

[1] For further particulars, see Hufbauer and Adler, *op. cit.*, p. 524 and Table 4.2. See also Table 1 in Appendix B to this chapter.

[2] It should be observed that nowhere in the Reddaway study is an attempt made to evaluate the marginal balance-of-payments return of foreign investment. Instead, the authors choose to relate the *average* annual purchases of *all* UK foreign subsidiaries from the UK for the period 1955/64 to the *average* net operating assets of these subsidaries and then apply this ratio to an *increase* of net operating assets of £100. (See, e.g., Table X. 1 and XII. 1.) We are told, however, that between 1956 and 1963, during which time the foreign assets of UK firms in fifteen specified countries increased by £539·8m., the purchases of input items by subsidiaries of UK manufacturing companies rose by £23m., while that of goods for resale fell by £7·6m. (See Tables VI. 3 and VI. 4.)

The efficiency of foreign investment (*a*) from the viewpoint of the individual firm

So much for an evaluation of the return on UK foreign investment. We now turn to consider whether or not, in recent years, the UK has been distributing its capital assets and/or increases in capital assets (*a*) between home and overseas and (*b*) between different countries in the 'optimum' way. From the viewpoint of the individual firm, we define the 'optimum' way as that distribution which maximizes the rate of return on capital (discounted for risk) at the margin $r'_{fpg} = r'_{dpg}$. What is the evidence that this is being achieved?

Once again, the published data only partially allow us to answer this question. For, first, the information we have is expressed in average terms; second, it is too global to be very meaningful; third, it is available only in respect of part of $\bar{r}_{dp}$ and $\bar{r}_{fp}$; fourth, it makes no allowance for differences in capital gearing of home and overseas investment; and fifth, in respect of $\bar{r}_{dp}$, various deductions must be made before a true $\bar{r}$ can be calculated. We have discussed the implications of the first three inadequacies in the previous section. We must now deal briefly with (4) and (5).

Differences in the rates of return on the total capital invested between firms may reflect differences in financial structure or gearing as well as efficiency in resource allocation. In the case of UK firms investing overseas, this shows itself in a higher ratio of net worth to total liabilities actually owned by UK firms than that recorded by UK firms at home.[1] This is because UK firms abroad prefer to invest only in equity, and borrow as much debt capital as possible from local sources. The differences in gearing of home and overseas companies is shown in Table 13. These imply that part of the higher return on the *total* assets of UK subsidiaries is due to their favourable financial structure.[2] Capital invested abroad is made to act as a catalyst for local investment in a way it cannot do at home.

[1] For example, in 1964, the percentage of interest paid on loan capital to the total earnings of UK branches and subsidiaries overseas (net of tax) worked out at only 1·4 per cent: the corresponding percentage derived from the consolidated accounts of the larger public UK companies in that year was 7·0 per cent.

[2] Most of the discussion in this article has taken capital to mean *net* rather than total assets. This is simply because both the Board of Trade and the Reddaway data define capital in this way. But from the viewpoint of the profitability of home and foreign investment it is *total* assets, i.e. net assets plus current liabilities, which is the relevant denominator. For part of the task of the efficient investor is to finance his capital in the most economic way.

TABLE 13

Average Rates of Return on UK Capital Invested at Home and Overseas 1960/64

	1960	1961	1962	1963	1964	Average 1960/64
United Kingdom						
Net income (b.t.)/Total assets	11·1	9·7	9·0	9·5	10·2	9·9
Net income (b.t.)/Net assets	15·0	13·2	12·1	12·9	14·1	13·5
Net income (a.t.)/Total assets	6·3	5·4	5·0	5·3	5·6	5·5
Net income (a.t.)/Net assets	8·5	7·4	6·8	7·2	7·7	7·5
Overseas (All countries)						
Net income (a.t.)/Net assets	8·2	7·4	7·6	8·1	8·5	8·0

Source: UK data *Statistics on Incomes, Prices, Employment and Production.* Net income (before tax) is defined as trading profit less depreciation plus income from investments and other income. Net income (after tax) is defined as disposable income plus interest on long-term liabilities net of tax. Net assets are defined as fixed assets (less accumulated depreciation) plus current assets less current liabilities and provisions, except provision for future tax.

Foreign investment data: *Board of Trade Journal*, 26/1/68. The UK data are derived from the balance sheets of about 2,000 quoted companies engaged mainly in manufacturing, distribution, construction, transport and other services, who owned assets of £0·5m. or more or earned income of $50,000 or more in 1960. The foreign investment data exclude those of companies engaged in the oil industry and in banking and insurance.

The average returns earned on capital by the leading UK public companies are published regularly. Unfortunately, as they stand, they are not a completely reliable indication of the profitability of UK companies in the UK. First, they incorporate the capital and earnings of the *foreign* operations of the companies in question (including royalties and fees): Second, included in the domestic capital and profits are the earnings of foreign-owned companies in the UK which, in general, are higher than those of competitive UK firms. Third, and operating in the opposite direction to the two factors just mentioned, the domestic profitability ratios are gross of the tax which has to be paid to the UK Exchequer on remitted profits from foreign subsidiaries, where the UK tax rate is more than the tax rate in the country in which the profits were earned. Fourth, no account is taken of the various indirect benefits and costs of foreign investment contained in the profits of the investing company.

Table 13 presents such published data as are available on the comparative rates of return earned on UK capital at home or abroad for the period 1960/64. These show $\bar{r}_{fpg}$ (or, more accurately $\bar{r}_{fp(1)}$) to be slightly higher than $\bar{r}_{dpg}(\bar{r}_{dp})$. But when these data are amended to incorporate the first three of the adjustments mentioned in the previous paragraph the superior profitability of foreign investment is clearly demonstrated. It is also interesting to observe that the trend of profitability is in favour of overseas investment.

Tables 14 and 15 suggest that this better performance of UK firms abroad is partly a structural phenomenon. Those industries which operate *both* at home and abroad, e.g. vehicles, electrical engineering, non-electrical engineering, paper, almost invariably record a higher $\bar{r}_{dp}$, although, as already pointed out, they are also the ones which often benefit the most from foreign investment in other directions.

However, not only is it argued that from the viewpoint of the individual firm, home and foreign investment are rarely competitive with each other; but that the average profitability of domestic investment is an imperfect reflection of the (private) opportunity cost of foreign investment.

Assuming that the marginal efficiency of domestic capital is equal to its cost (i.e. the firm is already investing as much as it wants to), then a reduction in the impetus overseas will not necessarily result in more investment at home. But this does not mean that the opportunity cost of foreign investment is zero. For the investing firm still has the choice of (*a*) not borrowing so much capital or reducing its short-term debts, and (*b*) enlarging its portfolio of short- or long-term assets. Let us then define $\bar{r}_{dp(\min)}$ as the long-term rate of interest

TABLE 14

Average Rates of Return on UK Private Capital Invested at Home and Overseas by Brod Industrial Groups 1960/64

Profits/Net Assets Per Cent[1]

	1960		1961		1962		1963		1964		Average 1960/64	
	UK	Overseas	UK	Overseas	UK	Overseas	UK	Overseas	UK	Overseas	UK	Overseas
Manufacturing	8·8	8·0	7·4	7·5	6·7	8·2	6·1	8·3	6·7	9·3	7·2	8·3
Electrical and mechanical engineering	7·7	2·6	6·9	4·6	4·5	4·5	5·8	3·4	6·5	5·0	6·7	4·0
Vehicles, shipbuilding and marine engineering	9·8	2·4	6·7	0·1	5·5	2·1	6·3	2·6	7·1	−2·3	7·1	1·0
Other manufacturing	8·9	9·5	7·6	8·5	6·8	9·3	6·2	9·5	6·7	10·8	7·2	9·5
Construction	8·5	6·4	8·4	10·4	8·5	5·8	8·4	7·5	9·5	9·1	8·7	7·8
Distribution	9·4	7·2	8·7	5·9	8·5	5·0	7·7	5·7	7·8	8·0	8·4	6·4
Transport and communications	8·5	12·8	6·7	11·5	8·0	7·1	7·2	9·0	7·0	8·0	7·5	9·7

[1]For definitions, see footnote to Table 14.

Source: Overseas data – *Board of Trade Journal*, 26/1/68. UK data – derived from *Statistics on Income, Prices, Employment and Production*, March 1964 and June 1966.

TABLE 15

Average Profitability of UK Capital Invested at Home and Overseas 1956/64

	$\bar{r}_{f(1)}$[1]	$\bar{r}_{dp}$[2]
Chemicals and allied trades	8·4	7·8[3]
Textiles	7·7	7·3
Food, drink, tobacco and household products	8·8	8·7[4]
Vehicles and components	5·0	9·2
Metal and metal products	7·4	8·6
Paper	7·7	8·3
Electrical engineering	5·4	8·2
Non-electrical engineering	4·5	8·6
Total (manufacturing)	8·1	8·4

[1] Foreign profitability represents rate of return to UK stake. Domestic profitability is calculated by dividing the net income earned in each year 1956/64 by the assets at the end of that year and averaging the result. For detailed definition see footnote to Table 14.

[2] Including income earned from overseas operations.

[3] Including oil companies.

[4] Food, drink and tobacco only.

Source: *Statistics on Incomes, Prices, Employment and Production. Reddaway Report*, Table XI.1.

which can be earned on Government bonds (net of tax). For the period 1960/65, $r_{dp(\min)}$ averaged 4 per cent. It can be seen from Tables 14 and 15 that some industries did not even earn this rate of return from their foreign investments. And of the 3,667 overseas companies supplying data to the Board of Trade in its survey, 1535 or 42 per cent earned 5 per cent or less on their capital in 1965.

Earlier tables (particularly Tables 4 to 7) have already revealed the wide differences in both the average and marginal profitability of British investment by country. When allowance is made for the other forms of income accruing to the investing company (see, for example, data in Table 12), these differences are reduced but by no means eliminated. There are, of course, a variety of reasons why these differences persist, not least the age, size and industrial distribution of the firms concerned. Again, it must be remembered that investment in one country is not necessarily competitive with investment in another; a copper-mining investment in Zambia in the 1960s can hardly be regarded as a substitute for an investment in a textiles factory in the US in the 1890s! To establish the extent of any in disequilibrium which might exist in the geographical distribution of UK assets, we would need to compare the profitability of enterprises in similar industries set up in a similar time period. Neither the Reddaway nor the published Board of Trade data enable us to do this.

The efficiency of foreign investment (*b*) from the viewpoint of the community

(a) The social product 'opportunity cost'

We shall confine our attention in this section to the allocation of private investment between home and overseas. A comparison of unadjusted profitability ratios ($\bar{r}_{ds}$ and $\bar{r}_{fs(1)}$) shown in Table 13 suggests that companies over-invest abroad and under-invest at home. This is mainly due to the fact that $\bar{r}_{ds}$ is calculated gross of (UK) tax while $\bar{r}_{fs}$ is net of (overseas) tax. But to what extent do the published figures of domestic profits/assets ratio (gross of tax), fairly reflect the true 'opportunity cost' of foreign investment? Assuming for the moment they do, then, when the various adjustments to domestic and foreign rates of return are taken into account,[1] domestic investment is seen to be marginally more profitable than that overseas investment. But much will depend on the assumptions made about three things:

(*a*) UK Government policy;
(*b*) the state of the (UK) capital market;
(*c*) institutional constraints.

First, Government policy. In this connection, it is important to distinguish between 'actual' and 'potential' opportunity costs. Thus the value of resources diverted from *overseas* to *home* investment will depend *inter alia* on *whether or not* the Government makes domestic investment more attractive at the same time it makes foreign investment less attractive. If it does, then the *existing* profitability of domestic investment $\bar{r}_{fp}$ might be a fair guide to the opportunity cost of foreign investment, assuming average and marginal profitability are the same. If it does not, then the opportunity cost will be less, as the increased supply of capital will tend to force down the

[1] In addition to those mentioned on pp. 30–31, it should be noted that part of the taxes levied by the UK Government and included in the (social) return on home investment will in fact be used on the provision of various community-type services, roads, lighting, etc. Strictly speaking, this expenditure should be deducted from the taxes levied on the domestic profits of UK companies.

rate of interest. If foreign investment is financed by borrowing from abroad, then the opportunity cost will be the interest charge on that capital.

Secondly, if there is disequilibrium in the capital market due, for example, to a rationing of loanable funds by other than the price mechanism, the existing domestic rates of return may be a fair reflection of opportunity cost. If, on the other hand, full equilibrium exists, the cost of alternative resource allocation will be that much less. In this case, an addition to private domestic investment will only occur if the marginal efficiency of capital is increased by a change either in businessmen's expectations or the rate of interest, which may only be possible if there is a change in Government policy. Failing a diversion of funds in the private sector, then the Government itself might speed up its own investment programme, e.g. in hospital, school, road building, etc., or allow more consumer goods to be produced.

Thirdly, a firm's investment programme will be influenced by its attitudes towards growth and diversification, i.e. the alternative courses of action it allows itself to pursue. Some firms in the UK may not be earning as high a rate of return on their capital as they could simply because they are not prepared to diversify their activities outside their immediate technological and/or marketing horizons. Should these (self-imposed) constraints on resource allocation be removed or loosened – as they might well be if alternative avenues of investment were blocked or made less profitable[1], the appropriate domestic opportunity cost would increase.

In attempting to assess the social costs and benefits of foreign investment two quite distinct questions are relevant:

(*a*) is British industry, in general, investing too much or too little overseas, assuming that the resources available for investment at home and abroad are fixed? This is purely a problem of investment allocation;

(*b*) is British industry investing too much or too little overseas, assuming only that the total resources of the UK economy are fixed? This is a problem of much wider import and cannot be answered without a clear specification of the Government policy assumed.

[1] It cannot be coincidence that since the 1965 budget which introduced measures which had the effect of making foreign investment less attractive *vis-à-vis* domestic investment, two of the largest of UK foreign investors have diversified into completely new activities in the UK.

The answer to (*a*) is that, if one judges the efficiency of resource allocation in the UK in terms of the way in which capital adjusts to the profit stimulus, and regards the complete mobility of resources as desirable – there is probably too much UK investment overseas in traditional-type industries and not enough investment at home in the newer technologically based industries. If, however, one accepts the institutional constraints mentioned earlier and also bears in mind the different financial structure of UK firms at home and abroad, there is probably no such misallocation, and, if there is, it is minimal.

The answer to (*b*) is that there is probably too little investment both at home and overseas. One of the background papers prepared by NEDC for the Prime Minister's productivity conference in September 1966 revealed most clearly that the countries which invested the highest proportion of their national product in the period 1955/64 were those which grew the fastest. The relevant statistics are contained in Table 16. For some years now, many UK economists have

TABLE 16

Output, Output per Head and Investment Ratios 1955/64
(Annual Averages)

Country	Per Cent Change Output	Per Cent Change Output per Head	Investment/GNP Ratios All Investment	Investment/GNP Ratios Excluding Dwellings
Japan	10·4	8·8	28·8	21·5
West Germany	6·3	5·0	23·7	18·4
Italy	5·7	5·6	21·6	15·6
Sweden	5·4	3·9	22·8	17·4
France	5·2	4·9	19·2	14·3
Denmark	5·0	3·8	18·7	15·4
Belgium	3·6	3·0	18·4	13·7
Britain	3·1	2·6	15·8	12·7
United States	3·1	2·0	17·1	12·2

Source: Paper prepared by NEDC for Prime Minister's Conference on Productivity, September 27, 1966.

been arguing for both more and better investment by British industry. For this to be achieved, the Government must create the right economic climate for businessmen to want and to be able to achieve it. And this is primarily a matter of policy. Overseas investment is one particular use of the nation's scarce resources and there is an opportunity cost involved in using resources in this direction rather than any other. In theory, this opportunity cost could be the fruit of almost any other pattern of resource allocation. In practice, given the constraints of the market, it will be the policy of the Government which decides what this should be.

(b) The balance-of-payments 'opportunity cost'

Here we need to distinguish between two kinds of opportunity cost of investing overseas. First the balance-of-payments effect of the alternative use of resources in the host country: second, the balance-of-payments effect of the alternative use of resources by the investing country.

The Reddaway enquiry assumed that:

(i) had not the UK investment been made in the host countries concerned, investment of an equivalent amount would have been made by firms of other nationalities, and

(ii) if the resources had been invested at home, this would have had no or a minimal effect on the balance of payments.

This means that the only foreign exchange 'cost' to be set against exchange earnings (E_{fs}) is the external financing charge. Reddaway puts this charge at 4½ per cent (it could, of course, be much higher or lower or even zero). This reduces the average balance-of-payments return for the period 1955/64 from 9·8 per cent (11·4 per cent with capital appreciation, valuing fixed assets on a replacement cost basis) to between 5 per cent and 7 per cent respectively). But it must be remembered that these calculations exclude certain other balance-of-payments effects as mentioned earlier, which, if included, would probably reduce the net $\bar{e}_{fs}$ still further. Moreover, it is possible to choose other 'alternative positions' of the host country in the absence of UK investment, e.g. no new investment at all, which are less favourable to UK exports.[1]

The question now arises: What is likely to be the effect on the UK balance of payments of any resource re-allocation in the UK consequential upon an increase or decrease in foreign investment? If the capital to finance foreign investment is simply borrowed from abroad in the first instance, the repercussions on the domestic economy will be negligible or zero. In all other cases, they will be positive; by how much, and in what direction, depending upon the

[1] By the same token, other 'alternative positions' may be assumed which are more favourable to UK exports. See W. Manser, 'The Reddaway report – not the last word on foreign investment,' *Westminster Bank Review*, August 1967.

state of the economy and the macro-economic policy pursued by the Government. If, in a full employment situation, a cutback in foreign investment diverts resources from sectors which are (net) balance-of-payment spenders to those which are (net) balance-of-payments earners, the resulting net gain to the balance of payments may be greater than that achieved by foreign investment. In a situation of less than full employment, the net balance-of-payments gain is almost certainly to be positive.

The Reddaway report makes the convenient, though, in our opinion, not very plausible, assumption that any change in the volume or composition of domestic output consequent upon a cutback in foreign investment will not affect UK exports as, since exports are assumed to be demand-determined, firms are already exporting all they wish to at the prevailing prices. The implications of this assumption are, first that a change in the volume of composition of domestic output does not affect the conditions of supplying exports from the UK; second, that, in fact, UK producers are supplying all the exports demanded of them, e.g. that orders are not being lost due to long delivery dates, etc.

Such empirical evidence as we have on this latter assumption suggests that it is false – at least in the recent experience of the UK. The work of several UK economists[1] all points to a negative correlation between the pressure of internal demand and the volume of export orders in certain key UK industries, e.g. machine tools – the suggestion being that, if output could be increased by one means or another, or home demand reduced, more exports would be earned.

An increase in the supply of capital for domestic investment may affect the conditions of supply of UK exports in various ways. Apart from any effect it may have on the supply price of capital, it may effect the production opportunities of firms by making possible a more rapid rate of technological innovation and the introduction of new products and processes. But once again firms must be induced to increase their output for exports by the appropriate Government policy.

Any conclusions on the relative balance-of-payments 'pay-off' between home and overseas investment must then depend on the macroeconomic assumptions made. Perhaps, in making such comparison, it is again useful to consider the implications of alternative export/capital ratios. One of these is the zero figure assumed by the

[1] J. Ball, J. R. Eaton and M. Steuer, 'The relationship between United Kingdom export performance in manufacturing industry and the internal pressure of demand,' *Economic Journal*, Vol. LXXVI, September 1966.

TABLE 17

Estimated Benefits of UK Foreign Investment in Various Countries Classified by Type of Benefi
(Rankings in Order of Benefit)

	(*a*) The return on capital							(*b*) The balance of payments			
	(*a*) $\bar{r}_{fp}$				(*b*) $\bar{r}_{d'p}$			$\bar{e}_{fs}$			Overall Perfor-mance
	(i) $\bar{r}_{fp(i)}$	(ii) $\bar{r}_{fp(ii)}$	(iii) $\bar{r}_{fp(iii)}$	(iv) $\bar{r}_{fp}$	(i) $\bar{r}_{d'p(i)}$	(ii) $\bar{r}_{d'p(iii)}$	(iii) $\bar{r}_{d'p(v)}$	(i) $\bar{e}_{fs}{}^{*}_{(i)}$	(ii) $\bar{e}_{fs}{}^{*}_{(iic,iid)}$	(iii) $\bar{e}_{fs}{}^{*}_{(ii)}$	
North America											
USA	6	8	8	7	3	7	1	13	12	9	5
Canada	10	14	12	13	3	6	1	11	11	11	9
Western Europe											
EEC											
Germany	1	5	1	1	1	n.a.	1	12	8	1	1
France	14	6	14	15	4	12	1	13	14	15	15
Italy	4	3	5	4	n.a.	n.a.	1	9	15	11	7
EFTA											
Denmark	11	2	11	11	n.a.	n.a.	13	6	6	9	
Switzerland											
South and Central America											
Argentina	15	12	7	14	n.a.	8	1	7	9	14	14
Brazil	11	6	6	8	n.a.	10	1	8	12	13	12

Commonwealth											
Australia	8	10	4	6	4	11	1	10	10	7	4
New Zealand											
South Africa	5	11	2	3	7	9	1	5	3	4	3
India	9	13	10	9	6	5	14	4	6	6	8
Malaysia	2	8	3	2	n.a.	1	15	2	5	2	2
Jamaica	7	15	14	12	n.a.	3	12	3	1	4	11
Ghana	3	1	12	5	n.a.	4	1	n.a.	2	3	6
Nigeria	13	3	9	10	n.a.	2	1	1	4	8	11

Notation

$\bar{r}_{fp}$ (i) Profits and interest/net assets 1955/64.
(ii) Royalties/net assets 1955/64.
(iii) Capital appreciation/net assets 1955/64.
(iv) $r_{fp(i)/(iii)}$ combined 1955/64.

$\bar{r}_{d'p}$ (i) Technological feedback effect.
(ii) Price and supply conditions of imports effect.[1]
(v) Differential taxation effect.

$\bar{e}_{fs}*$ (i) Export of capital goods from UK 1955/64. (UK ownership effect.)
$\bar{e}_{fs}*$ (ii*c*) Export of input items from UK 1955/64. (UK ownership effect.)
$\bar{e}_{fs}*$ (ii*d*) Exports of finished goods from UK 1955/64. (UK ownership effect – *Reddaway Report*.)
$\bar{e}_{fs}*$ (ii) Total visible and invisible exports resulting from UK investment – i.e. including profits and interest 1955/64. (UK ownership effect.)

Source: Tables 7 and 12.

[1] In deriving these ranks we assumed, (*a*) that investment in agriculture and materials exploitations is likely to have favourable rather than unfavourable effects on the price and supply conditions of UK imports, and (*b*) that this is likely to be greater in countries where there is more UK investment than where there is less, then it is possible to rank countries by their potential benefit to the invest-company in this respect. Column 6 presents such impressions as we have been able to derive here. The ranking is based on the percentage of the total UK capital invested in agriculture and mining in different countries in 1965.

Reddaway report; another is the average or marginal export/capital ratios (E/K or $\Delta E/\Delta K$) of UK manufacturing industry. This, at present is running around 15 per cent. Obviously which ratio is chosen makes a big difference to the balance-of-payments efficiency of foreign investment. But even this calculation takes no account of terms-of-trade effect of domestic investment about which (empirically at least) virtually nothing is known. Moreover, there is no evidence to suggest that, on *average*, foreign investment reaps a net advantage to the UK balance-of-payments for at least eight to ten years. Certainly the opportunity cost of foreign investment would seem to be considerably higher than that suggested by the Reddaway report.

Conclusion

We know quite a bit more about the costs and benefits of UK foreign direct investment to the investing country than we did in 1960 but our knowledge is still very incomplete. We also know something about the 'opportunity cost' of foreign investment, but so much here depends on the particular economic circumstances at the time and Government policies pursued. We know almost nothing about how far foreign investment is the *best way* of exploiting overseas markets, compared with licensing agreements and the like.

Table 17 presents a summary of the various forms of 'returns' on UK capital invested in fifteen countries derived almost entirely from data in the Reddaway report. In this case we have not given the actual rates of return but simply ranked countries according to the value, or estimated value, of these returns to the investing company or country. The final column attempts a very rough-and-ready index of overall performance, taking into account various other considerations, e.g. the political stability of the host country and the industrial composition of the investment.[1] This final table shows that there is little to choose in the general ranking between the developed and developing countries.

If the recently published Board of Trade statistics and the data contained in the Reddaway report have shown that some of the UK Government's recent short-term controls on foreign investment are not without justification (though they can tell us nothing of the efficiency of such a policy compared with other ways of curing a balance-of-payments deficit!), on the long-term merits and demerits of the present level of UK foreign investment, the debate still continues.

[1] On the lines of R. B. Stobaugh, Jr. 'How to analyse foreign investment climates,' *Harvard Business Review*, Sept./Oct. 1969, pp. 100–108.

REFERENCES

R. J. Ball, J. R. Eaton and M. D. Steuer. 'The relationship between United Kingdom export performance in manufacturing industry and the internal pressure of demand,' *Economic Journal*, Vol. LXXVI, September 1966.

J. Behrman. *Direct Manufacturing Investment Exports and the Balance of Payments*, National Foreign Trade Council, 1968.

Board of Trade. 'Overseas investment,' *Board of Trade Journal*, June 30, 1967.

Board of Trade. 'Book values of overseas investments,' *Board of Trade Journal*, January 26, 1968.

Board of Trade. 'Overseas transactions—trade credit and royalties,' *Board of Trade Journal*, July 21, 1967.

J. H. Dunning. 'Does foreign investment pay?' *Moorgate and Wall Street*, September 1964.

J. H. Dunning. 'Further thoughts on foreign investment,' *Moorgate and Wall Street*, September 1966.

J. H. Dunning. 'U.K. and U.S. foreign investment. A comparative study,' *National Provincial Bank Review*, August 1968.

J. H. Dunning. 'The Reddaway and Hufbauer/Alder reports,' *Banker's Magazine*, May, June and July 1969.

J. H. Dunning and D. C. Rowan. 'British direct investment in Western Europe,' *Banca Nazionale del Lavoro. Quarterly Review* 73, June 1965.

M. Frankel. 'Home versus foreign investment; a case against capital exports,' *Kyklos*, Vol. XVIII, 1965.

G. C. Hufbauer and F. M. Adler. *Overseas Manufacturing Investment and the Balance of Payments*, Tax policy research study No. 1, U.S. Treasury Department, 1968.

W. Manser. 'The Reddaway report—not the last work on foreign investment,' *Westminster Bank Review*, August 1967.

I. F. Pearce and D. C. Rowan. 'A framework for research into the real effects of international capital movements,' *Essays in Honour of Marco Fanno*, ed. T. Bagiotti, Padova, 1966.

J. Polk, I. W. Meister and L. A. Veit. *US Production Abroad and the US Balance of Payments*, National Industrial Conference Board, 1966.

W. B. Reddaway, S. J. Potter and C. T. Taylor. *Effects of U.K. Direct Investment Overseas*, Cambridge University Press, 1967 and 1968.

D. Snider. 'The case for capital controls to relieve the US balance of payments,' *American Economic Review*, June 1964, pp. 346–58.

R. B. Stobaugh, Jr. 'How to analyse foreign investment climates.' *Harvard Business Review*, Sept./Oct. 1969, pp. 100–108.

APPENDIX A

THE CHOICE BETWEEN HOME AND FOREIGN INVESTMENT: SOME THEORETICAL ISSUES*

(*a*) *Long-term aspects*

The problem of the overall allocation of investment between investment overseas on the one hand and investment at home upon the other has received extensive discussion in the literature. The writings on this issue tend to fall into two groups.

The first group of writers approaches the problem as one of resource allocation in a perfectly competitive world which is taken to be in long-term full employment equilibrium.[1] External equilibrium is assumed to be maintained without cost to the lending country – that is there is no transfer problem. Production functions in each country are taken to be homogeneous of degree one in the factor inputs and invariant with respect to foreign investment. Given a model of this type it is, *on the basis of invariant terms of trade*, possible to show that the marginal social product of investment overseas will be less than the marginal social product of investment at home. In short, that 'under competitive conditions capital-rich countries tie up too great a proportion of their resources in foreign investures.'[2]

This theoretical conclusion is strengthened by the fact that while the tax on profits arising out of investment at home accrues to the home government, the tax on profits arising out of investment abroad accrues, in general, to the foreign government.

* First published in *Banca Nazionale del Lavoro*, June 1965. This section of the article, originally entitled 'British direct investment in Western Europe', is substantially the work of my co-author of this article, Professor D. C. Rowan.

[1] See, for example, A. E. Jasay, 'The social choice between home and overseas investment,' *Economic Journal*, LXXI, 1960, pp. 105–13; G. D. A. MacDougall, 'The benefits and costs of private investment abroad. A theoretical approach,' *Economic Record*, 36, 1, 1960; M. C. Kemp, *The Pure Theory of International Trade*, Prentice Hall, 1964; P. B. Simpson, 'Foreign investment and the national economic advantage: a theoretical analysis,' in R. F. Mikesell (ed.), *US Private and Government Investment Abroad*, University of Oregon books, 1962.

[2] M. C. Kemp, *op. cit.*

Unfortunately, even on their own assumptions, these conclusions are not acceptable. For, in general, in a perfectly competitive world of the type postulated, an act of foreign investment is likely to change the terms of trade. Where the investing country engages extensively in international trade the effect of any change in the terms of trade will have a significant influence on the marginal social product of overseas investment. It follows, therefore, that in comparing the marginal social products of investment at home and abroad the behaviour of the terms of trade is likely to be crucial. The difficulty now arises, however, that in a perfectly competitive model of long-run equilibrium it is not possible to predict the sign of any change in the terms of trade even when the model is simplified by assuming only two countries (each producing an exportable, an importable and a non-traded good) without making strong additional assumptions regarding the parameters of the demand and supply functions involved. The approach to the problem along the lines of resource allocation in long-term full employment equilibrium thus yields an indeterminate result and eliminates any *a priori* presumption regarding the relative merits of investment at home and abroad.[1]

The second line of approach to the problem begins by pointing out the very restrictive assumptions which are the basis of the long-run equilibrium analyses.[2] The conclusion derived from this line of attack on the problem is given in the following quotation.

> 'Once the assumptions of perfect competition, divisibility of factors and products, diminishing marginal productivity of capital, constant terms of trade and adjustments to equilibrium positions are abandoned, it is impossible to say with certainty whether, from a rational point of view, investing abroad is preferable to investing at home, or whether foreign capital should be attracted into or kept out of the country. Much depends on the industries and the conditions in which the investment takes place.'[3]

We may thus conclude that whether we approach the problem of the social choice between domestic and foreign investment along the traditional lines of long-run static full employment equilibrium analysis or in a more agnostic and sceptical spirit, the only general

[1] I. F. Pearce and D. C. Rowan, 'A framework for research into the real effects of international capital movements,' published in T. Bagiotti (ed.), *Essays in Honour of Marco Fanno*, Padova, 1966.

[2] T. Balogh and P. Streeten, 'Domestic versus foreign investment,' *Bulletin of Oxford University Institute of Statistics*, August 1960.

[3] Balogh and Streeten, *op. cit.*, p. 223.

conclusion is that no general conclusion is possible. Moreover, we cannot hope to resolve the dilemma by appealing to the 'facts' for, though a static long-run theory can be developed in terms of measurable parameters independent of the problem itself, there are as yet no estimates of the numerical magnitude of them. Equally, though we have data on average rates of return, such as are set out in Chapter 2, the relevance of these to the problem in hand is by no means beyond dispute.

To see this, consider our own data. The rate of return, gross of tax but net of depreciation, on the net assets of about 2,000 British public companies was, on average over the period 1960/64, 13·5 per cent. If this is taken to be a reasonable approximation to the marginal social product of domestic investment, which involves assuming average rates and marginal rates of return to be equal, the apparent social rate of return on domestic investment in this period was some 5·5 per cent above the apparent social rate of return on overseas investment (on the same assumption) which, for the same period, averaged 8·0 per cent.

This calculation, which seeks to estimate the marginal social rate of return on direct overseas investment by the marginal private rate of return net of overseas tax is, however, easily upset even if we continue to assume that the average rates, which are observable, are good estimates of the marginal rates. This is so, amongst other reasons, because as we have seen overseas investment may change the terms of trade.

Suppose, for example, that, as a result of overseas investment, the terms of trade are 1 per cent *worse* than they otherwise would have been. Since a 1 per cent change in the terms of trade is worth £50–60 m. a year to the United Kingdom then, by assumption, this sum must be subtracted from the recorded earnings of overseas investment to obtain the 'social' earnings. Such a subtraction would reduce the apparent social rate of return, estimated on the lines set out above, by about one-quarter – say to between 6–6¼ per cent. Conversely, if the terms of trade had *improved* by 1 per cent the apparent social rate of return on overseas investment would need to be increased to between 9½–10 per cent.

In addition, as the previous essay has shown, there are various other benefits associated with foreign investment, e.g. royalty payments and the feedback of technological and managerial knowhow. These are not easily quantifiable but it is possible, that if allowance could be made for them, it would bring the adjusted average rate of return on overseas investment close to the apparent social rate of return on domestic investment. This is because these benefits, in so far as they are reflected in the profits of the investing companies, are already included in our estimates of the domestic rate of return (and ought not to be) and are not included at all in our estimates of the overseas rate of return (where they ought to be).

Thus though it may be correct, in some sense, to argue that: 'Unless the direct and indirect yields of investment abroad are very high, there is some presumption that, from a national point of view, domestic investment is preferable at the margin,'[1] there appears to be, in practice, no method of giving a meaning to 'very high' or identifying 'the margin'. Equally it is not at all easy to see, in this context, what precisely is meant by 'yields' or how they can be measured.

On the basis of the long-run or 'allocative' approach therefore, it seems that nothing can be said with any confidence. The present scale of British direct investment overseas may be optimal (in the sense defined above) or it may not. If it is not, we have no way either of showing this to be the case or of saying whether it is too great or too small.[2]

(b) *Short-term aspects*

So much for an outline of the long-run or 'allocative' approach to the problem of assessing the costs and benefits of direct overseas investment. As we saw above, this approach, though well established in the literature, permits no firm conclusion to be drawn regarding the relative marginal social rates of return on domestic and overseas investment because even if we accept the relatively simple model presented by MacDougall, we cannot, in the absence of quantitative evidence regarding the magnitude of the parameters of the demand and supply functions involved, determine the sign or magnitude of the change in the terms of trade.

In addition, it is not entirely clear that the basic assumptions of the long-run model are applicable to the contemporary British (or United States) problem. This model, it is recalled, assumes that real resources are transferred by the investing country. It follows that, given this assumption, domestic and overseas investment are

[1] Balogh and Streeten, *op. cit.*

[2] In his Budget for 1965 the Chancellor of the Exchequer (Rt. Hon. James Callaghan, M.P.) used figures very similar to those given in this paper in announcing policy changes designed to restrict direct overseas investment. *Hansard* (April 6, 1965), cols. 261–65.

alternative uses of available resources and hence that it is appropriate to frame the problem in allocative terms. In the British case, the balance-of-payments is not invariably in equilibrium. Over the cycle there has been a tendency to severe deficits during 'expansion phases'. There is also some evidence of the existence of a 'fundamental' – as opposed to temporary or cyclical – disequilibrium. Hence, in part, British direct investment has been financed not by the generation of a current account but by borrowing. Since direct investment outside the sterling area – and thus in Western Europe – is subject to exchange control, it is necessary for the authorities to formulate criteria by which applications for official exchange from companies contemplating overseas investment can be judged. In view of the persistent nature of the United Kingdom's external difficulties it is not surprising that the criteria employed emphasize the impact of investment on the balance of payments.

According to the budget statement of an earlier Chancellor of the Exchequer, applications for official exchange with which to finance direct investment outside the sterling area are now examined from two points of view. The relevant passages of the Chancellor's statement are as follows:

> 'First, the project must bring a substantial continuing return to the United Kingdom balance of payments – for example, in additional export earnings. Secondly, there must be good prospects that the overall return to the balance of payments will, within the short-term, equal or exceed the capital outflow'.
>
> 'In all cases where official exchange is allowed in future, or has been allowed since July 1961, the Bank of England will call for periodic reports to show how the return actually achieved in exports or otherwise compares with the expectations, on the basis of which permission was given for the use of official exchange.'[1]

The two criteria set out in the first paragraph quoted can fairly readily be formulated in a way which may be helpful.

Suppose we write the value of the investment project as I_f and assume that some proportion (λ) of the initial expenditure (I_f) will, in fact, be carried out in sterling – let us say for the purchase of British goods. The initial foreign exchange requirement is then:

$$I_f(1 - \lambda).$$

In practice, this foreign exchange can be obtained from two sources. The first is exchange in the hands of the authorities (official exchange).

[1] *Hansard* (April 6, 1965), col. 263.

The second is the accruing foreign exchange receipts of the applicant firm derived from the profits of its past overseas investments which have not been remitted to the United Kingdom. For a firm making its initial overseas investment the latter item is zero. Moreover, even when it is not zero, since the profits *could* have been remitted, the foreign exchange cost of the investment must still be taken as $I_f(1 - \lambda)$ since this is, in effect, the debit item on the balance of payments arising out of the overseas investment of I_f. For simplicity, therefore, we shall assume that the whole of the foreign exchange, $I_f(1 - \lambda)$, falls to be provided by the authorities.

In each of the i years of its life the investment (I_f) will yield returns in foreign current of Q_1. For each year these yield a rate of gross profit defined by:

$$P_i \equiv \frac{Q_i}{I_f}$$

so that the earnings, in any year i, coming from gross profit are:

$$P_i I_f \quad \text{where} \quad i = 1, 2, \ldots n.$$

Of these gross profits some part (t) will be taken in tax by the foreign government and some part (d) of the profits after tax will be retained in reserves overseas. Hence, in year 1 the *remitted* profits are:

$$I_f \,.\, P_i(1 - t)(1 - d)$$

If the foreign investment has an impact on exports – as a whole – and we write the increase in UK exports in year 1 resulting from the investment as ΔE_1 we have:

$$I_f \,.\, P_1(1 - t) + \Delta E_1$$

as the foreign exchange generated by the investment and

$$I_f \,.\, P_1(1 - t)(1 - d) + \Delta E_1$$

as the foreign exchange remitted as a result of the investment.

Proceeding on these lines and writing,

$$\Delta E_i \equiv e_i I_f$$

we can define the 'marginal rate of return (in terms of foreign exchange) on the initial foreign exchange expenditure' by the following equation:

$$I_f(1 - \lambda) = \sum_{i=1}^{i=n} \frac{I_f P_i(1 - t)(1 - d) + I_f \,.\, e_i}{(1 + r)^i} \quad \ldots \quad (1)$$

where r denotes the 'marginal efficiency of foreign investment in terms of foreign exchange.'

This formula is, rather obviously, a crude approximation to the proper definition of r since it neglects the foreign exchange remitted in years 2 to n out of the earnings on reserves held overseas. For large values of n it is, however, a close approximation to the correct value and, even for values of n around 10, possibly the sort of value the authorities have in mind in defining the 'short-run,' the error involved in using (1) is not too great to be acceptable.

It seems as if the first criterion mentioned by the Chancellor implies a concept of this kind even though equation (1) underestimates r. Presumably since the annual cost of the investment (in terms of foreign exchange) is the interest which has to be paid to foreigners to obtain $I_f(1 = \lambda)$ – let us call it i_s – the *prima facie* requirement for approval is:

$$r - i_s > 0$$

provided i_s is defined net of the tax charged on interest payable to foreigners.[1]

It is worth noting that this condition could be satisfied even if all the P_i were zero (or even negative) provided the ΔE_i were large enough. Conversely it could hold if all the ΔE_i were zero or negative if the P_i were large enough. All that $r - i_s > 0$ implies is that if the foreign investment is carried out with funds borrowed at the rate i_s then, after a deficit of $I_f(1 = \lambda)$ in period 0, there is 'a continuing net return to the United Kingdom balance of payments'. Obviously the condition does not imply optimal resource allocation in the sense of the long-run analysis.

Suppose all the $P_i(1 - t)$ are equal and approximate the present average rate of return on direct investment of 8 per cent. Then $P(1 - t)(1 - d)$ would be slightly in excess of 4 per cent. This gives a value of r, if all the ΔE_i are zero and $\lambda = 0$ less than 4 per cent. This in its turn is probably not far from the average net cost of borrowing. It follows that the value of the ΔE_i is likely to be crucial as is the value of λ.

Borrowing abroad reduces the international liquidity of the United Kingdom. This is particularly the case since much borrowing

[1] Strictly the relevant cost is the marginal interest cost of inducing foreigners to hold additional short-term sterling liabilities. For an estimate of this cost in the case of the USA consult H. P. Gray. 'Marginal cost of hot money,' *Journal of Political Economy*, April 1964, pp. 189–92. Gray put the marginal cost of attracting short-term funds at above 10 per cent.

is at short-term. It thus increases the risk of speculative attack on the pound. The second criterion mentioned by the Chancellor seems to represent an attempt to take account of this risk by requiring a short 'pay-off' period in terms of foreign exchange. Formally this requirement may be written:

$$\sum_{i=1}^{i=s} I_f P_i(1-t)(1-d) + \Delta E_i \geq I_f(1-\lambda) \cdots \qquad (2)$$

where $s \leq n$ is the number of years which constitute the 'short term'.

There is, of course, no information as to the length, in terms of years, of this 'short-term' within which 'there must be good prospects that the overall return to the balance of payments must equal or exceed the capital outflow'. Suppose, however, that it was 10 years, $s = 10$ – which is almost certainly a very generous estimate – then, if λ is close to zero, rather less than half the value of initial deficit will be accounted for by remitted profits, and if $s = 5$ less than a quarter. Once again it is the values of the ΔE_i which appear to be crucial. This, of course, assumes that all the P_i are equal. If they are not, what matters for any given r, is how the ΔE_i and P_i are distributed over the s years taken by the authorities to define the 'short term' mentioned by the Chancellor.

This attempt to formulate the Chancellor's criteria explicitly is plainly something of an oversimplification. Nevertheless it does seem to show the rationale of the importance attached by the exchange control authorities to λ and the ΔE_i. Our exposition is not, of course, either an analysis or a justification of the crtieria but simply an interpretation, Thus far, indeed, our discussion has been virtually devoid of economics.

If we now introduce a little economics we can immediately see the formidable difficulties standing in the way of estimating, for any particular investment, the P_i and the ΔE_i.

As far as the P_i are concerned the difficulties, though formidable, are familiar for, by definition,

$$P_i = \frac{Q_i}{I_f}$$

where Q_i is simply the return expected in year i from the investment I_f. Hence in so far as firms can estimate the Q_i – as if they are profit maximizers they must attempt to do in order to programme their investment – they can also estimate the P_i. How good their estimates are likely to be is another matter.

Estimating the ΔE_i is an entirely different problem. First of all the

ΔE_i which are relevant are *not* the increases in the exports of the investing firms, they are the increases in *total* British exports. Since the exports of the investing firm may increase at the expense of the exports of its British competitors, the estimates of the ΔE_i provided by the applicant may well be entirely misleading to the authorities.

There is also the problem of defining precisely what is meant by the ΔE_i. Since ΔE is dated and the dating is crucial in (2) some dynamic process is obviously envisaged. Moreover, it is clear that the ΔE_i, to have any meaning, must be the increase in British exports attributable to the single investment I_f alone. They are, in other words, an example of a *ceteris paribus* effect. It follows, therefore, that to obtain meaningful estimates of the relevant ΔE_i we need to be able to say by how much exports would have risen (or fallen) if the investment (I_f) had *not* taken place. This implies a quantitatively estimated dynamic model of both the investing (borrowing) country and the rest of the world. This, obviously enough, is not available. It is, however, a sobering thought that, even on restrictive assumptions, to obtain worthwhile estimates of the ΔE_i requires us to know not only the values of the parameters of the demand and supply functions of the static model of Pearce and Rowan[1] but also the time form of each response.[2]

In view of all this it seems that the authorities, in applying criteria (1) and (2) must, at least implicitly, be making some strong assumptions which enable them to use the ΔE_i of the investing firm as estimates of the ΔE_i of the economy as a whole. However, these are not necessarily of any obvious relevance to the social decision. Hence, the review of past forecasts, foreshadowed by the Chancellor, though possibly throwing some light on firms forecasting abilities, will not, necessarily, be a good guide to the correctness of earlier official decisions. Nor are the claims of increased exports by firms investing overseas necessarily of much relevance either. In these circumstances the authorities, who cannot avoid the task of making a decision, are scarcely open to criticism for adopting the criteria they have. Not until there has been far more research and a systematic attempt to estimate the parameters of a model which is believed to be relevant and is accepted as such can more useful criteria be developed.

[1] See ref. 1, page 99.

[2] According to the Southampton enquiry UK exports of finished and unfinished goods to European manufacturing subsidiaries amounted to nearly £8m. in 1962. These exports represented some 9 per cent of the net assets of the UK subsidiaries and associates in Western Europe included in the sample.

APPENDIX B

THE REDDAWAY AND HUFBAUER/ADLER REPORTS AND THE 'ALTERNATIVE POSITION' TO FOREIGN INVESTMENT*

The effects of foreign investment

Perhaps the most significant contribution of both the Reddaway and Hufbauer/Adler studies is their attempt to estimate the *effects* of foreign direct investment. In both cases, this is done by comparing the impact of foreign investment on resource formation in both the investing and host countries with that which might have otherwise occurred. But, while – as we have seen – Professor Reddaway gives detailed considerations to only one form of alternative resource formation, the American economists consider three, which they call respectively, the *classical* and *anti-classical* and the *reverse classical* substitution models.

The *classical* substitution model postulates that a unit of capital invested abroad will cause a unit net addition to capital formation in the host country, but a unit net decline in capital formation at home. Under *reverse classical* assumptions, foreign investment fully substitutes for other investment in the recipient country but causes no net decline in capital formation at home. In both these models international capital flows do not affect the total volume of investment – only its geographical distribution. By contrast, the *anti-classical* model postulates that foreign investment increases world capital formation. Under this formulation, no substitution takes place at home or abroad: foreign investment increases plant capacity abroad but has no effect on capital formation at home.[1]

Which of the above alternatives is likely to be the most plausible in practice, depends on the further assumptions one makes about

* First published as part of a review article in the *Bankers' Magazine*, May, June and July 1969.

[1] To complete the picture, Hufbauer and Adler add the case where outward investment occurs at the expense of domestic investment, displacing investment in the host country. Such an assumption implies that direct investment *decreases* world capital formation – not a very likely eventuality.

aims and achievements of macro-economic policy in both investing and host countries. If both countries are always successful in maintaining full employment, and an equilibrium exists between planned savings and investment, then clearly a change in the capital formation by one firm must be offset by expenditure elsewhere – be this investment or consumption. In this event, the *reverse classical* assumption seems to fit. If, on the other hand, the investing country is successful in this policy, but there is unemployment in the host country, the *anti-classical* model would appear the more realistic.

Unfortunately, the matter is not quite as simple as this. For first, even where *total* investment in the host country is unchanged by inward investment, its composition may be, and this could have important consequences for the investing country. Second, measures introduced by the host Government to achieve its macro-economic policy, following the increase in foreign investment, may indirectly effect the return to the existing capital stock.

We illustrate these points from the viewpoint of resource formation in the *host* country, using the *reverse classical* model. The implication is that, in the absence of UK investment, there would have been an equivalent amount of investment by domestic and/or other foreign firms. The Cambridge economists specifically make the assumption that competitors would have produced roughly equal output (*Interim Report*, p. 211), e.g. if Dunlop's had not set up a rubber tyre factory in Canada, Goodyear or Firestone would have done so – this suggesting that market forces would have brought about a similar quantity and pattern of investment. The effects on the recurrent exports of the investing country of such an investment are then the *actual* exports of the UK to Dunlop's Canadian subsidiary, less those which would have occurred had Goodyear or Firestone produced in Canada.

It is not difficult to think of some situations where this assumption seems very sensible, particularly where competing firms are of comparable size and efficiency. Its wider implications, however, do not appear to have been fully appreciated by either Professor Reddaway or Professors Hufbauer and Adler. These are, first, that the market for the goods produced by the competing firms is autonomously determined; the greater the share (or increase in share) of one, the less that of others. Second, it implies that firms are *equally able to exploit* a particular market situation; this, in fact, is most unlikely to be the case in conditions of monopoly or imperfect oligopoly. Indeed, one of the features which distinguishes direct from portfolio overseas investment is that when a firm sets up an overseas operation it does so to exploit a peculiar technical, managerial, financial or marketing advantage it possesses over its competitors, or potential competitors.[1] There is also the question of the *size* of competing firms. One cannot really argue that General Motors, with assets of £2500m. is really in the same competitive class as even the largest European car company, i.e. British Motors, with assets of £500m.[2] Third, the *reverse classical* model assumes that enterprises *judge* market opportunities the same, and are motivated in their investment behaviour by the same objectives. Again one questions the validity of this and wonders, if this is the case, why there are so many US takeovers of Continental European firms and so few UK takeovers.[3]

Intuitively, one finds the assumption of a perfectly elastic supply of direct investment difficult to accept: even if a unit of money capital is the same whoever is investing it, the other components of direct investment, e.g. technical expertise and entrepreneurial talent, are not. Moreover, taken to its local extreme, it implies that the $17 billion of US investment in foreign manufacturing industry since 1950 has made no difference to the total volume of world manufacturing investment; that the Canadian economy would have undertaken the same capital formation with or without US investment; that there is no real capital shortage in the less developed countries of the world.

Quite apart from this, for sheer practical or policy reason, one firm may not be able, or indeed wish, to invest more than a certain amount of capital in a particular market at a given time. Unilever may be prepared to invest £10m. in a detergent plant in India in a particular year, but, unless conditions dramatically changed, not more than this amount. If Procter and Gamble then start producing as well, this will not be at the expense of additional investment by Unilever. Where companies invest in retaliation to investment by competitors this may well result in a net increase in capital formation. This situation also applies where the host Government will not

[1] C. Kindleberger, *American Business Abroad*, Yale University Press, 1969.

[2] To be fair to Reddaway, he is using this particular model to measure the effects of UK foreign investment, which is only about one-fifth of US foreign investment. This means that any competitive relationship which exists between firms in the two countries is likely to be highly asymmetrical!

[3] Neither Professor Reddaway nor the US economists appear to distinguish between the balance-of-payments effect of a UK (or US) firm taking over an existing foreign enterprise and those arising from the establishment of a completely new enterprise. *A priori*, the *reverse classical* model seems much less appropriate in the first case than in the second.

allow any one foreign company (or group of foreign companies) to produce more than a certain proportion of the total domestic output.

Summarizing then, the plausibility of the *reverse classical* model rests, first, on the ability of the host Government to pursue an investment policy geared to full employment, but independent of the amount of (inward) foreign investment. If it is successful in this, then from the viewpoint of its effects on the investing country, it is the type of investment which would be undertaken in the absence of UK investment which is crucially important – e.g. whether it is competitive or non-competitive. We have suggested that, by its very nature, direct investment by any one company is unlikely to be completely substitutable for that of another, and that, in today's world environment, the market strategy of most of the larger international investors (and certainly those dealt with by Reddaway in his report) is likely to be interdependent of, and sometimes complementary to, those of their competitors.

It is, perhaps, a weakness of the Reddaway study that, although well recognized (pp. 254–5, *Final Report*) the implications of alternative assumptions were not explicitly pursued – and particularly the hypothesis that foreign direct investment adds to capital formation in the host country. Hufbauer and Adler examine this possibility in both their *classical* and *anti-classical* models. However, while the American economists allow a net increase in capital formation, they impose the constraint that total market activity within the host country is autonomously determined and independent of inward investment. This means that any increase in expenditure generated by the extra capital must be caused by a decline in expenditure elsewhere in the economy. The authors assume that the reduction will fall entirely on imports (in the *reverse classical* model it falls on the output of competitors). If Ford's (US) produces in the UK and sells £50m. of cars each year, this is assumed to result in a fall in imports (of cars or other goods) of the same amount. The extent to which imports from the *investing* country will be affected depends on the host country's marginal propensity to import from that country; the higher the proportion of imports bought from the investing country, the more the latter's exports are likely to be replaced by any investment it makes in the host country.

Though of respectable Keynesian lineage, it is unfortunate that the authors should concentrate their attention on this particular formulation of the capital generating model. For the only situation under which their analysis would apply is where full employment exists in the host country *and* the structure or resources are being used at their optimum. In unemployment, clearly idle resources exist and foreign investment will generate an additional output, equal to the investing enterprises' capital/output ratio, and subsequently by a multiple of this. Even in conditions of full employment, it is not clear why *only* imports must fall and not that of other forms of expenditure. Admittedly, inward investment will lead to some import substitution but, as often as not, even after a very short time, the value of the additional output it makes possible will considerably exceed the quantity of similar goods previously imported; there is then no obvious reason why subsequent increases should be at the expense of imports.

In estimating the balance-of-payments effect of US foreign manufacturing investment, Professors Hufbauer and Adler use a variety of statistical techniques, but basically they assume that, for every $1m. increase in output produced by US subsidiaries, imports from the US will fall by $1m. multiplied by the proportion of total imports of similar goods, originating from that country. Now, taken to its extreme, this assumption implies that, since the sales of US manufacturing subsidiaries abroad are five times those of US manufacturing exports, and these latter account for one-fifth of world manufacturing imports, that, in the absence of US investment, American exports would be roughly double their present value. Or, putting it in a UK context, without the presence of US subsidiaries, the sales of which amount to 10 per cent of all manufacturing output, the total value of US imported manufactured goods in 1966 would have been 125 per cent greater.[1] Clearly if one accepts the universal applicability of this assumption, one gets as absurd answers as one obtains from the *reverse classical* models.

In our opinion, both the models discussed highlight the unreality of always assuming a full employment situation in the host country for estimating the balance-of-payments effects of overseas investment. Both groups of authors appear to have tied themselves into a Keynesian straitjacket in this respect.

Once the assumption of full employment is dropped, one gets an entirely different *anti-classical* model, although even here the results will differ according to assumptions made of competitors' behaviour and the transactions of subsidiaries. In the simplest case, assuming, in the absence of UK investment, that (*a*) no other investment would

[1] These calculations, of course, ignore the various other balance-of-payments effects of foreign investment.

have occurred, (*b*) the import content of ouput produced is zero, and (*c*) all this output is sold in the home market, then there is no *necessary* reason for imports from the investing country to be effected at all.[1] If the output produced by the UK subsidiaries are non-competitive with UK exports, e.g. as in the case of oil and mining investments, then the net effect would be an increase in imports from the UK equal to the increase in income multiplied by the marginal propensity to import ratio. If production is competitive with imports, then there may be some export replacement effect, but this means expenditure is released for other purposes in the host country, and part of this could (but not necessarily would) be spent on other UK imports, including finished goods imported by the foreign subsidiaries for resale.

One question not asked by the Reddaway team was 'What do you consider the balance-of-payments effects of your investment would be, assuming, in its absence, there would have been no comparable investment by other firms – or indeed any form of compensating expenditure?' This would seem to me to effect the calculations published by Reddaway in three ways. (He pays brief attention to two of these on pp. 254–5 of the *Final Report*.) First, the actual purchases of *input* items by UK subsidiaries from the UK would be no mere appropriate measure of the 'effects of UK ownership,' as, without such investment, no comparable output would have been produced. This would increase this value of these exports from the UK (in the period 1955/64) to 6 per cent from 4½ per cent of the net operating assets of UK subsidiaries.[2] Second, there would be a general increase in imports from the investing country due to the income-generating effects of UK investment. This would vary between host countries, but in general, in relation to the investment made would be small. Third, there is the likely reactions on the purchase of finished goods for resale. This is by far the most difficult item to calculate. For, in a sense, the *reverse classical* model assumed by the Cambridge economists in fact makes two separate assumptions. First, that there is *no* foreign UK investment overseas, and second that an equivalent investment is undertaken by competitive companies. Only the second of these, strictly speaking, measures the 'effects of UK ownership': the first simply evaluates the effect of the absence of any foreign investment – which is essentially what the *classical* and *anti-classical* models try to do.

[1] Apart, that is, from those arising from the initial capital transfer effect.

[2] This latter figure being the difference between the actual imports of UK subsidiaries and those which competitor producers would have made from the UK.

In the absence of UK investment, the question as to whether the exports of UK finished goods are lower (or higher) than they would be if a competitive firm invested overseas depends mainly on the extent to which the goods produced are substitutable for each other, and whether or not foreign investment induces any change in the import policy of the host country – in other words, the competitiveness of importing goods compared with producing them locally.[1]

It would be difficult to estimate this particular impact. One way might be to study the effect of a foreign investment by one country on the imports of a competing country, e.g. what would be the repercussions of the export of B.M.C. cars from UK to Germany, if General Motors set up a subsidiary in Germany? In this case there is an *a priori* likelihood that UK exports would be reduced. It follows then, as the author himself points out, that the particular alternative position assumed by Reddaway is particularly favourable to the effect of UK exports of finished goods, simply because, in the absence of competitors, exports from the investing country would have been greater.

What then is the most realistic alternative position to assume? Any model that postulates that *all* output generated by foreign direct investment is additional to that which would have been produced in its absence is also unlikely to be generally applicable. In post-war years, for example, there appears to be little correlation between the rate of growth output in particular countries and their imports of foreign capital. Japan is the classic case of an economy that seems to have managed without foreign investment. Much seems to depend here on whether or not host countries can obtain the employment and growth stimulating effects of foreign investment by alternative means. Nor must one neglect the effect of foreign investment on resource allocation and efficiency as well as resource utilization.

My own opinion is that no *one* model can adequately explain the effects of not investing – unless it contains the ingredients of each of the models discussed. In most cases, one suspects that a reduction

[1] Neither Professor Reddaway nor the American economists make a distinction between an increase in investment due to the establishment of a completely new UK or US venture abroad and that due to an increase in investment of an existing enterprise. This is a pity, as I would have thought that that so called export replacement effect (i.e. of finished goods) which in the Reddaway model works out at −2 per cent of net operating assets, would have been considerably greater for the first group of firms than the second – if for no other reason than that once overseas production has got firmly established this effect would have largely worked itself out; in others the true marginal export replacement effect may be considerably less than −2 per cent.

in foreign investment by one country will lead to *some* additional imports of competitive products from the investing country; and to *some* reduction in the rate of capital formation in the host country. No generalization on the precise combination of these variables seems possible. It will vary *inter alia* according to the economic conditions of the host country, the character of the investment and the nature of competition between the investing (and prospective investing) firms.[1]

One possible solution to the problem is to present a model which is a hybrid of the *reverse* and *anti-classical* models. This is, in fact, what Professor J. Behrman has sought to do in his comments on the Hufbauer/Adler report in *Direct Manufacturing Investment and the Balance of Payments*.[2] Behrman argues that, in conditions of international oligopoly, a foreign investment by one enterprise, instead of replacing, may trigger off an investment by a competitor, i.e. that firms are more likely to enter rather than stay out of markets in which their competitors are operating. For the *initiating* firm then, the balance-of-payments effect of not investing is the difference between the transactions involved when *both* the initiating firm and its competitors are producing in the market in question, and those which would have occurred had *neither* company invested. To the *follower*, it is the difference between the transactions involved when both groups of firms invest and that when only the initiating firm invests. Both of these models can be formulated, with or without the assumption that foreign investment does not affect the level of market activity in the host country. Remove this constraint, and we have a situation where the impact of foreign investment is to *add* to the capital formation and output of the host country, but at the same time be accompanied by a similar amount of investment by a competitor.

[1] It may, however, be useful to remind readers, at this point in the argument, that in neither study is any attempt made to assess the actual 'incremental' balance-of-payments returns to foreign investment. Both groups of economists, for example, are concerned with the *difference* it makes to the exports of the investing country at a given moment of time, or over a period of time, whether a foreign investment is made or not, but not with the difference between the exports actually made prior to the investment and those subsequent to the investment. I do not wish to quarrel with this approach; simply to point out that, on a different context, the authors of the reports are applying the organic theory of investment discussed earlier. If there is a positive balance-of-payments through *not* investing, i.e. exports will be less (or more) than they were previously, why not a positive profitability effect as well?

[2] National Foreign Trade Council, New York, 1969.

The net balance-of-payments effects of an increment of foreign investment will differ according to whether one is concerned with an *initiating* or a *following* firm. For both types of investors, however, none of the actual inputs of components imported from the investing country would have been imported in the absence of such investment, since a competitor would either have invested in any case, or not at all (as in the *classical*, and *anti-classical* model). However, while for an *initiating* firm, the export displacement effect will be the difference between the finished goods it *and* the *following* firm actually buy from the investing country, *and* those which would have occurred without *either* firm making the investment; in the case of the *following* firm, the alternative position is the exports which would have been made if *only* a competitor firm had invested. Added to these effects there are balance-of-payments repercussions of the additional spending power created in the host country as a result of foreign investment.[1] These are dealt with most succinctly by Professors Hufbauer and Adler[2] using a model first developed by Professor Harry Johnson.[3] They show that under *classical substitution* assumptions, the US trade balance benefits from an increase in income generated from between 8·2 per cent to 26·8 per cent of the initial capital outflow, depending on the recipient region in question.

An idea of the difference a mixed alternative position might make to one's estimates of the balance-of-payments effect is given in Table 1. Using the same data as did Hufbauer and Adler, the nearest one

[1] It is here where the American economists appear to introduce the income-generating effect of inward investment under the *classical* and *anti-classical* assumptions. Their argument seems to run something like this: any increase in the *gross* output resulting from foreign investment will reduce imports from the investing country by this amount multiplied by the marginal propensity to import from that country. But, concurrently, the capital transfer will induce a rise in the *net* output of the host country, part of which will be saved, part spent on domestic output and part on imported goods. It is this latter parameter that the US economists estimate as the 'multiplier' effects investment. In some cases this formulation gives rise to some very unlikely results. For example, under the *classical* model for every additional $100 of capital *controlled* by US firms in Canada, Hufbauer and Adler calculate that there is an export displacement effect of $89 and an income-generating effect which in the first year is $8 and subsequent years $19. This suggests that, apart from the various other balance-of-payments effects, as a result of the $4,300m. of US investment in Canada between 1951 and 1964, the US trade balance could be worsened by up to $3,000m. per annum.

[2] See particularly pp. 52–8.

[3] H. G. Johnson, 'The transfer problem and exchange stability,' *Journal of Political Economy*, Vol. LXIV, June 1956.

TABLE 1

'Best Guess' Estimates of Selected Balance-of-Payments Returns of UK and US Direct Foreign Investment in Manufacturing Industry

	Reddaway Data (*UK* 1956/63) (1) *Percentage of Net Operating Assets Controlled by UK Firms Abroad*			(2) *Percentage of UK Share of Net Operating Assets Controlled*			*Hufbauer/Adler Data* (*US* 1957/64) (1) *Percentage of Total Assets Controlled by US from Abroad*			(2) *Percentage of US Share of Total Assets Controlled*		
	Model			*Model*			*Model*			*Model*		
	A.C.	R.C.	I.G.	A.C.	R.C.	I.G.	A.C.	R.C.	I.G.	A.C.	R.C.	I.G.
Initial Effect												
1. Capital equipment exports	14	10	14	21	15	21	27	3	27	49	5½	49
2. Immediate 'multiplier' effect[1]	n.a.	n.a.	n.a.	n.a.	n.a.	n.a.	2½	3	2½	5	5½	5
Specific Recurrent Effect												
1. Exports of parts and components	6	4½	6	8½	6½	8½	5	1	5	9	1½	9
2. Exports of finished goods (export displacement effect)	−20[6]	−3	−3	−30	−4½	−4½	−51	2½	2½	−93	5	5
3. Trade propensity effect[2]	n.a.	n.a.	n.a.	n.a.	n.a.	n.a.	6	—	6	11	—	1
4. Profits and interest	7½	7½	7½	8	8	8	12	12	12[7]	12	12	12
5. Royalties, fees and services[3]	½	½	½	½	½	½	1½	1½	1½	2½	2½	2½
6. Imports by investing country from subsidiaries[4]	n.a.	n.a.	n.a.	n.a.	n.a.	n.a.	−5	−4½	−5	−9	−8	−9
	−6	9½	11	−13	10½	12½	−31½	12½	22	−67½	13	30½
Non-specific Recurrent Effect												
1. Sustained multiplier effect[5]	n.a.	n.a.	n.a.	n.a.	n.a.	n.a.	7	−3	−5	15	−3	7
	−6	9½	11	−13	10½	12½	−24½	9½	17	−52½	10	23½
Recoupment period (approximate years)	Never	8	6½	Never	7	6	Never	8	4½	Never	7½	3½

[1] Attempts to measure the balance of payments repercussions (to investing country) of an increase in income in the host country consequent upon the capital transfer (see Hufbauer and Adler p. 52, ff).

[2] This effect acknowledges the more general trade effects which accompany any expansion of overseas sales. Under

[3] We have assumed that the royalties and fees are largely independent of the alternative assumptions made, taking as our estimates those contained in Table XII.4 (p. 373) of Reddaway and Table 3.9 (p. 29) of Hufbauer and Adler. Those of Reddaway are estimated net of royalties and fees which might have been earned in the absence of UK investment: The Hufbauer and Adler data assume that in

[4] US estimates are derived from figures on (*a*) US imports per unit of subsidiary sales and (*b*) US imports per unit of native firm sales in various recipient regions (see Hufbauer and Adler, p. 31, ff).

[5] The sustained multiplier effect estimates the multiplier effect of the continuing influence of the various specific balance of payments effect on income flows in the host

can get is to assume, along with Behrman, that the *reverse classical* model applies to the export displacement component but that the *classical* or *anti-classical* model (which allows an increase in capital formation) is more appropriate for the other components. The effect this has on the recoupment period of an export of unit of US capital is to lower this under the *reverse classical* model (which is the most favourable of the three)[1] from 9 to 6 years.[2] Assuming a similar ratio applied in the case of the UK foreign investment, this would reduce the recoupment period from 14½ years to 10 years.[3]

One final point. As already mentioned, the Reddaway assumptions may, in general, be more appropriate for the UK than the US economy. It is obvious, with the US exporting six times more capital than the UK in the period 1960/66, that, in the absence of this investment, UK firms could not have filled the gap; the reverse argument, however, does not hold good. On the other hand, if it is true that UK investors tend to follow rather than lead US investors abroad, one cannot automatically argue that, in the latter's absence, there would have been more UK investment. All this points to the need for far more study on the relationship of actions between international firms before any decisive conclusion can be made on the balance-of-payments effect of direct investment. In spite of the admirable contributions of both groups of economists and the particularly persuasive logic of Professor Reddaway, my own feeling is that no general theory of alternative behaviour (or at least the *effects* of alternative behaviour) is possible but, that we should be able to classify alternative assumptions, and hence the effects of foreign investment, by two or three main variables – such as (*a*) whether full employment exists in the host country and (*b*) the market structure faced by investing (and potentially investing) firms.

[1] This is because under the *classical* and *anti-classical* models there is a very large export replacement effect of finished goods.

[2] This is further lowered to 2½ years when the balance-of-payments effects are related to US investment *owned* abroad, rather than those *controlled*.

[3] 6 years when related to UK assets *owned*. Both calculations only include income actually remitted to the investing country.

Opposite

[6] This figure is very much a guess. It is based on the approximate UK share of the imports of manufactured goods into countries in which the UK has a substantial investment stake. For further details in a US context see Hufbauer and Adler, p. 32, ff.

[7] In the absence of other data, we assume that the return on non-US capital is the same as that on US capital in US controlled firms. In fact, it is likely to be somewhat less.

3

FURTHER THOUGHTS ON FOREIGN INVESTMENT*

Introduction

Writing on 'Does foreign investment pay?' in the Autumn of 1964,[1] I tried to pinpoint some of the main economic criteria on which I considered any evaluation of foreign investment to an investing country should be based. Almost all I wrote then seems to hold good, but on reflection, following further discussions with businessmen, a study of the latest literature published on the subject,[2] and with the current economic situation of this country particularly in mind, I would add two other propositions, which I seek to elucidate here. These are:

(i) Because of the imperfections of economic knowledge and the inadequacy of empirical data, it is virtually impossible to say as of now, with any accuracy, whether or not, *in general*, overseas investment by UK companies yields a higher or lower social dividend than domestic investment.

(ii) In the light of (i), and the UK's current economic situation, further discussions of the 'either/or' type are probably of secondary value. The crucial issue is not that of the competing claims of home and foreign investment, but rather, how one or both of these might be increased by a reallocation of the community's *total* resources.

By way of introduction, however, it might be helpful to consider *why* there is such a divergence of opinion about the merits of foreign direct investment, which, incidentally, is just as marked and

* First published in *Moorgate and Wall Street*, Autumn 1966. Parts of an earlier article published in Autumn 1964 are also included in this chapter.

[1] *Moorgate and Wall Street*.

[2] See particularly, Polk, Meister and Veit (1965), Frankel (1965), Behrman (1965 and 1966), Krause and Dam (1964), Pearce and Rowan (1966).

widespread in the US as in the UK.[1] It seems to me there are four quite distinct areas of disagreement. First, conclusions on the worthwhileness of foreign investment may diverge because the case is argued on different grounds. This may be because the underlying assumptions are different, e.g. the determinants of investment behaviour or the role attributed to Government in influencing such behaviour; or that the problem is tackled from different viewpoints, e.g. that of a particular firm or industry, cf. that of the community as a whole; or that one is examining only one aspect of the effects of foreign investment, e.g. on the balance of payments, and not its implications as a whole: or that one is evaluating these implications from a different time period, e.g. the short run cf. the long run. Many disagreements and misunderstandings, particularly between politicians and businessmen, are of this nature. They arise, simply because the assumptions and terms of reference of the argument are different.

The second area of conflict lies in the *interpretation* of the quantitative or qualitative data available on overseas investment and alternative patterns of resource allocation: partly this is a question of the reliability and usefulness of the published statistics, and partly of appraising their economic significance. Such conflicts of opinion as these can only be resolved by a more extensive coverage of the facts of foreign investment and more research (on the lines of the Reddaway enquiry) into the economics behind the facts.

The third cause of disagreement is more subtle and more difficult to settle by clarifying objectives or by eliciting facts. It arises, both at the individual firm and community level, whenever foreign investment is seen to produce both desirable and undesirable effects which are difficult to quantify in relation to each other. To take one instance, suppose that private investment abroad is shown to be less profitable than home investment but to contribute more to the UK balance of payments? How does one assess the value of a pound's worth of additional exports in terms of a pound's worth loss of output? On what criteria does one judge which is the more socially desirable? This, of course, leads us into much wider issues of economic policy, as indeed does the fourth area of disagreement, which again we illustrate by way of an example, not completely divorced from reality! Suppose the Government is faced with a substantial balance-of-payments deficit and sets itself the prime task of eliminating

[1] As shown, for example, in the varied evidence given before the Senate Committee on Finance when this whole issue was debated in 1962. See *Revenue Act of* 1962. Hearings before the Senate Committee on Finance, 87. Cong. 2nd sess. (1962).

this deficit. Now there are various ways by which this objective might be achieved, only one of which is a reduction of the outflow of funds on capital account. The more obvious alternatives include devaluation, quantitative limitations of imports, a reduction of Government overseas expenditure of foreign aid, internal deflation of real income and prices and so on.[1] Genuine differences may or do arise on the efficacy of these alternative courses of action but they involve much wider issues of policy than the foreign investment problem *per se*. Similarly, there are many other ways of increasing home investment or advancing the UK's rate of growth than by restricting investment abroad. Which of these are, in fact, implemented is again very much a matter of Government policy. Indeed, I am increasingly persuaded that the debate on foreign investment has been too narrowly focused and has assumed certain things as given – e.g. as the share of *total* investment in the national product – which it is not necessarily right to assume as given – since it is in the power of the Government, through its economic policy, to affect.

In trying to isolate some of the various reasons for disagreement on the subject of foreign investment, I have had in mind healing the breach between those of different views. I want now to turn to one or two of the more specific areas of disagreement, and try and formulate a series of propositions which, I would like to think, are acceptable to all discussants.

The divergence between the social and private effects of foreign investment

The first of my propositions is this. In most circumstances, *there is likely to be a divergence between the private and social, or community, costs and benefits of overseas investment.* It seems to me an elementary but basic fact, that, in this particular sphere of economic activity, it is not *necessarily* true that what is the best course of action for businessmen to pursue (still less for any particular businessman) is the best for the community as a whole. This is so for three main reasons. First, to the community, the value of any investment is the increase in the *total real* output generated by that investment,[2] irrespective of how it is distributed: to the businessman it is measured by that part of the total output which accrues to the investing

[1] Some of these alternatives are discussed in an article by D. Snider (1964).

[2] i.e. including the effect on the output of other firms in the community, adjusted as necessary, for any price changes which occur as a direct result of such an investment.

company in the form of *net money profits after tax*. The two may not coincide – indeed they are unlikely to do so: depending on the economic circumstances of the time, it is possible for the optimum rate of foreign investment to be smaller or greater than the private rate. Second, the policies and actions of individual businessmen cannot be considered in isolation to each other. For example, when considering the impact of foreign investment on the balance of payments, there is no reason, necessarily, to suppose that because the exports of a particular UK company increase (or decline less rapidly) following the establishment of an overseas subsidiary, that the country's exports as a whole will be similarly affected. Only if one assumes 'other things being the same' will this be true; normally, however, social exports will be more or less than private exports. Third, there are a variety of economies and diseconomies, external to the individual firm, which arise from outward investment: the operation of a UK mining company overseas may mean that the supplies of essential raw materials are ensured, stabilized or reduced in price, not only for the investing company, but for UK industry as a whole: on the other hand, if a foreign manufacturing subsidiary of a British company should develop marketing contacts in third countries on any scale, this could be at the direct expense of the exports not only of its parent company but of its competitors in Britain.

How far the private rate of return of capital is an adequate social measure of the product of foreign investment will partly depend on the economic conditions at the time. Where there is full employment, an increase in domestic investment can only be achieved without inflationary pressure if it is financed by additional savings or borrowing from abroad. In these conditions, the social dividend of home investment is its profitability (as defined earlier) plus or minus the *difference* in the earnings accruing to the other factor services (mainly labour) by using them in this particular way rather than any other – e.g. the production of consumer goods. On the other hand, if the Government chooses, or allows, the new investment to be financed out of inflation, the *money* rate of return of that investment will clearly exaggerate the *real* rate of return, by an amount which, taking into account its secondary effects, could be quite considerable. In such circumstances as these, foreign investment, by relieving the pressure on domestic resources, may well yield a return which will be 'pure gain to the standard of living'.[1] Where unemployment in the

[1] Chairman's statement to shareholders of Beecham Group Ltd. 28/7/65. See *Annual Report of Beecham Group Ltd.*, 1964/5, p. 8.

investing country exists, there is an additional benefit to be derived from domestic investment, since the community gains the whole of the extra output attributable to labour. This means that, unless there are very substantial external economies associated with foreign investment, it is most unlikely that such resource allocation will yield as high a social product as domestic investment, as the latter is always greater than the former by the additional employee compensation (less unemployment benefits). But as far as the *individual firm* is concerned, the alternative attractions of home and overseas investment may differ comparatively little with changes in general (as opposed to particular) economic circumstances.

The possibility of a conflict between private and social interests is, however, one thing: the likelihood of its actual occurrence is another. The United Kingdom is currently faced with a situation of full (or near full) employment: thus any divergence between private and social interests is less than it might have been in the inter-war years. At the same time, while the *average* rate of return net of tax on both home (or more strictly home *plus* foreign) and foreign investment has averaged around 8 per cent in recent years, the rate of return gross of tax in the UK has averaged 13·7 per cent – and, as a further point of interest – the gap is a fairly consistent one. The question remains, however, (i) how reliable are these figures and (ii) to what extent can they be taken as a true indication of the worthwhileness of home and foreign investment. We return to both of these points later in this chapter.

A second instance where there may be a difference in outlook on the benefits of overseas investment is seen when one examines this problem in a dynamic context. Investment is one of the main determinants of productivity gains and innovating developments – the fruits of which are seen, principally, in higher profits (*gross* of tax) and employee compensation – and, occasionally, lower prices. But whereas, with home investment, the community enjoys *all* these gains, in the case of overseas investment the rewards are confined – so it is argued – to the increase in the profits of the investing firms *net* of tax, and to any reduction in import prices. This is one of the most important differences between investing resources at home and abroad which has been stressed by Schonfield (1963) Streeten and Balogh (1960), and Jasay (1960) in this country, and has led some American economists to the conclusion that to be advantageous to the domestic economy, foreign investment must yield a premium sufficiently in excess of what home investment would have yielded to compensate for the development benefits foregone (Frankel

1965). Ignoring the indirect benefits or external economies of foreign investment, such a premium would normally be equal to the value of the additional productivity created less the share accruing to capital (net of tax). It is pointed out that, historically, this premium has been a high one, and in the context of today's growth oriented world environment, that a nation – particularly one as involved in international competition as the UK – cannot afford to export part of the resources necessary for domestic growth, except in so far as, by indirect means, investment overseas contributes towards such growth. We now turn to consider whether, in fact, UK investment overseas has been a net growth stimulator or not.

Factors influencing the worthwhileness of foreign investment

My second proposition is this: *the rate of return earned on overseas investment is not necessarily a good guide to the value of such investment either from the investing company's or the investing country's viewpoint.*

We discuss this proposition under a number of headings. First, and basic to our argument, is the recognition that to an individual enterprise, as to the economy as a whole, the effects of a particular overseas investment cannot be isolated from its effects on the company's (or country's) profitability as a whole. This, of course, is self-evident in the case of a company which derives 90 per cent of its income from its foreign operations, but the average figure for UK foreign investors is much less than this – between 25 per cent and 40 per cent for companies which engage in similar activities abroad as at home. Moreover, it is not difficult to think of examples where the profits earned by an overseas branch or subsidiary are a very imperfect pointer to the true worth of that operation to the investing company. Income earned abroad, as well as reflecting the efficiency of the local subsidiary, may equally be a function of intro-group accounting practices and pricing policies, and the extent to which it is subsidized in knowledge and services by the parent company: in countries of rapid inflation, seemingly high profits may be almost completely wiped out by foreign exchange losses. And so it is possible that one subsidiary, earning only 5 per cent on its capital, may be highly valued because it is remitting large royalties, buying goods from its parent company at above arm's-length prices, and supplying it with vital technical and managerial knowhow; while another, earning 20 per cent, may be doing so only at the cost of an erosion of its capital through inflation and because it is largely parasitic on its parent company for its research and management services.

This is one reason why too much should not be read into the published statistics. It is possible to make some minor adjustments, as we attempted to do in the previous study. It is almost certain, however, that the social value of foreign investment as shown in the published statistics is understated. When, for example, one *deducts* from the *total* profits recorded by UK companies at home and overseas (i) the profits derived from their foreign activities (net of foreign tax), and (ii) those earned by foreign companies in the UK (who themselves have very few overseas investments); and when one *adds* to the profits of foreign investment (i) the differential between the foreign tax and UK when the latter is greater than the former, and (ii) the share of royalties and fees paid by the subsidiaries which can be regarded as a surplus above the cost of providing the services, the gap between the social rate of return on home and overseas investment is considerably narrowed.

Second, account must be taken of the differences in the financial structure or gearing of home and overseas investment. It is frequently pointed out by business interests that foreign investment provides a more lucrative use of UK capital where it takes the form of equity rather than debt finance. The ratio of UK-*owned* equity to UK-*owned* debt capital is, in fact, much higher in respect of company investment overseas than at home. This means that the return on the UK share of *total* assets *controlled* (but not necessarily *owned*) by British capitalists overseas, *vis-à-vis* that earned on domestic investment, is relatively more favourable than the corresponding return on net assets or net worth. How much so is indicated by the fact that the differential between the (social) rate of return on *total* assets at home and overseas is much less than that on *net* assets; for example it was only 3·1 per cent in 1964. Neither is the gearing of the capital structure irrelevant to the balance of payments: for, whereas the quantity of machinery, components and finished goods imported by a subsidiary from the UK may be independent of the ownership of its loan capital, the net contribution of the investment on the (UK) balance of payments will clearly vary with the proportion of it which is British financed. Other things being equal, it will always be beneficial to the investing firm and the investing community to borrow as much debt capital as it can from local sources.

Third, there is the objection that *average* rates of return are not always a good guide to the efficiency of investment allocation. There are two schools of thought on this question. The one argues that it is the marginal rate of return which is the decisive factor, i.e. the incremental profits earned expressed as a proportion of the

What form was Egyptian?

incremental investment made. The other argues that part of foreign investment is undertaken not to exploit new markets, innovations or products but to protect the value of the existing capital employed. This is the *organic* theory of investment which we explained in some detail in the previous essay. Where a firm or industry is innovating rapidly and competition is directed towards product or process development, firms are forced to engage in net investment, not only so that they might grow but that they might maintain their existing position. Remembering too, that many markets are dominated by international firms and that the running is made by them, the pressure to 'keep up with the Jones's' investment-wise is very marked. Mr H. G. Lazell, ex-Chairman of the Beecham Group, has suggested (Lazell 1965) that many of the world's most modern industries, e.g. pharmaceuticals, motor cars, computers, etc., were dominated by international subsidiary companies and that any attempt to restrict the foreign operations of British firms would simply confer a valuable advantage on their international competitors, including those manufacturing in the UK market.[1]

Fourth, and perhaps the most important point of all, the profits recorded of foreign subsidiaries or associate companies ignore the various other benefits and costs of direct investment overseas which are an important component of consolidated profits of the investing company. These are the external economies and diseconomies of foreign investment which are equally important to the community as to the individual firms. We have examined some of these in other studies.[2] Both in Europe and North America, UK firms have benefited from the access to knowledge of new products, techniques, materials and managerial methods which might not otherwise be obtained, and, in the US, from operating in a more competitive economic environment than that to which they are usually accustomed.[3] The advantages of vertical backward integration do

[1] H. G. Lazell, 'The role of the international company,' *The National Liberal Forum*, 9/11/65.

[2] See, e.g., Chapter 2, and J. H. Dunning and D. C. Rowan, 'British direct investment in Western Europe', *Banco Nazionale del Lavoro Quarterly Review*, June 1965.

[3] Different approaches to factor deployment may result in another form of technical feedback. For example, the impetus to mechanize is greater in the US and Canada due to the higher price of labour and more extensive markets, but it is also true that the production methods so induced can be used with profit in the UK. This is a case of new production techniques being forced on the overseas subsidiary or associate company due to its particular structure of factor prices, but which the UK parent company finds it profitable to adopt.

not appear to be as prominent today as in the nineteenth century, even though such integration, e.g. as in the oil, wood pulp, rubber and non-ferrous metal industries, was probably the leading impetus for the original investment. Most UK subsidiaries in these fields sell their output more to other firms in the UK or in other countries as to their parent companies.

On the other hand, there are other less easily measurable benefits linked with foreign investment. Part of the earnings of the UK construction industry overseas, of consultant engineers, architects and designers, of advertising agents and so on are directly or indirectly derived from the operation of overseas subsidiaries. Some of these and those of other invisible activities, e.g. banking, transport, insurance, merchanting and brokerage, which may represent a cost to the foreign subsidiary, nevertheless appear as a credit item on our balance-of-payments account. In other words, the effects of foreign investment to a particular country cannot be isolated from its impact on its many other and varied external trading activities. Indeed, because of the UK's dependence on foreign trade, and particularly on the invisible component of this trade, these fringe benefits are almost certainly of more than marginal importance.

But, perhaps, most recent attention both here and in the US has been focused on the repercussions of foreign investment on visible exports. This has been because, in seeking ways to reduce their countries' balance-of-payments deficit, both the British and American Treasury have tended to look to cuts in foreign investment as a possible source of currency savings – not only in the short term but in the medium term to long term as well. The representatives of business have replied, most forcibly, that foreign investment, far from weakening the balance of payments, strengthens it. In the US many thousands of words have been written and spoken in support of this hypothesis,[1] and in particular, that, through (i) the generation of exports of capital equipment, raw materials component services and finished goods from the US to foreign subsidiaries, and (ii) the stabilization and cheapening of imports of raw materials into the US from foreign subsidiaries, the balance of payments has been improved. In the UK, a reading of recent company reports shows that

[1] See particularly *Revenue Act*, 1962. Hearing before Senate Committee on Finance, 87. Cong. 2nd Sess. (1962). For an analytical appreciation of these views see A. Gerlof Homan (1962).

much of the recent justification of overseas investment has been expressed in terms of its contribution to exports.[1]

Here again, it is important to distinguish between the company and community viewpoint. From a company viewpoint, it is relatively easy to show when overseas investment is associated with more (or less) exports; possible, but more difficult, to show when it leads to more (or less) exports than would have been achieved had no investment been made; but virtually impossible to show, at least from company data, whether the exports of the community are greater or less. To calculate this latter amount, it is necessary to make some fairly stringent assumptions about what the impact of any alternative resource allocation would have been. Two hypotheses readily come to mind: (i) that exports will be unaffected by any alternative pattern of resource allocation, (ii) that exports are increased by the same proportion as the (domestic) investment/export ratio of the UK economy as a whole. To assume (i) implies that any redistribution of resources will have no effect on the proficiency of supplying UK goods and that there is no excess demand for UK exports: to assume (ii) implies that the marginal investment/export ratio is the same as the average.

Enquiries conducted at an individual firm level, however careful or comprehensive they may be, can never provide a conclusive answer to which (if either) of these hypotheses is correct, though they may be strongly suggestive – and undoubtedly tell us much of which types and geographical distribution of overseas investment are most likely to advance UK exports. The Reddaway enquiry has certainly helped advance our knowledge in this respect, but without knowledge of any changes in Government policy which may, themselves, effect the pattern of alternative resource allocation consequent upon a fall (or rise) in overseas investment, it is almost impossible to assess the *net* affect of such investment on the balance of payments. Nevertheless, it would be interesting to know whether firms in particular industries which invest most overseas, export more, or are responsible for more exports, than firms which invest least overseas; whether the exports of industries or particular countries which are

[1] Some of these reports make very interesting reading, and most clearly indicate the importance attached by many of our leading companies to their overseas activities. See, for example, the reports of the Beecham Group (1964 and 1965), Booker Brothers (1964), Bowater (1965), British Match (1965), British American Tobacco (1965), Dunlop (1964 and 1965), General Electric (1965), Guest, Keen and Nettlefold (1965), Imperial Chemical Industries (1964), and Rio Tinto Zinc (1965).

substantial foreign investors are growing faster than those of industries or countries which do not invest overseas; whether or not UK exports to particular countries are related to UK investment in these countries and so on.

In this chapter we offer three points of evidence. The first is that, as Table 1 reveals, there is no evidence that, *as a whole*,

ABLE 1

Export Performance of Leading UK Foreign Investors 1964, and all UK Firms 1963

Industry	*Exports as per cent of Sales*	
	Leading Investors 1964	*All Firms* 1963
Food, drink and tobacco	15·9	4·3
Chemicals	13·7	18·8
Electrical engineering	21·7	19·8
Engineering	19·2	29·2
Vehicles	28·1	33·4
Textiles	16·0	17·7
Paper, etc.	4·1	6·1

Source: *Leading Investors*: Individual company accounts.
All Firms: *Census of Production* 1963 and information supplied to author by Board of Trade.

Sales are defined as the value of gross output produced in the UK: exports of the value of this output sold overseas. In some cases adjustments have had to be made to the figures presented in company accounts to exclude sales of overseas subsidiaries and to include all types of UK exports.

the leading overseas investors in UK industry export more or less than other firms. On the other hand, *in particular industries*, noticeably food, drink and tobacco, the leading investors record a distinctly better export performance than their competitors; in others, e.g. general engineering, a distinctly poorer performance.

Secondly, there is little reason to suppose that the geographical distribution of capital exports and the export of goods are closely related to each other. Table 2 portrays the growth of the foreign capital stake ($\dot{K}$) of the US and UK in various countries in recent years, and the change in (i) their merchandise exports ($\dot{E}$) and (ii) their share of world merchandise exports, ($\dot{E}/\dot{E}_W$) to these same countries. The correlation coefficient between $\dot{K}_{US}$ and $\dot{E}_{US}$ for the period

TABLE 2

The Relationship between Foreign Investment and the Export of Goods: the United States 1950/63 and the UK 1957/63

Capital Stake 1960/63 (1950/53 = 100) ($\dot{K}_{US}$)		United States Merchandise Exports 1960/63 (1950/53 = 100) ($\dot{E}_{US}$)		Change in Average Share of US to World Exports ($\dot{E}/_{US}\dot{E}_W$)		Capital Stake 1963 (1957 = 100) ($\dot{K}_{UK}$)		United Kingdom Merchandise Exports 1963 (1957 = 100) ($\dot{E}_{UK}$)		Change in Average Share of UK to World Exports ($\dot{E}_{UK}/\dot{E}_W$)	
(A) *Above average investment in and increase in exports to:*						Switzerland	550·0	Italy	214·9	France	118·0
Japan	1,784·6	Netherlands	280·5	Australia	205·4	Germany	360·1	Switzerland	190·1	Switzerland	114·8
Switzerland	937·5	Germany	271·3	Argentina	193·3	Argentina	239·2	France	177·4	USA	102·9
Italy	815·4	Japan	269·0	India	133·7	Brazil	223·3	Germany	172·1	Italy	101·9
Venezuela	630·5	Australia	260·0	UK	125·6						
Germany	623·0	Denmark	234·0	Netherlands	121·3						
(B) *Around average investment in and increase in exports to:*						Netherlands	189·0	Netherlands	136·7	Argentina	100·8
Netherlands	439·2	Sweden	233·9	New Zealand	120·1	Denmark	180·0	USA	131·5	Brazil	100·5
Australia	417·8	India	214·8	Sweden	119·2	Belgium	170·2	Belgium	122·8	South Africa	96·3
France	384·7	Argentina	214·0	South Africa	116·0	Australia	163·1	Denmark	120·2	Germany	94·9
UK	377·6	Italy	205·9	Denmark	110·7	France	150·3	South Africa	112·2	Netherlands	87·2
Belgium	356·4	Switzerland	186·8	Brazil	109·3						
Norway	342·9	UK	177·6	Canada	95·1						
India	338·5	New Zealand	170·0	Belgium	91·1						
Colombia	309·1	France	163·4	Japan	90·5						
(C) *Below average investment in and increase in exports to:*						South Africa	142·1	Brazil	101·2	Belgium	86·4
Denmark	260·0	Belgium	155·8	Mexico	86·0	New Zealand	137·9	Australia	99·3	India	80·9
Mexico	253·0	Canada	147·3	Colombia	85·6	India	133·3	Canada	86·4	New Zealand	76·2
New Zealand	245·7	Mexico	129·6	Germany	78·7	USA	129·9	New Zealand	81·9	Australia	76·0
Canada	244·1	South Africa	126·6	France	77·3	Canada	123·3	India	76·9	Denmark	75·5
South Africa	235·8	Norway	122·4	Switzerland	75·9	Italy	111·1	Argentina	75·5	Canada	73·1
Argentina	187·8	Venezuela	109·4	Italy	74·9						
Brazil	151·8	Colombia	98·4	Venezuela	71·6						
Sweden	84·1	Brazil	90·8	Norway	60·9						

Sources:

Capital Stake: *Survey of Current Business* (US) and *Board of Trade Journal* (UK). Exports of world merchandise to particular countries: *IMF Balance of Payments Yearbook.*

Exports of Merchandise: *Statistical Yearbook of US* and *Annual Abstract of Statistics* (*UK*).

1950/53 to 1960/63 worked out at 0·43, and that between $\dot{K}_{US}$ and $\dot{E}_{US}/\dot{E}_{W}$ to $-0{\cdot}38$; the corresponding coefficients between $\dot{K}_{UK}$, and $\dot{E}_{UK}$, and between $\dot{K}_{UK}$ and $\dot{E}_{UK}/\dot{E}_{W}$ for the period 1957/63 were 0·19 and 0·12 respectively. By contrast, in particular instances, one observes quite close relationships. For Canada, Germany, India, Japan, Mexico, New Zealand and South Africa the ranking of $\dot{K}$ and $\dot{E}$ is broadly the same; while in the case of Argentina, Brazil (UK data), Denmark (US data), Italy (UK data) and Venezuela the export of capital and goods would appear to be substitutable to rather than complementary with each other. If Tables 1 and 2 permit any generalization at all, it is that no generalization of the relationship between UK overseas investment and (recurrent) export of goods is possible: each case must be considered on its own merits.

Thirdly, if one examines the statistics published on trade credit, one sees that at the end of 1964 the net trade credit extended by UK firms to their overseas branches, subsidiaries and associates (excluding the oil companies) amounted to £479m. or rather more than a third of all credit outstanding on UK exports.[1] Without details of the comparative incidence and turnover of credit extended by UK foreign investors and that of other UK exporters, it is difficult to give a meaningful interpretation to this figure – particularly as some of the overseas affiliates are simply sales and distribution ventures operating on behalf of the UK firm. But taking a credit turnover of twice a year as a low estimate and a turnover of four times a year as a high estimate[2] the proportion of total UK exports sold by UK investors to their overseas affiliates is seen to vary from 21·8 per cent to 43·6 per cent of all exports. These proportions, of course, do not include exports direct to UK subsidiaries from other UK firms, which, particularly in the capital equipment field, are often quite important.

Finally, in this section, we turn to examine the profitability of the leading UK foreign investors compared with that of the industry of which they are part. Are they faster or slower growers than the average firm? Table 3 presents details of the comparative performance of some 60 British firms who between them are thought to

[1] International Trade Credit 1963 and 1964. *Board of Trade Journal*, June 17, 1966.

[2] It is, for example, estimated that, in 1964, 60 per cent of the credit extended by UK companies to *unrelated* companies overseas was far less than six months, and the balance for over six months. From conversations with executives of UK companies with subsidiaries overseas, it would seem that a rather higher proportion of credit extended to *related* companies is of a longer term character.

TABLE 3

Comparative Profitability and Growth of Assets of Leading UK Foreign Investors and the Rest of UK Industry

Industry	*Profitability* 1958/60 *Average Per Cent*		1961/63 *Average Per Cent*		*Growth of Net Assets* *end* 1957/*end* 1960 1957 = 100		*end* 1960/*end* 1963 1960 = 100	
	Group A	Group B	Group A	Group B	Group A	Group B	Group A	Group B
Food, drink, tobacco	20·7	16·9	20·4	16·2	27·6	22·3	33·9	23·3
Chemical and allied	19·0	20·3	17·4	15·1	26·2	37·1	22·9	−3·9
Electrical engineering	14·4 } 14·0	22·5	13·5	18·6	27·4 } 23·3	47·7	19·8	19·2
Non-electrical engineering	13·2 }		10·7	19·3	14·5 }		13·9	1·5
Vehicles	22·0	24·5	15·9	13·2	36·0	33·9	34·2	−34·0
Textiles	16·9	14·1	18·4	12·9	24·5	−0·2	43·9	−6·4
Paper, etc.	14·4	20·5	13·6	19·1	46·0	31·1	27·1	17·4
Other manufacturing	20·0	20·8	16·3	15·8	32·7	46·4	10·1	17·5
All manufacturing	17·6	19·5	16·4	16·5	28·0	25·3	26·9	5·4

Note: Group A comprises the leading UK foreign investors; Group B the rest of some 1,000 or so UK public companies.

Source: All data have been derived from *Company Assets and Income* 1957, and *Company Assets, Income and Finance* 1960 and 1963, H.M.S.O.

account for about 75 per cent of all UK investment in overseas manufacturing industry. It reveals a mixed picture. Whereas the growth of the foreign investors appears to have been universally faster than the industrial average since 1960, their profitability is above average only in the food, drink and tobacco, chemicals and textiles industries – and is considerably less in both the electrical and non-electrical industries. It would seem then, from this Table that while overseas investment is an important contributory factor to the growth of UK industry it does not necessarily lead to an improvement in its profitability. We now turn to examine some of the implications of this statement.

The opportunity cost of foreign investment

The third proposition – in this case twin propositions – which I want to put forward is, in a sense, the most important of all. It is this. *The cost of a particular overseas investment project is very rarely to be assessed in terms of domestic investment opportunities forgone by the investing firm in the UK. The opportunity cost of overseas investment in general is dependent, to a large extent, on the particular economic policy pursued by the Government of the day.*

One of the things which it is difficult for an academic economist to accept or fully appreciate is the widespread opinion held by businessmen that domestic and overseas investment are *not* competitive with each other; that any reduction in foreign investment which might result from, e.g., the introduction of the Corporation Tax will not necessarily lead to an increase in home investment; that most of the larger international investors (and probably 80 per cent of the £6,500/7,000m. of the total UK direct capital stake overseas is accounted for by 50 firms) – are not short of financial resources to undertake worthwhile investment projects either at home or abroad; that the constraint on investment at home is not a lack of capital but lack of profitable outlets and/or of management and skilled labour to exploit those outlets. This behaviour pattern, of course, is a little worrying as it appears, at first sight, to run counter to accepted economic theory, which argues that businessmen will aim to equalize the incremental return on their capital in all directions, and that if the relative profitability of resource allocation in one direction changes, so will the distribution of investment. This conflict is resolved, however, when one realizes that the theory (i) seeks more to explain the way in which business enterprises as a whole allocate their resources rather than a particular business enterprise, and (ii) assumes complete mobility of resources between firms and industries. In practice, and from the viewpoint of the individual firm, there is no reason to suppose that either the cost of borrowing capital or the opportunities for domestic investment will be affected by curtailing foreign investment – except, perhaps, in so far as its exports are concerned. Neither will there be a reallocation of investment between particular domestic industries. The constraints which precluded capital from earning the same marginal return on each line of activity before, remained unchanged. If a capital exporter already specializes in only one not very profitable activity in the UK, it is hardly likely to engage in more lucrative diversification if its foreign activities are curtailed.

This point is an important one and worth pursuing in a little more detail. Suppose a particular British firm has only two investment opportunities open to it – (i) to produce shoes in the UK, (ii) to produce shoes abroad. Suppose the borrowing rate of interest in the UK is 4 per cent. Then if the firm wishes to maximize its profits it will go on borrowing money as long as his incremental profit (net of tax) at both home and abroad is above 4 per cent – making the appropriate discount for risk. If a discriminatory tax is now placed on the earnings of its overseas subsidiaries, this will make it less profitable for the firm to make shoes abroad, but will not, of itself, make it more profitable to produce shoes at home. What, then, will the firm do with the funds it might otherwise have invested abroad – either by way of retained earnings or new capital from the UK? Had it been intended to finance this investment by borrowing, clearly the firm would borrow less: if from consolidated profits or liquid reserves, then it may channel the money into the (UK) money market until a more profitable avenue of investment appears; or it may even increase the dividend paid out to its shareholders. Assuming the firm to have been in equilibrium in the home market, before the tax on overseas earnings was levied, these are the only alternatives of resource reallocation open to it.

If it was in disequilibrium, however, other opportunities are opened up. First, if the firm was being forced to ration investment projects undertaken at home – simply because of sheer unavailability of capital, or a managerial or technical inability to cope with more than a certain number of projects over a given time period, then a cancellation of an investment project higher up the scale may lead to one farther down the scale taking its place. Second, the firm may reconsider its policy toward diversification and its mobility of resource allocation. If the more obvious outlets to expansion are closed, more serious thought may be given to the less obvious, although, from a social viewpoint, there is little evidence that resources are being allocated in such a way that incremental returns are equalized. Table 4 reveals that in the period 1958/59 to 1963/64 there was little relationship between the marginal profitability and incremental investments of the larger UK public companies.[1] Even

TABLE 4

Investment, Average and Marginal Profitability of Selected UK Industries 1959/64

Industry	*Growth of Investment* 1959/64 Per Cent	*Average Profitability* 1959/64 Per Cent	*Marginal Profitability* 1958–59/1963–64 Per Cent
Food	47·6	14·8	11·4
Drink	59·3	14·5	12·9
Tobacco	20·8	15·0	23·9
Chemicals and allied industries	29·3	13·7	11·0
Metal manufacture	21·4	12·0	−9·2
Non-electrical engineering	30·0	13·3	5·7
Electrical engineering	40·8	14·1	14·6
Ship building and marine engineering	13·3	6·9	−49·1
Vehicles	9·5	16·7	−17·2
Metal goods not specified elsewhere	43·8	17·7	9·5
Textiles	19·4	13·0	23·5
Leather, leather goods and furs	4·5	13·0	203·4
Clothing and footwear	77·8	15·7	9·1
Bricks, pottery, cement, etc.	80·8	15·9	16·4
Timber, furniture, etc.	52·2	15·4	10·2
Paper, printing and publishing	51·7	13·3	11·5
Other manufacturing	23·0	13·8	14·8
All manufacturing	34·5	14·1	9·4
Construction	62·4	17·6	16·8

Source: *Statistics on Incomes, Prices, Employment and Production*, June 1962 and June 1966.

Definitions: Growth of investment is percentage growth in net assets. Average profitability is average of income/asset ratio for 1959 and 1964 where income is net income (before tax) plus interest on long-term liabilities.

Marginal profitability is ratio of average 1963/64 income minus average 1958/59 income to average 1963/64 assets minus average 1958/59 assets.

[1] The coefficient of correlation between these two variables worked out at 0·07; that between in growth of investment and average profitability to 0·57. It should be noted, however, that the data on marginal profitability reflect both changes in the profitability of existing investment as well as the profitability of new investment.

though the divergence between the average rates of return in particular industries appears fairly small, and allowing for accounting discrepancies, it would seem doubtful if the distribution of new capital is as lucrative as it should be. Different industries clearly earn different rates of profit at the margin, even allowing for differential risk discounts. This, in turn, would suggest that either businessmen are inefficient in their choice of investment or that there are institutional constraints on the mobility of capital.

The *fact* of this immobility of capital may help to explain why some firms do not earn as high a profit as they might do in the UK. The *reason* for the immobility is probably contained in the policy of firms towards product and/or market diversification – and, indeed, of its very attitude to growth and development. For, in the last resort, the opportunity cost of a firm's resource allocation is limited by the alternative courses of action it allows itself to pursue. Various theories have been put forward to explain the scope of business diversification[1], but the one which seems to come nearest to business practice is that a firm will not, in general, extend its activities beyond its technological or marketing horizons. This means that, apart from the industrial holding type of company, a firm, in a particular industry, may well choose to grow horizontally through extending its activities overseas than by branching out to new and unfamiliar lines of production or marketing at home. This, combined with the historical structure of UK foreign investment would help to explain why such a high proportion, probably two-thirds, of such investment in manufacturing industry is in traditional type industries, e.g. textiles, food processing, tobacco, heavy engineering, etc., and why global figures, which take no account of the industrial distribution of home and foreign investment, can be so misleading.

If one accepts this constraint of a firm's activities, it is easy to appreciate why, from a micro-viewpoint, overseas and home investment are not necessarily competitive with each other. A firm's investment opportunities are limited by its technical and marketing ability to diversify: if these are fully met at home, then the opportunity cost of investing overseas is zero – or at least only the short-term rate of interest.

But this does not mean that from a *community's* viewpoint, the opportunity cost of foreign investment is low. For, as shown earlier, when a firm finds it reduces its commitments to invest overseas it will either borrow less capital or purchase short-term assets in the money

[1] These are summarized by Lloyd Amey (1964).

market. Whatever it does, the capital market benefits from the availability of more funds than it otherwise would have had, which can be used to finance additional private domestic (or indeed other foreign) investment. Whether or not it is used in this way will primarily depend on if the capital market is in equilibrium. If it is not, or if the supply of capital is being rationed by other than the market mechanism, e.g. by a complete clamp-down on bank loans, then less foreign investment could mean more domestic investment without a change either in (i) demand or cost expectations, or (ii) the rate of interest. If the market *is* in equilibrium, then an addition to private domestic investment can only occur if the marginal efficiency of capital is increased by a change in one or other of these variables, which may only be possible if there is a change in Government policy. Failing a diversion of funds to the private sector, then the Government itself might speed up its own investment programme, e.g. in hospitals, schools, roads, etc. – or allow more consumer goods to be produced. The effect of the reduction in overseas investment on the balance of payments will, of course, differ according to *type* of alternative resource allocation made. And, once one gets into certain areas of social investment, it is extremely difficult to make a sensible quantitative evaluation of costs and benefits. But the point which must be stressed is that, except where a foreign investment is financed by borrowing from abroad, it must always have a positive opportunity cost. In particular, investment abroad by an advanced industrial nation should never be regarded as a soft option for domestic investment in the development of new products, processes and materials upon which that nation's future prosperity and international strength might depend.

Let me summarize my argument so far:

1. Assuming that it is possible to find an acceptable definition of the worthwhileness of overseas investment, then to the investing firm, equilibrium will be reached when the (adjusted) incremental return earned on such an investment, suitably discounted for risk, is equal to that which could have been earned from any alternative pattern of resource allocation considered desirable by the investing company. Such a return is imperfectly reflected in the published data of the earnings of UK companies overseas because they are (*a*) too global to be really useful, (*b*) expressed in average terms, and (*c*) exclude the external benefits (and costs) of foreign investment which are hidden in the profits earned on consolidated accounts by the investing company.

2. To the community, the right level of foreign investment is that

which represents the best return on resource allocation, and this has to satisfy two criteria:

(*a*) the equalization of income earned at the margin – *net* of tax abroad and *gross* at home, suitably adjusted to allow for the 'organic' theory of investment approach. This assumes a mobility of resource allocation between industries in the UK which, in fact, is not being achieved.

(*b*) that foreign investment induces a growth rate in the investing country equivalent to any alternative pattern of resource allocations.

In recent years, a third criteria of desirability has been added:

(*c*) that foreign investment should result in as little strain as possible on the balance of payments – both in the short and long run.

3. There is no evidence that, from the viewpoint of the individual investing firm, and accepting the constraints of resource allocation, the UK is misallocating its resources by investing too much overseas. Indeed, when the full facts of the situation are known, British companies may well be seen to be investing too little overseas, and that, because of this, the Corporation Tax will be damaging to their long-run profitability and growth prospects. To the extent too, that the larger of UK foreign investors look upon their international activities, not only as a source of foreign exchange earnings, but as a vital part of their competitive strength *vis-à-vis* other multinational companies – particularly those of American parentage – any curtailment of these operations might have affects much wider than those on the foreign investment itself. The linkages between outward investment and UK invisible exports also need further exploration.

4. From a social viewpoint, foreign investment is one particular use of the nation's scarce resources and there is an opportunity cost involved in using resources in this direction rather than any other. In theory, this opportunity cost could be the fruit of almost any other pattern of resource allocation. In practice, given the constraints of the market, it will be the policy of the Government which decides what this should be. For it is able, by various devices, to decide whether foreign investment should be 'paid for' out of domestic investment or consumption, out of its own overseas expenditure or out of the countries' foreign exchange reserves. If I am not completely sure about the balance of advantage between foreign and domestic

investment, I am certain that attention has been unduly focused on a very limited range of solutions to the UK current economic problems. It would seem that foreign investment has been made something of a scapegoat, in so far as it is has been assumed that its cost is always less domestic investment. Very well. It is possible that more home investment and less foreign investment would yield a higher national dividend. But preferable to this particular pattern of resource allocation may be another which yields both more home and foreign investment, but a reduced output of consumer goods and/or a cut-back in Government commitments overseas. I have yet to see the costs and benefits of foreign investment fully reasoned in these terms.

The terms of trade

Up to this point I have ignored the *terms of trade* – the effect of overseas investment on the price of imports and exports. This is a field in which the empirical evidence, at least in so far as the investing country is concerned, is slight;[1] we shall do no more than summarize how, in principle, overseas investment may affect the prices of imports and exports.[2]

(a) The price of imports

Overseas investment in resource exploitation ventures will usually reduce the price of imports of the investing country as the supply of these products by recipient countries increases. Much depends on whether the industries in question are producing under increasing or decreasing costs and the proportion of the total output produced by the investing firm. On the other hand – and this applies particularly where there are unemployed resources in the host country – the additional income created by such investment *may* be spent on goods at present being exported to the investing country, thus (in the short run at least) raising their price and turning the terms of trade against that country. Had the investment been undertaken at home, the immediate effect would vary according to whether there was full employment or not. If the former, then the effect on the demand for imports would depend on the import-component of the new investment *vis-à-vis* that which would otherwise have been produced;

[1] i.e. in respect of recent years. The nineteenth-century relationship between trade and investment is much better documented. See, e.g., A. K. Cairncross (1953).

[2] We will also confine ourselves to the *primary* effects of such investment.

if the latter, imports will rise by the import-component of the investment and hence, *ceteris paribus*, the terms of trade would move against the importer. If the output produced by the new investment is import-replacing in character, then a reduced demand may cause prices to fall. Again, the long-run effect in both instances will depend on the elasticity of the supply of the imports the demand for which has changed.

(*b*) *The price of exports*

Initially, an investment abroad will increase or not affect the demand for capital goods exported by the investing country. To the extent that it increases exports, the terms of trade will move in favour of the investing country. Subsequently, if the overseas investment is in import-replacing industries, the demand for those goods from the investing country will tend to fall and the price of exports likewise; the reverse will occur if the investment is in import-complementing industries. On the other hand, the raised incomes resulting from such investment may increase the demand for goods from the investing country, thus raising the price of exports. On the supply side, where investment is *horizontal* in character, i.e. in the same industry abroad as at home, it is possible that the increased efficiency of the recipient country might enable it to increase its exports to third countries at the expense of the exports of the investing country. Counteracting this tendency, is the fact that through the technical feedback the productive efficiency of the *investing country* is improved and thus the price of exports may well fall. On the other side, had the investment been undertaken at home, exports would have risen by the export-component of the increased production and, very probably, the efficiency of production as well.

How far an adverse movement in the terms of trade is a good or bad thing, in terms of the balance of payments, largely depends on whether the price movements are induced by changes in demand or changes in supply. Obviously, *given* the *conditions* of demand and supply, it is desirable that the UK should obtain her imports at cheapest cost and sell her exports for the highest prices. But taking account of *changes* in the conditions of demand and supply this conclusion need not necessarily hold. Thus, it is likely to be a much better thing for the balance of payment if, as a result of an improvement in technology or production efficiency (due to the technical feedback from overseas investment), the UK is able to reduce the price of her exports, even though this worsens her terms of trade, than if she were forced to raise her export prices, through decreased efficiency (or increased costs), although this would result in an improvement in the terms of trade.

Conclusion

There is one final point I should like to make. I have argued that the question 'does foreign investment pay?' is largely meaningless unless we specify from *whose* viewpoint, from *which* viewpoint, from which time period and in terms of what alternatives we are asking. It is also important to know whether the global data available on the performance of UK investors overseas, e.g. as shown in the rate of return capital, is broadly representative of the constituent firms. For example, if one looks at the profitability (net income after tax to net assets) of UK companies in Germany, one sees that, for the period 1958/62 it averaged around 28 per cent: if, however, one excludes the profits and assets of the two most successful large companies in Germany, the rate of return drops by more than a third – to around 18 per cent. This means that the global figure of profitability is not representative of the majority of UK firms operating in Germany.

Perhaps the main reason why it is necessary to know the extent to which there are variations in the profits earned by UK firms in particular countries and industries is that this could have important policy implications. Let me illustrate. If, on average, it is shown that foreign investment, in relation to other forms of resource allocation, ought to be curtailed, there are broadly two ways this could be achieved. First, a general measure could be introduced, e.g. an increase in the taxation of foreign earnings or a complete embargo on all forms of new investment; this will probably bring about the desired results, but in a completely indiscriminate fashion and without regard to the degree of profitability of the potential investors. Alternatively it is possible to make use of selective measures which attempt to curtail the type of investment which is the least profitable while not harming the investment which is the most profitable. Now, among the factors influencing the choice of measure adopted will be the extent to which the experience of UK firms operating overseas are broadly the same or different. If the former is true, a general measure will operate fairly enough: if the latter, it *could* do more harm than good. And, the fact is that the experiences of UK business investors overseas are extremely diverse. In some countries, handsome profits are earned; in others, losses are made; whereas UK mining and some manufacturing ventures have, on the whole, done very well, the returns recorded by most kinds of engineering firms have been extremely disappointing. Some subsidiaries, such as the majority of sales ventures, make possible immediate and substantial exports from the UK; others tend to replace exports and take a long time to earn any profits. UK companies with investment in advanced industrial countries are more likely to benefit from a feedback in technical and managerial expertise than those whose activities are concentrated in the less developed areas; on the other hand these latter may offer a greater growth potential. The impact of an investment, financed by a comparatively small amount of UK equity capital associated with a large amount of local debt capital, may be quite different on the balance of payments than that where all but a small part of the current debt is UK owned. Companies which depend exclusively on foreign activities for their income, e.g. the mining and plantation enterprises, can hardly be considered in the same light as those whose purpose in venturing abroad is to advance their UK exports.

These are just some aspects of the diversity of both the kinds and effects of UK direct investment abroad. They suggest that any general attempts to effect a particular economic policy can never produce the desired results in all cases – perhaps not even in the majority of cases: on the other hand, one can sympathize with the Government in trying to frame any selective policy towards foreign investment which, when carried to its extreme, would mean the consideration of each case on its merits. But this, in fact, is what is being done when the Bank of England considers applications for foreign currency to underwrite new capital exports from the UK. Why not equally apply similar criteria for the retained earnings component of investment over say, £500,000 a year? This would take care of about 85 per cent of all such investment overseas and involve a detailed examination of the activities of only about 100 companies. Would such companies object to such a procedure – in place of more blanket type controls? Not, I suspect, if they had a say in the framing of the questions and of the criteria on which they were based. And in the end, if the argument of this chapter is correct, there may be more surprises in store for the custodians of our national purse than for the firms which help supply this purse.

REFERENCES

L. Amey. 'Diversified manufacturing business,' *Journal of the Royal Statistical Society*, Series A, Vol. 127, June 1964.

J. N. Behrman (1965). 'Foreign investment muddle: the perils of *ad hoccery*,' *Columbia Journal of World Business*, Vol. 1, Fall 1965.

J. N. Behrman (1966). 'Foreign private investment and the Government's efforts to reduce the balance-of-payments deficit,' *Journal of Finance*, Vol. XXI, No. 2, May 1966.

A. K. Cairncross. *Home and foreign investment* 1870/1914, Cambridge University Press, 1953.

M. Frankel. 'Home versus foreign investment: a case against capital export,' *Kyklos*, Vol. XVIII, 1965.

A. Gerloff Homan. *Some measures and interpretations of the effect of the operation of U.S. foreign enterprises on the U.S. balance of payments*, paper presented at the annual meeting of the Western Economic Association at the University of California, Los Angeles, August 1962.

A. E. Jasay. 'The social choice between home and overseas investment,' *Economic Journal*, Vol. LXXI, March 1960.

L. B. Krause and K. W. Dam. *Federal tax treatment of foreign income*, The Brookings Institution, 1964.

H. G. Lazell. 'The role of the international company,' *The National Liberal Forum*, 9/11/65.

I. F. Pearce and D. C. Rowan. 'A framework for research into the real effects of international capital movements,' in T. Bagiotti, *Essays in Honour of Marco Fanno*, Padova, 1966.

J. Polk, I. W. Meister and L. A. Veit. 'U.S. production abroad and the U.S. balance of payments,' *National Industrial Conference Board*, New York, 1966.

A. Shonfield. *British economic policy since the war*, Penguin, 1963.

D. Snider. 'The case for capital controls to relieve the U.S. balance of payments,' *American Economic Review*, Vol. LIV, June 1964.

P. Streeten and T. Balogh. 'Domestic *v.* foreign investment,' *Bulletin of the Oxford University Institute of Statistics*, Vol. 22, August 1960.

4

BRITISH INVESTMENT IN THE UNITED STATES 1860/1913*

I

This chapter has two main objects: first to construct a continuous statistical series of British capital exports to the United States between 1860 and 1913; and, second, to examine the relationship between this series and other economic variables, with a view to shedding some light on (i) the main determinants of UK investment in the US during this period, (ii) the extent to which this capital flow affected the pace and pattern of the economic development of both the host and investing countries.

II

In an attempt to assess the growth of UK investment in the US between 1860 and 1913, we find two main sets of data at our disposal. The first consists of two series relating respectively to total UK capital exports and US capital imports. The former series, compiled by A. H. Imlah (1958), covers the whole of our period and gives annual estimates, both of net foreign investment (foreign investment by the UK minus investment by foreigners in the UK) and of the cumulative value of capital invested abroad by the UK. A complementary series by Matthew Simon (1960) presents annual data of the net capital movements into or out of the US for the period 1861 to 1900, with the net accumulating balance of indebtedness at June 30 each year. Both series were derived in a similar way, and, in each case, the export or import of capital is largely a residual figure in the balance of payments. The Simon series has been updated to 1913 by the US Bureau of the Census (1960).

* This study is part of a wider piece of research into the role of British capital in the development of the US, financed by the Rockefeller Foundation. I am greatly indebted to T. C. Coram and F. J. B. Stilwell for their help in the preparation of the diagrams and statistics in this chapter.

The other data available are those published by various American and British writers, on (*a*) the total UK investment or the cumulative UK capital stake in the US at particular points of time between 1860 and 1913, these being calculated either directly, or by capitalizing income received by UK investors, as revealed by tax returns;[1] and (*b*) some of the more important components of total investment in North America, e.g. new portfolio investment throughout the period (Simon 1967). With these two sets of data we shall attempt to construct a series of UK capital exports to the US over the period 1860/1913.

TABLE 1

Foreign Investment in US and of UK: Imlah and Simon Series
$m.

	Aggregate Credits and Debits		*Net New Investment*	
Year	*Net Balance of US Indebtedness*	*UK Accum. Credit Abroad*	*In US from from Abroad*	*By UK Abroad*
1861	483·6	1,915		
2	482·5	1,971	−1·1	56
3	495·1	2,100	12·6	129
4	605·7	2,211	110·6	111
5	674·4	2,380	68·7	169
6	768·8	2,541	94·4	161
7	914·4	2,746	145·6	205
8	987·1	2,923	72·7	177
9	1,156·3	3,150	169·2	227
1870	1,255·7	3,365	99·4	215
1	1,356·6	3,711	100·9	356
2	1,599·4	4,187	242·8	476
3	1,782·3	4,582	182·9	395
4	1,864·5	4,927	82·2	345
5	1,951·4	5,176	86·9	249
6	1,953·2	5,289	1·8	113
7	1,895·9	5,353	−54·3	64
8	1,734·0	5,435	−161·9	82
9	1,573·8	5,607	−160·2	172

[1] In particular, see the sources quoted in Simon (1960). Also Madden (1957), Williamson (1964), Cairncross (1953) and Brinley Thomas (1967).

TABLE 1—*continued*

1880	1,603·2	5,780	29·4	173
1	1,562·4	6,099	−40·8	319
2	1,671·9	6,385	109·5	286
3	1,723·0	6,622	41·1	237
4	1,828·3	6,974	105·3	352
5	1,861·2	7,276	32·9	302
6	1,997·1	7,660	135·9	384
7	2,227·3	8,086	230·2	426
8	2,512·3	8,533	285·0	447
9	2,713·9	8,926	201·6	393
1890	2,906·5	9,405	192·6	479
1	3,041·0	9,742	134·5	335
2	3,081·8	10,029	40·8	287
3	3,227·2	10,287	145·4	258
4	3,161·2	10,476	−66·0	189
5	3,298·2	10,669	137·0	193
6	3,338·0	10,945	39·8	276
7	3,314·9	11,147	−23·1	202
8	3,036·4	11,259	−278·5	112
9	2,787·3	11,465	−249·1	206
1900	2,569·3	11,649	−218·0	184
1	2,324·3	11,814	−245·0	165
2	2,189·3	11,976	−135·0	162
3	2,168·3	12,193	−21·0	217
4	2,158·3	12,445	−10·0	252
5	2,075·3	12,841	−83·0	396
6	2,143·3	13,412	68·0	571
7	2,214·3	14,160	71·0	784
8	2,168·3	14,912	−46·0	752
9	2,227·3	15,571	59·0	659
1910	2,482·3	16,385	255·0	814
1	2,530·3	17,341	48·0	956
2	2,553·3	18,299	23·0	958
3	2,640·3	19,389	87·0	1,090

(i) 1861/1900

Source: M. Simon, 'The United States Balance of Payments 1861/1900,' pp. 629–715, in *Trends in the American Economy in the Nineteenth Century*, NBER Princeton, 1960.

(ii) 1900/13

Historical Statistics of the United States, Washington, 1960, p. 564. A. H. Imlah, *Economic Elements in the Pax Britannica*, Cambridge Press, 1958.

We begin by presenting, in Table 1 and Diagram 1, the data on (*a*) net new investment, and (*b*) aggregate credits or debits, contained in the Imlah and Simon/US Bureau of the Census series. A first glance at these figures shows a general similarity in the movement

DIAGRAM 1

International Investment Position of UK and US 1861–1913.

(Imlah and Simon US Bureau series.)

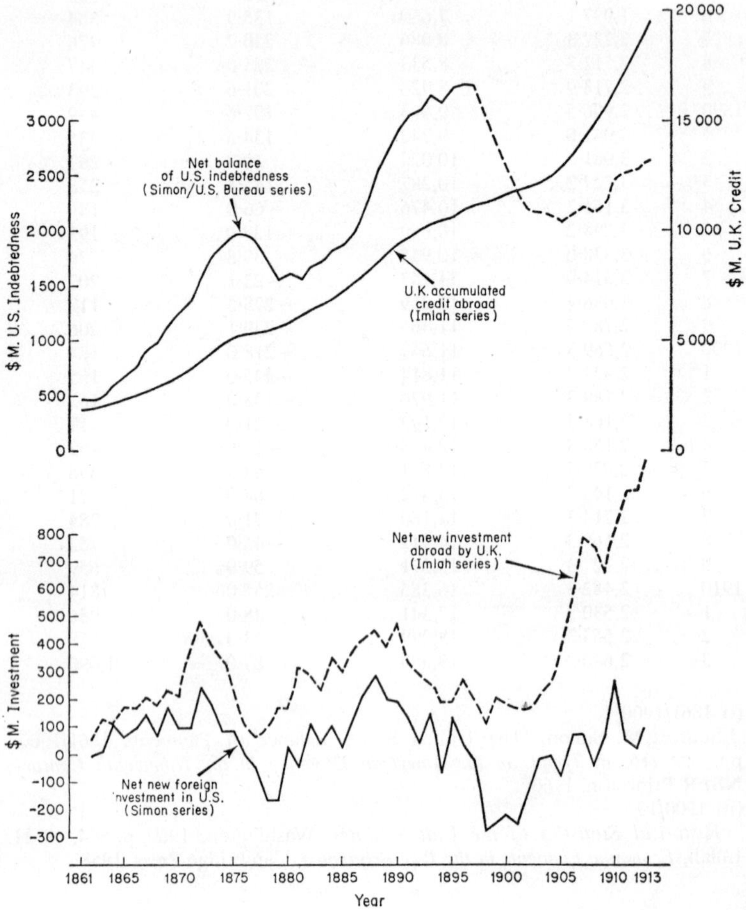

Source: Table 1.

of capital out of the UK and into the US, although the fluctuations appear to be more marked in the American series. In the 1860s, for example, we see substantial capital movements in both cases, culminating in 1872 with a peak outflow of investment from the UK and inflow of capital to the US. The period from 1873 to the end of the decade is seen to be one of falling investment in both series – with a net outflow of capital being recorded by the US between 1876 and 1879. The trough of new investment was reached in 1877 in the Imlah series and 1878 in the Simon series. The 1880s saw a new wave of capital exports from the UK and capital imports into the US, with each series moving to a new peak at the end of the decade. This was again followed by a period of retrenchment in foreign investment by the UK and one of net disinvestment by foreigners in the US; both series reach a new trough around the turn of the century. By contrast, in the first years of the twentieth century, the movement of both capital exports and capital imports is strongly upwards.

A straightforward linear coefficient of correlation between the Imlah and Simon/US Bureau time-series works out at +0·922.

However, if one separates the trend from the series by way of nine-year moving averages and then calculates the association of the deviations so derived from the original values, the coefficient is reduced to 0·255. Alternatively, correlating the first differences of the two series, i.e. the data on net new investment, the coefficient is seen to be 0·349. The correlation coefficient for the trend itself (or, strictly speaking, the trend plus residual fluctuations) is 0·997.[1]

That there is not a closer association between the fluctuations in the Imlah and Simon series, and that the data (as they stand) are of little assistance, even as a starting point, in estimating movements of UK investment in America is not surprising. For such investment, is, after all, only one of the determining components of each series, and it is clearly quite possible for either the total UK capital invested overseas, or the total foreign capital invested in the US, to change without British investment in the US changing, or for the latter to rise or fall without there being any alteration in total capital movements. Only if the *share* (or rate of change in the share) of UK capital exports destined for the US, or that of US capital imports from the UK remained

[1] It is interesting to compare the relationships obtained with those which may be computed from the Imlah/North series for the period 1820/60 (see also *Trends in the American Economy in the Nineteenth Century*, *op. cit.*). Here the correlation coefficient works out at 0·980 for the original value of the series, 0·308 for the relative deviations from the trend, and 0·999 for the trend itself.

constant could one take global figures of the Imlah/Simon type as a reasonable proxy of UK investment in America.[1]

A second difficulty in using the Imlah/Simon figures as they stand, is that they are both *net* of capital movements in the reverse direction, i.e. net of capital imports in the case of the UK and of capital exports in the case of the US. This means that a decrease in capital exports as recorded by Imlah could be due either to a rise in foreign investment in the UK or to a fall in overseas investment, or a combination of the two; a fall in net foreign investment in the US may be the result of an increase in investment abroad rather than a reduced flow of capital from overseas. Since we wish to estimate the *gross* UK investment in the US, some adjustment is required to the Imlah/Simon figures *before* any estimate of the UK/US share is possible. Before the Civil War, both imports of capital by the UK and exports of capital by the US were so insignificant that they could have had little bearing on fluctuations in trans-Atlantic investment. The situation is not quite so clear-cut for the period under discussion, chiefly because of the emergence of the US as an important overseas lender. Indeed, from 1890 onwards US capital exports were growing at a faster rate than her capital imports and in twelve of the sixteen years between 1897 and 1914 there was a net *export* of capital from the US (US Bureau of the Census 1960).

We tackle this second problem first. In the construction of his time series, Imlah is chiefly concerned with *net* movements in the various components of the balance of payments; however, in seeking a check to his own estimates of Britain's cumulative credit position overseas at particular points of time, he draws upon the estimates of other authorities who usually present their data unadjusted for any foreign investment in the UK (Jenks 1938, Hobson 1914, Feis 1930). Based on a calculation of Sir George Paish (1909 and 1911) of interest and dividends received by foreigners on publicly issued securities in the UK for the year 1907, and his own 'guesstimate' of the income earned on private foreign investment in this country, Imlah puts foreign holdings in Britain at that time at 10 per cent of the value of all British foreign investment. Working backwards to earlier

[1] We will examine the data available on the relative importance of such investment from both countries' viewpoint more fully later; for the moment, we observe that the fluctuations in the distribution of British investment overseas in the pre-1860 period is one of, if not the most important reason for the low correlation between the Imlah/North series. Indeed they ranged from under 10 per cent of the total capital exports in the early 'twenties and forties' to nearer 60 per cent in the middle 'forties and fifties'.

estimates of Jenks, Giffen, Seyd, etc.,[1] he continues to assume that this proportion is a reasonable figure to deduct to obtain the *net* accumulated balance abroad, although, as he admits, it is based on little more than impression and guess-work. Accepting this proportion of 10 per cent – which clearly must have fluctuated from year to year, we have then adjusted the Imlah series throughout by multiplying each figure by 10/9ths to obtain estimates of gross UK overseas investment.

The situation is more complicated with the American data, as the importance of capital exports has changed over the years. We have four starting figures, each provided by Cleona Lewis (1938). The first is for 1869, at which date Lewis puts the value of American foreign assets at between \$50 and \$100 million (roughly 5 per cent of her liabilities); the second is for the end of 1897 by which time compared with a net foreign indebtedness of about \$3·175 million[2] US foreign assets had risen to \$685 million (roughly 20 per cent of gross liabilities). Between these two dates, it would seem, both from the picture given by Lewis in her book, and extrapolating backwards from the data available on the income earned on foreign investments in the years 1900/14, that there was little significant expansion in American investment overseas until the 1880s, when a substantial amount of direct investment was made in Canadian and European manufacturing outlets, mining ventures in Canada and Latin America, sugar plantations in Cuba, and railroads and public utilities in various countries (Southard 1932, Marshall, Southard and Knight 1936). We thus make the assumption that from 1861 to 1880 the (gross) outflow of capital from America was (on average) equal to 5 per cent the (gross) inflow of foreign capital: that between 1881 and 1890 its share increased by ½ per cent per year (compound) to reach 10 per cent in 1890 and in the following six years by 1 per cent per year to 16 per cent in 1896. The third estimate by Lewis of America's foreign assets is that for the end of 1908, when these were valued at \$2,525 million – a very substantial increase over the past decade and now representing a sum greater than the *net* indebtedness of the US and 53·5 per cent of the *gross* indebtedness. Finally, Lewis puts the foreign assets of the US on July 1st, 1914, at \$3,514 million – about 58 per cent of the country's gross indebtedness. Taking these figures as base, we then assume that, between 1897 and 1906, the proportion of US foreign investment to gross foreign indebtedness

[1] For detailed sources see Imlah (1958) and Cairncross (1953).
[2] The midpoint between the (June) 1897 and 1898 figures of Simon.

rose very sharply (but at an even rate) to 50 per cent, and from 1907 to 1913 more slowly to 57 per cent in 1913. When the Simon and US Bureau of Census figures are amended in this way, we believe they give a reasonably accurate picture of the total US import of foreign capital between 1860 and 1913.

Next, what of the proportion of the total UK capital exports directed to the US and of the total capital imports of the US originating from the UK? To assess these, we look first at the few statistical estimates which have been made of UK investment in the US at various dates between 1860 and 1913. When these are related to the (amended) Imlah/Simon series, the resulting proportions may be taken to represent a kind of trend picture. We, then, attempt to estimate the proportion for the intervening years by reference to movements in the geographical distribution of UK capital exports and US capital imports, as may be inferred from the literature.

Table 2 below sets out the only reliable, or reasonably reliable, estimates we have been able to find of the accumulated UK capital stake in the US. Even these, as can be seen by the brief particulars given at the end of the table, are based on incomplete data. Columns 3 and 5 of the table express these figures as a proportion of the total stock of UK capital exports and US capital imports in the years in question. When we examine these proportions, we see that, apart from the year 1870, the share of UK investment attracted to the US remained very steady around the 20 per cent level throughout the period, while the British share of American capital imports fell very slightly from around 75 per cent in 1854 to 72 per cent in 1899 and then dropped markedly due to very substantial Continental European investment in the years following the turn of the century.

The only substantial variation from the trend of values of the UK capital export figures is for the year 1870. We look at this variation a little more closely in the light of the data available on British overseas investment in the surrounding period. The 1860s and early 1870s were a period of substantial capital movements from the UK to all parts of the world, but the US, particularly after 1865, was the chief attraction. There were three reasons for this: first the resurgence of American railroad growth (between 1869 and 1874 two-fifths of all securities issued by UK private companies operating abroad were in respect of US railroads [Jenks 1944, 1951, Adler 1958]); second, the considerable outflow of UK capital for mining ventures in the Rocky Mountains, some 67 UK companies being registered between 1870 and 1873 to engage in mining activities in Colorado, Nevada and Utah (Spence 1958); third, and perhaps the most important,

TABLE 2

Selective Estimates of UK Capital in the United States
$m.

Date	*UK Capital in US*		*Total UK Capital Abroad*	*Percentage of* 1 *to* 2	*Total Foreign Investment in US*	*Percentage of* 1 *to* 5
			Imlah (*adjusted*)		*North/Simon/US Bureau* (*adjusted*)	
1838	174	(Jenks)	846	21	261	67
1851	225	(B. Thomas)	1,177	20	241	94
1854	275	(Jenks)	1,323	21	360	76
1870	1,000	(Cairncross)	3,739	27	1,329	75
1885	1,500	(Cairncross)	8,084	19	2,001	75
1899	2,500	(Bacon)	12,739	20	3,484	72
1908	3,500	(Paish)	16,658	21	6,500	54
1913	3,885	(Paish)	21,543	18	7,200	54

Source: A. K. Cairncross, *Home and Foreign Investment* 1870/1910, Cambridge, 1953; L. H. Jenks, *The Migration of British Capital to* 1875, London and New York, 1938; G. Paish, 'Great Britain's capital investment in individual colonial and foreign countries,' *Journal of the Royal Statistical Society*, Vol. LXXIV, 1911; Brinley Thomas, *Migration and Economic Growth*, Cambridge, 1954.

the bargain prices at which UK investors were able to obtain American Government bonds in the years immediately following the Civil War. In this latter connection, it has been estimated that $700 million of such bonds were held in Europe by 1868, for which the American sellers had not received more than 57½ per cent – the low price being due mostly to the depreciation of the dollar after the war (McGrane 1935). British investors held the bulk of these bonds, which they purchased direct either from the US or from Germany at the time of the Franco-Prussian war. Some of the Southern States also borrowed from the UK for purposes of reconstruction. The broad quantitative implications of these events is suggested by the global structure of US and UK capital trends. In the period 1861/74, total foreign investment in the US amounted to $1,454 million, 43·7 per cent of total UK capital exports. Whereas in 1861, the accumulated foreign indebtedness of the US was only 21·1 per cent of the accumulated capital stake abroad of the UK, by 1874 the proportion had risen to 35·9 per cent. With these facts in mind, it does not seem unreasonable to suppose that the American share of UK capital exports gradually rose from its 20 per cent trend line in 1861 to 30 per cent in 1871/74, the peak years of US capital imports.

In the years that followed, a reverse movement took place. There were few new American investments in the rest of the decade after 1874 – indeed the Simon series suggests there was a net disinvestment up to 1882 – although Britain continued to add to her Indian and Australian holdings. When the export of capital was resumed on a large scale in the 1880s, it was Canada and Australia that first proved the main attractions and then the Argentine. Cairncross estimated that in 1885, 'fully half' the UK foreign investments were within the Empire compared with only one-third fifteen years earlier (Cairncross 1953). In the eleven preceding years, while the foreign indebtedness of the US had remained almost unchanged, foreign investment in Canada and Australia rose by $873·1 million (North 1962). Once again, these trends are reflected in both the Imlah and Simon series, with the proportion of US capital imports to UK capital exports falling quite steeply in the late 1870s, after which it remained steady until the mid 1880s. For the purposes of our exercise, then we assume a decline in the US share of UK capital exports, from 30 per cent in 1874 to 20 per cent in 1882, the decline being most marked in the late 1870s.

The years from 1885 to 1890 were boom years in the export of capital from the UK, with particularly substantial investments being made in South America and South Africa. A collapse in overseas lending came in 1890/91 with an outbreak of a revolt in Buenos Aires which had widespread repercussions. This was followed by a slump in South African mining shares and economic paralysis in Australia (Hobson 1914). In the US, while business was adversely affected by the McKinley tariff and a currency crisis, there were compensatory factors sufficient to boost slightly the *share* of British capital invested in the US. These included a boom in real estate companies and mining activities – both of which attracted much UK capital (Clements 1960) – and a flurry of UK investment in all forms of US manufacturing industry, particularly between 1888 and 1891 (Clements 1953, 1955; Coram 1967). Though such investment dwindled in the latter part of the decade, its place was taken by a renewal of interest in railroad expansion. To allow for this short-term increase in the share of UK capital exported to the US, we assume that from 1887 to 1891 the proportion rises from 20 to 25 per cent in yearly increments of 1 per cent and then between 1893/98 drops back, again by equal instalments, to 20 per cent. In the fourteen years of the twentieth century, UK overseas investment rose again very steeply, particularly between 1905 and 1913. The US appears to have shared in this expansion rather less than other areas (with South America and Canada gaining the most), and, for this reason, we assume a steadily falling proportion of aggregate investment from 20 per cent in 1898 to 17 per cent in 1931.[1]

Concerning the share of foreign investments in the US, the data are almost non-existent, and any assessment – at least as regards the *trend* of the share up to 1899 – can be little more than an intelligent guess. The evidence, such as it is, suggests that in 1860 at least 90 per cent of all foreign investment in the US was British (North 1960) and that the derived proportion of 75 per cent for 1854 from the Jenks/Imlah data is almost certainly an underestimate. That there were some fairly substantial investments by Continental European capitalists in the 1860s (particularly German and Dutch) there is no doubt; equally it is quite certain that a fairly high proportion of these were repatriated in the following decade at the time of the Franco-Prussian War (Lewis 1938). Both the Germans and the French subsequently assumed important roles as international lenders, but only the former ever invested large sums in the United States; by 1898, according to a German source, some $2,035 million

[1] Once again it is most unlikely that the trend of the share was as smooth as is suggested here; between 1898 and 1912, for example, there was some quite substantial disinvestment of British funds in US in spite of continuous upward movement in exports of British capital as a whole.

marks of a total foreign capital stake of between $7,035 and $7,735 million, had been invested in North America (Satorius, n.d.). Non-European investment was negligible right up to the First World War. With these facts in mind, we consider the derived share of UK capital in the US of 75 per cent for 1870 and 1885 is probably on the low side; it is, indeed, doubtful that, except for short periods, the proportion of UK capital in the US ever fell below 80 per cent until after 1880. The assumptions we think more realistic about the UK share of the foreign indebtedness of the US (using the [amended] Simon/US Bureau figures) are as follows. For the period 1861/80, a falling share of ½ per cent per annum from 90 per cent in 1861 to 80 per cent in 1880; a constant share of 80 per cent between 1881 and 1884, and then a falling share of ½ per cent per annum for the period 1885 to 1898 and 1 per cent in 1899 to bring the UK share in 1899 to 72 per cent – in line with the estimate contained in Table 2. For the remainder of the period, we assume a decline in the UK share of 1 per cent per annum, as this was a time in which there were substantial Continental European investment in the US. We are only too aware of the crudity of this procedure, and, particularly, that the UK share in the 60's might be exaggerated as a consequence.

Our estimates of the growth of the UK capital stock in the US derived from the calculations in Table 2, and based on (*a*) the Imlah and (*b*) the Simon/US Bureau time series[1] are presented in Table 3 and Diagrams 2 and 3. It can be seen from these figures, and a comparison between them in Column 3, that, apart from the periods 1866 to 1872, 1886 to 1888 and 1895 to 1899, the correspondence between them is sufficiently close (the average differences is less than ±5 per cent) to allow a reasonable series of UK capital stock (and changes in stock) in the US to be computed. Bearing in mind differences in definition and methods of calculation of the initial Imlah/Simon series, the final resemblance is very close. The (linear) coefficient of correlation between the two series now works out at 0·997, that of the fluctuations at 0·556, that of the first differences of the series (i.e. investment flows) at 0·785 and that of the trend itself 0·999. We therefore propose to assume the mid-point of these series as correct and take these as final estimates of the UK capital stock in the US.

Finally, how do figures of our constructed series compare with the various direct estimates made of the Anglo-American component

[1] The Simon data figures had to be adjusted from mid-year to end-year for comparability with the data derived from Imlah.

TABLE 3

Growth of UK Investment in US 1861–1913

Year	UK Capital Stock in the US (*a*) Estimate Derived from Simon's Series $m.	(*b*) Estimate Derived from Imlah's Series $m.	(*c*) $b \div a \times 100$ Per Cent	(*d*) Final Series $\frac{a+b}{2}$ $m.	Annual UK investment in the US $m.
1861	447·3	425·6	94·9	436	
2	450·1	459·9	102·2	455	19
3	514·1	513·3	99·8	514	59
4	594·5	564·9	95·0	580	66
5	666·4	634·6	95·2	651	71
6	772·8	705·8	91·3	739	88
7	868·1	793·3	91·4	831	92
8	972·8	876·7	90·1	925	94
9	1,088·5	980·0	90·0	1,035	110
1870	1,172·0	1,083·1	92·4	1,128	93
1	1,318·2	1,236·0	93·8	1,277	149
2	1,499·3	1,395·6	93·1	1,447	170
3	1,607·4	1,527·3	95·0	1,567	120
4	1,671·9	1,642·2	98·2	1,657	90
5	1,700·6	1,667·8	96·4	1,684	27
6	1,666·4	1,645·3	98·7	1,656	−28
7	1,562·1	1,605·7	102·8	1,584	−72
8	1,414·8	1,508·3	106·6	1,462	−122
9	1,350·2	1,431·5	106·0	1,391	−71
1880	1,340·6	1,412·8	105·4	1,377	−14
1	1,372·8	1,423·0	103·7	1,398	21
2	1,448·6	1,418·8	97·9	1,434	36
3	1,523·5	1,471·4	96·6	1,497	63
4	1,586·2	1,549·6	97·7	1,568	71
5	1,657·3	1,616·8	97·6	1,637	69
6	1,812·9	1,702·0	93·9	1,757	120
7	2,032·2	1,886·6	92·8	1,959	202
8	2,238·8	2,085·6	93·2	2,162	203
9	2,405·4	2,280·9	94·8	2,343	181
1890	2,550·3	2,507·8	98·3	2,529	186
1	2,638·8	2,706·0	102·6	2,672	143
2	2,731·1	2,785·8	102·0	2,758	86
3	2,778·8	2,857·3	102·8	2,818	60
4	2,823·9	2,793·4	98·9	2,809	−9
5	2,915·7	2,726·2	93·5	2,821	12
6	2,938·1	2,675·2	91·1	2,807	−14

TABLE 3—*continued*

7	2,801·4	2,600·6	92·8	2,701	−106
8	2,750·6	2,501·8	91·0	2,626	−75
9	2,664·9	2,522·1	94·6	2,593	−33
1900	2,582·1	2,536·8	98·2	2,559	−34
1	2,529·7	2,546·6	100·7	2,538	−21
2	2,554·9	2,554·9	100·0	2,555	17
3	2,620·9	2,574·1	98·2	2,598	43
4	2,663·1	2,599·7	97·6	2,631	33
5	2,728·6	2,653·8	97·3	2,691	60
6	2,841·0	2,742·0	96·5	2,793	102
7	2,913·9	2,863·4	98·3	2,889	96
8	2,975·4	2,982·4	100·2	2,979	90
9	3,148·2	3,079·6	97·8	3,114	135
1910	3,310·7	3,204·1	96·8	3,257	143
1	3,396·5	3,352·6	98·7	3,375	118
2	3,489·1	3,497·1	100·2	3,493	118
3	3,637·8	3,662·3	100·7	3,650	157

of British capital exports and American capital imports? As regards the *stock* of capital, the data presented in Table 2 show that, apart from the year 1908, and allowing for the degree of error inherent in any balance-of-payments estimates and the incompleteness of most direct estimates, the similarities between the sets of figures are very close. For a detailed explanation of the divergences the reader is invited to consult the Imlah/Simon articles. Diagram 4 compares our estimates of the *flow* of capital with the only other sources known to us – viz. J. J. Madden's estimates of the total UK capital exports to the US between (nominal) value of UK holdings of US securities 1860/80 (Madden 1963) and Matthew Simon's estimates of new British portfolio investment in *North America* 1865/1914 (Simon 1967). Thus regard these figures as a reasonable approximation both of the *stock* and *flow* of UK capital in the US and use these as a basis for further analysis.

III

The question next arises: What are the main causes behind these movements of UK capital to the US? The problem can be tackled from two angles – the quantitative and the qualitative; we shall attempt both. First we examine some of the economic variables which it is reasonable to suppose might be associated with trans-Atlantic

DIAGRAM 2
Accumulated UK Capital Stake in US.

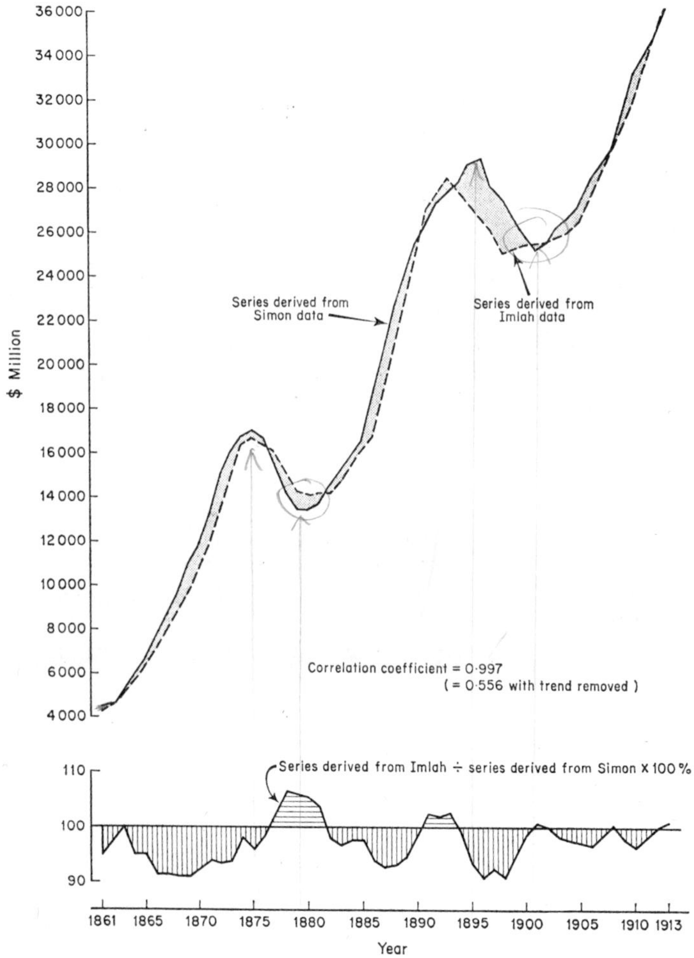

Source: Table 3.

DIAGRAM 3

UK Investment in US (Flow).

Correlation coefficient = 0·785

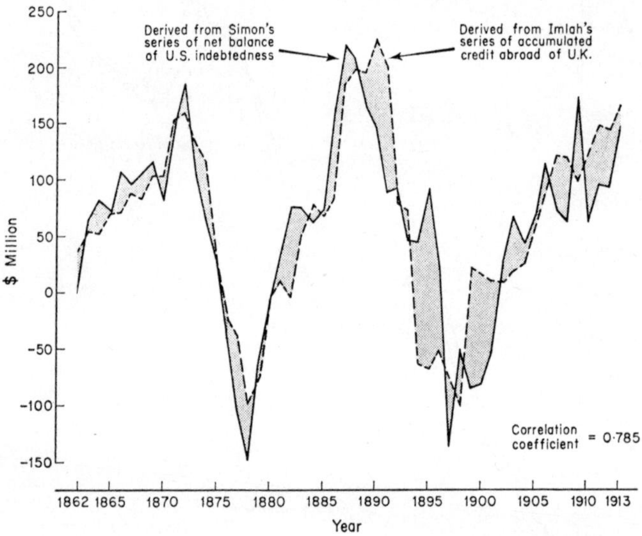

Source: Table 3.

DIAGRAM 4

Comparison of our final estimate of UK Investment in US with related series.

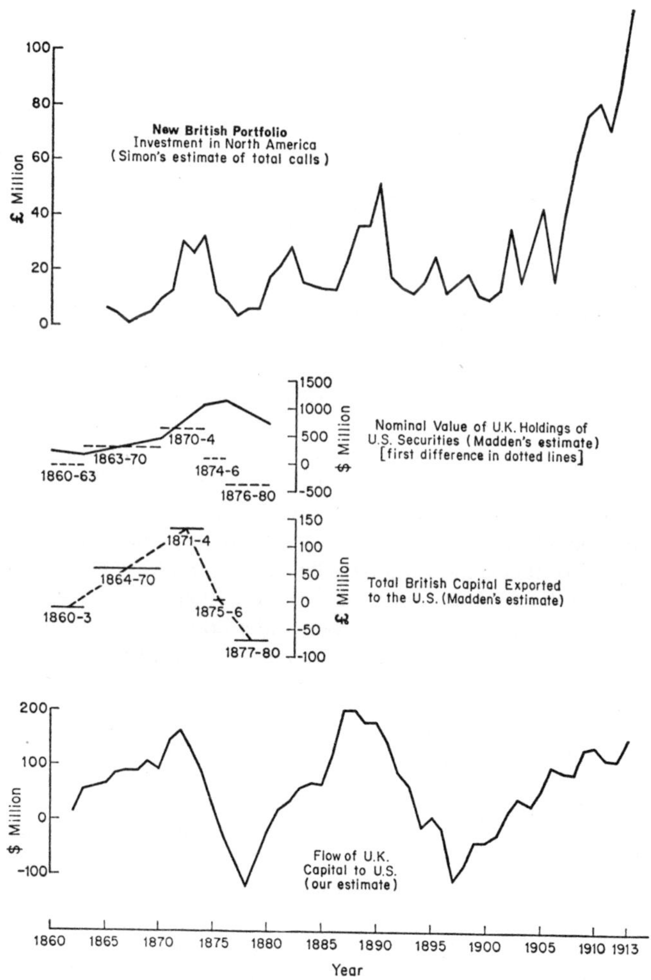

Source: Simon (1967), Madden (1957).

capital movements; second we test the association with simple regression and correlation analysis; third, where the association is statistically significant, we seek to establish whether there is any causal relationship between the variables in question.

In his book *Migration and Economic Growth: A Study of Great Britain and the Atlantic Economy*,[1] Professor Brinley Thomas sought to relate trans-Atlantic movements of labour and capital in the second half of the nineteenth century to economic conditions, or changes in conditions, in the investing and recipient countries. Other writers have since taken up this theme and have analysed the swings in economic fortune of the UK and US in more detail, stressing particularly the relationship between home and foreign investment of the UK, exports, rates of return on capital, terms of trade and international migration (Williamson 1964, Matthews 1959, Simon 1967, Brinley Thomas 1967). We propose to adopt a similar approach here, using the data derived in Section II.

First, we postulate a particular *supply* relationship in which UK investment in the US is one of the independent variables. The hypothesis here is that the pace of US economic growth is a function of the trans-Atlantic movement of productive factors. We take as our two independent variables (i) UK investment in the US, and (ii) European migration to the US – each for the period 1860/1913. The difficulty arises when we try and define US growth. There is no direct measure available; continuous series of the US national product, or index of industrial production, do not date back far enough. We have various proxy variables to draw upon but all have their limitations. We examine four of these – viz. (i) railway miles added (the railway was a prime factor in US economic development right up to the turn of the century); (ii) bituminous coal production; (iii) index of manufacturing production; and (iv) index of new building. The data for these variables are given in Table 2 in the Appendix, but the relevant time series are graphically portrayed in Diagram 5. Using linear equations, various sets of simple and multiple correlation coefficients we derived from the data, and the results are given below in Table 4.

It can be seen that only when new building is used as the dependent variable is there a reasonable correlation between UK investment and immigration and US economic growth.

This, perhaps, is not surprising for two reasons; first, no time lag is assumed to exist between investment and growth; second, through-

[1] Cambridge, 1954.

DIAGRAM 5

Relationship between US growth and the trans-Atlantic movement of labour and capital.

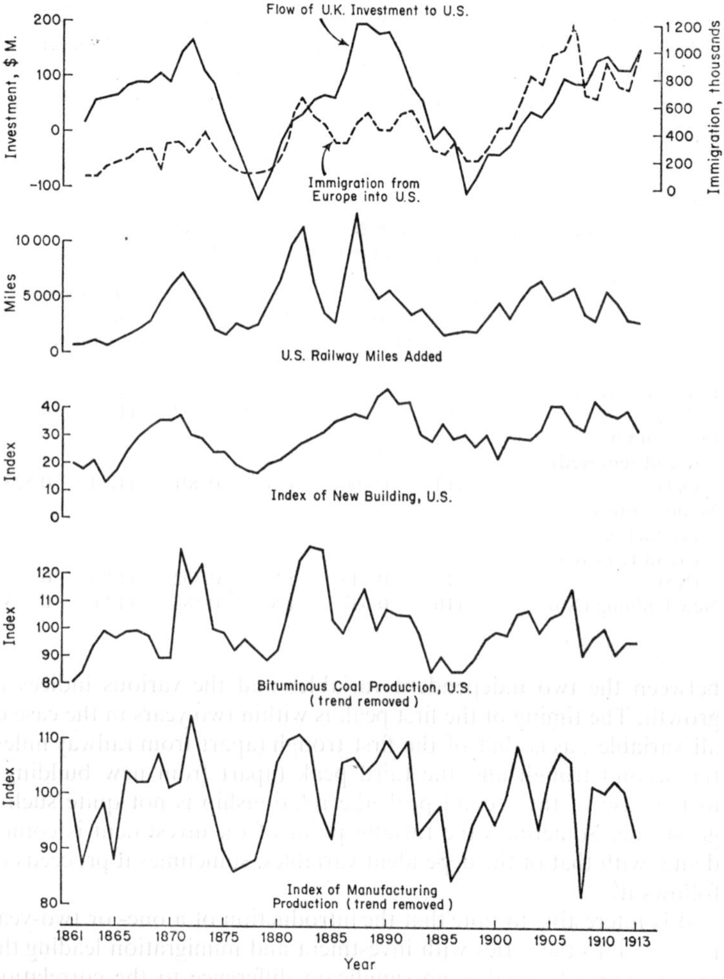

Sources: Miles of Railroad Track added – Original data from Simon Kuznets, *Secular movements in Production and Prices*, pp. 526–27.

Bituminous Coal output – Original data from US Bureau of the Census: *Historical Statistics of the United States* as listed in Brinley Thomas, *Migration*, Appendix 4, Table 97, with trend removed index.

Manufacturing Production – Edwin Frickey, *Production in the United States* 1860–1914, Tables 6 and 7, pp. 54, 60.

Building – Original data taken from J. R. Riggleman, *Building Cycles in the United States* 1830–1935 (unpublished Ph.D. dissertation, the Johns Hopkins University) as listed in Brinley Thomas, *Migration*, Appendix 4, Table 108.

Immigration – *Annual Report of Commissioner General of Immigration* (*U.S.*) 1926. Listed in *Historical Statistics of the United States*, US Bureau of the Census.

See also Appendix, Table 2.

out this particular period, the share of UK investment to gross domestic investment in the US was never more than 10 per cent.[1]

Between 1860 and 1913, there were two distinct peaks of UK investment in the US, in 1872 and 1887, and one less obvious 'twin' type peak in the 1906/10 period; and there were two clear troughs in 1878 and 1897. Table 5 below, shows that there is quite a close relationship

TABLE 4

Correlation Coefficients (r) between Trans-Atlantic Factor Movements and US Growth 1860/1913

	UK Investment (X1)		*European Immigration (X2)*		*Investment and Immigration (X1 and X2)*	
Railway miles added (X3)	r13	0·369	r23	0·432	r12.3	0·479
Coal output (trend removed) (X4)	r14	0·466	r24	0·401	r12.4	0·523
Manufacturing production (trend removed) (X5)	r15	0·543	r25	0·302	r12.5	0·577
New building (X6)	r16	0·637	r26	0·583	r12.6	0·723

between the two independent variables and the various indices of growth. The timing of the first peak is within two years in the case of all variables, as is that of the first trough (apart from railway miles) the second trough and the third peak (apart from new building); in the case of the second peak the relationship is not quite such a good one. Sometimes the turning point of UK investment is coincidental with that of the dependent variables, sometimes it proceeds or follows it.

It is interesting to note that the introduction of a one- or two-year time lag into the series with investment and immigration leading the growth variables makes no significant difference to the correlation coefficients.

Again, this is not entirely unexpected – at least in respect of the railway mileage and new building indices of growth – as these two variables are essentially components of investment likely to be influenced by (or to influence) the same variables as non-resident

[1] For further details see Table 2 in the Appendix.

investment. With manufacturing production, the position is different in as much as this is partly influenced by past investment; but, here too, no clear picture emerges. In all cases, however, the fit of the

TABLE 5

Peaks and Troughs of Selected Variables in the US Economy 1860/1913

	Peak	*Trough*	*Peak*	*Trough*	*Peak*
X1. US investment	1872	1878	1887	1897	1906 and 1910
X2. European immigration	1873	1878	1882	1898	1907 and 1911
X3. Railway miles	1871	1875	1887	1898	1907 and 1910
X4. Coal production (trend removed)	1871	1879	1883	1897	1907 and 1910
X5. Manufacturing output (trend removed)	1872	1876	1889	1896	1906 and 1911
X6. New building	1871	1878	1890	1900	1906 and 1909

Source: Table 2 in the Appendix.

relationships is improved by applying a five-year moving average to the data, and the new coefficients of correlation in Table 6. Even so there is still no evidence that foreign investment leads US growth, although it is clearly associated with it.

TABLE 6

Correlation Coefficients (r) between Trans-Atlantic Factor Movements and US Growth 1860/1913

(5 year moving average)

	UK Investment X1		*European Immigration X2*		*Investment and Immigration X1 and X2*	
Railway miles added (X3)	r13	0·371	r23	0·451	r12.3	0·507
Coal output (trend removed) (X4)	r14	0·550	r24	0·424	r12.4	0·558
Manufacturing production (trend removed) (X5)	r15	0·605	r25	0·441	r12.5	0·621
New building (X6)	r16	0·683	r26	0·658	r12.6	0·820

Second, we treat UK investment in the US as the dependent variable and seek to quantify some of its main determinants. We proceed on the assumption that such determinants contain both a 'pull' and a 'push' element, which reflect the economic conditions in both the investing and host countries. We postulate two types of equation based respectively on the two most commonly suggested motives for investment – (*a*) profitability, and (*b*) growth. We examine, first, the proposition that (i) the absolute amount of UK investment in the US (I_{US}), and (ii) the *share* of UK investment in the US relative to that in the UK (I_{US}/I_{UK}) is functionally related to the relative profitability of US and UK investment (R_{US}/R_{UK}).

We obtained the data in respect of I_{US} directly from the series earlier computed. For UK we took the net capital formation figures provided by C. R. Feinstein in his article 'Income and investment in the United Kingdom 1856/1914' (Feinstein 1961). Since no comparable information was available on the rates of return on capital in the US and the UK, we took as our surrogate for R_{US} an index of common stock prices in the US and that for R_{UK} an index of share prices in the UK as derived from P. Rousseaux and K. C. Smith and G. F. Horne cited by Brinley Thomas.[1] The relationship between these series is depicted in Diagram 6. The correlation coefficient between I_{US} and R_{US}/R_{UK} works out at 0·596 and that between I_{US}/I_{UK} and R_{US}/R_{UK} 0·425. The corresponding regression equations are:

$$(1871/1913) I_{US} = -2{\cdot}744 + 3{\cdot}253 R_{US}/R_{UK}$$
$$(0{\cdot}7077)$$

and

$$(1871/1913) I_{US/UK} = -2{\cdot}346 + 2{\cdot}953 R_{US}/R_{UK}$$
$$(0{\cdot}9813)$$

Table 7 shows that introducing a time-lag of one year for the investment data improves the fit of two series quite considerably with the correlation coefficients rising to 0·635 and 0·589. The new regression equations are:

$$(1871/1913) I_{US}{}^{t} = -3{\cdot}355 + 3{\cdot}794 R_{US}{}^{t-1}/R_{UK}{}^{t-1}$$
$$(0{\cdot}6298)$$

$$(1871/1913) I_{US/UK}{}^{t} = -3{\cdot}593 + 4{\cdot}064 R_{US}{}^{t-1}/R_{UK}{}^{t-1}$$
$$(0{\cdot}8692)$$

[1] See P. Rousseaux, *Les mouvements de fond de l'economices Anglaise* 1800/1913, Louvain, 1938, p. 272: K. C. Smith and G. F. Horne, 'An index number of securities 1867/1914,' *London and Cambridge Economic Service Special Memorandum* No. 37, June 1934; B. Thomas (1954), *op cit.*, Appendix 4, Table 99, p. 289.

We finally tested the relationship between the two series after applying a five-year moving average to the data. The best fit was again obtained by using a time-lag of one year and I_{US} (rather than

TABLE 7

Correlation Coefficients between UK Investment and US and Relative Share Prices

	Investment Indices	
Share Prices	$I_{US}(X1)$	$I_{US}/I_{UK}(X2)$
(*a*) R_{US}/R_{UK}	0·596	0·425
(*b*) $R_{US}{}^{t-1}/R_{UK}{}^{t-1}$	0·685	0·589

I_{US}/I_{UK}) as the dependent variable.[1] The correlation coefficient is 0·713 and the regression equation:

$$(1871/1913) I_{US}{}^{t*} = -2{\cdot}642 + 3{\cdot}416(R_{US}{}^{t-1}/R_{UK}{}^{t-1*})$$
$$(0{\cdot}6083)$$

where

$$* = \text{5-year moving average}$$

The second set of relationships postulates that UK investment in the US or the share of UK investment in the US relative to that in the UK is a function of the absolute or relative rate of growth in the US ($\dot{O}_{US}$ or $\dot{O}_{US}/\dot{O}_{UK}$.) Again, since we do not have any direct measure of this variable for the US, we are forced to choose between a number of alternatives. These are listed in Table 9 where it is seen that a non-lagged investment/growth relationship shows up best when the relative share of new building in the US (X8) is associated with UK investment in the US (X1).

Normally, of course, one would expect investment to lag growth by one or more years. But a quick look at Diagram 6 reveals that, if anything, US/UK building (X8) lags rather than leads investment (X1) although the best fit is obtained without lags or leads. This, as suggested earlier, is probably a reflection of the interdependence

[1] Williamson used a two-year time-lag for UK share prices and a three-year time-lag for American railroad stock prices and obtained the following relationship, which is much superior to ours.

$$1873/1911 \quad K^t = 112{\cdot}42 + 420{\cdot}71\beta_{US}{}^{t-3} - 552{\cdot}39\rho_{GB}{}^{t-2}$$
$$(64{\cdot}41) \qquad (72{\cdot}52)$$

where $K^t = K^2\, 0{\cdot}083$, the level of net capital inflows from all countries.

DIAGRAM 6

Relationship between UK Investment in US and relative growth and profitability in the UK and US.

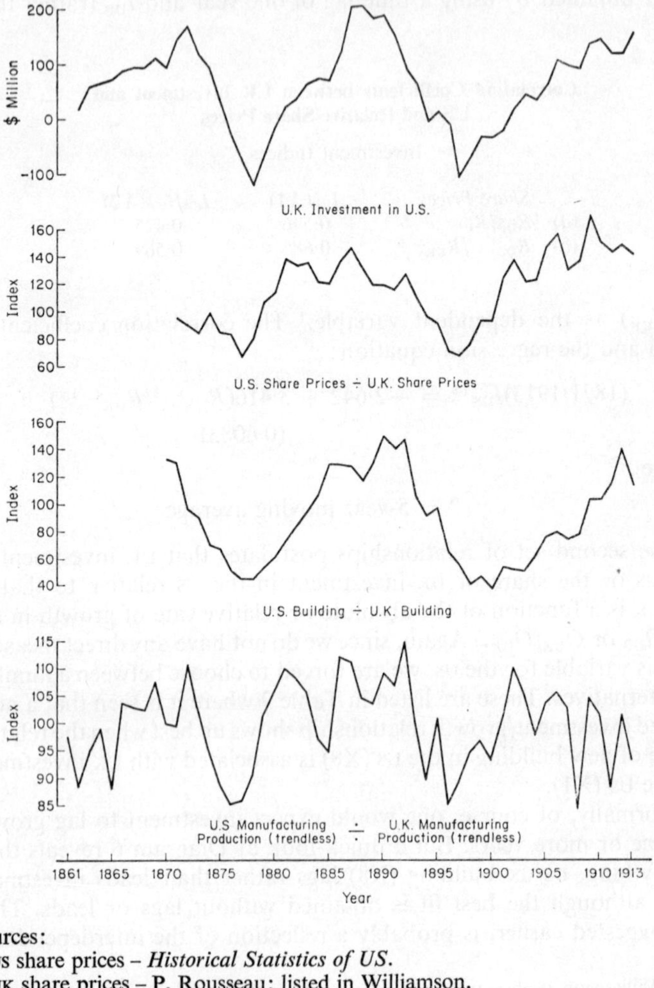

Sources:

US share prices – *Historical Statistics of US.*
UK share prices – P. Rousseau; listed in Williamson.
US building – J. R. Riggleman; listed in Williamson.
UK building – Mitchell and Deane.
US manufacturing production – E. Frickey; listed in Williamson.
UK manufacturing production – Mitchell and Deane.

See also Appendix, Table 3.

of the two variables. By contrast, manufacturing production (X9) appears to lead investment; when $X9^{t-1}$ and $X1^{t}$ are related to each other, the correlation coefficient is 0·627. Manufacturing production is, of course, the most volatile of the series under discussion: the best fit of all between X9 and X1 is obtained by smoothing out the

TABLE 8

Correlation Coefficients between UK Investment in US and Various Growth Indices

(Investment Indices)

Growth Indices	$I_{US}(X1)$	$I_{US}/I_{UK}(X2)$
(1) $\dot{O}_{US}$		
(*a*) Railway miles (X4)	0·369	0·047
(*b*) Coal output (trend removed) (X5)	0·466	0·433
(*c*) New building (X6)	0·637	0·315
(*d*) Manufacturing production (trend removed) (X7)	0·543	0·460
(2) $\dot{O}_{US}/\dot{O}_{UK}$		
(*a*) New building (X8)	0·804	0·658
(*b*) Manufacturing production US/UK (trend removed) (X9)	0·513	0·392

X9 series by five years moving averages and then relating $X9^{t-1}$ to $X1^{t}$, r then becomes 0·676.

In summary then, the two growth variables which are associated the closest with UK investment in the US in the period 1860/1913 (X1) are (i) building with no time lead or lag ($X8^{t}$), and (ii) a five-year moving average of manufacturing output (with trend removed) with a time lead of $X9^{t-1*}$.

The appropriate regression equations are:

$$(1871/1913) I_{US}{}^{t} = -2{\cdot}100 + 3{\cdot}583 \dot{O}_{US}{}^{t}/\dot{O}_{UK}{}^{t}$$
$$(0{\cdot}4130)$$

and

$$(1871/1913) I_{US}{}^{t} = -18{\cdot}66 + 19{\cdot}66^{t-1*} \dot{O}_{US}{}^{t-1*}/\dot{O}_{UK}{}^{t-1*}$$
$$(3{\cdot}350)$$

We finally attempted a series of multi-correlations using the profit and growth variables that gave the best results.

TABLE 9

Correlation Coefficients between UK Investment in US and Combined Profit and Growth Indices 1871/1913

(Investment Indices)

Profit and Growth Indices	$I_{US}^t/(X1^t)$	$I_{US}^t/I_{UK}^t(X2^t)$
(1) Share prices US/UK leading by one year $(R_{US}^{t-1}/R_{UK}^{t-1})(X3^{t-1})$ and New building US/UK $(\dot{O}_{US}^t/\dot{O}_{UK}^t)(X8^t)$	0·837	0·636
(2) Share prices US/UK leading by one year $(R_{US}^{t-1}/R_{UK}^{t-1})(X3^{t-1})$ and Manufacturing output (trend removed – 5-year moving average) $(\dot{O}_{US}^{t-1*}/\dot{O}_{UK}^{t-1*})(X9^{t-1})$	0·762	0·630

The appropriate regression equations are as follows:

$$(1871/1917)I_{US}^t = -3{\cdot}334 + \underset{(0{\cdot}6672)}{1{\cdot}660}R_{US}^{t-1}/R_{UK}^{t-1} + \underset{(0{\cdot}5472)}{2{\cdot}674}\dot{O}_{US}^t/\dot{O}_{UK}$$

$$(1871/1913)I_{US}^t = -13{\cdot}84 + \underset{(0{\cdot}7038)}{2{\cdot}430}R_{US}^{t-1}/R_{UK}^{t-1} + \underset{(3{\cdot}699)}{12{\cdot}08}\dot{O}_{US}^{t-1*}/\dot{O}_{UK}^{t-1*}$$

The conclusion of these exercises is that UK investment in the US over the half century before the First World War was most closely associated with *relative* US/UK movements in three main variables, viz. (1) share prices, (2) new building activity, and (3) manufacturing output. The evidence suggests that while movements in (1) and (3) tended to influence rather than be influenced by UK investment, movements in (2) were so closely interdependent with UK investment that each was probably the result of some more fundamental influence at work – although there is a hint that the cutback in the inflow of UK capital in late 1880s and its recovery a decade later preceded movements in this particular investment series by a year or more.

It is, perhaps, disappointing that we have not been able to offer a better explanation of the export of UK capital to the US in the period under review. The correlation coefficients derived are not very impressive, particularly when one allows for the usual problems associated with using time-series data. Other writers, notably Williamson (1964), have had more success in relating net capital (K^t) inflows from all countries to net capital expenditures on US railroads ($I_{US}{}^t$) and UK home investment ($I_{GB}{}^t$). For the period 1871/1914 the correlation coefficient of the relationship worked out at 0·654 and for the period 1891/1914 at 0·891.[1]

IV

Having looked into some of the relationships between movements in UK investment in the US and other variables, we turn briefly to summarize the significance of such movements to US and UK economic development.

The United States

Table 10 expresses the accumulated UK capital stake in the US to gross national product and *per capita* of population, averaged over 5-year intervals for the period 1869/1914, and the actual investment in the same years as a proportion to domestic gross and net capital formation. It can be seen that, in terms of these magnitudes, the role of UK investment has tended to be decreasingly significant, but at a fluctuating rate. In particular, we see UK capital inflows being associated with a surge of US development in two main periods, viz. 1869/76 and 1882/91. Both periods were those of investment boom which was financed in no mean extent from the UK. The other surge in development occurred at the end of the century and in the period 1906 to 1914. Here, although there were substantial imports of foreign (particularly UK) capital, the boom was largely internally financed. It should be stressed that the figures quoted in Table 12 relate to gross capital flows from the UK. Simon Kuznets has shown that when US capital exports are taken into account the US became

The relevant regression equations were as follows:

$$1871\text{–}1914\,K^t = 914{\cdot}45 - 0{\cdot}6303 I_{US}{}^t - 8{\cdot}8473 I_{GB}{}^t$$
$$(0{\cdot}2000) \qquad (0{\cdot}1556)$$

and

$$1891\text{–}1914\,K^t = 699{\cdot}2 + 0{\cdot}4047 I_{US}{}^t - 6{\cdot}6934 I_{GB}{}^t$$
$$(0{\cdot}1628) \qquad (1{\cdot}3884)$$

J. G. Williamson, *American Growth and the Balance of Payments* 1820/1913, 1964.

TABLE 10

UK Participation in the US Economy, 1869–1911
(All figures are averages for the periods)

Year	GNP US at Current Prices	UK Investment in US		UK Capital Stock in US as a Proportion of		UK New Investment in US as a Proportion of US Domestic Investment	
		Capital Stock	New Investment	GNP	Population	Gross	Net
	$ billion	$m.	$m.	Percent	Ratio	Percent	Percent
1869–73	6·71	1,291	128·4	0·19	3·17	9·6	15·7
1872–76	7·53	1,602	75·8	0·21	3·63	5·8	7·8
1877–81	9·18	1,442	−51·6	0·16	2·94	−2·8	−4·4
1882–86	11·30	1,579	71·8	0·16	2·86	3·2	6·8
1887–91	12·30	2,333	183·0	0·19	3·78	6·8	12·7
1892–96	13·60	2,803	27·0	0·21	4·01	0·9	1·6
1897–01	17·30	2,604	−53·8	0·15	3·47	−1·4	−2·5
1902–06	24·20	2,654	50·1	0·11	3·23	0·9	1·7
1907–11	31·60	3,123	116·4	0·10	3·42	1·8	3·7

Source: GNP and Capital Formation US: S. Kuznets, *Capital in the American Economy: Its Formation and Financing*, 1961, and J. Kendrick, *Productivity Growth in the United States*, NBER, 1960. Population: US Bureau of Census Historical Statistics of US.

a net exporter of capital in the 1890s (Kuznets 1961). Between 1869 and 1878, net foreign investment in the US accounted for 10·7 per cent of domestic net capital formation, 6·2 per cent of domestic gross capital formation and 1·3 per cent of gross national product. The percentages for the following decade were 3·0 per cent, 1·8 per cent and 0·4 per cent. In the ten years 1889/98, however, there was a net capital outflow of 1·1 per cent, 0·6 per cent and 0·1 per cent of the above variables and for the following decade 8·8 per cent, 4·7 per cent and 1·0 per cent. These figures, of course, make no allowance for the cost of servicing foreign investment. J. Knapp (1957) has argued that although the net stock of US foreign indebtedness rose from $200m. in 1843 to $3·700m. in 1914, the net payments of interest and dividends amounted to $5·800m. in the same period. There was thus no real transfer of goods into the US, taking one year with another. W. A. Lewis and P. J. O'Leary (1955) state the view even more strongly that British investments were unimportant in that they averaged between 1874 and 1895 less than 1 per cent of US gross national product.

While each of these latter approaches contains an element of truth, they are misleading in that they understate the catalytic affect of investment at the right time. For so often it is the impact of foreign investment on the key industry or sector in which it is concentrated which sets the pace for economic growth; in any case, and this applies particularly where direct investments are concerned, it is impossible to isolate the effects of an inflow of capital from the knowledge and expertise which accompany it.

Looking at the broad association of UK investment with US economic development, we see four distinct phases of capital inflow. The first is from 1863 or thereabouts to 1872. This was a period of rapid internal growth and considerable foreign investment mainly in Federal and State Bonds and the railroads. Throughout these years, the US had an unfavourable balance of payments. The expansion came to a head in 1872, and the years which followed up to 1879 reflected the second phase where investment was falling as several states and railway companies defaulted and capital returned to Europe (or was diverted to Australia and India). The US had a favourable balance of payments for this period. In 1879, capital imports were resumed and during the 1880s it is reckoned that Europe contributed two-fifths of the total investment in American railroads; in all, over the period 1883/90, over $1 billion were invested by Europe in the US. A crisis developed in this latter year when the American market became loaded with railway securities; a depressed state of trade which lasted until 1897. During these years there was a net disinvestment of European money and a favourable balance of payments for the US. The fourth period starts in 1896 with money being invested in US railways and public utilities; it was a short-lived boom at first, but after a period of retrenchment in the early twentieth century, imports of capital were resumed in quantity around 1906 which lasted up to the First World War. Another 1 billion dollars of capital was poured in from Europe although, over the period as a whole, net disinvestment occurred owing to a substantial outflow of funds to Canada and Europe.

The United Kingdom

We first look at the importance of UK investment in the US as expressed as a proportion of net capital formation at home. On average, it appears that about 8 per cent of UK net domestic capital formation was directed to the US over the period 1861/1913 though the proportion fluctuated from −14 per cent in 1897 to +32 per cent in 1872. There would seem to be no evidence that exports of capital are associated with unemployment – indeed, if anything, the reverse is the case – although it is true that there is an inverse correlation between net fixed capital formation in the UK and UK investment in the US of −0·372 (see Diagram 7). It would seem reasonable to conclude that foreign investment stimulated rather than retarded domestic activity. The link is through the export industries, the correlation coefficient between the annual UK export of goods and capital to all countries in the period 1861/1914 being 0·726. The coefficient in respect of the export of goods and capital to the US is somewhat less, 0·510, but still quite significant. Diagram 8 illustrates these two relationships in more detail. The chain of causation between capital exports and their economic repercussions on the investing and recipient countries is not always easy to disentangle. Mostly, however, it would seem that the initial impetus originated from the US in the form of an increased demand for goods and services and/or capital resulting from a surge of internal expansion, which itself was triggered off by such factors as increased immigration, technological innovation, discovery of mineral wealth or territorial expansion. This caused a balance-of-payments deficit – either due to the increased imports of goods and services, or the transfer effect of an export of money capital paid for by the export of goods. In either event, the increased export of goods raised domestic income through export industries thereby compensating for the slack in expansion

DIAGRAM 7

Relationship between UK Investment in US and Growth of the UK Economy.

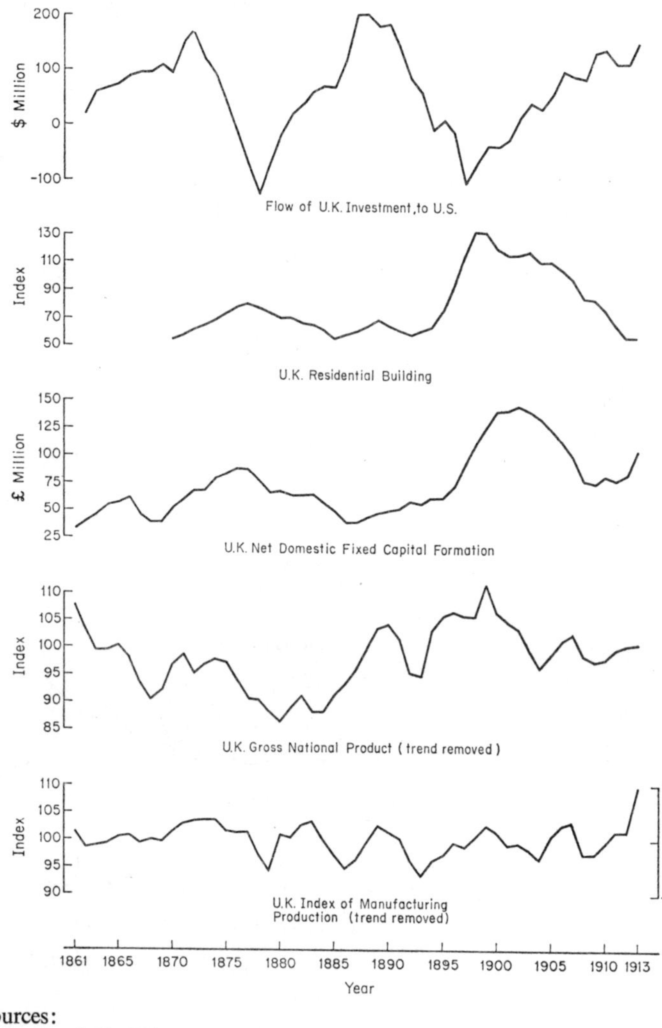

Sources:

Residential building – A. K. Cairncross, *Home and foreign investment* 1870–1913, p. 213.

Net fixed capital formation – C. H. Feinstein, 'Income and Investment in the United Kingdom, 1856–1914,' *Economic Journal*, June 1961.

Net National Income (trendless) – A. L. Bowley's cost-of-living index (*Wages and Income since* 1860, Cambridge, 1937, pp. 121–22).

Manufacturing production (trendless) – W. G. Hoffman, *British Industry* 1700–1950, Oxford, 1955.

See also Appendix, Table 4.

DIAGRAM 8

Relationship between UK export of goods and export of capital.

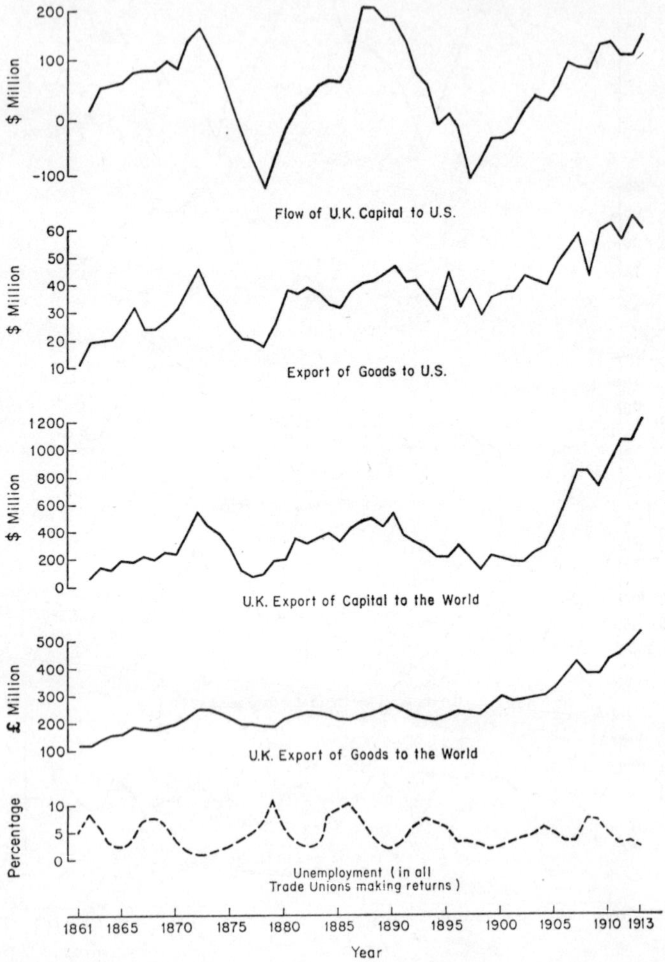

Sources:

Export of goods to the world – *Annual statement of trade.*

Export of capital to the world – A. H. Imlah, *Economic elements in the Pax Britannica.*

Export of goods to the US – *Historical statistics of the US*, by the US Bureau of the Census.

See also Appendix, Table 5.

Unemployment – Sessional Paper, 1905, LXXXIV, 1861–1903, then Abstract of Labour Statistics.

resulting from the diversion of investment out of the country. Subsequently, with a break in the growth of the US, UK investment at home rises with British real income rising faster as capital exports are reduced. For example, in the 1870s and 1890s, capital formation in UK was at its peak when capital exports were low. On the other hand, in the 1880s and 1890s, capital exports were high but activity at home was low.

This fluctuating ratio between home and foreign investment is a feature of the UK economy in years 1860/1914. Inevitably it both affected, and was affected by, the terms of trade; indeed one writer has gone as far as to say that the distribution of UK investment at home and abroad ultimately depended upon the terms of trade, unfavourable terms of trade encouraging overseas investment and favourable terms of trade encouraging home investment. Testing this hypothesis, we find no significant relationship either between movements of UK capital to the US and the UK terms of trade, or between this same movement and the US terms of trade. The reason is that UK investment in US was not centred in raw materials but in railway building which caused the fall in price of agriculture products. In general, it appears that short-term movements in home and foreign investment move in sympathy with one another: in the long term they move in opposite directions.

The impact of UK capital exports to the US has, moreover, changed with the years. Thus, J. J. Madden (1963) has calculated that 60 to 65 per cent of fluctuations in British capital exports over the period 1860/80 were due to fluctuations in US demands for capital. In the later period the domination is not as great, as the proportion of US imports of capital originating from the UK falls. Cairncross (1953) has argued that it was foreign rather than home investment that pulled the UK out of most depressions before 1914. It is most noticeable that there is an inverse correlation between exports of capital and building construction by local authorities, and investment in railways. There is a complementary relationship between the exports of capital and machinery. An inverse correlation exists between machinery retained for home use and capital exports. There is some relationship between employment and capital exports. Peaks and troughs are fairly closely associated with an increase in employment associated with increase in capital exports (Hobson 1914). Williamson, in his paper, notes that 'the net exports of British capital is positively correlated with the export of goods and negatively correlated with the trade balance deficit, home investment and deflated imports.' On the average capital exports lead deflated exports by two years . . . and home investment leading capital by one or two years.

REFERENCES

D. Adler. *British Investment in U.S. Railroads*, Ph.D. thesis, University of Cambridge, 1958.

N. T. Bacon. 'America's international indebtedness,' *Yale Review*, Vol IX, No. 3, November 1897.

T. Coram. *The Role of British Capital in the Development of the United states*, M.Sc.(Econ.) thesis, University of Southampton, 1967.

A. K. Cairncross. *Home and Foreign Investment* 1870/1910, Cambridge, 1953.

R. Clements (1953). 'British controlled enterprise in the West, 1870–90,' *Agricultural History*, Vol. XXVII, October 1953.

R. Clements (1955). 'The farmer's attitude towards British investment in American industry,' *Journal of Economic History*, Vol. XV, 1955.

R. Clements (1960). 'British investment in the trans-Mississippi West 1870/1914,' *Pacific History Review*, February 1960.

C. H. Feinstein. 'Income and investment in the United Kingdom 1856/1914,' *Economic Journal*, Vol. LXXXI, June 1961.

H. Feis. *Europe, the World's Banker*, 1870/1914, Yale University Press, 1930.

C. Hobson. *The Export of Capital*, Constable, London, 1914.

A. H. Imlah. *Economic Elements in the Pax Britannica*, Cambridge (Mass.), 1958.

L. H. Jenks (1938). *Migration of British Capital to* 1875, London and New York, 1938.

L. H. Jenks (1944). 'Railroads as a force in American development,' *Journal of Economic History*, Vol. IV, May 1944.

L. H. Jenks (1951). 'Britain and American railway development,' *Journal of Economic History*, Vol. XI, August, 1951.

J. Knapp. 'Capital exports and growth,' *Economic Journal*, Vol. LXVIII, September 1957.

S. Kuznets. *Capital in the American Economy: its Formation and Financing*, Princeton, 1961.

C. Lewis. *America's Stake in International Investment*, New York, 1938.

W. A. Lewis and P. J. O'Leary. 'Secular swings in production and trade 1870/1913,' *The Manchester School of Economic and Social Studies*, Vol. XIII, May 1955.

J. Madden. *British Investment in the United States* 1860–80, Ph.D. thesis, University of Cambridge, 1963.

H. Marshall, F. A. Southard and K. W. Knight. *Canadian-American Industry*, New Haven, 1936.

R. C. O. Matthews. *The Business Cycle*, Chicago, 1959.

R. C. McGrane. *Foreign Bondholders and American State Debts*, New York, 1935.

B. R. Mitchell and P. Deane, *Abstract of British Historical Statistics*, Cambridge University Press, 1962.

D. North (1956). 'International capital flows and the development of the American West,' *Journal of Economic History*, Vol. XVI, December 1956.

D. North (1960). 'The United States balance of payments 1790/1860,' in *Trends in the American Economy in the Nineteenth Century*, National Bureau of Economic Research, Princeton, 1960.

D. C. North (1962). 'International capital movements in historical perspective,' in *U.S. Private and Government Investment Abroad* (ed.) R. Mikesell, University of Oregon, 1962.

G. Paish (1909). 'Great Britain's investment in other lands,' *Journal of the Royal Statistical Society*, Vol. LXXII, 1909.

G. Paish (1911). 'Great Britain's capital investment in individual, colonial and foreign countries,' *Journal of the Royal Statistical Society*, Vol. LXIV, 1911.

P. Rousseaux. *Les mouvements de fond de l'économie Anglaise*, 1800/1913, Louvain, 1938.

A. Satorius. 'Freiherrn von Wattershauser,' quoted by D. North in 'International Capital movements in historical perspective,' in *U.S. Private and Government Investment Abroad* (ed.) R. Mikesell, University of Oregon, 1962.

S. B. Saul. *Studies in British Overseas Trade* 1870/1914, Liverpool, 1960.

M. Simon (1960). 'The United States balance of payments 1862/1900,' in *Trends in the American Economy in the Nineteenth Century*, National Bureau of Economic Research, Princeton, 1960.

M. Simon (1967). 'The pattern of new British portfolio investment 1865/1914,' in J. H. Adler (ed.), *Capital Movements and Economic Development*, Macmillan, 1967.

F. Southard. *American industry in Europe*, New York, 1932.

C. Spence. *British Investment and the American Mining Frontier*, Ithaca, 1958.

Brinley Thomas (1954). *Migration and Economic Growth: a Study of Great Britain and the Atlantic Economy*, Cambridge, 1954.

Brinley Thomas (1967). 'The historical record of international capital movements to 1913,' in J. H. Adler (ed.), *Capital Movements and Economic Development*, Macmillan, 1967.

U.S. Bureau of the Census. *Historical Abstract of the United States*, Washington, 1960.

J. G. Williamson. *American Growth and the Balance of Payments*, 1820/1913, Carolina, 1964.

APPENDIX TO CHAPTER 4
(Supplementary Statistical Data)

TABLE 1

Calculation of Final Series of UK Investment in US 1861/1913 (all figures in $m.)

	Derived from Simon's series					Derived from Imlah's series							
	(1)	(2)	(3)	(4)	(5)*	(6)	(7)	(8)	(9)	(10)	(11)	(12)	(13)
Year	Net Balance of US Indebtedness	US Inv. Abroad as Percentage Foreign Inv. in US	Total Foreign Inv. in US	UK Share Foreign Inv. in US	UK Inv. in US	UK Accum. Credit Abroad	Foreign Inv. in UK as per cent of UK Inv. Abroad	UK Foreign Investment	Share of UK Foreign Inv. going to US	UK Inv. in US	$\frac{(10)}{(5)} \times 100\%$	Final Series of UK Inv. in US (Stock)	Final Series of UK Inv. in US (Flow)
1861	483·6	5·0	509·1	90·0	447·3	1,915	10	2,128	20·0	425·6	94·9	436	
2	482·5	5·0	507·9	59·5	450·1	1,971	10	2,190	21·0	459·9	102·2	455	19
3	495·1	5·0	521·1	89·0	514·1	2,100	10	2,333	22·0	513·3	99·8	514	59
4	605·7	5·0	637·8	88·5	594·5	2,211	10	2,456	23·0	564·9	95·0	580	66
5	674·4	5·0	709·9	88·0	666·4	2,380	10	2,644	24·0	634·6	95·2	651	71
6	768·8	5·0	809·3	87·5	772·8	2,541	10	2,823	25·0	705·8	91·3	739	88
7	914·4	5·0	962·5	87·0	868·1	2,746	10	3,051	26·0	793·3	91·4	831	92
8	987·1	5·0	1,039·1	86·5	972·8	2,923	10	3,247	27·0	876·7	90·1	925	94
9	1,156·3	5·0	1,217·2	86·0	1,088·5	3,150	10	3,500	28·0	980·0	90·0	1,035	110

1870	1,255·7	5·0	1,321·8	85·5	1,172·0	3,365	10	3,735	29·0	1,083·1	92·4	1,128	93
1	1,356·6	5·0	1,428·0	85·0	1,318·2	3,711	10	4,120	30·0	1,236·0	93·8	1,277	149
2	1,599·4	5·0	1,683·4	84·5	1,499·3	4,187	10	4,652	30·0	1,395·6	93·1	1,447	170
3	1,782·3	5·0	1,876·1	84·0	1,607·4	4,582	10	5,091	30·0	1,527·3	95·0	1,567	120
4	1,864·5	5·0	1,962·6	83·5	1,671·9	4,927	10	5,474	30·0	1,642·2	98·2	1,657	90
5	1,951·4	5·0	2,054·1	83·0	1,700·6	5,176	10	5,751	29·0	1,667·8	96·4	1,684	27
6	1,953·2	5·0	2,056·0	82·5	1,666·4	5,289	10	5,876	28·0	1,645·3	98·7	1,656	−28
7	1,895·9	5·0	1,995·7	82·0	1,562·1	5,353	10	5,947	27·0	1,605·7	102·8	1,584	−72
8	1,734·0	5·0	1,825·3	81·5	1,414·5	5,435	10	6,033	25·0	1,508·3	106·6	1,462	−122
9	1,573·8	5·0	1,656·6	81·0	1,350·2	5,607	10	6,224	23·0	1,431·5	106·0	1,391	−71
1880	1,603·2	5·0	1,687·6	80·5	1,340·6	5,780	10	6,422	22·0	1,412·8	105·4	1,377	−14
1	1,562·4	5·5	1,653·3	80·0	1,372·8	6,099	10	6,776	21·0	1,423·0	103·7	1,398	21
2	1,671·9	6·0	1,778·6	80·0	1,448·6	6,385	10	7,094	20·0	1,418·8	97·9	1,434	36
3	1,723·0	6·5	1,842·8	80·0	1,523·5	6,622	10	7,357	20·0	1,471·4	96·6	1,497	63
4	1,828·3	7·0	1,965·9	80·0	1,586·2	6,974	10	7,748	20·0	1,549·6	97·7	1,568	71
5	1,861·2	7·5	2,012·1	79·5	1,657·3	7,276	10	8,084	20·0	1,616·8	97·6	1,637	69
6	1,997·1	8·0	2,170·8	79·0	1,812·9	7,660	10	8,510	20·0	1,702·0	93·9	1,757	120
7	2,227·3	8·5	2,434·2	78·5	2,032·2	8,086	10	8,984	21·0	1,886·6	92·8	1,959	202
8	2,512·3	9·0	2,760·8	78·0	2,238·8	8,533	10	9,480	22·0	2,085·6	93·2	2,162	203
9	2,713·9	9·5	2,998·8	77·5	2,405·4	8,926	10	9,917	23·0	2,280·9	94·8	2,343	181

TABLE 1 (*Contd*)

Year	Derived from Simon's series					Derived from Imlah's series							
	(1) Net Balance of US Indebtedness	(2) US Inv. Abroad as Percentage Foreign Inv. in US	(3) Total Foreign Inv. in US	(4) UK Share of Foreign Inv. in US	(5)* UK Inv. in US	(6) UK Accum. Credit Abroad	(7) Foreign Inv. in UK as per cent of UK Inv. Abroad	(8) UK Foreign Investment	(9) Share of UK Foreign Inv. going to US	(10) UK Inv. in US	(11) $\frac{(10)}{(5)} \times 100\%$	(12) Final Series of UK Inv. in US (Stock)	(13) (Flow)
1890	2,906·5	10·0	3,229·4	77·0	2,550·3	9,405	10	10,449	24·0	2,507·8	98·3	2,529	186
1	3,041·0	11·0	3,416·9	76·5	2,638·8	9,742	10	10,824	25·0	2,706·0	102·6	2,672	143
2	3,081·8	12·0	3,502·0	76·0	2,731·1	10,029	10	11,143	25·0	2,785·8	102·0	2,758	86
3	3,227·2	13·0	3,709·4	75·5	2,778·8	10,287	10	11,429	25·0	2,857·3	102·8	2,818	60
4	3,161·2	14·0	3,675·8	75·0	2,823·9	10,476	10	11,639	24·0	2,793·4	98·9	2,809	−9
5	3,298·2	15·0	3,880·2	74·5	2,915·7	10,669	10	11,853	23·0	2,726·2	93·5	2,821	12
6	3,338·0	16·0	3,973·8	74·0	2,938·1	10,945	10	12,160	22·0	2,675·2	91·1	2,807	−14
7	3,314·9	17·8	3,864·7	73·5	2,801·4	11,147	10	12,384	21·0	2,600·6	92·8	2,701	−106
8	3,036·4	22·7	3,767·9	73·0	2,750·6	11,259	10	12,509	20·0	2,501·8	91·0	2,626	−75
9	2,787·3	27·6	3,701·3	72·0	2,664·9	11,465	10	12,738	19·8	2,522·1	94·6	2,593	−33

1900	2,569·3	32·7	3,636·8	71·0	2,582·1	11,649	10	12,943	19·6	2,536·8	98·2	2,559	−34
1	2,324·3	37·6	3,613·8	70·0	2,529·7	11,814	10	13,127	19·4	2,546·6	100·7	2,538	−21
2	2,189·3	41·2	3,702·8	69·0	2,554·9	11,976	10	13,307	19·2	2,554·9	100·0	2,555	17
3	2,168·3	44·0	3,854·3	68·0	2,620·9	12,193	10	13,548	19·0	2,574·1	98·2	2,598	43
4	2,158·3	49·0	3,974·8	67·0	2,663·1	12,445	10	13,828	18·8	2,599·7	97·6	2,631	33
5	2,075·3	49·0	4,134·3	66·0	2,728·6	12,841	10	14,268	18·6	2,653·8	97·3	2,691	60
6	2,143·3	50·2	4,370·8	65·0	2,841·0	13,412	10	14,902	18·4	2,742·0	96·5	2,793	102
7	2,214·3	51·8	4,550·3	64·0	2,913·9	14,160	10	15,733	18·2	2,863·4	98·3	2,889	96
8	2,168·3	53·5	4,722·8	63·0	2,975·4	14,912	10	16,569	18·0	2,982·4	100·2	2,979	90
9	2,227·3	53·6	5,077·8	62·0	3,148·2	15,571	10	17,301	17·8	3,079·6	97·8	3,114	135
1910	2,482·3	53·8	5,427·3	61·0	3,310·7	16,385	10	18,205	17·6	3,204·1	96·8	3,257	143
1	2,530·3	55·1	5,660·8	60·0	3,396·5	17,341	10	19,268	17·4	3,352·6	98·7	3,375	118
2	2,553·3	56·1	5,913·8	59·0	3,489·1	18,299	10	20,332	17·0	3,497·1	100·2	3,493	118
3	2,640·3	57·0	6,165·8	59·0	3,637·8	19,389	10	21,543	17·0	3,662·3	100·7	3,650	157

* Adjusted from mid-year to end year . . . for comparability with series of UK Investment in US derived from Imlah's data.

TABLE 2

Indicators of the Growth of the US Economy

Year	Miles of Railroad Track Added	Index of Bituminous Coal Production (trend removed)	Index of Manufacturing Production (trend removed)	Index of Building Permits	Immigration into the US from Europe
1861	660	79	99	20·0	81,200
2	834	84	77	18·0	83,710
3	1,050	93	94	20·5	163,733
4	732	99	98	13·5	185,233
5	1,177	97	88	17·5	214,048
6	1,716	99	104	25·0	278,916
7	2,249	99	102	29·5	283,751
8	2,979	98	102	33·0	130,090
9	4,615	89	107	35·5	315,963
1870	6,078	89	101	35·5	328,626
1	7,379	129	102	37·5	265,145
2	5,870	117	114	30·0	352,155
3	4,097	123	106	29·0	397,541
4	2,117	100	98	24·5	262,783
5	1,711	98	90	24·5	182,961
6	2,712	92	86	20·0	120,920
7	2,274	97	87	18·0	106,195
8	2,665	92	88	17·0	101,612
9	4,809	89	95	20·0	134,259
1880	6,711	92	106	21·5	348,691
1	9,846	107	110	25·0	528,545
2	11,569	125	111	28·0	648,186
3	6,745	130	109	30·0	522,587
4	3,923	129	97	32·0	453,686
5	2,975	104	92	36·0	353,083
6	8,018	99	106	37·5	329,529
7	12,876	108	107	38·5	482,829
8	6,900	115	104	37·0	538,131
9	5,162	100	106	44·5	434,790
1890	5,915	108	110	48·0	445,680
1	4,844	106	107	42·5	546,085
2	3,656	106	110	43·0	570,876
3	4,143	99	93	31·5	429,324
4	2,899	85	86	29·0	277,052
5	1,895	90	98	35·5	250,342
6	2,053	86	85	30·0	329,067
7	2,163	85	88	31·5	216,397
8	2,026	90	95	27·0	217,786
9	3,466	97	99	31·0	297,349

TABLE 2—*continued*

1900	4,628	99	95	22·5	424,700
1	3,324	99	100	30·5	469,237
2	4,965	106	109	30·0	619,068
3	6,169	108	103	29·5	814,507
4	6,690	99	94	33·5	767,933
5	5,084	105	104	42·0	974,273
6	5,565	107	108	42·0	1,018,365
7	6,188	116	106	35·5	1,199,566
8	3,897	91	82	33·0	691,901
9	3,238	98	102	43·5	654,875
1900	5,908	101	101	39·5	926,291
1	4,740	92	103	38·0	764,757
2	3,301	96	102	40·5	718,875
3	3,003	96	93	33·0	1,055,855

Sources: Miles of Railroad Track added: Original data from Simon Kuznets, *Secular Movements in Production and Prices*, pp. 526–27.

Bituminous Coal output: Original data from US Bureau of the Census, *Historical Statistics of the United States*, as listed in Thomas, *Migration*, Appendix 4, Table 97, with trend removed.

Manufacturing Production: Edwin Frickey, *Production in the United States* 1860–1914, Tables 6 and 7, pp. 54, 60.

Building: Original data taken from J. R. Riggleman, *Building Cycles in the United States* 1830/1935 (unpublished Ph.D. dissertation, the Johns Hopkins University) as listed in Brinley Thomas, *Migration*, Appendix 4, Table 108. Expressed in terms of dollars of 1913 purchasing power per capita.

Immigration: *Annual Report of Commissioner General Immigration (U.S.)*, 1926. Listed in *Historical Statistics of the United States*, US Bureau of the Census.

TABLE 3

Relative Growth and Profitability of the US and UK (Indices)

Year	US Share Prices ÷ UK Share Prices Index	US New Building ÷ UK New Building Index	US Manufac. Prodn. (trendless) ÷ UK Manufac. Prodn. (trendless) Index
1861			97·4
2			88·3
3			94·9
4			98·8
5			87·6
6			103·2
7			102·9
8			102·0
9			107·4
1870			99·7
1	95·8	130	99·1
2	91·4	96	110·5
3	85·0	90	102·3
4	99·4	70	94·7
5	85·6	66	88·6
6	83·8	50	85·1
7	68·2	44	85·9
8	79·6	44	90·3
9	105·6	54	101·0
1880	113·2	60	105·1
1	137·4	72	109·8
2	134·0	84	108·0
3	135·6	92	105·7
4	120·0	104	97·0
5	118·0	128	94·7
6	135·6	128	111·7
7	145·6	126	111·0
8	121·6	114	104·4
9	119·6	128	103·4
1890	118·4	148	108·9
1	114·4	138	106·8
2	127·6	146	114·5
3	108·6	104	99·6
4	97·2	90	89·5
5	90·6	94	100·8
6	70·0	64	85·3
7	67·0	54	89·0
8	76·0	40	94·6
9	92·6	46	96·4

TABLE 3—*continued*

1900	91·8	36	93·7
1	123·4	52	101·0
2	134·8	50	109·9
3	118·2	50	105·0
4	122·6	60	97·3
5	147·4	74	103·3
6	155·4	78	105·2
7	128·6	72	102·7
8	136·4	76	84·2
9	170·4	162	104·5
1910	150·8	102	101·4
1	142·4	114	88·6
2	147·8	138	101·3
3	140·6	112	93·0

Sources: US share prices: *Historical Statistics of the U.S.*
UK share prices: P. Rousseau – listed in Williamson.

US building: J. R. Riggleman – listed in Williamson.
UK building: B. R. Mitchell and P. Deane – *Abstract of British Historical Statistics.*

US manufacturing production: E. Frickey – listed in Williamson.
UK manufacturing production: Mitchell and Deane.

TABLE 4

Indices of the Prosperity of the UK Economy

Year	Residential Building 1907 = 100	Net Fixed Capital Formation £m.	Net National Income (trend removed)	Manufac. Prodn. (trend removed)	Unemployment (in all Trade Unions making returns) %
1861		33	107·8	101·6	5·2
2		41	103·6	98·5	8·4
3		46	199·3	99·0	6·0
4		54	99·5	99·2	2·7
5		56	100·3	100·4	2·1
6		61	98·1	100·8	3·3
7		45	93·6	99·1	7·4
8		39	90·5	100·0	7·9
9		38	92·1	99·6	6·7
1870	54	51	96·8	101·3	3·9
1	58	59	98·7	102·9	1·6
2	63	68	95·0	103·2	0·9
3	65	68	96·9	103·6	1·2
4	70	80	97·7	103·5	1·7
5	74	83	97·0	101·6	2·4
6	79	88	93·9	101·1	3·7
7	81	87	90·5	101·3	4·7
8	78	75	90·5	97·4	6·8
9	74	65	88·4	94·1	11·4
1880	71	67	86·3	100·9	5·5
1	70	63	89·1	100·2	3·5
2	67	64	91·1	102·8	2·3
3	65	64	88·4	103·1	2·6
4	61	57	88·4	100·0	8·1
5	56	49	91·4	97·2	9·3
6	59	39	93·1	94·9	10·2
7	61	39	96·0	96·4	7·6
8	65	43	99·8	99·6	4·9
9	70	48	103·6	102·5	2·1
1890	65	50	104·1	101·0	2·1
1	62	52	101·2	100·2	3·5
2	59	58	95·3	96·1	6·3
3	61	56	94·8	93·4	7·5
4	65	61	103·1	96·1	6·9
5	76	62	105·8	97·2	5·8
6	94	72	106·5	99·6	3·3
7	117	91	105·8	98·9	3·3
8	134	111	105·6	100·4	2·8
9	134	125	111·6	102·7	2·0

TABLE 4—*continued*

1900	122	141	106·7	101·4	2·5
1	117	142	104·7	99·0	3·3
2	118	146	103·7	99·2	4·0
3	120	141	99·6	98·1	4·7
4	113	134	96·2	96·6	6·0
5	113	123	98·7	100·7	5·0
6	107	113	101·4	102·7	3·6
7	100	100	102·6	103·2	3·7
8	87	77	98·4	97·4	7·8
9	85	75	97·6	97·6	7·7
1910	78	81	98·0	99·6	4·7
1	67	78	99·9	101·6	3·0
2	59	84	100·5	101·7	3·2
3	59	105	100·8	109·7	2·1

Sources: Residential building: A. K. Cairncross, *Home and Foreign Investment* 1870–1913, p. 213.

Net fixed capital formation: C. H. Feinstein, 'Income and investment in the United Kingdom, 1856–1914,' *Economic Journal*, June 1961.

Net National Income (trendless): A. L. Bowley's cost of living index (*Wages and Income since* 1860, Cambridge, 1937, pp. 121–22).

Manufacturing production (trendless): W. G. Hoffman, *British Industry* 1700–1950, Oxford, 1955.

Unemployment: Sessional Paper 1905, LXXXIV 1861–1903, then Abstract of Labour Statistics.

TABLE 5

Export of Goods and Capital from UK (£m)

Year	Export of Goods to the World	Export of Capital to the World	Export of Goods to the US
1861	125·1	2,128	11·0
2	124·0	2,190	19·2
3	146·6	2,333	19·7
4	160·4	2,456	20·2
5	165·8	2,644	25·2
6	188·9	2,823	31·8
7	181·0	3,051	24·1
8	179·7	3,247	23·8
9	190·0	3,500	26·8
1870	199·6	3,735	31·3
1	223·1	4,120	38·7
2	256·3	4,652	45·9
3	255·2	5,091	36·7
4	239·6	5,474	32·2
5	223·5	5,751	25·1
6	200·6	5,876	20·2
7	198·9	5,947	19·9
8	192·8	6,033	17·5
9	191·5	6,224	25·5
1880	223·1	6,422	38·0
1	234·0	6,776	36·8
2	241·5	7,094	38·7
3	239·8	7,357	36·7
4	233·0	7,748	32·7
5	213·1	8,084	31·1
6	212·7	8,510	37·6
7	221·9	8,984	40·2
8	234·5	9,480	41·2
9	248·9	9,917	43·9
1890	263·5	10,449	46·3
1	247·2	10,824	41·1
2	227·1	11,143	41·4
3	218·1	11,429	35·7
4	215·8	11,639	30·8
5	225·9	11,853	44·1
6	240·2	12,160	32·0
7	234·2	12,384	37·9
8	233·4	12,509	28·5
9	264·5	12,738	35·0

TABLE 5—*continued*

1900	291·2	12,943	37·3
1	280·0	13,127	37·7
2	283·4	13,307	43·1
3	290·8	13,548	41·6
4	300·7	13,828	39·3
5	329·8	14,268	47·3
6	375·6	14,902	53·2
7	426·0	15,733	58·1
8	377·1	16,569	42·5
9	378·2	17,301	59·3
1910	430·4	18,205	62·2
1	454·1	19,268	56·1
2	487·2	20,332	64·6
3	525·3	21,543	59·5

Sources: Export of goods to the world: 'U.K. Annual statements of trade.'
Export of capital to the world: A. H. Imlah, *Economic elements in the Pax Britannica.*
Export of goods to the US: *Historical Statistics of the US.*

5

UK CAPITAL EXPORTS AND CANADIAN ECONOMIC DEVELOPMENT*

Introduction

One of the features of world economic development in the twentieth century is the increasing extent to which it has been promoted and sustained by the international flow of capital and knowledge. Nowhere is this more strikingly illustrated than in the case of Canada. It is, of course, possible to cite numerous examples of how, in the past, foreign investment has played a leading role in financing the initial or take-off period of development in particular economies.[1] Usually, however, once the necessary conditions have been achieved to ensure regular and self-reinforcing growth, the significance of capital imports *vis-à-vis* domestic capital formation gradually falls. In Canada this has not happened. No other modern industrial country has such a large proportion of its economic wealth owned and controlled by foreigners, or such a high *per capita* international debt. For more than sixty years now, apart from the period of depression and war between 1930 and 1945, and latterly since 1962, capital imports have regularly financed between a quarter and a third of Canadian private fixed investment, and during the five years between 1956 and 1960, the proportion (33 per cent) was higher than for any other similar period during the past thirty years.

The explanation of Canada's continued attraction for, and unusually high dependence on, foreign capital as an instrument of growth, lies partly in the unique economic and geographical relationship of the country to the two main capital-exporting countries of the present century – the UK and the US – and partly in her possession of a substantial reservoir of valuable minerals and raw materials essential to world (and in particular US) industrial development.

* First published in *Moorgate and Wall Street*, Spring 1962: Since then expanded and updated. Part of this chapter is based on an analysis of British manufacturing subsidiaries in Canada undertaken by the author in 1961 and 1962. This study was financed by The Rockefeller Foundation.

[1] W. W. Rostow, *The Stages of Economic Growth*, Cambridge University Press, 1961.

At the same time, the nature of the debtor–creditor relationship evolved between Canada and the rest of the world in the last half-century, mirrors very accurately the two main changes which have occurred in the wider sphere of international lending over the same period. These are, first, the supersession of Britain by the US as the leading supplier of foreign capital and, second, the growing significance of direct, in place of portfolio, investment as the main form of lending.

In 1914, for example, Britain accounted for one-half the world's supply of international capital, an amount nearly five times that provided by the US: her share of a total foreign investment in Canada of $3,837m. was 72 per cent while that of the US was 23 per cent. Today, the relative position of the two countries is almost the reverse. Of the gross outflow of private long-term finance from the main capital-supplying countries between 1955 and 1965, the US was responsible for nearly two-thirds and the UK for about one-fifth. In Canada, of a total non-resident investment at the end of 1964 of $27,354m. the British contribution was 13 per cent and the American 78 per cent. Over the same period, and particularly since 1945, the establishment of overseas subsidiaries and branch plants has ousted the purchase of foreign securities as the main form of capital export. Before the First World War, direct investment accounted for less than 10 per cent of British and only 40 per cent of American overseas lending: by 1960, these proportions had risen to at least one-half and 72 per cent respectively. In Canada, 58 per cent of all non-resident investment was of this kind in 1964, compared with 12 per cent in 1914.

This chapter deals mainly with the role of British direct capital exports in Canada's economic growth from the viewpoint of the investing country. Where possible, comparative trends in US investment are also discussed: these not only help to put the significance of UK investment in a proper perspective, but also provide us with some of the basic data upon which it is possible to judge the results and impact of such investment.

The part played by non-resident capital in Canada's economic development since 1900 is briefly summarized in Table 1. First, the accumulated foreign investment stake is expressed as a proportion of gross national product, second, new foreign investment is related to private gross fixed formation (excluding residential construction)[1] and, third, the net annual capital inflow (capital imports

[1] Since foreign investment is net of depreciation, Column 8 underestimates its true contribution to domestic capital formation.

TABLE 1

Foreign Investment and Canadian Economic Development 1900/64

	Total $m.	*US* $m.	*Investment Percentage of US to Total*	*UK* $m.	*Percentage of UK to Total*	*Percentage of Foreign Investment to GNP*	*Percentage of Foreign Investment to Private Fixed Investment*	*Percentage of Net Capital Inflow (—) to Total Imports*
1900	1,232	168	14	1,050	85			
1914	3,837	881	23	2,778	72	166·6		
1918	4,536	1,630	36	2,729	60	111·1		
1926	6,003	3,196	53	2,637	44	111·3		
1930	7,614	4,660	61	2,766	36	137·0	52·6	—9·8
1933	7,365	4,492	61	2,683	36	208·3	neg.*	—9·4
1939	6,913	4,151	60	2,476	36	120·5	neg.	+11·8
1945	7,092	4,990	70	1,750	25	60·0	4·1	+37·0
1946	7,181	5,158	72	1,670	23	60·0	8·7	+12·0
1950	8,664	6,549	76	1,750	20	48·1	24·1	—7·2
1955	13,473	10,275	76	2,356	18	49·7	20·3	—10·3
1956	15,569	11,789	76	2,668	17	50·9	36·1	—17·2
1957	17,464	13,264	76	2,917	17	54·7	31·1	—16·8
1958	19,010	14,441	76	3,088	16	57·8	27·2	—14·7
1959	20,857	15,826	76	3,199	15	59·7	31·6	—18·0
1960	22,214	16,718	75	3,359	15	61·2	23·8	—14·4
1961	23,606	18,001	76	3,381	14	63·0	24·4	—14·6
1962	24,889	19,155	77	3,399	14	61·3	21·3	—11·1
1963	26,134	20,479	78	3,331	13	60·1	19·1	—7·0
1964	27,354	21,443	78	3,463	13	57·7	15·6	—7·2

* Negative.

Source: Dominion Bureau of Statistics, *The Canadian Balance of International Payments* 1963/65 and *National Income and*

less exports) is expressed as a ratio of total current payments made abroad. The Table confirms the trends to which we have already referred and shows the continuing significance of foreign capital as an instrument of Canadian economic growth. Since 1960 or thereabouts, however, the inflow of capital has slowed down as both US and UK enterprises have found it more attractive to invest elsewhere in the world.[1] At the same time, Canada has considerably added to her own foreign investments. The net effect of these trends has been to reduce a net capital inflow of \$5,871m. between 1956 and 1960 to \$3,590m. between 1960 and 1964.

Table 2 depicts, more particularly, the relative expansion of UK and US investment in Canada and highlights the growing prominence of direct investment over the years.

Historical development

Although there had been earlier periods of substantial foreign investment in Canada, particularly between 1851 and 1858 when the greater part of the \$60m. required for railways and canals was supplied by the United Kingdom,[2] the years between 1906 and 1914 are best remembered as those in which the inflow of capital made its most critical impact on the economy's development. While the initial impetus to the period of expansion which followed was the rise in agricultural (and particularly wheat) prices, which, together with important mineral discoveries, led to the opening up of the Canadian west and the introduction of new farming and mining techniques, it was facilitated and accelerated by foreign capital.[3] Of the total non-resident investment in these years, the UK accounted for two-thirds and the US for 27 per cent.

At the same time, the real transfer of capital, i.e. in the form of export of goods, was mainly effected via the US rather than the UK. Thus, while between 1900 and 1913, total Canadian borrowing from the UK totalled \$1,754m. compared with \$630m. from the US, the import surplus on current account with the UK was only

[1] See particularly Table 2.2 in Chapter 2.

[2] C. K. Hobson, *The Export of Capital*, Constable, 1914, p. 136. For a comprehensive discussion of the role of British investment in Canada, see R. N. Beattie, *Some Aspects of British Investment in British North America* 1850/64 (unpublished M.A. thesis, University of Toronto, 1946).

[3] P. Hartland, 'Factors in economic growth in Canada,' *Journal of Economic History*, Vol. XV, No. 1, 1955.

TABLE 2

UK and US Direct and Portfolio Investment in Canada 1926/64

	UK Investment $m					*US Investment* $m				
	Direct	1926 = 100	*Portfolio*[1]	1926 = 100	*Percentage of Direct to Total*	*Direct*	1926 = 100	*Portfolio*	1926 = 100	*Percentage of Direct to Total*
1926	336	100·0	2,301	100·0	13	1,403	100·0	1,793	100·0	44
1930	392	116·6	2,374	103·2	14	1,993	142·0	2,667	148·7	42
1933	376	111·9	2,307	100·3	14	1,933	137·8	2,559	142·7	42
1939	366	108·9	2,110	91·7	15	1,881	134·1	2,270	126·6	45
1945	348	103·6	1,402	61·2	20	2,304	164·2	2,686	149·8	46
1950	468	139·4	1,335	58·3	26	3,426	244·2	3,123	174·2	53
1955	891	265·3	1,465	63·6	36	6,513	464·4	3,762	209·8	63
1956	1,048	311·9	1,620	70·4	40	7,392	527·0	4,397	245·2	62
1957	1,163	346·3	1,755	76·3	40	8,472	603·8	4,792	267·2	64
1958	1,296	385·7	1,792	77·9	42	9,045	644·7	5,391	300·7	63
1959	1,384	411·9	1,815	78·9	43	9,912	706·5	5,899	329·0	63
1960	1,535	456·8	1,824	79·3	46	10,549	751·8	6,169	344·1	63
1961	1,613	480·0	1,768	76·8	48	11,284	804·3	6,717	374·6	63
1962	1,706	507·7	1,693	73·6	50	12,006	855·7	7,149	398·7	63
1963	1,737	517·0	1,594	69·3	52	12,754	909·1	7,725	430·8	62
1964	1,944	578·6	1,519	66·0	56	12,901	919·5	8,542	476·4	60

[1] And other long-term investments, for example: investment in real estate, mortgages, etc.
Source: Dominion Bureau of Statistics.

$152m. compared with $1,704m. with the US.[1] The closer proximity of Canada to her Southern neighbours and the greater similarity between the structures of their two economies (the US had experienced a similar take-off period in her development sixty to seventy years previously) forged between them a link which has strengthened with the years, and is now, according to some Canadians, more akin to a chain! From the start, while capital exports from Britain mainly took the form of absentee portfolio holdings, those from the US were accompanied by managerial and technological control, and represented the geographical extension of the operations of established American business units. Between 1900 and 1913, 55 per cent of all US capital in Canada was invested in the setting up of branch plant enterprises compared with only 11 per cent of British money. If British capital, invested in railways and public utilities securities, laid the foundations of Canadian growth in these years, American enterprise has been one of the greatest beneficiaries.[2]

In the years following the First World War, US direct investment in Canada steadily increased while the New York money market made available increasingly large sums of portfolio capital – once again, largely for industry and the exploitation of natural resources. By contrast, and much to the disappointment of the Canadians, British capital exports were only a fraction of those before 1914. Quite apart from her reduced ability to invest overseas and the higher yields being paid on gilt-edged securities in the London market, the nationalization dispute over the Grand Trunk Railway (in which there were considerable sums of UK capital invested) antagonized British investors and made them reluctant to extend their portfolio holdings. At the same time, an attempt was made, in these years, to follow the lead of the US and invest more money directly in subsidiaries and branch plants. By 1930, it was reported that there were seventy UK subsidiaries operating in Canadian manufacturing industries. On the whole, these ventures do not appear to have been successful. 'The blundering Englishman has blundered nowhere more blindly than in Canada,' reported the *Financial Post* in 1926. 'British investors and firms have lost millions in Canada chiefly through making mistakes that they would have never made at home.'

[1] For further particulars see J. A. Stovel, *Canada in the World Economy*. Harvard University Press, 1959, pp. 108ff, and J. Viner, *Canada's balance of international indebtedness* 1900/1913, Harvard University Press, 1924.

[2] It also appears that US investors were better choosers of profitable investment outlets than their UK counterparts. See 'US investors faster at seizing opportunities in Canada than British ones,' *The Statist*, 14/2/1903.

Too often, it would seem a subsidiary was established or purchased without proper investigation of market conditions and prospects, and then managed from London.

By 1926, the American capital stake in Canada exceeded that of the UK, and by 1930 it was more than half as much again. Such was the expansion of US investment that, by this latter year, US interests owned and controlled some 40 per cent of all capital invested in Canadian manufacturing, mining and smelting. The years which followed were a period of retrenchment, and by the time US or UK capital exports were once again on the increase – encouraged *inter alia* by a liberal Canadian tax policy – the Second World War had broken out. It ended with the unrivalled supremacy of the US as chief foreign investor in Canada. While the US added \$839m. to her Canadian holdings between 1939 and 1945, Britain was forced to liquidate \$726m. to purchase essential war supplies. The withdrawal of British capital would have been much greater had not the Canadian Government made the UK a gift of \$1,000m. in 1942 and extended \$2,000m. in mutual aid between 1943 and 1945. In addition a \$700m. interest-free loan was granted on the collateral of UK-held Canadian securities of an equivalent value. It was agreed at the time that, as and when these securities were sold or redeemed by UK investors, the proceeds should be employed to repay the loan. In 1946, however, the Canadian Government gave permission for such proceeds to be used for new direct investment in Canada. Little advantage was taken of this offer and, in 1953, by which time \$511m. of the original loan had been repaid, a new agreement was entered into by which the balance of the loan would be repaid in five years while, in the meantime, a certain amount of switching of portfolios would be allowed.

Post-war growth

The post-war history of British capital exports to Canada centres almost exclusively around the growth of direct investments.[1] Not until 1953, was there any net increase in the value of portfolio holdings (in spite of a very substantial loan made by the UK Government to the Aluminium Company of Canada); since that date there has

[1] Defined in this instance as the book value of the UK share of capital stock, surpluses and long-term debt of Canadian companies (or unincorporated UK branches) in which there is a British equity holding of 50 per cent or more. A few instances of concerns in which effective control is held by a parent firm with less than 50 per cent of the stock are also included. See Canada's *International Investment Position* 1926/54, Dominion Bureau of Statistics.

been a steady rise in values, although inflation is partly responsible for this. Direct investments also expanded slowly at first. There were more profitable outlets for funds at home and elsewhere in the Sterling Area, and the Government was reluctant to sanction dollars for foreign investment unless it could be shown that a quick return of dividends or interest was likely or the UK balance of payments would otherwise be strengthened. Although direct investments in Canada rose by $120m. in the first five years after the war, a good proportion of this amount represented earnings re-invested by pre-1945 established firms. Some forty manufacturing subsidiaries were set up with British capital in this period, including some firms in the heavy engineering industry 'in order to salt some of UK's industrial defence potential away from the shadow of the Russian bear.'[1] In the main, these were fairly small and exploratory investments, but one or two were very substantial and of great importance to the Canadian economy. Such, for example, was the entry of Hawker-Siddeley, through A. V. Roe Canada Ltd., into the Canadian aircraft industry; within ten years this company and its subsidiaries were employing 20,000 Canadians and undertaking 75 per cent of the aeronautical research in Canada.

By 1953, the UK economy had recovered sufficiently for the Government to release more funds for investment in Canada. Two years later, the Economic Secretary to the Treasury stated quite specifically that dollars would now be made readily available for all kinds of direct investment in Canada, which would advance UK exports, ensure essential raw materials supplies and promise a good rate of return.[2] In the meantime, for various reasons, but mainly as a result of the tremendous publicity given to Canada as 'the land of the future', and the exhortations of official and semi-official bodies in Britain to earn more dollars, UK companies were becoming increasingly mesmerized by the prospects of investing in the Dominion. Overnight, Canada was transformed into a Mecca for British capital; the country of glittering promise where it was impossible to fail. Despite warnings, firms, without any prior experience of overseas operations, rushed to set up or purchase a Canadian production unit without any realistic assessment of the market potential or the particular problems involved. Daily, new subsidiaries of UK firms were reported in the financial press; investment trusts and brokerage houses mushroomed and the rate of investment growth rose from $68m. in 1953

[1] *Financial Post*, 21/10/50.
[2] *Board of Trade Journal*, 12/11/55.

to $147m. in 1954, $132m. in 1955 and $157m. in 1956. By 1957 the number of manufacturing units directly or indirectly controlled by British capital had reached 349 (compared with 140 in 1945), and the number of merchandizing companies 362 (compared with 136 in 1945). The corresponding figures for 1964 were 419 and 402 respectively.

Over and above these general factors making for the expansion of British investment, there were a number of special considerations, three of which might be briefly mentioned. First, at the end of the war, the request of the Canadian Government for British capital and knowledge to help develop a domestic aircraft industry encouraged many UK firms to set up branch plants. Hawker Siddeley, leading the way in 1945, was shortly to be followed by a score or more of other British airframe and aero-engine companies and firms supplying components and ancillary products, e.g. Joseph Lucas. Until 1959, the Canadian aircraft industry had been largely financed by British capital. The cancellation in that year of a most important contract with A. V. Roe Canada involving the Arrow supersonic fighter, and the reorientation of Canadian defence thinking along American lines radically changed the situation and was a serious blow to British companies in Canada. At present, the Canadian aircraft industry is limited to supplying short-range or public utility aircraft, the manufacture of spares and replacements, and undertaking repair, maintenance and contract work, some of which is for the American Government.

A second special inducement was provided by the St Lawrence Seaway project, to which a large number of British civil engineering and constructional companies responded by establishing branch units in Canada and tendering for contracts. But, the results were disappointing; the competitiveness of the market was misjudged, the adaptations required in techniques and methods underestimated and the system of tendering not understood. Some companies soon withdrew, others weathered the storm, ploughed in additional capital, branched out into new fields and are now among the leading firms in the construction industry.

Third, a substantial Canadian programme was undertaken by the Rio Tinto company between 1955 and 1959 to develop uranium mines in northern Ontario. The initial stimulus for this venture, in which Canadian and US capital was also involved, originated from the US Atomic Energy Commission, which contracted for substantial quantities of uranium oxide, initially up to 1962 and 1963 but with a possibility of subsequent renewal. By 1959, $400m. – about one-eighth of it British money – had been invested in ten uranium mines and a completely new township, Elliott Lake, built to house 9,000 miners and their families. But, at the end of that year, the Commission announced it would not be exercising its options for further purchases of uranium. This decision necessitated a complete reappraisal of the situation by the Rio Tinto company; productive capacity was cut back and considerable hardship and inconvenience caused to the people of Elliott Lake.

More generally, the great proportion of British post-war investment in Canada has been directed to either the exploitation of resources, e.g. aluminium, oil, iron, timber, etc., or to manufacturing industry. Though the number of investments is greatest in merchandizing, finance, real estate, etc., the value of investments in manufacturing, mining and oil, hereafter referred to as the goods industries, accounted for 69 per cent of the total investment in 1964 and 72 per cent of the growth since 1945.

The motives for these capital exports fall into a number of fairly distinct categories. First, there is a kind of investment best described as international backward integration, which seeks to safeguard supplies or reduce the price of important raw materials to the investing company or other UK companies: subsidiaries operating the newsprint, aluminium, and oil and metal industries are of this kind. At the other extreme, there is the type of capital export which aims to advance the overseas sales of the investing company. One in seven British firms who invested in Canada between 1945 and 1960 appear to have been promoted to do so for one or other of these reasons.

The imposition or increase in tariffs, or other obstacles to export, induced one in four investments, while the need to provide on-the-spot design, contracting or servicing facilities was cited as the most important impetus by firms supplying capital goods. To some companies, the various advantages of being the first domestic manufacturer of a particular product (such as the tariff protection that could sometimes be claimed) provided the main attraction of investing in Canada. Other reasons included unfavourable conditions for expansion at home, the break-up of international licensing agreements, the belief that cost conditions favour local manufacturing (rather than export), the direct invitation from Government bodies or other firms, and the need to counteract US competition.[1] In general, it is very rare to find only one motive leading a firm to invest

[1] J. Brecher and S. S. Reisman, *Canadian-United States Economic Relations*, Royal Commission on Canada's economic prospects 1957; T. E. Pennie, *The Canadian Market for British Exports and Investments*, 1945/53, M.A. (Economics) Thesis, McGill University, 1954, pp. 111–17.

in Canada, although the general prospect of long-term growth figures twice as often as any other single explanation for the rise in UK capital exports to that country since the war.

The scope of U.K. investment in Canada

The present structure of British investment in Canada and the main changes which have taken place in recent years are depicted in Table 3. Perhaps the feature most worthy of comment here, is the trend towards a more diversified pattern of manufacturing investments, and the growing interest shown by British companies in the primary or extractive industries. Some 80 per cent of the direct investment in these groups since the war is seen to have occurred in five main industries – wood and paper, iron and steel, chemicals, oil, and mining. Oil investments, which in 1945 were negligible, accounted for more than one-fifth of the UK direct capital stake in 1964 and 46 per cent of new investment in the previous six years. Well over three-quarters of the UK interests in manufacturing are concentrated in the capital or intermediate goods industries, a considerably higher proportion than in 1945. Outside manufacturing and mining, the number of merchandizing investments has also grown rapidly.

Table 4 adopts a slightly different classification of industries, but one which helps us to assess the relative contribution of British and US investment to the total. In addition, the industries in question have been subdivided according to their national, i.e. Canadian, rate of expansion between 1949 and 1963. Here, we see that 50·5 per cent of UK investment in 1959 was within those industries expanding more than the national average (as compared with 63·6 per cent of US investment and 53·5 per cent of Canadian investment). Excluding oil investments, these proportions fall to 27·1 per cent, 29·0 per cent and 28·3 per cent respectively. A rather higher proportion of UK capital than US or Canadian capital appears to be invested in the less dynamic industries, although this is partly a reflection of historical forces. An interesting difference between the structure of Canadian and British industry is that the engineering and vehicles industry, which employs a third of the labour force in the UK, occupies a much less significant role in Canada. In fact, the five industries mentioned on p. 202, which account for four-fifths of the total British investment in the goods industries, employ less than a third of the industrial labour force in the UK. By contrast, the similarities between the US and Canadian industrial structure are more marked than the differences.

TABLE 3

Industrial Distribution of UK Investment in Canada 1945/64

	All Investment						*Direct Investment*					
	1945	1951	1955	1959	1964	1945 = 100	1945	1951	1955	1959	1964	1945 = 100
Manufacturing												
Vegetable products	66	80	106	131	158	239·4	60	74	91	117	152	253·3
Animal products	6	5	6	7	6	100·0	3	3	4	6	6	200·0
Textiles	38	52	55	59	47	123·7	26	38	45	49	39	150·0
Wood and paper products	64	140	155	159	244	381·3	30	109	124	127	192	640·0
Iron and steel products	12	28	103	194	203	1,691·7	4	14	87	180	185	4,625·0
Non-ferrous metals	64	91	153	192	182	284·4	8	10	27	64	59	737·5
Non-metallic minerals	8	20	32	45	49	612·5	4	15	26	34	31	775·0
Chemicals and allied products	36	60	132	153	183	508·3	19	30	129	150	177	931·6
Miscellaneous manufactures	2	12	4	5	5	250·0	2	12	4	5	4	200·0
	296	488	746	945	1,077	363·9	156	305	537	732	845	541·7
Petroleum and natural gas	7	7	31	162	436	6,228·6	—	4	23	116	390	—
Other mining and smelting	60	58	86	160	211	351·7	22	18	26	68	104	472·7
Public utilities												
(including railways)	896	760	784	908	585	65·2	16	16	33	40	14	87·5
Merchandizing	57	102	145	225	273	478·9	51	97	139	219	268	525·5
Financial institutions	186	142	241	413	501	269·4	98	48	109	168	265	171·4
Other enterprises	6	10	25	45	60	1,000·0	5	9	24	41	58	1,160·0
Miscellaneous investments	85	65	157	200	209	245·9	—	—	—	—	—	—
	1,750	1,778	2,356	3,199	3,463	197·9	348	497	890	1,384	1,944	558·6

Source: Dominion Bureau of Statistics.

TABLE 4

Industrial Distribution of UK, US and Canadian Investment in Canada and Ownership of Assets, 1963

	Industrial Production 1949 = 100	*UK Investment* ($m.)	*Percentage of Investment in Each Group to Total*			*Percentage of Total Investment Owned by Residents on Firms in*		
			UK	*US*	*Canada*	*UK*	*US*	*Canada*
A. *Industries which have expanded since 1949 above national average:*								
Petroleum products	319·7	380	23·4	32·8	25·2	5	54	36
Mining and smelting	294·4	161	9·9	17·1	14·2	4	54	38
Chemicals	244·1	180	11·1	5·2	4·8	13	47	37
Automobiles and parts	228·9	1	0·1	4·3	0·5	—	91	9
Electrical apparatus	223·5	32	2·0	3·6	2·0	5	62	30
Primary iron and steel	216·7	65	4·0	0·6	6·8	7	8	80
		819	50·5	63·6	53·5			
B. *Industries which have expanded since 1949 around the national average:*								
Rubber products	190·5	13	0·8	1·5	0·3	6	81	13
Beverages	177·6	12	0·7	1·1	4·2	2	23	74
		25	1·5	2·6	4·5			
C. *Industries which have expanded since 1949 below the national average:*								
Other industries	168·3	492	30·3	23·8	24·6	8	41	47
Pulp and paper	163·8	153	9·4	8·6	10·8	7	44	48
Textiles	159·5	46	2·8	0·8	5·5	6	14	80
Transportation and equipment[1]	88·6	86	5·3	0·5	1·0	34	25	41
		777	47·8	33·7	41·9			
All industry	195·9	1,621	100·0	100·0	100·0	7	48	41

[1] Other than automobiles and parts.

Table 4 also shows that, in most industries, the American stake is much more important than the British, the chief exception being in the transportation equipment industry (mainly aircraft in this instance) and, even here, the US share is growing and the British falling. Of the total capital engaged in the goods industries, 48 per cent is owned in the US, 41 per cent in Canada and 7 per cent in the UK.

TABLE 5

Number and Average Size of UK and US Direct Investment in Canada 1964*

	UK Firms		*US Firms*	
	No.	*Average Value* ($m.)	*No.*	*Average Value* ($m.)
Manufacturing				
Vegetable products	69	2·2	175	3·3
Animal products	11	0·5	62	2·4
Textiles	25	1·6	101	0·9
Wood and paper products	75	2·6	257	4·2
Iron and steel products	106	1·7	637	2·4
Non-ferrous metals	46	1·3	334	2·8
Non-metallic minerals	25	1·2	77	2·0
Chemicals and allied products	54	3·3	384	2·1
Miscellaneous manufacturers	8	0·5	149	0·8
	419	2·0	2,176	2·5
Petroleum and natural gas	37	10·5	478	7·3
Mining and smelting	52	2·0	314	5·6
Total, all goods industries	508	2·6	2,968	3·6

* Both first- and second-stage investments are included in this total.
Source: Dominion Bureau of Statistics.

The American pre-eminence is seen to be most marked in the automobile, rubber and electrical industries, and the least in primary iron and steel, transportation equipment and textiles industries. It is this dominance which the Canadians are so concerned about and are trying to counteract.

In certain industries, American capital is highly concentrated. This may be seen by examining the size of US ventures as well as their value. Table 5 shows the number of Canadian concerns controlled in the US and the UK, and the average size of investment in particular industries. Except in the textiles, chemical and oil industries, the average US subsidiary is seen to be somewhat larger than its

UK counterpart. Since 1959, the average UK investment has tended to become smaller and the average US investment larger. These figures, however, tell us nothing about the frequency distribution of such firms. A better indication is given by examining the nationality of the six largest enterprises in leading Canadian industries. These data are presented in Table 6. Once again the leading role of US companies is clearly emphasized.

TABLE 6

Output and Country of Control of Six Largest Firms in Selected Canadian Industries, 1959

	Percentage of net Output	*Country of Control*		
		Canada	*US*	*UK*
Petroleum				
(*a*) Crude	68	—	5	1[1]
(*b*) Refining	93	1	3	2
Mining				
(*a*) Nickel-copper	100	3	3	—
(*b*) Lead-zinc	86	4	1	1
(*c*) Copper-gold	88	4	2	—
(*d*) Iron ore	100	3	3	—
(*e*) Aluminium[2]	100	—	1	1
(*f*) Asbestos	94	3	2	1
(*g*) Gypsum	97	2	3	1
Manufacturing				
(*a*) Pulp and paper	46	3	1	2
(*b*) Chemicals				
(i) Fertilizers[3]	92	2	2	1
(ii) Acids	63	1	3	2
(*c*) Electrical apparatus	52	2	4	—
(*d*) Primary iron and steel	84	3	1	2
(*e*) Automobiles	97	6	—	—
(*f*) Rubber goods	77	4	1	1
(*g*) Railway rolling stock	84	2	3	1
(*h*) Primary textiles				
(i) Synthetic fibres[3]	100	3	—	2
(ii) Other	90	6	—	—
(*i*) Agricultural implements[4]	91	2	2	—

[1] An Anglo-Dutch concern. [2] Two firms only. [3] Five firms only. [4] Four firms only.

Source: Royal Commission on Canada's Economic Prospects: *Canada/United States Economic Relations*, by I. Brecher and S. S. Reisman (brought up to date where possible).

An examination of the scope of the most important UK investments in Canada shows a wide diversity of interests. In the pulp and paper industry the combined net worth of Bowater Company and Albert Reed in 1965 was more than $200m. with the former company being one of the four most important suppliers of newsprint.[1] Shell-Oil (an Anglo-Dutch concern, 50 per cent of whose capital is owned by the Shell Oil Co. of US and the balance of Royal Dutch Shell in the UK) is the third largest company in the petroleum industry and a leading producer of chemical insecticides and sulphur. Since 1953, the B.P. Group has invested approximately $205m. in exploration, refining and marketing in Canada. B.P. now holds a 62½ per cent interest in Triad Oil Company of Calgary and operates two refineries and a network of 1,750 service stations in Ontario and Quebec. Canadian Industries, a subsidiary of I.C.I. which originated in 1954 as a result of the break-up of an earlier enterprise of the same name jointly owned by I.C.I. and Dupont, and Electric Reduction of Canada (a subsidiary of Albright and Wilson) are primary suppliers of basic chemicals. In the iron and steel and transportation equipment industries, A. V. Roe Canada, both on its own account and through its various subsidiaries, e.g. Dominion Steel and Coal Corporation, controls assets worth more than $280m.

As has already been mentioned, UK firms are strongly represented in the Canadian aircraft industry. De Havilland, Bristol Aeroplane, Rolls Royce, Fairey Aviation and others, have all invested substantial sums of money in one branch of the industry or another. Courtaulds is one of the three leading firms in the man-made fibres industry and Dunlop the fifth largest in the rubber goods industry. Two other UK companies with a multi-million-dollar stake in Canada are Vickers Ltd. which, through a controlling interest in Canadian Vickers, operates ship-building and repairing plants in Quebec, and Tate and Lyle, which in 1955 bought a majority holding in Canada and Dominion Sugar Company and now operates the largest sugar-refining plant in Eastern Canada. In the electrical apparatus industry, Canadian Marconi, which supplies domestic and industrial radio equipment, and John Inglis, which produces a wide range of household appliances and heavy electrical gear, are both controlled by English Electric. Unilever still remains a leading company in the detergent,

[1] Though in the case of Bowater, it should be noted that the Canadian company – the Bowater company of North America – is the 'first-stage' investment for all the parent companies North American operations. A substantial part of the Canadian investment in fact, represents the interests of subsidiary companies in the US.

fats and processed foods fields and over one-half the chocolate and confectionery produced in Canada is supplied by subsidiaries of Cadbury's and Rowntree's. With Rio Tinto and Canadian Aluminium (the latter is a subsidiary of British Aluminium) the companies mentioned in this and the preceding paragraph account for 85 per cent of the total British investment in the manufacturing and extractive industries.

Apart from these companies controlled from the UK, there are a number of important minority holdings in the tobacco, iron and steel and cement industries. Within more specialised branches of Canadian industry, the impact of UK firms is no less marked, although the size of the investment is often much smaller. Such companies,

TABLE 7

Size Structure of UK and US Investments in Canada, 1960

	UK			*US*		
	Number	*Total Invest-ment* ($m.)	*UK Share* ($m.)	*Number*	*Total Invest-ment* ($m.)	*US Share* ($m.)
More than $25m.	7	556	360	92	9,015	6,825
$10m.–$25m.	14	232	160	92	1,441	1,163
$1m.–$10m.	88	240	203	712	2,244	1,992
Under $1m.	308	76	65	2,780	665	569
Totals	417	1,104	788	3,676	13,365	10,549

Source: Dominion Bureau of Statistics.

for example, supply important shares of the confectionery, biscuits, evaporated milk, matches, glass, wallpaper, meat extracts, toys, shoe polish and asbestos products manufactured in Canada. Outside the goods industries, there are important British interests in insurance, real estate and constructional activities.

The great majority of UK investments are much less spectacular both in size and significance. Table 7 reveals that of the 417 Canadian enterprises controlled by UK capital at the end of 1960, 95 per cent owned assets worth less than $10m. and 74 per cent assets less than $1m. The size structure of US investments is broadly similar. At the same time, a good proportion of the larger companies controlled from England operate subsidiaries of their own. Hawker Siddeley's interests in Canada, for example, extend over a score of separate enterprises. In all, there were 419 Canadian concerns in manufacturing directly or indirectly controlled by UK investors at the end of 1964. In addition, there were 89 oil and mining companies, 104 insurance companies, 80 real estate firms, 30 public utilities, 51 other financial institutions, 402 merchandising companies and 225 miscellaneous investments similarly controlled making a grand total of 1,400.

Contrary to the age-profile of UK investments in the US, the greater proportion of British firms in Canada are post-war in origin. As shown in Table 8, at the end of 1945, there were 391 first-stage and 58 second-stage UK investments in Canada. By 1964, these figures had risen to 877 and 523 respectively. The particularly rapid expansion of second-stage investments is explained partly by the purchase by British companies of Canadian concerns already owning more than one subsidiary, and partly by the formation of new companies by existing Canadian affiliates. In the goods industries, the rise in investment has been particularly marked. Seven of the UK largest firms referred to on p. 204 have been acquired since 1945. Between that date and 1964, the value of UK direct investments in Canada rose by 459 per cent. This is a faster rate of growth than UK investment in the US, though well short of that of US and Canadian investment in the UK. Again, unlike the post-war expansion of the US investment in Britain, the greater part of the increase in British investment in Canada has taken the form of new capital flows from Britain. Of the increase in all non-resident investment in Canada between 1946 and 1960, 50 per cent represented capital inflows and the balance reinvested profits and other factors affecting the total value.[1] For the US companies, the proportion of new capital flows was 47 per cent, and for the UK 54 per cent.[2]

In general, most of the sizeable UK investments in Canada in recent years have been initiated by the purchase or part purchase of local enterprises. In 1960, some 37 per cent of the first-stage investments of 175 UK companies involving 64 per cent of total investment, and 31 per cent involving 66 per cent of post-war investments, were of this kind. The balance, comprising newly established enterprises,

[1] For example new issues, retirements, borrowing, investment abroad, etc., and other factors including revaluations, reclassifications and similar accounting adjustments. See Statement 12B (p. 35) of *The Canadian Balance of Payments and International Investment Position*, Dominion Bureau of Statistics, March 1962.

[2] Estimated from Statement 12B referred to above.

TABLE 8

Number and Value of UK Investments in Canada by Broad Industrial Groups 1945/64

<table>
<tr><th></th><th colspan="2">1945</th><th colspan="2">1954</th><th colspan="2">1959</th><th colspan="2">1964</th></tr>
<tr><th></th><th>Number</th><th>Value ($m.)</th><th>Number</th><th>Value ($m.)</th><th>Number</th><th>Value ($m.)</th><th>Number</th><th>Value ($m.)</th></tr>
<tr><td>Manufacturing</td><td>140</td><td>156</td><td>294</td><td>457</td><td>379</td><td>732</td><td>419</td><td>845</td></tr>
<tr><td>Petroleum and natural gas</td><td rowspan="2">13</td><td rowspan="2">22</td><td rowspan="2">22</td><td rowspan="2">20</td><td>26</td><td>116</td><td>37</td><td>390</td></tr>
<tr><td>Mining and smelting</td><td>61</td><td>68</td><td>52</td><td>104</td></tr>
<tr><td>Utilities</td><td>6</td><td>16</td><td>24</td><td>15</td><td>43</td><td>40</td><td>36</td><td>14</td></tr>
<tr><td>Merchandising</td><td>136</td><td>51</td><td>298</td><td>130</td><td>380</td><td>219</td><td>402</td><td>268</td></tr>
<tr><td>Financial institutions</td><td>140</td><td>98</td><td>174</td><td>94</td><td>230</td><td>168</td><td>279</td><td>265</td></tr>
<tr><td>Other</td><td>20</td><td>5</td><td>60</td><td>19</td><td>158</td><td>41</td><td>175</td><td>58</td></tr>
<tr><td></td><td>455</td><td>348</td><td>872</td><td>735</td><td>1,277</td><td>1,384</td><td>1,400</td><td>1,944</td></tr>
<tr><td>Of which first-stage investments</td><td>397</td><td></td><td>712</td><td></td><td>776</td><td></td><td>877</td><td></td></tr>
</table>

Source: Dominion Bureau of Statistics.

were mostly much smaller in size. While the great majority of US controlled companies in Canada are wholly owned subsidiaries, in one out of three British investments there is some local equity participation.

In 1960, this amounted on average to 21·3 per cent in manufacturing, 38·7 per cent in mining and smelting and 20·5 per cent in all industries. The corresponding figures for American controlled firms were 11·0 per cent and 18·2 per cent respectively.[1] Of the total capital controlled by UK firms, 34 per cent was provided locally, 16 per cent of which was equity and 18 per cent loan capital. The corresponding figures of local participation in US firms were 18 per cent, 9 per cent and 9 per cent respectively. Local participation appears to be especially concentrated in the chemical, iron and steel, and non-ferrous metals industries.

In post-war years, the British Treasury has particularly favoured those applications for dollars to invest in Canada, where it is expected that a substantial part of the loan capital will be raised locally. Figures from the Dominion Bureau of Statistics reveal that $1,331m. of the $1,944m. of direct investments of British firms in 1964 comprised capital stock and surpluses, and the balance debentures or other long-term investments[2]. The financial structure of US investment in Canada is much the same. However, there are more important differences between individual industries. Those which are new, fast growing and/or capital-intensive, e.g. petroleum refining, aluminium and uranium extraction, pulp and paper, etc., have raised considerably more local debt capital than the older, and less rapidly expanding trades. As regards portfolio investments, in 1964, apart from $111m. of UK capital invested in Government and municipal bonds, $394m. was directed to bonds and debentures in business enterprises (of which Canadian Railways accounted for $257m.) while $754m. consisted of capital stock. Up to 1959, there was a noticeable swing by UK investors away from Government or semi-official debt to industrial equities, but in the last five years these have also declined in value.[3]

Some 70 per cent of the UK controlled manufacturing establishments were located in Ontario and Quebec in 1961 and these were responsible for 83 per cent of total manufacturing sales. The Atlantic

[1] *Canadian Balance of Payments 1961 and 1962*, August 1964, particularly Statement 35, pp. 85–6.

[2] Taking into account local participation of both equity and debt capital, the total net assets controlled by UK firms in 1964 was close on $2,500m.

[3] Partly due to the UK Government's sales of some of its dollar securities.

Provinces accounted for 9 per cent of all factories and the Prairie Provinces and British Columbia the balance. The geographical pattern of US investment was broadly similar, though somewhat more concentrated in Western Canada.[1]

Managerial structure

Financial and managerial control are by no means synonymous. It is quite possible for the majority of the equity of a company to be held by a foreign investor, but for policy formulation and decision-taking to be largely management. The reverse may equally be true. Much depends upon the basic philosophy of the investing company towards its overseas operations, and the extent to which these are interwoven with the policy and programmes of the group as a whole.

Among the variables which have been suggested as possible determinants of the allocation of decision-taking responsibility between parent and subsidiary enterprises, we might mention: the nature and range of the products supplied, the extent to which production and/or marketing sales methods are familiar to local skills and experience, the age and size of the subsidiary (*vis-à-vis* its parent), the extent of foreign ownership, the personalities of the leading decision-takers, whether or not the subsidiary is part of an international network, the prosperity of the subsidiary, environmental factors in the country of operation, and the nationality of the parent company.[2] The extent and character of control exercised by the parent company will also vary according to the area of decision-taking; it may be considerable, for example, in the field of financial decision-taking and export policies, but negligible in personnel and production planning.

There are various ways in which the extent of control exercised by the parent company may be assessed. One index frequently used is the proportion of local nationals on its Board of Directors. In sixty of the 120 UK firms which gave information on this point in a 1961 analysis, North American directors outnumbered UK directors: in sixteen cases, the two nationalities were equally represented and

[1] For full details, see Statement 76 (pp. 94–5) of *The Canadian Balance of International Payments*, 1963, 1964, 1965, Dominion Bureau of Statistics 1967.

[2] The literature is quite extensive on this subject. See particularly E. Barlow, *Management of foreign manufacturing subsidiaries*, Cambridge (Mass.), 1953; E. B. Lovell, *Managing foreign-based corporations*, New York, 1963; J. B. Fayerweather, *Management of international operations*, New York, 1960.

in forty-four cases there were more British than Canadian directors. This would suggest a reasonable degree of local participation at Board level – far more so than in US controlled firms. In only four enterprises were there no Canadian nationals on the Board and in seven there were no British. As might be expected, the composition of the subsidiary's Board of Directors varies slightly with the age and size of firm, the share of UK ownership and the type of industry. The proportion of non-resident directors falls as the age of the firm increases and share of UK ownership increases; Canadian directors are slightly more frequent on the Boards of larger firms but this may be due to the fact that a higher proportion of such firms originated by the purchase or part-purchase of a Canadian company, which tends to be more fully represented with local management.

Insofar as the Managing Director (or President) of the foreign subsidiary is the key link between the Board of Directors of the parent company (of which he may or may not be a member), and the day-to-day management of the subsidiary, and can shape the local board's decision-taking more than any other member, his nationality and relationship with the parent company is often of crucial importance. While it does not necessarily follow that a UK Managing Director will administer and control the subsidiary more on the lines of the UK parent than would a Canadian national, in practice this would seem to be the case. However, where there is an inadequate supply of local talent or experience available, the UK subsidiary may have no alternative but to appoint a non-resident as chief executive. Many years elapse before local men of sufficient expertise and experience are available. Until comparatively recently, the senior executives of UK subsidiaries in the Canadian rubber tyre and motor vehicles industries, both of which are more than 90 per cent controlled by non-residents, were entirely US or British.

Apart from where it is company policy to appoint a UK chief executive or it is desirable for other special reasons, a Canadian national is usually preferred as first choice once the subsidiary has become firmly established. Some sixty-four of the 120 companies in our analysis were controlled by a Canadian Managing Director and fifty-six by British. As one would expect, the presence of UK Managing Directors is strongly correlated with the size of the UK shareholding, and is more pronounced in the case of newly established subsidiaries than with 'take-over' investments.

In fifty-four of the 120 firms in the sample (45 per cent) UK citizens were also employed in other senior executive positions. Table 9 gives particulars of the main avenues of employment for each personnel. The figures in the left-hand column represent the number of subsidiaries employing UK executives in the capacity stated, not the actual number of UK executives employed in those capacities. In seven companies each of these departments was headed by a UK national; otherwise such personnel (usually recruited from within the parent company's organization) were most frequently found either in an administrative or technological capacity. By contrast,

TABLE 9

Proportion of Canadian Firms Employing UK Nationals in Senior Management Positions

	Firms Employing UK Citizens	*Percentage of all Firms*
Managerial policy and administration	35	29·2
Finance and capital expenditure	21	17·5
Product innovation and development	22	18·3
Production planning and budgetary control	19	15·8
Plant supervision and manufacturing	34	28·3
Personnel	15	12·5
Sales and Marketing	24	20·0

Source: Survey conducted by author 1961/62.

the personnel department, where an appreciation of local conditions and procedures is so important, is headed in seven cases out of eight by a Canadian; for the same reason, one might have expected fewer Britishers to be responsible for sales and marketing. However, where the product being sold is either completely new to the Canadian economy or highly technical and/or requires after-sales servicing, there is often insufficient local expertise or experience to draw upon. Most consumer goods firms, on the other hand, are headed by a Canadian sales director.

Suffice to point out here that UK control over decision taking – in the sense that the subsidiary has to consult the parent company on such decisions – is strongest in the fields of general managerial policy, capital expenditure, production methods and export policy, and least in personnel policy and marketing methods. A number of UK firms operate close liaison with their Canadian subsidiaries without exerting any control. In others, there is a Central Co-ordinating Committee on both sides of the Atlantic through which all important policy questions are channelled. Thus rather than consultation between departments, i.e. between production managers, all matters of Anglo-Canadian interest are dealt with centrally. In general, however, the extent of control exercised by the parent company is considerably less than in the case of US investment in the UK. The dependence of subsidiaries on the expertise and judgement of the parent company tends to be greatest where control is most pronounced.

Productivity, costs and exports

Of the 185 Canadian subsidiaries analysed in our 1961 study, about one-half produced products sufficiently similar to those produced by their UK associates to allow reasonable productivity and cost comparisons to be made, though in only 10 per cent of cases were the products absolutely identical. Most confectionery and biscuit subsidiaries, for example, manufacture the 'bread and butter' lines in their Canadian plants and import specialities from their parent companies: items of electrical equipment supplied to UK specifications require modifications due to Canadian voltage differences; the availability and price of particular raw materials, and the idiosyncrasies of the Canadian market also govern the character of the end-products supplied. In some instances, the products supplied in the two countries are completely different. Apart from oil refining, all the resource exploitation investments fall into this category and some of the acquired manufacturing investments as well. Moreover, since the majority of UK parent companies are older and considerably larger than their Canadian counterparts, their production is usually more vertically integrated. Some of the more recently established UK manufacturing subsidiaries are little more than assembling units. Such differences in product content and range, and production processes make meaningful comparisons of productivity and costs difficult to make: our own analysis inevitably suffers from these limitations, and the data we present in Table 10 and 11 must be treated with some caution.

Some sixty-one (42·7 per cent) of 143 firms giving information on this point considered that where a comparable product, or range of products, was produced in both the UK and Canadian factories, the manufacturing methods employed were identical or near identical; seventy-six (53·1 per cent) stated that the methods were basically the same but that marginal adjustments to factor-mix or scale of production were necessary and six (4·2 per cent), that quite different manufacturing methods were used. It is interesting to compare these proportions with those applicable to US subsidiaries operating in the

UK – 14·1 per cent, 70·3 per cent and 15·6 per cent respectively.[1] Whether this means that US subsidiaries are better able to adapt their production methods to the economic environment of the country in which they are operating than UK subsidiaries, or there is less need for such adaptation in the latter than in the former case, or that, assuming the character of manufacturing methods is partly a function of the extent of parental control and that UK subsidiaries in Canada are more subject to such influence than US subsidiaries in Britain, it is difficult to say. Certainly the extent of parental control appears to influence operating methods to some degree at least.

Unfortunately, very few UK subsidiaries in Canada make detailed studies of Anglo-Canadian productivity or production costs, partly due to the difficulties involved and partly to a widespread scepticism of the practical usefulness of such measures. Some ninety-nine firms in our sample were, however, able to give some idea of physical output per head and production costs in Canada and the UK, and the results are presented in Table 10. The data relate to some 120 products which are produced in both countries in 1959/60 by the same, or very similar, methods of production. No cardinal measure of productivity was requested, but a range of Canadian production costs, relative to UK costs, was specified and the subsidiaries were asked to indicate which was the most appropriate for their particular operations. In the accompanying table we have cross-classified productivity (physical output per man-year) with unit production costs (ex-factory). As can be seen, differences in the former appear to be little more than marginal in the great majority of cases, while production costs in Canada are at least 5 per cent more than those in the UK in three-quarters of the sample. One interesting feature of these comparisons is that they show the affiliates of UK firms in Canada in a less favourable light (*vis-à-vis* their parent companies) than those in the US,[2] largely, one suspects, because the under-utilization of plant is so much more pronounced in the former case. Indeed, apart from the additional labour charges, the high excess capacity is, perhaps, the main reason for the unfavourable production costs. When questioned on this point, no less than seven out of ten UK firms operating in Canada mentioned that the burden of plant and administrative overheads was considerably greater in that country than in the UK. In addition, lack of experience, higher transport

[1] J. H. Dunning, *American Investment in British manufacturing industry*, Allen & Unwin, 1958, p. 150.

[2] See Chapter 6, p. 250.

TABLE 10

Anglo-Canadian Productivity and Cost Comparisons 1959/60

		Productivity in Canada Compared with UK					
		Considerably Higher	*Slightly Higher*	*About the Same*	*Slightly Lower*	*Considerably Lower*	*Total*
	50–74	1	—	—	—	—	1
	75–94	1	2	2	—	—	5
	95–104	1	5	5	3	—	14
Production	105–124	4	8	17	4	—	33
costs in	125–149	1	6	8	5	2	22
Canada	150–199	—	1	16	2	—	19
(UK = 100)	200 and over	—	1	2	—	2	5
	Totals	8	23	50	14	4	99

Source: Data provided to author by individual firms.

and depreciation costs, lower volumes of output making for sub-optimum scales of plant – all these, and others, were cited as reasons for lower productivity and higher costs in Canada: only in a few cases were these considerations outweighed by the benefits of cheaper raw materials and power, and more intensive mechanization induced by higher labour costs.

We now turn to examine some of the possible reasons for the differences in productivity tests revealed in Table 10.

1. *Size of market*

Coupled with data on productivity, some thirty-five firms also gave particulars of the relative volumes of output of ninety-five products supplied by their Canadian and UK plants. In only seven cases was the output more or less the same in the Canadian plant, in eight cases between 50 and 99 per cent, in twenty-three cases between 25 and 49 per cent, in thirty-five cases between 10 and 24 per cent and in twenty-two cases below 10 per cent; the UK/Canadian output ratio was varied from 15:1 to 400:1. A cross-classification between volume and productivity ratios shows little correlation between the two variables; almost as many Canadian subsidiaries, with outputs substantially below their parent company, recorded a higher output per man-year performance than that of their parent company, as recorded a lower productivity. The relationship between volume and costs ratios is a little closer but still inconclusive. Our analysis appears to give only limited support to the widely held thesis that size conveys important productivity gains or savings in costs, although this was certainly one of the most frequent explanations cited for lower productivity or higher costs in Canada by UK businessmen; moreover, the 1960 study of the National Industrial Conference Board into the experiences of US subsidiaries abroad also found that lower costs '. . . were more frequently associated with the relatively larger foreign operations than with smaller activities abroad'[1] and 'where the foreign plant in relatively much smaller, the likelihood is that its costs are more frequently above domestic levels.'[2] How far this applies to British firms operating in Canada may be seen by comparing the structure of relative costs in US and UK enterprises in that country. Whereas, in only 4 per cent of cases could products be manufactured more cheaply in

[1] *Costs and Competition: American Experience Abroad*, p. 127.
[2] *op. cit.*, p. 130.

Canada than in the UK, 17 per cent of the products studied by the Conference Board were produced in Canada at a lower cost than in the US. Some 86 per cent of the products in our sample cost more to produce in Canada than in the UK, compared with 67 per cent in US firms.

There are two other ways in which market size and structure may effect productivity. One concerns the comparative size of UK firms in Canada, *vis-à-vis* other firms; the other the proportion of capacity operated by parent and subsidiary plants. We have already seen that apart from the score or so largest companies, the average size (in terms of assets employed) of UK subsidiaries in Canada is generally smaller than that of US subsidiaries and about the same as Canadian companies. In some industries, e.g. the industrial machinery and electrical equipment trades, these size differences operate to the detriment of UK efficiency: there is evidence of considerable under-utilization of capital. Equally, if not more important, the fact that the parent companies of US subsidiaries are often so much larger than those of UK subsidiaries means that important economies of finance and risk which arise from size are often available to, and adopted with profit by, the smaller Canadian companies. In general, *ceteris paribus*, the larger the parent company, the better able it is to finance, and bear the risks of, a given size of investment. A \$10m. investment to a firm with assets of \$500m. can be undertaken with less risk to shareholders' profits than the same investment of a firm with assets of only \$50m. Such considerations as these may, in part, explain why UK firms have not achieved a larger *share* of the Canadian market and grown larger *vis-à-vis* their parent companies.

2. *Different factor-mix*

Second, labour productivity is a function of the way in which factor inputs are co-ordinated. Other things being equal, the more capital is used per unit of labour to produce a given output, the higher labour productivity will be. In turn, the composition of the factor-mix reflects the structure of factor prices, and the expertise and organizing efficiency of management.

In some industries, particularly the processing industries, manufacturing methods are often inflexible and independent of the level of output and structure of factor prices; in others, e.g. most kinds of engineering and metal production, there is scope for adjustments to factor-mix. Of the reasons given by the companies in our sample for their higher labour productivity in Canada, the greater capital intensity induced by the higher labour/capital price ratio in that country was amongst the most important in only one in twelve cases, but these included firms in the heavy electrical equipment, rubber products, man-made fibres, and pulp and paper industries. On the other hand, there was a widespread tendency of UK subsidiaries to pay more attention to labour economies than material economies.

3. *Differences in technical knowledge and managerial efficiency*
The third, and perhaps most important, reason for possible differences in the productivity of firms falls under the general heading of knowledge and managerial efficiency. Even when the market characteristics and structure of input prices facing firms are identical, one may still record a higher productivity than the other. This is because the more productive firm is either (*a*) a possessor of superior knowledge or (*b*) more efficient in its factor use.

In the case of parent and branch enterprises where knowledge is freely communicated, it might be supposed that any differences in productivity under this heading must be largely due to differences in managerial efficiency. However, the fact that UK subsidiaries in Canada operate in a more advanced technological and economic environment than the investing companies means that additional knowledge is sometimes available to the subsidiary, the application of which may result in its labour productivity rising relative to that of the parent plant. Moreover, plants differ in age, and since each new factory built is usually equipped with the latest machinery and equipment, their productivity will naturally differ. One of the reasons most frequently claimed by UK subsidiaries in Canada for their higher productivity is that the design and layout of their plant and the technological efficiency of their equipment is superior to that of the parent company, simply because they are newer. This was particularly evident in such trades as biscuit making, cosmetics, plastic containers, paints, tinned milk, paper, aircraft, oil refining and man-made fibres. In the Canadian rubber tyres industry, a saving in material costs was effected by the more advanced techniques in the production of tyres from reclaimed rubber. In all, one firm in four gave 'more advanced technology' or 'better plant layout and machine deployment' as incorporated in a newer factory as the chief reason for their higher productivity in Canada. On the other hand, lack of certain types of skill and knowledge in Canada explain why other factories record a lower productivity.

4. *The efficiency of individual factor inputs*

(*a*) *Labour*. Of the fifty firms citing reasons for differences in their Anglo-Canadian productivity, twenty-four claimed that labour was more efficient in Canada, and three that it was more efficient in the UK. More specifically, the following components of labour efficiency were observed, according to whether they favoured the Canadian or UK firms.

TABLE 11

Differences in Labour Efficiency in Canadian and UK Plants, 1959/60

	Favouring Canadian Plant	*Favouring UK Plant*
Labour efficiency (general)	4	0
Trade union difficulties, restrictive practices or other labour problems	12	0
Labour turnover and time spent in training	5	2
Labour absenteeism	6	2
Attitude of labour towards incentives and work	15	0
Quality of supervisory labour.	2	4
Quality of non-supervisory labour	0	2
Experience	0	6
Total	44	16

Source: Data provided to author by individual firms.

Although the evidence is very scant, and the majority of UK firms in Canada did not even mention this factor as being an important cause of productivity differences, labour efficiency would seem to be slightly higher in Canada than in the UK. This does not necessarily mean that the industrial UK worker is less productive than his Canadian counterpart. Labour turnover and absenteeism, trade-union difficulties and the attitude to incentives and work are as much a function of the general environment as the intelligence, effort and co-operation of the individual worker. The higher unemployment experienced in Canada than in the UK for most of the post-war period has tended to discourage both labour absenteeism and labour turnover, while the impetus to work efficiently has probably raised personnel output. There appear to be fewer union difficulties in Canada: although every two or three years, labour contracts are negotiated and bitter disputes may occur, in the intervening period, co-operation between labour and management, e.g. as regards the introduction of new machinery processes, etc., is much better than in the UK. Again, the average Canadian responds well to incentives as he seems more anxious to raise his living standards than his UK counterpart. On the other hand, there is no evidence to suggest that once trained and experienced there is much difference in the basic quality of UK and Canadian workers and supervisors – if anything, the UK worker has the slight advantage in this respect.

(*b*) *Materials*. The material content of any particular product will differ according to the price structure and availability of the alternatives which could be used. Nowhere does this apply more than in the sphere of raw and semi-processed materials, the supply conditions of which vary so markedly between countries. Products made of steel in one country may more cheaply be made of aluminium in another; where locally produced timber is plentifully available, plastic substitutes may be used less; natural-based rubber may be the preferred choice in one country – synthetic rubber in the other; it may be economic to purchase nylon thread for industrial uses in one case and rayon thread in another, and so on. Sometimes the choice of material affects the speed and efficiency of the production process and/or the quality of the end product. One in ten firms in our sample claimed that the better quality raw materials available in Canada raised productivity by reducing the amount of machinery or processing time. Both tube and sheet steel were better finished and of a superior quality, requiring less polishing or buffing; Canadian ceramic materials require only one firing compared with two which is common practice in England.

5. *The efficiency of the allocation of factor inputs*

Differences in efficiency in this respect reflect the quality of management and its attitude towards cost minimization and productivity maximization. There is no clear evidence that the nationality of the president or managing director of the Canadian subsidiary substantially affects productivity in UK subsidiaries one way or the other. It would, however, seem that the impetus to operate at optimum efficiency is more pronounced in Canada than in the UK due to the intensity of competition and urgency to keep costs down. The market is less protected than in Britain; some firms which enjoy a monopoly or near-monopoly position in the UK (and often the profits which go with it) find they are faced with the fiercest competition in Canada, and are forced to be more cost and efficiency conscious than they might otherwise have been.

Few companies were prepared to offer any comments on the managerial efficiency of their subsidiary companies. Only one firm commented that 'management in Canada was inefficient from top to bottom', while another argued that the Canadian plant was treated by the parent company 'as a convenience, only requiring it to produce that which the parent company could not or would not produce'. The relationship between managerial efficiency and profitability is further taken up in Chapter 9.

The small Canadian market and its disappointing rate of growth in recent years has naturally induced firms to look elsewhere for outlets in which to expand and, in particular, to the US. In this respect, several UK subsidiaries have been extremely successful, exporting to America from Canada rather than the UK, partly because the product manufactured by the Canadian firm has certain advantageous features over its UK counterpart, and partly because it can be supplied at a lower price. In general, however, exports of such companies from Canada are small and no attempt is made to compete with the parent enterprise in other markets than the US. Six out of ten subsidiaries exported nothing at all in 1960 and only one in ten exported more than 10 per cent of its output. Manufacturing exports of Canadian subsidiaries of US firms are equally small, much to the concern of some Canadians who regard the control exercised by the parent companies in this direction as too high a price to pay for the capital and knowledge made available.

The performance of U.K. firms in Canada

A survey undertaken by the Dominion Bureau of Statistics, covering 1961, extracted some interesting data on the performance of foreign-owned enterprises in Canada. Some of this data are presented in Tables 12 and 13. Table 13 reveals that Canadian industry, as a whole, US subsidiaries record a higher output per head and wages per employee than both UK-owned all-Canadian enterprises, and that other foreign enterprises do almost as well. These differences are partly explained by the much higher investment per employee in US and other foreign enterprises (which in turn reflects the industrial composition of such investment) and partly by the fact that, relative to Canadian firms at least, they tend to be more concentrated in the larger enterprises where productivity is highest.[1]

[1] The value added per employee in US enterprises with an aggregate investment of $25m. or more was $13,087 in 1961 compared with $10,611 in enterprises with investments of $1 to $25m. The corresponding figures for UK enterprises were $9,877m. and $8,736m. UK Firms with an aggregate investment of more than $1m. employed 6·1 per cent of the employees in all enterprises in Canada, paid out 6·9 per cent, the salaries and wages were responsible for 6·8 per cent of the net output produced and 6·5 per cent of the total sales.

The comparative profitability of US and UK enterprises in Canada since 1960, as shown in Table 1 of the appendix to Chapter 6 confirms the data in Table 12 of this chapter, although it tells us nothing about the reasons for such differences. The size structure of the two groups of firms is broadly similar, but there are some differences in industrial composition. Unfortunately, the official statistics do not give an industrial breakdown of the data contained in Table 12 for British firms. The best one can do is to compare such a breakdown of US firms with that of all other foreign firms, of which the UK component (in terms of investment) is about four-fifths. This is done in Table 13, which shows, first that, in almost every line of activity, US enterprises perform better than UK and other foreign enterprises – and presumably, since the value added per employee, other foreign enterprises is about the same as in US enterprises, considerably better than their UK counterparts[1] – and second that these differences cannot be explained by a higher investment per employee. Indeed, if anything, UK and other foreign enterprises in Canada would appear to be over-capitalized.

TABLE 12

Comparative Performance of Foreign and Canadian Enterprises, 1961

Foreign Enterprises with more than $1m. Investment

	US Controlled	*UK Controlled*	*Other Foreign Countries Controlled*	*All Enterprises in Canada*
Number of establishments	1,104	289	71	32,415
Total employees	284,444	77,163	10,826	1,264,946
Average number of employees per establishment	258	267	153	39
Value added per employer	11,999	9,406	11,904	8,445
Sales per employee	27,758	20,329	30,212	19,165
Aggregate investment per employee	18,600	14,500	40,300	9,700

Source: *The Canadian Balance of Payments 1963, 1964 and 1965 and Internationa Investment Position*, p. 91, 1967.

[1] The net output less salaries and wages/investment ratio – is intended to be a very rough proxy for the rate of return on capital, gross of tax and depreciation. Since, however, these are all exceptionally high profitability ratios one suspects there are other components of net output (value added) apart from employee compensation and the return of capital not specified in the DBS Statement.

The results of British direct investment in Canada since 1945 have been very disappointing, although they have improved slightly in recent years. Our own analysis shows that, expressed as a proportion of their net worth, the average profits (net of tax) earned by British-controlled companies engaged in the Canadian goods industries over the five-year period 1955/56 to 1959/60 was 4·9 per cent.[1] For manufacturing investments alone the ratio was 6·8 per cent and for mining investments – 0·5 per cent. These rates of return take into consideration the net losses made by public companies over the period but not those of private companies. In this latter case, returns are treated as zero. Companies set up since 1957 are not included in the sample; neither are companies which ceased production or sold out to local (or US) interests before 1959. This means that the proportion of one in four companies which actually recorded a net loss over the five-year period is almost certainly an underestimate of the total number of unprofitable British companies.[2]

How do these profit ratios compare with those earned by Canadian industry in general and by American capital in particular? As regards the former, three sources of data are available. For manufacturing industry, the Canadian Manufacturers' Association undertake a yearly survey of the financial results of 1,000 or so Canadian companies of various sizes and industrial spread, on the basis of information provided by individual firms. For the period of 1955/60 profits averaged 8·1 per cent of net worth. Second, since 1957, the Canadian Bank of Commerce has published selected corporate ratios, derived from taxation returns, and covering all companies with total assets of $500,000 or more, or annual profits of $25,000.[3] For the three-year period 1957/59 the ratio of profits to net worth averaged 10·4 per cent for manufacturing industry, 5·9 per cent for mining (including petroleum) and 8·6 per cent for all goods industries. The corresponding ratios expressed as a proportion of net assets were 9·7 per cent, 5·7 per cent and 8·1 per cent respectively. Third, the annual examination by the *Financial Post* of the financial returns of leading public companies shows that the ratio of profits to net

[1] For further details see Chapter 6.

[2] Elsewhere, viz. Chapter 2 and particularly Table 2.7, we have shown that except in France, of all countries in which substantial sums of UK capital have been invested, Canada has yielded the lowest rate of return in the period 1955/64. The combined rate of return ($\bar{r}_{fp}$) works out at 7·1 per cent, well below the average of 13·2 per cent.

[3] Companies recording losses are thus excluded from this analysis.

TABLE 13

Comparative Performance of Selected US-controlled Enterprise and Other Foreign-controlled Enterprises in Canadian Industry, 1961

	Net Output / *Employees* $		*Salaries and Wages* / *Employees* $		*Net Output-Salaries and Wages* / *Aggregate Investment* %		*Aggregate Investment* / *Employees* $	
	US	*Other*	*US*	*Other*	*US*	*Other*	*US*	*Other*
Vegetable products	12,706	11,833	4,235	4,089	56·6	45·0	14,971	17,223
Animal products	8,096	15,015	4,281	3,033	39·8	72·7	9,584	16,517
Textiles	7,285	6,381	3,238	3,828	45·4	21·3	8,904	11,996
Wood and paper products	11,384	9,938	5,008	5,014	21·0	16·7	30,421	29,723
Iron products	9,896	6,986	5,145	4,880	35·6	17.5	13,356	12,067
Non-ferrous metals	9,752	7,955	4,925	4,821	20·7	16·0	23,300	19,646
Non-metallic minerals	11,714	12,053	4,548	5,113	33·8	9·3	21,122	74,507
Chemicals and allied products	18,157	15,327	5,027	4,820	48·7	40·7	26,864	25,834
Miscellaneous manufactures	8,983	5,650	4,736	3,736	34·7	25·0	12,249	7,532
Totals	10,906	9,636	4,840	4,669	32·7	25·0	18,590	19,880

Source: Derived from data published in *The Canadian Balance of Payments 1963, 1964 & 1965* and *International Investment Position*, pp. 132/3, 1967.

worth of manufacturing corporations for the period 1955/60 was 9·6 per cent, compared with 9·3 per cent for oil enterprises and 9·4 per cent for all goods industries. Although the coverage of these three sources of data differs slightly, each shows the profit ratios of UK companies in an unfavourable light to those of Canadian industry in general. Table 14 attempts to break down these rates of return according to a number of broad industrial groups.

TABLE 14

Distribution of Profit Ratios* of UK and Canadian Firms by Industries

	UK Firms	*Canadian Firms*	
	Author's Estimate 1955/60	*Financial Post* 1955/60	*Bank of Commerce* 1957/59
Manufacturing			
Iron and steel products	7·3	9·0	11·8
Pulp and paper	7·4	10·9	8·1
Textiles and clothing	8·6	5·4	9·5
Foods and beverages	8·0	9·0	12·1
Chemicals	5·9		11·0
Non-ferrous metals	5·1	12·8	10·9
Other manufacturing industries	2·1		12·0
Total manufacturing	6·8	9·6	10·4
Oil and minerals	−0·5	9·3†	5·9
All goods industries	4·9	9·4	8·6

* Divided by net worth. † Petroleum only.

No detailed analysis has been published of the profitability of American companies in Canada. But the general picture is clear enough. According to statistics published by the US Department of Commerce, the average ratio of profits to net assets of US subsidiaries in the Canadian goods industries between 1955 and 1960 was 7·4 per cent. For manufacturing alone the ratio was 9·5 per cent and for the mining (including petroleum) 4·9 per cent. Unfortunately figures of the net worth of US investments are only available for the year 1957. If, however, one assumes that the ratio of net worth to net assets is the same for all other years as for 1957, the profit ratios would rise to 10·1 per cent, 12·8 per cent and 6·6 per cent respectively. In computing these figures net losses have been taken into consideration. Thus American firms find Canada a more profitable outlet either than British companies or Canadian industry in general.

What is the explanation of the unsatisfactory performance of UK firms in Canada? In part, such firms have suffered with others in the failure of the Canadian economy to maintain a satisfactory rate of expansion for most of the period since 1950, and from intensive foreign (and, in particular, Japanese) competition. It may be said that the resulting fall in profit margins has particularly affected post-war British subsidiaries since most of them arrived late on the Canadian scene in the 1950s, and had hardly become established before the economy lost some of its earlier vitality. A number of special reasons might also be adduced for the low profit ratios earned by British firms as compared with their American and Canadian competitors. British subsidiaries in the aircraft and ancillary industries suffered badly as a result of the switch in Canadian government defence policy mentioned earlier; other post-war UK investments have been of a kind which involve an exceptionally large capital outlay and yield satisfactory profits only after many years, e.g. oil and mineral exploitation; the average age of British firms is generally less than their American or Canadian counterparts; the problems of operating a branch unit from 3,000 miles away and the unfamiliarity with the distinctive features of the Canadian market are obstacles which do not have to be faced by local or US competitors; the cut-throat competition from American subsidiaries, backed by large financial reserves from the parent companies; all these reasons and others have been put forward by UK firms to explain their disappointing performance.

Yet, when all is said and done, the failure of most UK subsidiaries to earn more profits in Canada has been due, first to the inability of such firms to gauge the size, form and future prospects of the Canadian market correctly, and second, to their failure to compete effectively against Canadian and American firms and successfully to assimilate themselves into their local environment. Unfortunately, as we have seen elsewhere[1] the profit experiences of UK firms in Canada are by no means unique; rather are they symptomatic of a wider failure of UK industry to earn good profits overseas. To argue, from the evidence available, that American, or firms of other nationality, are generally more efficient than British firms may be going too far; on the other hand, the consistent failure of UK subsidiaries overseas to earn at least average profits must surely be no small reflection of the competitive ability (or lack of same) of the parent companies themselves. Admittedly, American industralists have had more

[1] See pp. 258–9.

experience of this particular type of overseas investment than the British, but this hardly explains why the former have been so often more successful in adapting themselves to the needs of the local market.

In Canada, this may partly be because the competitive conditions there are so much more like those of the US than those of the UK. Indeed, in their Canadian operations, some British firms have experienced the full force of dynamic competition for the first time since the war. Many have wilted under it; others have fought back and today successfully compete with the best of US and Canadian firms. But in so doing, dramatic changes in managerial procedures and thinking have often been necessitated – particularly in the field of marketing and product innovation. It is not enough for UK firms simply to duplicate their domestic activities in Canada in the belief that since these have proved reasonably successful at home, they will be likewise overseas. There might have been some truth in this way of thinking a century ago when Britain was the leading industrial country in the world, but in most cases it is little more than a fond hope today. Apart from where the products supplied are uniquely British, e.g. Scotch whisky, Wedgwood pottery, etc., thinking has to be completely re-oriented to meet the specific requirements of the country of investment in the light of the best sources of knowledge and techniques available. There is no room for inflexible or backward-looking management in Canada.

For the most of the post-war period – up to 1960 at least – British industry has been faced with a seller's market and variously protected from foreign and, in particular, American competition. Profits have been fairly easy to come by and, in consequence, one of the spurs to efficiency and innovation has been removed. While the more forward-looking firms have invested part of this good fortune in seeking ways and means to raise productivity or developing new or improved products, and in carving for themselves an expanding share in world markets, the others have been content to do little or nothing, making no real attempt to improve production and managerial methods, undertaking little product innovation or market research, and watching the more dynamic development of their overseas competitors with distant interest more than immediate concern. Is it thus surprising that not only Britain's share of world trade in manufactured goods continues to fall but that, when she exports her enterprise and knowledge (in the form of direct investment) to industrialized and toughly competitive markets, she is only partially successful in assimilating herself into the new economic environment and effectively competing against some of the world's most dynamic and efficiency-conscious firms?

Let no one suppose that there are no successful British subsidiaries operating in Canada. A number of subsidiaries regularly earn good profits under very severe competitive conditions. But the parent companies of each made careful appraisals of the market beforehand, examined in detail the competition likely to be faced (and, in the case of a purchase or part-purchase of a Canadian company, its financial status and the ability and reputation of the management and directorate), recognized the need for a complete adaptation of UK marketing methods and other managerial techniques to the situation in hand, accepted at once that British goods will not just sell themselves, were prepared to spend capital on breaking into and exploiting the market, employed the best senior executives that money could buy; in short, did not try to operate the local subsidiary 'on a shoestring', took a realistic look at the long-term prospects of the industry in question, were professional in management, and accepted the need to adapt completely their thinking and policies to the needs of this particular market.

It may be objected that too much emphasis has been placed on profitability as a measure of success of an overseas venture; that there are other considerations to be taken into account. For example, a low rate of return might be considered a reasonable price to pay in order to safeguard the future supplies of an essential raw material; or to increase (or maintain) the sales of the parent company; or to obtain the benefits from an exchange of technical or managerial know-how; or to preserve markets against competitors or other forms of discrimination in favour of indigenous industries. All these may be regarded as possible benefits of overseas investment over and above any profits, interest or fees earned.

There is some force in this argument. A case might be made out that unless British capital was invested in certain Canadian resource industries, e.g. aluminium, pulp and paper, etc., US firms would monopolize output, raise prices, and make it difficult for Britain to obtain supplies at all in time of particular need. Or, alternatively, such investment may be thought worth while if it leads not only to an initial, but a recurrent increase in exports from the investing country. When questioned about their experiences in 1960, some 40 per cent of 150 leading British manufacturing subsidiaries in Canada claimed that their exports of finished products had increased as a direct result of the investment, 44 per cent that exports had been unaffected and only 16 per cent that exports had dwindled. And, of this latter group, a third argued that these would have fallen in any event. In addition, two subsidiaries in five also imported raw materials, parts or semi-finished goods either from their parent companies or from other British firms.

While these latter exports may be expected to fall as the local companies become more self-sufficient, exports of the former kind are likely to be of more lasting significance. The usual case is where the local company produces a limited range of its parent plant's products and acts as a selling (and publicity) agent for the rest which it pays to import rather than to produce locally. This has not only been important in advancing UK exports of certain consumer goods, e.g. confectionery, biscuits, toys, textiles, etc., but also capital goods. When tendering for contracts a locally established manufacturer is likely to be more successful than a foreign company, even if a good proportion of the product has to be imported. For example, several UK electrical equipment subsidiaries have gained important orders by being on the spot in Canada, which have led to an increase in exports from their UK parent companies. A number of UK subsidiaries also act as agents or manufacture under licence for other UK firms (and some for US firms). As regards initial capital equipment, little appears to have been imported from Britain; Canadian industry can supply most of what is required and the US is on the doorstep.[1]

The technical benefits derived from investment in a more advanced industrial nation are not easily measured.[2] Nevertheless they are often significant. The Canadian economic environment is very similar to that of the US in many ways. The easy access to and better communications with the US enable UK subsidiaries in Canada to keep more abreast of the latest technical developments than their parent plants in England. In addition, the vigour of competition from, and the dynamic attitude to growth of, US manufacturers is more directly experienced; this forces UK firms to be of the highest possible efficiency and to be bold and imaginative in product innovation. Since, however, most research and development undertaken is in the UK, it follows that ideas and knowledge which originate

[1] Since this essay was first written, both the interim and final exports of W. B. Reddaway have been published. As shown in Chapter 3, Reddaway has estimated that in the period 1955/64 only \$4 of every additional \$100 invested by UK firms in Canada was spent on UK capital exports (compared with that which imports have been bought by a non-UK firm investing this amount). The effect on the exports of input items and finished goods was equally unimpressive, working out at only ½ per cent of the net operating assets of UK firms in Canada.

[2] But see Chapter 2, pp. 60–61.

from the Canadian subsidiary can often be developed and applied to the benefit of the parent company. In other cases, the intensity of Canadian competition has forced new cost-reducing techniques to be devised, which have since been successfully adopted by the parent company. Another substantial benefit derived from the experiences of Canadian subsidiaries has been in the field of marketing and selling techniques, particularly in respect of consumer goods products.

At the same time, the system by which such knowledge is exchanged between parent and subsidiary is often extremely poor: up to 1962 at any rate few UK firms made the best use of their Canadian experiences. In many instances, the parent company seems too proud to learn from its subsidiary, or indeed, accept that there is anything that the differences in the UK and Canadian economies automatically preclude any sensible comparisons of productivity, cost or manufacturing methods being made. Too often it is argued that nothing of value can be learned from marketing or selling methods, or that product innovations, however successful they may be in Canada, will 'just not go down well in this country'. But perhaps the most disturbing feature of all is the positive lack of interest which some UK companies display in their subsidiaries, once established. There is little or no attempt to understand, or even appreciate each other's problems, exchange ideas or personnel or engage in regular visits. Local managerial autonomy and close liaison of men and ideas seems to be regarded as mutually exclusive aims. The result is either a complete independence of policy between parent and branch ('as long as the subsidiary makes a reasonable profit we're quite happy not to interfere in any way' typifies this attitude) or an excessively rigid and detailed control exercised from the UK. A happy blending of these two extremes in approach is rarely achieved though, in recent years, an increasing number of British companies have been forced to re-examine the structure and organization of their Canadian ventures.[1]

In summary then – the post-war experience of British firms has not been as successful either as was hoped or as it might be. In 1961, some 45 per cent of all UK firms in the goods industries producing in Canada expressed the opinion that their investment has not come

[1] Again there is evidence that the criticisms expressed in this paragraph were less relevant in 1968 than in 1962. Latest Board of Trade figures (for 1965) reveal that the rate of return earned on UK direct investment in Canada (apart from petroleum, insurance and banking investments) averaged 6·4 per cent compared with 4·3 per cent in 1960. See *Board of Trade Journal*, 26/1/68.

up to their expectations. The proportion among post-war-established firms was even higher (59 per cent). Many companies have had to spend much more money on breaking into the Canadian market than they originally planned and the usual length of time before any profit is made is 4 to 5 years and a 'reasonable' profit (defined according to the firm's criterion) 6 to 7 years. Mistakes and teething troubles have been more numerous than with other overseas markets. The rate of failures has been high. The inter-war comment of the *Financial Post* relating to the blundering Englishman seems to have re-echoed down the years. When one also recalls the loss of tax revenue inherent in such investment, the fact that such capital exports have often been paid for in the form of valuable currency reserves (hence reducing the manoeuvrability of the UK economy in its bid for growth), and that the resources (or claims to resources) had they been wisely invested at home would have helped to raise industrial productivity above the level achieved, one perhaps may be forgiven for wondering whether the journey of many UK firms to Canada in recent years were really necessary (or indeed, desirable)! On the other hand, this judgement may be premature: who knows – in future years, Canada may be a very valuable source of invisible earnings to the UK.

REFERENCES

H. G. Aitken. *American Capital and Canadian Resources*, Harvard University Press (Mass.), 1961.

H. G. Aitken (ed.). *The American Economic Impact on Canada*, Duke University Press, Durham, N.C., 1959.

R. J. Ball. 'Capital imports and economic development,' *Kyklos*, Vol. XV, 1962.

Benjamin Barg. *A Study of United States Control in Canadian Secondary Industry*, unpublished Ph.D. thesis, Columbia University, 1960.

R. N. Beattie. *Some Aspect of British Investment in North America 1850/64*, unpublished M.A. thesis, University of Toronto, 1946.

I. Brecher. *Capital Flows between Canada and the United States*, Canadian-American Committee, Montreal, 1965.

I. Brecher and S. S. Reisman. *Canada – United States Economic Relations*, Royal Commission on Canada's economic prospects, Ottawa, 1957.

A. W. Currie. 'Canadian attitudes toward outside investors,' *The Canadian Banker*, Vol. 68, No. 1 (Spring 1961), pp. 22–35.

T. R. Gates and F. Linden. *Costs and Competition: American Experience Abroad*, The National Industrial Conference Board, 1961.

P. Hartland. 'Private enterprise and international capital,' *The Canadian Journal of Economic and Political Science*, Vol. XIX (1953), p. 70.

H. G. Johnson. *The Canadian Quandary: Economic Problems and Policies*, McGraw-Hill, Toronto, 1963.

F. A. Knox. 'United States capital investments in Canada,' *The American Economic Review*, Vol. XLVII, No. 2 (May, 1957), pp. 596–609.

J. Lindeman and D. Armstrong. *Policies and Practices of United States Subsidiaries in Canada*, Canadian-American Committee, Montreal, 1961.

H. Marshall, F. A. Southard Jr. and K. W. Taylor. *Canadian-American Industry: A Study in International Investment*, Yale University Press, New Haven, 1936.

R. G. Penner. 'The benefits of foreign investment in Canada 1950/56,' *Canadian Journal of Economics*, Vol. XXXII, 1966.

T. E. Pennie. *The Canadian Market for British Exports and Investments 1945/53*, unpublished M.A. (Economics) thesis, University of McGill, 1954.

A. E. Safarian (1964). 'The exports of American-owned enterprises in Canada,' *Papers and Proceedings of the American Economic Association*, Vol. LIX, No. 3 (May 1964), pp. 449–58. Comment by C. P. Kindleberger, pp. 474–77.

A. E. Safarian (1965). ''Foreign ownership and control of Canadian industry,' in Abraham Rotstein (ed.), *The Prospect of Change*, McGraw-Hill, Toronto, 1965.

A. E. Safarian (1966). *Foreign Ownership of Canadian Industry*, McGraw-Hill, 1966.

A. E. Safarian (1968). *The Performance of Foreign-owned Firms in Canada.* (Evidence presented to Watkins Committee.)

J. A. Stovel. *Canada in the World Economy*, Harvard University Press, Cambridge (Mass.), 1959.

J. Viner. *Canada's Balance of International Indebtedness 1900/13*, Harvard University Press, Cambridge (Mass.), 1924.

M. Watkins. 'Foreign ownership and the structure of Canadian industry,' *Report of the task force on the Structure of Canadian industry*, Ottawa, 1968.

6

THE PROFITABILITY OF BRITISH ENTERPRISE IN NORTH AMERICA*

In other chapters of this volume, we have drawn attention to the fact that in several countries of the world where British and American firms compete side by side in the same industry, the profit/capital ratio of the British companies is usually well below (usually between one-half and two-thirds of) the corresponding ratio earned by the American firms. Not only this; British companies also appear to be less successful in their choice of investment outlets than their US counterparts, as the proportion of British capital directed towards the high profit and rapid growth industries is, in general, considerably smaller than that of US capital. Both these phenomena appear to be present in Australia, Canada, the United States, the United Kingdom, India, South Africa and, in most of continental Western Europe as well.[1]

These facts, when originally published, stimulated widespread interest and comment. In general, however, two reactions predominated; first that the figures given were simply added confirmation of the decadence of British industry, and second, that comparisons of this kind were misleading in that there were special circumstances explaining the low profitability of British firms which had nothing to do with such firms' efficiency. The truth lies somewhere in between these two extremes, but at what point it is difficult to say. However, from our study of British firms in both Canada and the United States, certain points have emerged which enable us to evaluate, at least approximately, some of the more important causes of profitability differentials.

Broadly speaking, in our experience, there are three main reasons for the variations in the profit/capital ratios of particular firms of different nationality competing in the same country:

* First published in *Moorgate and Wall Street*, Spring 1963, and slightly amended.

[1] Latest figures (1965) show that in the US and Australia, UK firms are now as profitable as their US competitors. See Appendix to this chapter.

(*a*) differences in the *structure* of investments, e.g. timing, size, industrial and geographical spread and so on;

(*b*) differences in *definition, and managerial attitude* towards investment, e.g. in accounting and taxation procedures (particularly between parent and branch firms), payments made for services such as research and development, the interpretation and valuation of capital, the motivation behind overseas investment and its repercussions on the investing firm or country apart from the money profits earned, e.g. effects on exports, exchange of technical expertise, etc.

(*c*) differences in *managerial judgement, enterprise and efficiency* – which, for our purposes, may be treated as a residual after (*a*) and (*b*) have been taken into account.

This means that, quite apart from the effects of overseas investment on the growth and profits of the investing (as opposed to the invested-in) company, there are a whole range of factors which may influence the rate of return earned on a particular investment, apart from any element of managerial efficiency. Certainly the greater part of the superiority of most American industrial firms (measured in terms of real output per man-year) over their UK counterparts can be explained in terms of unavoidable or non-transferable factors, e.g. resource conditions, size and character of market, different factor-mix (consequent upon a higher labour/capital cost ratio) and so on. But to what extent is this true when comparisons are made of the productivity of American and British firms competing in the *same* country, i.e. where many of the factors accounting for the differences between such firms operating in their own countries no longer apply?

In seeking to answer this and similar questions, we look specifically into some of the possible explanations of the comparative profit structure of UK and domestically financed firms in North America. As can be seen from Table 1, there is a considerable difference between the rates of return earned on British and US direct investment in US industry and British and Canadian capital in Canadian industry. If it were generally the case that foreign-financed firms earned lower profits than their domestic competitors, this, in itself, would be an important reason. But the evidence we have suggests that at least in the UK and Canada, and possibly in India and Australia, the reverse is nearer the truth. Moreover, in cases where foreign firms appear to record lower profits than domestic firms – in the US, for example – it may well be that differences in profitability are due, not to the nationality of their ownership, but to certain structural differences between such firms and domestic companies in regard to such factors as the size and timing of investment.

The method adopted in this article is simple, viz., to relate the data available on the rates of return earned on UK capital in Canada and the US to selected variables which, *a priori*, we consider likely to influence the profitability of an enterprise. It may be that in

TABLE 1

Comparative Rates and Return in US and Canadian Manufacturing Industry, 1955/60

	Net Profits/Net Assets Ratio				
	US		*Canada*		
	UK Firms	*US Firms*	*UK Firms*	*Canadian Firms* (*a*)	*Canadian Firms* (*b*)[1]
Chemicals and allied trades	6·4	15·0	5·9	9·0	11·0
Food and kindred products	8·2	10·5	7·2	9·0	12·1
Iron and steel products / Non-ferrous metals	9·0	10·3	5·1	—	10·9
Textiles and clothing	5·0	6·5	6·4	5·4	9·5
Pulp and paper	7·9	10·6	8·3	10·9	8·1
Other manufacturing	5·2	n.a.	2·7	12·8	12·0
All manufacturing	7·3	11·7	6·6	9·6	10·4

Source: UK firms – author's research.
US firms – First National City Bank of New York.
Canadian firms – (*a*) *Financial Post* (only public companies).
(*b*) Canadian Bank of Commerce (all firms with assets of $500,000 or more or annual profits of at least $25,000).

certain cases the variables examined will prove to be unimportant influences, but even if we discover this, our knowledge is advanced. Also, because our research into British investment in Canada and the US was not originally designed to answer questions of this kind, it is possible that certain important determinants of profitability have been omitted from discussion. Nevertheless, since information on this subject is extremely scarce, we feel that any contribution, however limited, may be of some use to further understanding.[1]

[1] Since this article was first published, the Board of Trade has published some data on the profitability of UK firms overseas, classified by size, industrial structure and date of establishment of investment. See 'Book value of overseas investments,' *Board of Trade Journal*, 26/1/68. We present the relevant tables as an Addendum to this essay.

One point of definition. 'Profitability' is defined in this article as net profits (i.e. distributed plus re-invested profits net of tax) divided by net assets (i.e. total assets minus current liabilities). All values are taken from unadjusted company accounts and no allowance has been made for differences in depreciation procedures or capital revaluation. It is thus quite possible (though in our opinion, unlikely) that part of the explanation for the difference in Anglo-American profits might lie in the interpretation and valuation of balance sheet items. We hope to investigate this point further in a future research project.

The variables, or possible influences on profitability, we have chosen to consider in this article are:

(i) size structure of investment;
(ii) age profile of investment;
(iii) form or origin of investment;
(iv) relationship of the North American (i.e. invested-in) firm with the UK (i.e. investing) company.

In turn, this latter variable, of which managerial efficiency is an important aspect, is discussed under two headings:

(*a*) the extent of UK financial control, and
(*b*) the extent of UK managerial influence exercised over the judgement and decision-taking of the North American company.

1. *Size structure of investment*

One reason commonly suggested for the below-average profitability of UK firms in Canada and the US is that such firms operate at a size disadvantage compared with their domestic competitors. This suggestion is based on the twin assumptions that:

1. profitability is positively correlated with size;
2. the proportion of UK capital concentrated in small firms is higher than that of North American capital.

We take as the criterion of size the net assets of a company. There is some evidence that in North America large firms earn higher rates of return on capital than small firms. Table 2 indicates the average rates of profit for the period 1955/60 for UK and all firms in the US by size of assets.

Two points of interest emerge from this table:

(*a*) that for US industry in general, large firms are decidedly more profitable than small firms, but that there is no clear pattern for UK-financed firms;

(*b*) that in relation to US industry in general, UK firms with assets under \$2·5m. and between \$10m.–\$25m. come out best and those with assets between \$2·5m.–\$10m. worst.[1]

TABLE 2

Profitability of All Firms and UK Firms in US Manufacturing Industry by Size of Net Assets, 1955/60

	Net Profits/Net Assets Ratio	
$	*All Firms*	*UK Firms*
Under 1m.	6·9	8·6
1m.–4·9m.	7·9	7·8
5m.–9·9m.	8·6	4·3
10m.–50m.	9·3	9·0
50m. and over	11·0	8·0
All companies	10·2	7·6

Source: All firms – Federal Trade Commission. UK firms – Author's research (also Tables 3–16).

No data are available on the rates of return earned in Canadian industry by size except those recorded by UK-financed firms. These are given in Table 3, side by side with the rates of return earned by

TABLE 3

Profitability of UK Companies in North American Manufacturing Industry by Size of Net Assets, 1955/60

Net Assets ($)	*Net Profit/Net Assets Ratio*		
	Canada	*US*	*Both Countries*
Under 500,000	4·4	9·8	5·8
500–999,000	4·7	7·3	5·3
1–2·4m.	7·1	10·3	7·6
2·5–4·9m.	7·3	5·2	7·0
5·0–9·9m.	7·4	4·3	6·7
10–24m.	6·5	9·7	7·2
25–49m.	5·4	8·3	7·0
50–99m.	6·6	8·3	7·9
100m. and over	6·3	7·7	7·0
All companies	6·6	7·6	7·1

[1] Since there were only three firms in the \$5 – 9·9m. group (one of which recorded a loss for period 1955/60) the profit/assets ratio of 4·3 per cent should be treated with reserve.

UK firms in the US. It can be seen that, while there is some evidence that firms with very small investments in manufacturing (under the $1m. mark) do less well than firms with medium or large investments, there appear to be no such significant economies of size as are apparent, for example, in US industry.

It should be noted, however, that average losses recorded by UK firms for the period 1955/60 are treated as a zero profit[1] and thus the profit ratio for size groups which include an above-average proportion of unsuccessful firms overstates the true position. We give the proportion of UK firms in Canada and the US making profits and losses classified by four broad size categories in Table 4.

TABLE 4

Proportion of UK Firms in North American Manufacturing Industry Making Profits and Losses, 1955/60[a]

Investment Category	*Canada*		*US*		*Total*	
	Profits	*Losses*	*Profits*	*Losses*	*Profits*	*Losses*
Small (under $1m.)	66·1	33·9	81·0	19·0	69·9	20·1
Small/Medium ($1m.–$4·9m.)	86·4	15·6	91·7	8·3	88·0	12·0
Medium/Large ($5m.–$24·9m.)	80·6	19·4	87·5	12·5	86·2	13·8
Large ($25m. and over)	100·0	0·0	100·0	0·0	100·0	0·0
All firms	77·4	22·6	88·9	10·1	80·4	19·6

[a] Firms engaged entirely in petroleum production and in the extractive industries are excluded from consideration.

Here it is clearly shown that small UK firms in North America, and particularly in Canada, are not only less profitable than the average but are also much more likely to make losses. By and large the successful companies with an investment of less than $1m. are

[1] Although no details of the *size* of losses are available, according to the Board of Trade, 173 UK concerns operating in the United States earned profits and interest of £50·5 millions in 1965 and 49 made losses of £1·9 millions. In Canada, 270 firms recorded profits and interest of £38·7 millions and 62 made losses of £1·7 millions. The proportion of UK enterprises making losses in North America was almost identical with that recorded by other UK foreign investors, viz. 25 per cent. See *Board of Trade Journal*, 30/6/67.

either assemblers of partly finished goods imported from the UK, or are concentrated in those industries in which the size of optimum firm is comparatively small. The dispersion of profit-ratios among firms in the first two groups in Table 4 is also greater than in the second two groups.

It may be argued that global figures of this kind are of little value since we do not know whether the low profitability of UK firms among smaller firms in Canadian (and to a lesser extent US) industry is due to the fact that such firms are in industries subject to the economies of size, or simply that they are less efficient than their competitors in industries not subject to such economies.

TABLE 5

Profitability of UK Firms in North America by Industry and Size of Investment

(Net Profits/Net Assets Ratio)

	Net Assets			
Industry	*Under* $1m.	$1–5m.	$5–25m.	*Over* $25m.
Food, drink and tobacco	7·5	9·3	8·8	8·5
Chemicals and allied trades	3·4	8·0	5·8	8·2
Non-electrical metal products	5·8	6·3	7·4	4·7
Electrical metal products	5·3	2·9	5·1	—
Textiles and clothing	7·6	6·6	9·0	3·9
Wood and paper products	5·5	6·0	12·8	7·5
Other	6·5	5·5	5·6	—
Total	5·6	7·3	7·0	7·0

It would seem that the relationship between the size of a firm and its profitability varies between industries. Table 5 classifies the average profit/capital ratios of UK firms in North America by seven industrial groups and four size categories. While the number of firms in each of the twenty-eight 'cells' is too small to permit any firm conclusions, the data presented suggest that in the chemical and wood and paper industries large firms are certainly more profitable than small firms; that in the non-electrical metal products and food industries this is more likely to be the case than not;[1] and that in the electrical products, textiles and clothing and other goods trades, there is no real

[1] The 4·7 per cent in the over $25m. category represents the profitability of only one enterprise.

evidence of economies of size. UK investment is fairly evenly spread over these three groups in the ratio of 40:35:25.

TABLE 6

Distribution of UK Investment in Canadian and US Industry by Size of Net Assets,[a] 1961

$	*Canadian* Number of Firms	Total Investment $m.	%	*US* Number of Firms	Total Investment $m.	%
Under 500,000	43	8·2	0·8	17	4·4	0·4
500–999,000	36	25·4	2·5	13	8·5	0·7
1–2·4m.	35	54·3	5·4	6	12·1	1·0
2·5–4·9m.	19	65·3	6·4	7	25·6	2·1
5·0–9·9m.	9	65·8	6·5	4	28·9	2·4
10–24m.	11	154·7	15·3	5	67·9	5·7
25–49m.	3	91·0	9·0	6	194·2	16·2
50m. and over	4	548·0	54·1	4	859·0	71·5
	160	1,012·7	100·0	62	1,200·6	100·0

[a] Excluding wholly extractive industries but including companies engaged in petroleum production and refining.

2. Although in terms of *numbers* of firms, the distribution of investment in Canada and the US is strongly concentrated at the lower end of the scale (Table 6 reveals that just under one half of UK firms in Canada and the US control net assets of under $1m.), in terms of *value* of investment the opposite is the case. In the US, for example, the ten largest firms (each of which controls investments worth $25m. or more) account for 87·8 per cent of the total investment in manufacturing industry (including petroleum production and refining): in Canada investment is slightly more dispersed but firms in the two largest investment groups still account for 63·1 per cent of all UK-controlled investment. If anything, as shown in Table 7,

TABLE 7

Percentage Distribution of Investment in US Manufacturing Industry by Size of Net Assets

	$m. *Under* 1*m.*	1–4·9*m.*	5–9·9*m.*	10–24·9*m.*	25–49*m.*	50*m. and over*
All firms	6·1	6·8	3·6	5·8	5·5	72·2
UK firms	1·1	3·1	2·4	5·7	16·2	71·5

UK-financed firms in the US appear to be *more* concentrated in the larger investment groups than US industry in general. When related to the earlier data on profitability, these figures reveal that although the proportion of UK firms recording losses or very low profits in North America (particularly Canada) is quite high, since these firms are most highly concentrated in the smaller investment groups, the effect on the profits earned by all UK companies and hence the overall profit/capital ratio is likely to be quite small. Thus, if all UK firms with investments of over $10m., for example, made at least average profits in North America, then, even if the remaining firms made no profits at all, or even losses, the overall profit/capital ratio would be only slightly affected. As it is, however, the average profitability of UK firms in both Canada and the US is well below that of North American industry as a whole; hence we conclude that the argument which claims that the lack of success of UK enterprise in these countries is mainly or even substantially due to the smallness of their size *vis-à-vis* domestic (or, in the case of Canada, US) competition

(*a*) has little foundation as an explanation of the overall profit/capital ratio of such companies;
(*b*) *may* have some element of truth in explaining the comparatively high failure rate of UK companies.

2. *Age profile of investment*

The profit/capital ratio may also vary according to the age of the investment, age in this instance being defined as the number of years a particular US or Canadian enterprise has been controlled by UK capital. Quite apart from problems of distance and those inherent in investing in a new and sometimes unfamiliar environment, any manufacturing investment (especially one which involves the setting up of a completely new firm) takes time to become profitable; machinery and plant have to be assembled, markets tested and exploited, labour trained and so on. On an average, newly established North American subsidiaries in the post-war period have taken 4/5 years to make any profits and 6/7 years to make a 'reasonable' profit. Moreover, *ceteris paribus*, a firm newly set up with little experience and limited financial resources is likely to find it more difficult to weather the storm in times of economic difficulties than an older, firmly established enterprise more familiar with local conditions.

The questions we now seek to answer in respect of UK investments in North America are:

(i) how far do profit/capital ratios vary according to the age of the firm?

(ii) to what extent is the age profile of investments by UK firms in North America different from that of domestic investments?

TABLE 8

Profitability (1955/60) of UK Enterprises in North American Industry by Age of Investment

Date of Initial Investment	*Net Profits/Net Assets Ratio* Canada	US	Both Countries
Pre-1918	9·3	7·1	7·7
1918/39	8·6	9·4	8·9
1940/50	7·2	5·8	6·9
1951/53	5·2	9·0	5·5
1954/56	3·4	7·6	4·3
1957/59	2·7	6·4	3·4
All years	6·6	7·6	7·0

(i) Table 8 indicates a most marked difference in the profits earned by UK firms in Canada according to the date of the initial British investment. The pattern is much less obvious in the US but here, since the sample of firms considered is much smaller, the results are more subject to error. Combining the series, the overall trend is quite distinct. For firms set up (or bought out) by UK interests in the period up to 1939 (63 in our sample) the average profits earned between 1955 and 1960 were 8·1 per cent. Only two firms in this group recorded net losses over the period. Investments first made between 1940 and 1953 (62 in all) made average profits of 6·8 per cent (the 9 per cent for the US 1951/53 is unrepresentative as the sample comprised only three firms): 15 (or nearly one-quarter of the sample) made net losses over the years 1955/60. Of the 52 firms investing between 1954 and 1959, only 29 or 59 per cent made profits and (counting losses as zero) the overall profit/capital ratio of all firms worked out at 4·5 per cent.

Table 9 shows the age pattern of investment (i.e. it 'weights' the figures given in the previous table). Again, there are interesting differences between Canada and the US, e.g. the age structure of UK investment in the former country is more widely dispersed than that in the latter. Perhaps most significant is that while Canadian subsidiaries set up (or acquired) since 1954 accounted for 38 per cent of the total UK investment in 1961, the corresponding proportion for US subsidiaries is only 14 per cent. On these grounds it would certainly seem that one of the main reasons for the difference in

TABLE 9

Distribution of Total Net Assets Controlled by UK Firms in North American Industry by Age of Investment

Date of Initial Investment	*Canada* $m.	*Canada* Per Cent	*US* $m.	*US* Per Cent	*Both Countries* $m.	*Both Countries* Per Cent
Pre-1918	217·0	16·4	725·0[a]	57·9	942·0	36·6
1918/39	244·3	18·5	310·1	24·8	554·4	21·5
1940/50	280·6	21·2	11·2	0·9	291·8	11·3
1951/53	70·6	5·3	35·2	2·8	105·8	4·1
1954/56	369·7	27·9	130·8	10·5	500·5	19·3
1957/59	142·1	10·7	39·4	3·1	181·5	7·1
All years	1,324·3	100·0	1,251·7	100·0	2,576·0	100·0

[a] Only the UK share in the Shell Oil Company is included.

the profitability of UK investments in the US compared with Canada is the different age profile of such investments.

(ii) To carry this argument farther, more data are required of the age-profile of Canadian and US investments as a whole. Unfortunately, these are not available in a convenient form.

We do know, however, that:

(i) the percentage of the cumulative UK investment stake in Canada to (*a*) Canadian G.N.P. and (*b*) domestic capital formation has grown markedly over the past ten years and that in the US it has remained around constant.

(ii) the rate of increase in the *number* of new UK enterprises in Canada since 1951 has been vastly greater than of domestic enterprises, but that in the US it has been somewhat less.

We then conclude:

(*a*) that it is likely that part of the explanation of the low profitability of UK firms in Canada (but not in the US) is due to their younger age-profile *vis-à-vis* domestic firms. It is not possible to assess the weight of this factor as we do not have a detailed age breakdown of Canadian domestic investments.

(*b*) There is no evidence to suggest that recently established subsidiaries in North America are concentrated in the least profitable industries, though, on the whole, the average size of such investments is smaller than of those controlled by well-established firms. However, size for size, the younger the firm the lower its profit/capital ratio.

3. *Form of investment*

Broadly speaking, a UK investment in North America may be made in one of two ways:

1. a take-over, or partial take-over, of an existing US or Canadian company;
2. the establishment of a new company with or without the participation of local capital.

The method chosen will naturally depend upon the relative cost of acquiring new assets, managerial policy and the expected profitability of the two forms of investment, but the great advantage of a take-over is its 'package deal' character; in addition to plant and equipment one acquires goodwill, an established market and a trained labour force. On the other hand, if the purchasing company wishes its subsidiary to be a carbon copy of its UK parent, or where a completely new type of process or product unfamiliar to the local market is being introduced, a new subsidiary is often chosen as the more desirable vehicle. The choice will also depend upon the reason for the investment, and, in particular, whether the investing company contemplates exercising detailed managerial and technical control or treating its overseas venture simply as a financial investment.

TABLE 10

Profit/Capital Ratios of UK Firms in North American Industry by Origin of Investment (1955/60)

Origin of Investment	*Canada* *Number of Firms*	*Profit Ratio*[1]	*US* *Number of Firms*	*Profit Ratio*	*Both Countries* *Number of Firms*	*Profit Ratio*
(1) Take-over of existing firm	49	7·5	15	7·5	64	7·5
(2) New investment	86	5·2	37	7·4	123	5·8
Both types	135	6·0	52	7·5	187	6·4

[1] Unweighted average of firms in group.

The evidence on this subject as presented in Tables 10 and 11 suggests that, while in Canada the take-over type of investment has fared somewhat better than that which has involved the setting up of completely new companies or extending the interests of existing sales companies, this is not the case in the US: indeed, the proportion of newly formed subsidiaries earning more than 10 per cent is slightly higher than that of take-over companies. In Canada, both the profit/capital ratio and the proportion of profitable firms is lower for new subsidiaries than for taken-over companies. In the US there is little difference, either in the profit ratios or in the proportion of unprofitable firms, between the two types of investment.

TABLE 11

Number of UK Firms in North American Industry by Profit/Capital Ratio Groups and Type of Investment (1955/60)

		Losses	*Under 5%*	*5–9·9%*	*10% and over*	*Total*
Take-over of existing firm	Canada	6	13	19	11	49
	US	3	13	16	13	15
	Both countries	9	16	25	14	64
New investment	Canada	27	20	24	15	86
	US	5	5	17	10	37
	Both countries	32	25	41	25	123
All investment	Canada	33	33	43	16	135
	US	8	8	23	13	52
	Both countries	41	41	66	29	187

When the form of investment is related to the *age* and *size* of investment, it is clear that, in Canada at least, firms which are small, of recent (i.e. post-1950) origin, and which are newly established manufacturing units, have failed more often than any other kind of investment. It is also evident that the time elapsing before any profits are made is usually much longer in the case of new subsidiaries than with take-over investments.

4. *Relationships of the North American (i.e. invested-in) firm with UK (i.e. investing) company*

(*a*) UK *financial control.* To what extent do profit ratios vary with the proportion of capital of the invested-in firm controlled in the

UK? Are firms jointly owned by UK and US or UK and Canadian capital *more* or *less* likely to earn high profits than wholly owned subsidiaries? Here we examine the hypothesis that ownership of capital affects the profitability of a firm, in that firms with a substantial local shareholding are more likely to be autonomous in their policy and decision-taking than firms whose equity is entirely UK owned.

TABLE 12

Profitability of UK Firms in North American Industry by Ownership Patterns

Per cent of Equity held by UK Company	*Canada* *Number of Firms*	*Per Cent*	*US* *Number of Firms*	*Per Cent*	*Both Countries* *Number of Firms*	*Per Cent*
Under 50	7	5·6	5	8·3	12	6·8
51–74	21	7·2	5	8·1	36	7·3
75–99	17	6·4	8	7·5	25	6·8
100*	88	5·1	34	7·7	122	5·9
Total	135	6·6	52	7·6	187	7·0

* Including branches of UK companies.

Table 12 indicates that, in general, wholly owned subsidiaries in North America earn considerably lower profit ratios than jointly financed arms, except for – rather surprisingly – UK firms with minority (albeit substantial) holdings in Canada. Of the 88 firms which are 100 per cent UK subsidiaries in Canada, 22 made losses in the period 1955/60 – a slightly higher proportion than the jointly financed firms (10 out of 44). The corresponding numbers of firms recording losses in the US were 6 of 34 and 2 of 18.

The question now arises as to why such differences should occur? One possibility is that there is less control over decision-taking by the UK associate in the case of Anglo-American subsidiaries. We examine this possibility in the light of the managerial influences exerted by the parent company on the subsidiary.

(*b*) *UK managerial influence*. The data obtained on the comparative managerial techniques exercised by UK subsidiaries in US and Canadian industry sheds some (though, unfortunately, not much) light on the importance of this variable as a possible explanation of Anglo-American profit variations. The hypothesis we seek to test is this. If the inferior quality or lack of dynamism of UK management is one of the main causes of the poor rates of return of UK firms in North American industry, then one might expect that those subsidiaries which are (*a*) strongly controlled by their (UK) parent companies in decision-taking, and (*b*) follow closely their managerial practices and techniques, would earn *lower* profits than subsidiaries which are independent of UK influence and control and which are wholly US or Canadian in thinking and practice. The above interpretation is, of course, only one which could be placed on a particular pattern of subsidiary/parent managerial relationships. Independence could no less reflect a lack of interest and/or weakness of communication of knowledge and ideas between parent and subsidiary. Both of these defects were particularly evident in the experiences of UK enterprises in Canada. Moreover, we are only concerned with the aspects of managerial procedure (*a*) which can, in some sense, be subject to a numerical assessment and (*b*) on which data were obtained in the course of our researches.

We examine our hypothesis by reference to three main sets of profit/capital ratios, each related to a particular aspect of managerial procedure. Where we have computed averages we have taken the *unweighted* profit ratios throughout.

TABLE 13

Profit/Capital Ratios of UK Firms in North American Mamufacturing Industry by Nationality of Management (1955/60)

	Canada	*US*
(*a*) *Nationality of Chief Executive*		
UK	5·6	10·0
Canadian or UK	6·9	6·0
(*b*) *Composition of Board of Directors*		
One half or more UK	5·8	7·7
More than one-half Canadian or UK	6·7	7·0

1. *Nationality of main decision-takers*

(*a*) *The Managing Director or Chief Executive of the local company*

(i) As can be seen from Table 13, in Canada firms with a British chief executive earned slightly lower rates of return on their capital in 1955/60 than those under the control of a Canadian or US managing director.

(ii) In the US, subsidiaries so managed recorded considerably higher profit/capital ratios than those with American chief executives.

(*b*) *Composition of board of directors*

In subsidiaries with one-half or more of the members of the Board of Directors consisting of British nationals (these were usually senior executives of the UK company), the profitability is usually slightly less in Canada and slightly more in the US than in those subsidiaries where the majority of the Board are of Canadian or US nationality.

2. *Control exercised by UK over decision-taking*

Table 14 sets out the profit/capital ratios of UK firms in North America classified by the degree of control exercised over local managerial decision-taking by the parent or investing company. Seven aspects or functions of management have been considered: by 'decisions taken after approval from UK' we mean that all important issues of policy and control and development facing the subsidiary

TABLE 14

Profit/Capital Ratios (1955/60) of UK Firms in North American Industry by Control Exercised by Parent Company

	Major Decisions Undertaken			
	After Approval from UK		*Independently of UK*	
Management Function	*Canada*	*US*	*Canada*	*US*
Overall managerial policy	6·4	7·2	6·0	7·6
Capital expenditure	6·0	7·0	6·4	8·4
Product innovation and development	6·1	8·1	6·5	6·7
Production planning and budgetary control	5·0	7·8	6·6	7·1
Plant supervision and manufacturing methods	4·8	10·2	6·6	6·7
Wages policy and industrial relations	7·6	13·9	6·1	5·7
Marketing policy	6·6	11·4	6·2	5·7

have to be referred back to the UK associate for approval and/or comment. For example, the introduction of new products, methods of marketing, wage payments, and accounting procedures, all items of capital expenditure of over £50,000 or thereabouts; research and development programming; managerial attitudes to profits, growth and risk-taking; policies in respect of inventories, production planning, exports, costing and pricing, office administration and so on – decisions taken on all these matters would normally need parental approval in the case of a subsidiary under the control of the investing company. By 'decisions taken independently of the UK' we imply that the management of the local subsidiary is given much more autonomy and freedom to act as it thinks best in the local circumstances.

Canada. There appears to be a remarkable similarity in the profit/capital ratios earned by the two groups of subsidiaries. Companies which are given autonomy in their production planning and manufacturing methods appear to fare better than those subject to parental influence, while, rather surprisingly, in the field of wages policy and industrial relations subsidiaries more closely controlled in their decision-taking by their UK parents (admittedly only 9 per cent) earn higher profit/capital ratios than those which are autonomous in this field. Taking an average of these ratios, the 'independent' companies record a figure of 6·4 per cent and the 'controlled' companies 6·1 per cent. Clearly the difference is an insignificant one and no conclusions of value can be drawn save that, *from the viewpoint of this particular measure*, there is no evidence to support the hypothesis we are seeking to test.

United States. This conclusion is considerably strengthened when the US profit/capital ratios are examined. Here in 5 cases out of 7, controlled subsidiaries earn a higher rate of return on their capital than autonomous subsidiaries – a situation which hardly lends support to the argument that UK firms in the US are less efficient because they are controlled by UK management and, in consequence, decisions are taken in the light of UK thinking, judgement and attitudes rather than American. Admittedly, the number of firms giving information was much smaller than in the Canadian case, but it is interesting that the data we have contradict rather than uphold the above argument.

3. *Managerial techniques adopted by subsidiary*

Finally, let us examine the relationship between the profits of UK firms in North America and the extent to which such subsidiaries are influenced by the managerial practices of the parent company.

Table 15 presents the broad conclusions in respect of the seven managerial functions discussed earlier. Again, the classification of firms into the three categories of UK influence, viz. marked, moderate and negligible, is essentially a subjective one, the interpretation of which may vary slightly according to the firm or industry giving the information. Broadly speaking, by a *marked* managerial influence we mean that the subsidiary's managerial techniques and methods are decisively and consciously based on those of its parent company and that only minor adaptations are made to these to meet local requirements. By a *negligible* influence we mean that the Canadian or American subsidiary operates its managerial practices independently of its UK parent and does not (consciously) imitate

TABLE 15

Profit/Capital Ratios (1955/60) of UK Firms in North American Industry by Extent to which they are Influenced by Managerial Techniques of Parent Companies

	Markedly Influenced		*Moderately Influenced*		*Negligibly Influenced*	
	Canada	*US*	*Canada*	*US*	*Canada*	*US*
Overall managerial policy and thinking	6·3	8·6	6·2	5·7	6·4	7·0
Capital expenditure	6·1	7·0	6·4	7·2	6·6	7·3
Product innovation and development	6·2	8·1	5·4	5·3	8·0	7·1
Production planning and budgetary control	7·0	7·8	5·4	6·3	6·6	7·6
Plant supervision and manuturing methods	4·8	7·1	6·8	11·1	7·9	7·2
Wages policy and industrial relations	*	11·6	5·6	4·0	6·5	6·7
Marketing policy	6·4	11·2	6·8	4·9	6·1	7·0

* Sample too small to be of value; included under 'moderately influenced.'

or draw upon the latter's knowledge. By a *moderate* influence we mean that the inter-firm management relationship is somewhere between these two extremes.

Canada. It can be seen that the profit/capital ratios of four management functions, viz. overall policy, capital expenditure, production planning and marketing policy, are broadly the same irrespective of the degree of UK managerial influence exerted, but that in the US product innovation and manufacturing methods of the 'negligibly' influenced subsidiary earn the highest rate of return. Overall, the average profit/capital ratio for this latter group of firms works out at 6·9 per cent compared with 6·1 per cent for both the 'moderately influenced' and 'markedly influenced' subsidiaries.

United States. In general, subsidiaries which follow the managerial practice of their parent companies earn a higher return on their capital than those who do not. Particularly (and rather surprisingly) does this appear to be true in the case of labour relations and marketing policy. The average of the seven profit ratios for firms markedly influenced works out at 8·8 per cent, for those moderately influenced 6·3 per cent and for those negligibly influenced 7·1 per cent.

On the basis of the evidence presented in the preceding paragraph, there would seem little reason to suppose that the inefficiency of UK *managerial practices in decision-taking* is a significant factor in explaining the below-average profitability of UK firms in North America. This does not mean there may not be other aspects of managerial inefficiency, e.g. timing, form and choice of investment, weaknesses in the flow of communications between subsidiary and parent firm – only that the policy and technique of British management does not appear to be markedly at fault. This, of course, may well be because it is the most efficient UK firms that invest overseas.

In addition to those given in the above sections, there are various other possible explanations of a non-measurable character which might account for the poor post-war performance of UK firms in North America – and particularly in Canada. Some of these, which affect the *level* of profit/capital ratios as much as the comparative position of UK firms *vis-à-vis* their competitors, were examined in a previous chapter.[1]

Conclusions

The main conclusions of this chapter may be summarized as follows:

1. While size and profitability of investment appear to be positively associated in North America and the incidence of loss-making is strongly concentrated in the firms with the smallest investments, the size dispersion of UK investments in Canada and the US (in terms of net assets) is such that this is not an important explanation of the relatively low *average* profit/capital ratio of UK firms in relation to their domestic competitors.

2. There is strong evidence to suggest that age and profitability of UK investments in Canada are positively correlated and that the above-average concentration of UK capital in that country in the years since 1950 is an important reason for the low average profit/capital ratio of all firms. There is no such evidence to suggest this is the case in the US.

[1] See particularly p. 226.

3. In the US, UK investment is considerably less concentrated in growth industries than is domestic investment. This is probably the most important single reason for the differences in Anglo-US profitability. In Canada the structure of UK investments is broadly similar to that of resident investment.

4. UK firms which have invested in Canada by the purchase of existing companies have generally fared much better than newly established subsidiaries. There appears to be no pattern of this kind in the US.

5. On average, Anglo-Canadian and Anglo-American firms record slightly higher profits than fully owned UK subsidiaries.

6. There is little evidence to suggest that the inefficiency of UK management techniques or procedures is an important factor in explaining low profits, but due to weaknesses in the flow of knowledge and ideas between parent and subsidiary, mistakes in the timing and choice of investment, and inadequate pre-production planning, much capital has been wasted and many ventures have been less successful than they might have been.

7. There are several non-measurable and unforeseeable or unpredictable reasons for the difficulties faced by UK firms in Canada since the war.

8. One possible reason for (6) is that UK firms which invest overseas are among those which are the most efficient at home.

Finally, a brief comment on the implications of the above analysis for policy on overseas investment.

It does not necessarily follow that where UK industry earns lower profits than its competitors overseas that overseas investment ought to be discouraged, nor that where it earns higher profits such investment ought to be encouraged. Nor can it be argued that *because* the industrial distribution of UK investment in the US or Canada yields a lower average profit than resident investment that it is inefficiently distributed. It is quite possible that, *vis-à-vis* the rates of return on home investment, it is still most profitable[1] to invest abroad in the industries which *in the country of investment* yield below-average profits or in industries where profit/capital ratios of UK firms are less than those of its competitors. However, it may well be that *if* UK firms increased the profitability of their investments in North America to the level of their domestic competitors, then, assuming no change in the profitability of home investments, more

[1] In terms of the marginal rate of return on overseas *v.* domestic investment.

TABLE 16

Rates of Return* on Direct Investments by Industry, 1965

(Estimates for Companies Supplying Comparable Data for Earnings and Investments)

Book values of net assets attributable to the United Kingdom at end-1965 in £m.

Industry	Losses	per cent	0·5 per cent	0–10 per cent	10–20 per cent	over 20 per cent	Total
Agriculture:							
Numbers	17·0	8·0	64·0	70 0	36·0	33·0	228
Net assets	15·3	3·0	106·0	106·2	41·6	32·4	304·5
Percentage of net assets in industry	5·0	1·0	34·8	34·9	13·7	10·6	100·0
Mining:							
Numbers	10·0	4·0	9·0	11·0	17·0	33·0	84·0
Net assets	10·8	4·5	11·7	90·0	95·0	38·8	250·8
Percentage of net assets in industry	4·3	1·8	4·6	35·9	37·9	15·5	100·0
Electrical and mechanical engineering:							
Numbers	60·0	27·0	44·0	66·0	56·0	66·0	319·0
Net assets	21·0	4·3	63·6	58·8	35·4	20·3	203·4
Percentage of net assets in industry	10·3	2·1	31·3	28·9	17·4	10·0	100·0
Vehicles and shipbuilding:							
Numbers	8·0	13·0	9·0	15·0	17·0	6·0	68·0
Net assets	13·1	7·8	18·5	33·2	26·0	2·2	100·8
Percentage of net assets in industry	13·0	7·7	18·4	32·9	25·8	2·2	100·0
Other manufacturing:							
Numbers	151·0	91·0	166·0	227·0	298·0	227·0	1,160·0
Net assets	72·0	23·3	234·8	515·0	574·6	110·6	1,530·3
Percentage of net assets in industry	4·7	1·5	15·3	33·7	37·6	7·2	100·0
Construction:							
Numbers	31·0	30·0	16·0	13·0	14·0	35·0	139·0
Net assets	4·5	4·3	8·9	11·0	9·0	4·1	41·8
Percentage of net assets in industry	10·8	10·3	21·3	26·3	21·5	9·8	100·0
Distribution:							
Numbers	185·0	122·0	166·0	181·0	187·0	181·0	1,022·0
Net assets	45·4	10·1	163·7	217·9	117·9	31·2	586·2
Percentage of net assets in industry	7·8	1·7	27·9	37·2	20·1	5·3	100·0
Transport and communications:							
Numbers	47·0	17·0	16·0	15·0	16·0	38·0	149·0
Net assets	12·5	1·3	35·5	56·4	9·4	8·5	123·6
Percentage of net assets in industry	10·1	1·1	28·7	45·6	7·6	6·9	100·0
Other activities:							
Numbers	71·0	67·0	86·0	111·0	74·0	89·0	498·0
Net assets	40·1	9·5	114·4	178·2	69·8	23·8	435·8
Percentage of net assets in industry	9·2	2·2	26·2	40·9	16·0	5·5	100·0
Total:							
Numbers	580·0	379·0	576·0	709·0	715·0	708·0	3,667·0
Net assets	234·7	68·1	757·1	1,266·7	978·7	271·9	3,577·2
Percentage of total	6·6	1·9	21·2	35·4	27·3	7·6	100·0

* After overseas tax.

investment (or a smaller reduction in investment) in those countries would be justified.

Addendum

Tables 16/18 have been extracted from an article published in the *Board of Trade Journal* on January 26, 1968, entitled 'Book values of overseas investment'. The data reveal a number of interesting

TABLE 17

Rates of Return* on Direct Investments by Period of Establishment

(Estimates for Companies Supplying Comparable Data for Earnings and Investments)

Book values of net assets attributable to the United Kingdom at end-1965 in £m.

Period of Establishment	Losses	Nil	0–5 per cent	5–10 per cent	10–20 per cent	Over 20 per cent	Total
Before 1946:							
Numbers	163·0	76·0	245·0	290·0	302·0	238·0	1,314·0
Net assets	105·2	21·1	480·5	864·7	737·8	176·8	2,386·1
1946/55:							
Numbers	105·0	64·0	147·0	228·0	209·0	196·0	949·0
Net assets	40·8	12·0	124·1	241·4	129·6	56·1	604·0
1956/65:							
Numbers	312·0	239·0	184·0	191·0	204·0	274·0	1,404·0
Net assets	88·7	35·0	152·5	160·6	111·3	39·0	587·0
Total:							
Numbers	580·0	379·0	576·0	709·0	715·0	708·0	3,667·0
Net assets	234·7	68·1	757·1	1,266·7	978·7	271·9	3,577·2

* After overseas tax.

facts about the profitability of UK foreign investment, perhaps most striking of which is the very wide variation which exists in each class of investment. Among other points of interest, we might mention:

1. Of the industries classified, electrical and mechanical engineering, construction and transport and communications are most likely to do either badly or very well. The dispersion of rates of return in distribution and 'other activities' is more evenly spread. Some 39 per cent of mining companies earn more than 20 per cent on their capital, compared with 19 per cent in the case of all companies; by contrast 44 per cent of constructional enterprises either made no profits or a loss in 1965.

2. As might be expected, Table 17 depicts an inverse correlation between data of establishment and rate of return, a higher proportion of the more recently initiated investment showing losses, nil earnings or low rates of return. On the other hand, a slightly higher

proportion of enterprises set up since 1956 made over 20 per cent on their capital than those established before that date.

3. Variations on profitability in 1965 were less in larger companies than in small companies. A considerably higher proportion of those concerns with assets of less than £0·5m. earned more than 20 per cent on their capital or recorded losses than those with assets over

TABLE 18

Rates of Return* on Direct Investments by Size of Overseas Concern

(Estimates for Companies Supplying Comparable Data for Earnings and Investments)

Book values of net assets attributable to the United Kingdom at end-1965 in £m.

Size Range of Net Assets	Losses	Nil	0–5 per cent	5–10 per cent	10–20 per cent	Over 20 per cent	Total
Over £5 million:							
Numbers	57·0	16·0	28·0	57·0	34·0	5·0	131·0
Net assets	136·9	32·5	263·6	771·3	516·7	39·6	1,638·0
£1 million–£5 million:							
Numbers			147·0	156·0	147·0	61·0	577·0
Net assets			359·6	331·5	300·5	118·3	1,232·5
£0·5 million–£1 million:							
Numbers	54·0	14·0	92·0	132·0	111·0	65·0	468·0
Net assets	40·2	9·8	65·2	95·6	81·6	46·6	339·0
£0·25 million–£0·5 million:							
Numbers	76·0	30·0	126·0	114·0	138·0	94·0	578·0
Net assets	27,4	10·3	45·3	41·2	49·8	33·0	207·0
£0·1 million–£0·25 million:							
Numbers	1314·0	50·0	109·0	121·0	137·0	129·0	660·0
Net assets	19·1	8·0	19·1	20·5	23·3	21·5	111·5
Less than £0·1 million:							
Numbers	279·0	269·0	74·0	129·0	148·0	354·0	1,253·0
Net assets	11·1	7·5	4·3	6·6	6·8	12·9	49·2
Total:							
Numbers	580·0	379·0	576·0	709·0	715·0	708·0	3,667·0
Net assets	234·7	68·1	757·1	1,266·7	978·7	271·9	3,577·2

* After overseas tax.
Source of Tables 16 to 18: *Board of Trade Journal*, 26/1/68.

£0·5m. Some 47 per cent of the investments of subsidiaries with net assets of £5m. recorded a rate of return of between 5 and 10 per cent, compared with 26 per cent in the case of other companies.

No geographical breakdown of the data in Tables 16 to 18 has been published.

APPENDIX to Chapter 6

COMPARATIVE PROFITABILITY OF UK AND US ENTERPRISE ABROAD[1]

This Appendix looks into the comparative performance of US and UK firms in foreign countries.

Table 1 presents details of the net income (after tax)/*net* asset ratios of UK firms in various countries for the period 1960/65, and the net income (after tax)/*total* assets figures of US firms in similar countries over the same period. Unfortunately, no data are available on the *net* assets of US firms except for the year 1957, at which date they represented 90 per cent of total assets (the balance comprising current liabilities): to this extent, then, the rate of return on US investment will be understated compared with the profitability of UK investment.

The table shows that, in most countries, US firms achieve a higher rate of return on their capital and that, on average, for the period in question, they were 26·3 per cent more profitable. Had the geographical distribution of the investment of US firms been that of UK firms in 1965, the average return in that year (for US firms) would have been 10·5 per cent, 0·1 per cent lower than the actual return of 10·6 per cent, but 2·1 per cent more that UK firms actually earned. This suggests that most of the difference in profitability between UK and US investment is due not to the geographical distribution of such investment but to the better performance of US investors, firms in particular countries.

In its turn, this difference may be a reflection of various factors, some of which we shall now consider briefly. First, the *industrial composition* of the investment. Table 2, which presents the profitability of US and UK firms by broad industrial groups, shows that UK firms perform better than US firms in mining ventures and worse in other directions.[2] It follows then that in those countries in which the relative

[1] First published as part of an article 'UK and US investment abroad: a comparative study,' *National Provincial Bank Review*, August 1968.

[2] UK oil firms with assets of £918·9 million in foreign enterprises, earned a return of 13·0 per cent (after tax).

stake of mining investments is the highest, the differential between UK and US firms will be the lowest. Within manufacturing industry, there are no data published by the US Department of Commerce on the profitability of US investment, but studies on the profitability of US and UK firms in UK, US, Australian and Canadian manufacturing industry suggest that most of the differences which exist are due more to a higher return being earned *within* particular industries rather than the concentration of US firms in the more profitable industries. It is, however, true that a higher proportion of US than UK investments tend to be concentrated in the technological advanced industries of the host countries in which innovatory profits are most likely to be made, and in Europe, at least, they appear to be better choosers of growth *countries* than UK investors.

A second factor affecting the profitability of investment is its *age profile*. Board of Trade statistics reveal that there is an inverse correlation between the data of establishment and rate of return earned on UK investments, and a higher proportion of the more recently initiated investments make losses or achieve only very low rates of return. This is confirmed by the Reddaway study and also D. T. Brash in his study of US enterprises in Australian manufacturing industry.[1] By contrast, US investments in the UK set up between 1946 and 1955 seem to do rather better than those established before or since. That the older UK investments do so well is a little surprising, as these are often concentrated in the traditional and less profitable industries, e.g. textiles.

The *size of investment* is another variable affecting its profitability. In general, there is no evidence that large UK subsidiaries do better than small subsidiaries except that they are less likely to make losses. The average US investment abroad is considerably larger than that of the UK – particularly in industries where both nationalities are represented. In the computer, motor car and pharmaceutical industries this size differential gives the American firms a distinct advantage. Moreover, there is no doubt that the larger the size of the investing organization, the more internationally specialized and integrated it can become and the more its subsidiaries can benefit from access to technology, financial and management expertise and marketing outlets.

Profitability may also be influencing by *accounting and pricing practices* of the investing companies and their subsidiaries. This is particularly the case in resource, and other vertically integrated

[1] D. T. Brash, *American Investment in Australian Industry*, Canberra, Australian National University, 1966, pp. 241ff.

TABLE 1

Comparative Profitability (Net of Tax) of UK and US Firms Abroad 1960/65
[Excluding Petroleum]

Percentages

Area	1960 *UK*	1960 *US*	1961 *UK*	1961 *US*	1962 *UK*	1962 *US*	1963 *UK*	1963 *US*	1964 *UK*	1964 *US*	1965 *UK*	1965 *US*	*Average* 1960/65 *UK*	*Average* 1960/65 *US*
North America	5·2	7·3	5·0	6·3	5·6	7·7	7·3	7·9	8·0	8·8	8·5	8·6	6·6	7·8
Canada	4·3	7·3	4·0	6·3	4·6	7·7	5·1	7·9	6·1	8·8	6·4	8·6	5·1	7·8
United States	6·8	(9·1)[1]	6·6	(8·7)	7·2	(9·0)	10·6	(9·7)	10·8	(10·3)	11·5	(11·1)	8·9	(9·6)
Latin America	9·6	8·8	6·9	9·6	7·5	10·1	8·4	8·7	9·1	10·3	8·3	10·6	8·3	9·7
Argentina	12·4	9·7	5·3	13·5	4·5	10·0	6·0	6·3	10·4	10·3	7·7	13·4	7·7	10·5
Brazil	17·3	8·7	12·2	6·8	9·9	8·3	10·3	6·3	7·9	6·0	8·9	9·1	11·1	7·5
Other Countries	5·5	9·2	5·6	10·7	8·0	11·7	9·0	10·7	8·8	11·9	8·4	10·9	7·6	10·9
Western Europe	7·3	13·8	8·0	13·7	6·9	12·0	6·6	12·2	5·0	12·3	5·1	11·5	6·5	12·6
EEC	6·8	14·7	8·0	14·4	7·1	11·7	6·7	11·0	3·9	11·2	4·6	9·2	6·2	12·0
Belgium and Luxembourg	1·2	19·0	2·4	21·4	5·3	19·1	4·4	14·7	−4·0	14·0	1·3	10·3	1·8	16·4
France	3·3	3·1	4·1	6·9	2·4	5·7	5·5	5·6	3·8	6·5	2·6	5·1	3·6	5·5
Italy	0·6	12·9	3·6	9·5	−1·2	8·7	−2·8	9·2	−3·7	7·5	2·5	3·2	−1·7	8·5
Netherlands	7·7	11·9	9·9	11·0	7·5	10·1	5·1	11·0	2·1	12·3	5·0	12·6	6·2	11·5
Western Germany	25·0	18·6	22·3	19·8	19·2	15·5	15·2	14·8	12·0	15·3	9·5	12·9	17·2	16·2

Other Europe	8·7	13·2	8·0	13·4	6·4	12·2	6·4	13·1	7·8	13·1	6·4	13·3	7·3	13·1
Denmark	4·9	18·5	4·3	29·4	2·7	18·4	0·8	13·3	2·8	16·3	−0·6	14·5	2·5	18·4
Switzerland	20·8	20·6	15·9	23·0	5·3	21·1	7·7	24·1	9·9	17·4	11·9	15·0	11·9	20·0
United Kingdom	(8·5)[2]	12·2	(7·4)	11·4	(6·8)	9·9	(5·4)	11·1	(6·9)	11·9	n.a.	12·5	(7·4)[4]	11·3[4]
Other Countries	8·3	16·3	7·6	13·3	7·1	21·4	6·8	9·7	8·0	12·1	6·1	15·8	7·3	14·8
Rest of the World	9·4	16·8	8·3	14·6	8·5	10·3	8·7	13·9	9·4	13·5	9·1	13·6	8·9	13·1
Australia	7·3	11·8	5·0	8·1	6·1	10·3	6·6	10·0	7·0	8·3	7·7	7·5	6·6	9·3
India	8·4	8·8	8·3	12·2	8·4	11·7	6·7	6·8	6·9	9·8	7·6	11·9	7·7	10·2
Malaysia	17·8	n.a.	17·1	n.a.	14·8	11·7	15·3	n.a.	15·8	n.a.	14·5	n.a.	15·9	n.a.
New Zealand	7·4	20·8	4·2	19·0	6·3	17·0	4·8	n.a.	8·1	n.a.	7·5	n.a.	6·0	18·9
Rhodesia and Nyasaland	15·1	23·1	11·7	16·1	10·3	10·8	13·3	n.a.	17·3	n.a.	18·7	n.a.	12·4	16·7
South Africa	10·3	17·5	10·4	19·4	12·1	20·4	12·9	20·9	14·8	18·6	12·1	19·1	12·1	19·3
The World	8·2	10·4	7·4	10·0	7·6	10·3	8·1	10·2	8·5	10·9	8·4	10·6	8·0	10·1
[Including petroleum][3]	[9·2]	[10·8]	[8·3]	[10·7]	[8·8]	[11·4]	[9·9]	[11·3]	[9·9]	[11·4]	n.a.	[11·1]	[9·2][4]	[11·1][4]

N.B. Rates of return are calculated with reference to book values at *the end of the year*.

[1] Net income (after tax)/net *worth* ratio for leading US Corporations (including those in petroleum).
Source: First National City Bank of New York.

[2] Net income (after tax)/net assets ratio for UK public companies in manufacturing and distribution.

[3] UK data on petroleum assets and income taken from *Reddaway report*, p. 40.

[4] Average 1960/64.

Source: Board of Trade and US Department of Commerce.

TABLE 2

Comparative Rates of Return Earned by UK and US Direct Investment Abroad by Broad Industrial Groups, 1960/65

Percentages

	1960		1961		1962		1963		1964		1965		*Average* 1960/65	
	UK	*US*	*UK*	*US*	*UK*	*US*	*UK*	*US*	*UK*	*US*	*UK*	*US*	*UK*	*US*
Agriculture	9·4	[1]	8·1	[1]	9·6	[1]	7·8	[1]	7·6	[1]	6·8	[1]	8·2	[1]
Mining	19·8	13·1	18·1	11·7	17·2	11·5	19·2	10·7	12·6	14·2	13·4	15·1	16·7	12·7
Petroleum	10·6[2]	11·7	9·7[2]	11·9	11·4[2]	13·6	12·4[2]	13·3	11·0[2]	13·0	n.a.	11·9	11·0[3]	12·7
Manufacturing	8·0	10·5	7·4	9·9	8·2	9·9	8·3	10·3	9·3	10·8	9·0	10·8	8·4	10·4
Trade	7·2	[1]	5·9	[1]	5·0	[1]	5·7	[1]	8·0	[1]	7·8	[1]	6·6	[1]
Other	3·4	9·1	3·1	9·4	3·2	10·4	5·0	9·8	5·3	9·8	5·8	9·4	4·3	9·3
Total (excluding petroleum)	8·2	10·4	7·4	10·0	7·6	10·3	8·1	10·2	8·5	10·9	8·4	10·6	8·0	10·1
Total (including petroleum)	9·2	10·8	8·3	10·7	8·8	11·4	9·9	11·3	9·9	11·4	n.a.	11·1	9·2[3]	11·1[3]

[1] Included in 'Other'.
[2] Estimates of *Reddaway report*.
[3] Average 1960/64.
Source: Board of Trade and US Department of Commerce.

TABLE 3

UK and US Direct Investment Receipts of Royalties and Fees (Excluding Petroleum)

	1961		1965		1961		1965	
	UK	*US*	*UK*	*US*	*UK*	*US*	*UK*	*US*
	£m.	$m.	£m.	$m.	*Percentage of Total Assets*			
North America	0·1	88	6·1	176	0·0	1·0	0·7	1·5
Latin America	2·0	79	2·6	145	1·2	1·6	1·2	2·3
Europe	1·9	140	3·8	351	0·6	2·5	0·7	3·4
Other areas[1]	24·7	45	29·0	113	1·3	1·4	1·5	2·2
Total	28·7	353	41·5	786	0·9	1·6	1·0	2·3

[1] Almost entirely Overseas Sterling Area.

N.B. UK figures are net of payments made by UK companies to their foreign affiliates. It is not clear from the American data whether these are gross or net figures.

Source: Board of Trade and US Department of Commerce.

industries.[1] Unfortunately, we have no comparative data here, although it is known the profits of some US subsidiaries in the UK are inflated by the subsidized services they receive from their parent companies. Since a greater proportion of US investment is of more recent origin, the effects of inflation on capital values are likely to favour US rather than UK enterprises. In so far, too, as the incentive to shift profits away from the investing to the host country is probably greater in the case of the UK (because of the more unfavourable domestic tax structure) one might expect any bias in profits earned overseas to favour UK rather than US investors.[2]

Some information on the receipts of *royalties, fees and service* charges by US and UK firms is given in Table 3. These have become an increasingly important supplement to income earned on capital. In part a payment for services rendered, these (especially royalties) also represent an income resulting from overseas investment. Table 3 also reveals that the US receives proportionately more on royalties and fees than the UK, which again contradicts the suggestion that, relative to UK firms, US firms subsidize their foreign subsidiaries through undercharging for research and development.

A final point worthy of brief mention concerns the *motivation* of foreign investment. B. L. Johns has argued[3] that in Australia, not only is British investment concentrated in those industries where the specific advantages of foreign capital are most likely to be exploited,[4] e.g. banking, insurance, real estate, but that a higher proportion of it *vis-à-vis* US investment is *defensive* rather than *aggressive* in character, initiated by the desire to protect export markets, etc., rather than exploit innovating gains. On the other hand, part of the reason for the narrowing of the profitability gap between US and UK firms in Australia since 1960 may be due to the fact that the earlier monopoly profits of US firms have been substantially reduced by additional competition – both from imports and local firms.[5]

[1] Because of the increasing volume of intra-group transactions of multinational enterprises the profitability measure of performance for any part of an international organization is becoming more and more suspect. For a comprehensive examination of pricing policy in the international oil industry see E. Penrose, *The Large International Firm in Developing Countries*, Allen & Unwin, 1968.

[2] See Chapter 9 for further details.

[3] B. L. Johns, 'Private overseas investment in Australia: profitability and motivation,' *Economic Record*, Vol. 43, June 1967.

[4] See Chapter 7, p. 275.

[5] This point is well made in C. Kindleberger, *American Business Abroad*, Yale U.P., 1969, *c*. pp. 127ff.

It may also be interesting to compare the overall profitability of domestic and foreign investment of US and UK companies. Table 1 shows that, since 1960, the (private) rate of return (after tax) on UK investment overseas has been just about the same as that earned at home (see the bracketed figures). For US companies, domestic investment has gradually become a more attractive proposition with the passing of years.

This section has shown that US firms earn higher profits on their capital than UK firms in most foreign countries.[1] We have suggested that, from the limited evidence available, differences in definition, industrial composition, size, age, structure and accounting and charging procedures of the two groups of firms only partly account for these variations in profitability, and as much favour UK and US investors. This suggests that UK firms, in general, are not as efficient or as aggressively motivated abroad as their US competitors. There are, of course, notable exceptions and some UK firms earn extremely high rates of return. But the fact remains that if their average profitability in manufacturing industry had been as high as that of US investors in the period 1960/65, the absolute profits earned would have been, on average, £35·4 million or 12 per cent higher each year.

[1] US firms also earn higher rates of return than other *foreign* firms in the UK.

7

FOREIGN CAPITAL AND ECONOMIC GROWTH IN EUROPE

Introduction

It has long been recognized that foreign investment can play a major role in stimulating national economic growth. As Kuznets (1955), Rostow (1961), Berrill (1963) and others have shown, not only has the 'take-off' stage in the development of many countries been considerably accelerated by capital imports; when this same capital embodies, or is accompanied by, technological and managerial expertise, it can decisively effect the whole course and framework of economic progress.

In the nineteenth and early twentieth centuries, there was a parallel yet largely independent movement of capital and labour across national boundaries. Complementary to the migration of labour from Europe to North America flowed a substantial volume of investment funds. But the great bulk of this capital took the form of fixed-interest-bearing securities, issued by railroad companies and public authorities. Marketed by Anglo-American merchant bankers, and bought by thousands of individual and institutional investors in Britain, such portfolio investment was rarely accompanied by any management participation or the transference of knowledge from the investing to the host country (Coram, 1967). Such expertise and entrepreneurship as was exported from Europe was transmitted by the large numbers of highly skilled migrants who crossed the Atlantic; indeed, more often than not, this was their only asset on arrival in the US (Nurske 1954, Brinley Thomas 1967).

Today, the situation is quite different. Now, by far the larger part of private capital movements are accounted for by direct investments by multi-national corporations, which rarely involve open market transactions or give rise to associated movements in labour. When a country imports capital in the mid 1960s, it does not just increase its foreign reserves or claims on the investing country's resources. In most instances, it buys a package of factor inputs – a package containing technical expertise, managerial attitudes and investment funds. Most kinds of direct investment involve the transference of both *human* (or *knowledge*) capital and *money* capital (Kenen 1965): these can effect, for good or bad, not only the economic welfare of the investing firms and their subsidiaries but, depending on Government policy and the efficiency of the competitive mechanism, that of a large number of other institutions and individuals in the host economy as well (Watkins 1968).

A unique feature of movements in international business capital is that they often incorporate knowledge and skills which otherwise might not be transferred across national boundaries. Capital is the vehicle by which this knowledge is transmitted; it is, by no means, the only vehicle (Johnson 1968), but, it is certainly one of the most important (Root 1968). Indeed, in the last two decades, the multinational corporation has probably been more responsible for the dissemination of technological expertise than that of any other institution. It is not without significance that the industries which are the most research-intensive in the United States are those in which that country has a comparative trade advantage (Keesing 1966), and which derive the highest percentage of their profits from overseas operations (*Management Today* 1967). Between 1958 and 1964, the four most research-intensive industries in the US spent two and a half times more on new plant and equipment in Europe than fourteen other industries (Gruber, Metha and Vernon 1967). Due to the presence of US subsidiaries in the UK, British industry enjoys direct access to a far greater volume of trans-Atlantic research and development than it itself generates each year (Dunning 1958). In theory, it is possible for one nation to be entirely parasitic on another's knowledge: in practice, the concept of division of labour applies in this field as in any other.

The measurement of the *results* of new knowledge presents a host of conceptual and practical difficulties: the cost of *acquiring* new knowledge is easier to evaluate in terms of expenditure on research and development and/or royalty and licensing fees. Several writers (Williams 1967, Freeman and Young 1965) have shown that there is a close association between the research and development expenditure of particular industries (expressed as a proportion of their net output) and their rate of growth. While this does not necessarily imply a causal relationship – both variables may be dependent on some third factor – economists working on growth and productivity theory (Solow 1957,[1] Salter 1960, Kendrick 1960 and Brown 1966)

[1] Solow, for example, found that 90 per cent of the growth in output of the US between the turn of the century and 1950 was due to technical progress rather than to increases in capital formation and the labour supply.

generally accept that technological progress, which incorporates both changes in the structure of capital and advances in human skills (Grilliches and Jorgenson 1966), has been the main cause of advances in the productivity of industrial economies in recent years. Edward Denison (1967), in his impressive anatomy of European economic growth since 1950, comes to similar conclusions. Since quite often, improvements in the production function of firms within a particular industry, both of a capital widening and a capital deepening character, are initiated by the subsidiaries of foreign enterprises, the flow of knowledge capital may be an important ingredient of international productivity improvements, and, *pari passu*, international growth.

Clearly, where a technological gap exists between two industrial countries, broadly comparable in size and resource endowment, direct investments by corporations of the advanced country in the less advanced country are *prima facie* likely to be productivity improving and growth stimulating – particularly, when one remembers that it is usually the more outward looking and efficient enterprises within the investing country that venture abroad in the first place (*Management Today* 1969).

In this paper, we propose to test this proposition with respect to US and UK direct investment in Western Europe. We shall be concerned first with the dimensions and character of such participation. Second, we shall try and evaluate its effect on the pace and pattern of European economic development and external trade. Third, we shall look into some of the issues of policy problems raised by the growing participation by non-resident firms in various European countries – particularly those associated with the technological gap and brain drain. Fourth, we shall briefly examine the matter from the investing country's viewpoint and suggest the main reasons for the recent upsurge of both US and UK investment in Europe, and the likely trends in the near future.

The amount of US and UK investment in Western Europe 1958/65

In our analysis, we shall confine ourselves to the impact of Anglo-American investment in eleven European countries about which data are available. These countries account for more than 90 per cent of both UK investment and of US investment in Europe.

Table 1 summarizes the situation as a whole since 1958. The time constraint has been determined by the availability of UK data. The information on domestic capital formation has been obtained from various sources – and is not always directly comparable. For our purposes, however, it is broad magnitudes in which we are interested. Table 1 shows that US and UK investment combined (net of depreciation) expressed as a proportion of both foreign and domestic investment (gross of depreciation) varied between 1·1 per cent and 6·6

Definitions and Sources to Tables 1, 3, 4

1. *US direct investment in Europe*

From various US Surveys of Current Business. These figures cover the estimated net addition to US private capital investment in Europe through capital movements primarily from the parent company, and through the reinvestment of earnings. They do *not* include depreciation or government investment.

2. *UK direct investment in Europe*

From various Board of Trade Journals. Covers investment in overseas branches, subsidiaries and associated companies of UK enterprises other than those in oil, and, for 1958–62, insurance; does not include public investment or portfolio investment. Relates to *change* in UK private investment stake only, and thus does not cover the whole of the funds at the disposal of these overseas concerns and excludes depreciation provisions and local borrowing.

3. *Gross domestic fixed capital formation*

From various UN Statistical Yearbooks. Covers the value of purchase and own-account construction of fixed assets by enterprises, private non-profit institutions and general government. Expenditure by households on durable goods, other than new dwellings, is treated as private consumption expenditure. All expenses directly related to the acquisition of capital goods, such as transportation and installation charges, fees for engineering, legal and other sources are included.

There are thus notable discrepancies of definition between (1) and (2) and (3), particularly in the treatment of depreciation and government expenditure. These must be noted in the interpretation of Table 1. Unfortunately, however, no available source providing more suitable capital formation figures covers the whole of Europe. Table 2 shows figures for a limited number of countries for which more compatible capital formation figures could be obtained.

Definitions and Sources to Table 2

1. *US direct investment in Europe*

As for Tables 3 and 4.

2. *UK direct investment in Europe*

As for Tables 3 and 4.

3. *Net domestic fixed capital formation of enterprises*

Derived from Table II/15 of *Comptes Nationaux* 1955–65 (Office Statistique des Communautés Européennes). Basically covers UN definitions but excludes Government investment and depreciation.

TABLE 1

UK and US Direct Investment in Europe 1958/65

$m.

	(1) *Total UK Investment*	(2) *Total US Investment*	(3) *Total UK and US Investment*	(4) *Gross Domestic Fixed Capital Formation*	$\frac{(1)}{(4)}$ *Percent*	$\frac{(2)}{(4)}$ *Percent*	$\frac{(3)}{(4)}$ *Percent*
Europe (total)	872	9,807	10,679	673,900	0·13	1·46	1·59
EEC (total)	601	4,404	5,005	401,167	0·15	1·10	1·25
Belgium and Luxembourg	63	373	436	31,045	0·20	1·20	1·40
France	158	1,093	1,251	111,182	0·14	0·98	1·13
Germany	247	1,768	2,015	164,955	0·15	1·07	1·22
Italy	36	702	738	67,879	0·05	1·03	1·09
Netherlands	97	470	567	26,106	0·37	1·80	2·17
Other Europe (total)	270	5,401	5,671	272,733	0·10	1·98	2·08
UK	507*	3,105	3,612	104,030	0·49	2·99	3·47
Switzerland	89	1,352	1,441	21,690	0·41	6·23	6·64
Denmark	28	150	178	11,531	0·24	1·30	1·54

* Continental European Investment in UK.

TABLE 2

UK and US Direct Investment in EEC 1958/65

	(1) *Total UK Investment*	(2) *Total US Investment*	(3) *Total UK and US Investment*	(4) *Net Domestic Fixed Capital Formation of Enterprises*	$\frac{(1)}{(4)}$ *Percent*	$\frac{(2)}{(4)}$ *Percent*	$\frac{(3)}{(4)}$ *Percent*
EEC (total)	601	4,404	5,005	184,184	0·33	2·39	2·72
Belgium and Luxembourg	63	373	436	8,192	0·77	4·55	5·32
France	158	1,093	1,251	50,445	0·31	2·17	2·48
Germany	247	1,768	2,015	79,012	0·31	2·24	2·55
Italy	36	702	738	34,884	0·10	2·01	2·12
Netherlands	97	470	567	11,646	0·83	4·04	4·87

TABLE 3

UK and US Direct Investment in Europe 1958/61

$m.

	(1) Total UK Investment	(2) Total US Investment	(3) Total UK and US Investment	(4) Gross Domestic Fixed Capital Formation	$\frac{(1)}{(4)}$ Percent	$\frac{(2)}{(4)}$ Percent	$\frac{(3)}{(4)}$ Percent
Europe (total)	281	3,560	3,841	263,273	0·11	1·35	1·46
EEC (total)	203	1,344	1,547	153,342	0·13	0·88	1·01
Belgium and Luxembourg	31	68	99	12,731	0·24	0·53	0·78
France	54	358	412	41,530	0·13	0·86	0·99
Germany	80	588	668	62,085	0·13	0·95	1·08
Italy	24	213	237	26,652	0·09	0·80	0·89
Netherlands	13	118	131	10,344	0·13	1·14	1·27
Other Europe (total)	76	2,215	2,291	109,931	0·07	2·01	2·08
UK	195*	1,569	1,764	44,322	0·44	3·54	3·98
Switzerland	19	344	363	7,622	0·25	4·51	4·76
Denmark	7	56	63	4,305	0·16	1·30	1·46

* Continental European Investment in UK.

TABLE 4

UK and US Direct Investment in Europe 1962/65

$m.

	(1) *Total UK Investment*	(2) *Total US Investment*	(3) *Total UK and US Investment*	(4) *Gross Domestic Fixed Capital Formation*	$\frac{(1)}{(4)}$ *Percent*	$\frac{(2)}{(4)}$ *Percent*	$\frac{(3)}{(4)}$ *Percent*
Europe (total)	591	6,247	6,838	410,627	0·14	1·52	1·67
EEC (total)	398	3,060	3,458	247,825	0·16	1·24	1·40
Belgium and Luxembourg	32	305	337	18,314	0·18	1·67	1·84
France	104	736	840	69,652	0·15	1·06	1·21
Germany	167	1,180	1,347	102,870	0·16	1·15	1·31
Italy	12	489	501	41,227	0·03	1·19	1·22
Netherlands	84	352	436	15,762	0·53	2·23	2·77
Other Europe (total)	194	3,186	3,380	162,802	0·12	1·96	2·08
UK	312*	1,536	1,848	59,708	0·52	2·57	3·10
Switzerland	70	1,008	1,078	14,068	0·50	7·17	7·66
Denmark	21	94	115	7,226	0·29	1·30	1·59

* Continental European Investment in UK.

per cent, in the period 1958/65, and was most marked in three countries – Switzerland (the tax-haven centre of Europe) the UK and the Netherlands. It also reveals the dominating role of US investment in all countries: for every dollar invested by a British firm in Europe since 1958, the Americans have invested eleven dollars. Table 2 expresses this same investment as a proportion of the net fixed capital formation of enterprises in EEC countries; here its contribution is seen to be considerably greater.[1]

Tables 3 and 4 divide the data into two time periods – 1958/61 and 1962/65. These portray two things:

1. the growing role of both US and UK capital as a proportion of domestic capital formation in all European countries, *except* the UK;
2. the changing distribution of US capital both between the UK and EEC, and within EEC countries.

Tables 5 and 6 give further details of the trend of US and UK capital growth in Europe since 1950, and, *inter alia*, reveal a marked shift of interest of US investors away from the UK to the EEC countries in the latter part of the period. Between 1957 and 1966, while plant and equipment expenditure by US manufacturing firms in the UK rose by two and a half times, that in the EEC rose by eight times. Table 5 also shows that, in all countries, the rate of expansion by US firms has exceeded that of UK firms.

It should be observed that these data do not measure the net impact of US and UK capital on resources formation in the host countries as they ignore both the servicing cost of past investments (£100m. of new capital inflow less £150m. of profits and dividends, royalties and fees, etc., earned on past investments and repatriated is a net drain of resources of £50m.), and its demands on local capital markets. Since 1960, for every $2 of investment by US manufacturing subsidiaries financed from reinvested profits or capital outflow from the US $3 has been provided from local savings or the Euro-dollar market (US Department of Commerce 1967, Servan Schreiber 1968), and since President Johnson's curbs on US foreign investment in January 1968, the demands in European capital markets have been further intensified.

[1] A third index – the proportion of plant and equipment expenditure of foreign (US) firms to net fixed domestic capital formation is given in Table 18.

TABLE 5

Value of US and UK Direct Investment Capital Stock in Europe 1950/65

$m.

	US Direct Investment Stock			*Percent Growth*	*Percent Growth*	*UK Direct Investment Stock*		*Percent Growth*
	1950	1958	1965	1950/58	1959/65	1958	1965	1960/65
Europe (total)	1,585	4,362	13,985	275	320	836	1,537	184
EEC (total)	592	1,794	6,304	303	351	610	1,098	180
Belgium and Luxembourg	50	200	596	400	298	143	190	133
France	201	505	1,609	251	319	190	329	173
Germany	189	624	2,431	330	389	118	310	263
Italy	50	266	982	520	369	100	111	111
Netherlands	71	199	686	280	345	58	158	272
Denmark	31	46	200	148	435	23	48	209
Norway	23	52	152	226	292	18	29	161
Spain	29	46	275	159	598	58	101	174
Sweden	55	108	315	196	292	17	48	282
Switzerland	24	76	1,120	316	1,370	13	75	577
UK	788	2,061	5,123	261	248	—	—	—

The flow of new US investment and the earnings on past investment is presented in Tables 7 and 8. For the period 1950/66, in all European countries, except the UK, new investment (including undistributed earnings) exceeded the profits and dividends (whether remitted or not). During this period the EEC was a net gainer of resources to the

TABLE 6

Percentage of US Capital and New Investment in Europe between Countries 1950/65

	US Capital Stake Percent			*New Investment Percent*	
	1950	1958	1965	1950/53	1958/65
EEC (total)	35·4	41·1	45·1	44·4	46·0
France	12·7	11·6	11·5	10·9	11·5
Germany	11·9	14·3	17·4	15·7	18·8
Italy	3·1	6·1	7·0	7·8	7·4
Netherlands	4·5	4·6	4·9	4·6	5·1
Belgium and Luxembourg	3·1	4·6	4·3	5·4	4·1
UK	49·7	47·2	36·6	45·8	31·8
Switzerland	1·5	1·7	8·0	1·9	10·8
Sweden	3·5	2·5	2·3	1·9	2·2
Other Europe	9·9	7·5	8·0	6·0	8·3
	100·0	100·0	100·0	100·0	100·0

tune of $2,564m.; the UK exported $438m. more than it imported (*N.B.* this is *not* the net balance-of-payments effect). Comparable data for UK investment in Europe are given in Table 9.

Summarizing so far:

(i) foreign direct investment has been a fairly small component of total capital formation in most European economies in the last decade or so, but its importance is growing quite rapidly. US investment has increased faster than UK investment in the EEC but slower than UK investment in the EFTA.

(ii) there has been a marked redistribution of new US investment to EEC countries and Switzerland, away from the rest of Europe since 1957, although, even in Britain, expenditure on plant and equipment by US subsidiaries is growing considerably faster than local capital formation. (See Table 18 in the Appendix.)

(iii) the flow of new US investment into continental Europe has exceeded the outward flow of profits and dividends by a considerable margin, thus revealing a net inflow of real resources to Western Europe. At the same time US and UK firms have both made substantial demands on local capital markets and possibly kept interest ratios higher than they might otherwise have been. In the UK, the rate of capital growth by US firms has *fallen behind* the increase in earnings on past investment.

The character of foreign investment in Western Europe

The principal feature of non-resident investment in Western Europe is that it is strongly oriented towards the growth industries of the recipient countries. This brings with it important advantages both to the investing and the host countries.

From the viewpoint of the investing firms, the most commonly cited reasons for setting up foreign operations (*vis-à-vis* expansion at home) are (i) better market prospects, and (ii) increased profitability (Robinson 1961, Behrman 1962 and Basi 1963). Lawrence Krause (1968) has shown that US investment has been most directed to those industries in Western Europe which have grown the fastest. A different approach is taken by Stephen Hymer (1965), who suggests that US corporations invest abroad primarily to acquire control over foreign enterprises or markets, and in so doing strengthen their own international competition. Kindleberger (1969) supports this view and argues that direct investment will only take place when a firm wishes to exploit some special advantage it has over its competition, e.g. with respect to economies of integration or scale, patents, access to capital and/or markets, and the economic rent such advantages confer. Both Christopher Layton (1966) and Raymond Vernon (1966) stress the need of research-oriented and capital-intensive companies for large markets so that they can spread their expensive overheads and use their technological and management knowledge to the full. Raymond Mikesell (1967) sees the American penetration of Europe as a natural extension of domestic growth and a widening of the horizon of US firms following the establishment of the EEC and the consequential enlargement of the market; other writers, e.g. Balassa (1966), Maddison (1966) and Polk, Meister and Veit (1966), point to such participation as a defensive measure against

TABLE 7

Balance between New US Direct Investment in Europe and its Earnings 1950/65

$m.

	1950/65			1950/54			1954/58		
	New Investment (*a*)	*Total Earnings* (*b*)	(*a*)–(*b*)	*New Investment* (*a*)	*Total Earnings* (*b*)	(*a*)–(*b*)	*New Investment* (*a*)	*Total Earnings* (*b*)	(*a*)–(*b*)
Europe (total)	12,400	9,836	2,564	919	1,307	−388	1,858	2,086	−228
EEC (total)	5,743	3,542	2,201	399	404	−5	834	689	145
Belgium and Luxembourg	546	448	98	62	64	−2	88	84	4
France	1,408	832	576	118	150	−32	186	210	−24
Germany	2,242	1,646	596	96	89	7	339	256	83
Italy	932	290	642	61	45	16	155	76	79
Netherlands	615	326	289	62	56	6	66	63	3
Denmark	169	52	117	7	12	−5	8	13	−7
Norway	129	n.a.	n.a.	16	n.a.	n.a.	13	19	−6
Spain	246	110	136	19	15	4	−2	17	−19
Sweden	260	155	105	24	34	−10	29	32	−3
Switzerland	1,096	811	285	10	24	−14	42	51	−9
UK	4,335	4,773	−438	406	751	−345	867	1,217	−350

TABLE 7 (*Contd*)

Balance between New US Direct Investment in Europe and its Earnings 1950/65

$m.

	1958/62			1962/65		
	New Investment (*a*)	*Total Earnings* (*b*)	(*a*)–(*b*)	*New Investment* (*a*)	*Total Earnings* (*b*)	(*a*)–(*b*)
Europe (total)	3,974	3,159	815	5,649	3,284	2,365
EEC (total)	1,619	1,255	364	2,891	1,192	1,699
Belgium and Luxembourg	74	143	−69	322	157	165
France	440	235	205	664	237	427
Germany	705	660	45	1,102	641	461
Italy	257	123	134	459	46	413
Netherlands	144	95	49	343	112	231
Denmark	60	13	47	94	14	80
Norway	48	17	31	52	24	28
Spain	37	29	8	192	49	143
Sweden	50	36	14	157	53	104
Switzerland	395	276	119	649	461	188
UK	1,628	1,449	179	1,434	1,356	78

tariff barriers or other import restrictions and/or the activities of rival firms.[1]

Some of these objectives can be achieved by other means, e.g. direct exporting or the conclusion of licensing agreements. But in recent years, the conditions have increasingly favoured local production, the sales of US manufacturing subsidiaries in Europe have grown much faster than US manufacturing exports to Europe:

TABLE 8

Balance between New US Direct Investment in Europe (Total) and Its Earnings by Years

	Annual Investment (a)	*Annual Total Earnings* (b)	(a)–(b)
1951	259	302	−43
1952	166	305	−139
1953	224	316	−92
1954	270	384	−114
1955	365	474	−109
1956	516	483	33
1957	631	547	84
1958	428	582	−154
1959	750	709	41
1960	1,325	769	556
1961	1,057	837	220
1962	1,161	844	317
1963	1,443	996	447
1964	1,776	1,112	664
1965	1,867	1,176	691

between 1957 and 1964 the former rose by $10,186m. and the latter – with respect to similar goods – by $2,477m. (Hufbauer and Adler 1968). Armed with plentiful cash reserves from the US boom in the 1950s, but inhibited in their expansion in the US by anti-monopoly legislation, more and more American companies looked to overseas markets for growth. A study published in 1966 revealed that 77 per

[1] In this connection a quote from the annual report of the Tektronix Company (US) for 1964 is worth repeating (Williams, 1967): 'Manufacturing within the major European trading areas lets us provide customers there with our instruments at lower prices (by avoiding restrictive trade barriers). It does another important thing: it acts to guard our United States markets against foreign manufacturers, who, protected by trade barriers from vigorous competition in their own market or trade areas, could grow strong enough there to make inroads here also.'

TABLE 9

Balance between New UK Direct Investment in Europe and its Earnings 1958/65

£m.

	1958/65			1958/61			1962/65		
	New Investment (*a*)	*Total Earnings* (*b*)	(*a*)–(*b*)	*New Investment* (*a*)	*Total Earnings* (*b*)	(*a*)–(*b*)	*New Investment* (*a*)	*Total Earnings* (*b*)	(*a*)–(*b*)
Europe (total)	870	555	315	279	248	31	591	308	283
EEC (total)	600	379	221	203	175	28	377	204	193
Belgium and Luxembourg	64	26	38	31	12	19	33	14	19
France	159	69	90	55	27	28	104	42	62
Germany	246	243	3	80	111	−31	166	132	34
Italy	35	2	33	25	7	18	10	−5	15
Netherlands	96	39	57	12	17	−5	84	22	62
Switzerland	90	35	55	20	10	10	70	25	45
Denmark	28	7	21	7	5	2	21	2	1

cent of the leading 500 US industrial corporations have sizeable foreign investments, and most of these have plants in Western Europe (Bruck and Lees, 1966).

From the recipient country's viewpoint, the participation of foreign firms is likely to be welcome wherever they bring with them knowledge capital, access to new markets, balance-of-payments gains and a competitive stimulus to local producers (Watkins 1968). By contrast, constraints are often placed on inward investment, where its effect on a country's resource utilization and balance-of-payments position is thought likely to be adverse. Where an economy is fully extended, the import of capital may be inflationary – unless domestic spending is curtailed, or the investment brings about a more efficient use of resources. If the balance-of-payments situation is critical, efforts will be made to attract investments which are export-earning or import-saving; if growth or technological advance is the main aim, then the priorities of need may differ slightly. Where there is unemployment in the host country, a completely liberal policy may be pursued towards foreign investment; by contrast, where there is a strong political bias against non-resident ownership of activities, e.g. as in Japan until recently, foreign enterprise might be discouraged altogether. In the UK, and latterly in some Continental countries as well, the main thrust of a generally welcoming policy towards direct capital inflows (Dunning 1969a) has been to give a high priority to those very industries which host Governments are now concerned about being dominated by foreign capitalists, e.g. computers, electronics, pharmaceuticals, etc.

In a dynamic world economy, the operations of multi-national companies tend to be directed towards those activities in which they have a comparative technological or managerial advantage, but where the prospects for growth in the recipient country are promising.[1] More than three-quarters of the investment by UK and US firms in Western Europe is now concentrated in a half-dozen industries, viz. oil refining, electronics, office machinery, pharmaceuticals, computers and motor vehicles, and in each case the share of the total output supplied by such firms is substantial. American interests are also significant in a wide variety of consumer goods trades, which supply products on which people tend to spend a higher proportion of their income as their standard of living rises (refrigerators, packaged

[1] There are certain forms of foreign investment which do not fit into this category, e.g. investment in resource exploitation, and distributive outlets but it does apply to most of US investment in European manufacturing industry.

foods, cosmetics, etc.) and/or capital goods which contain a substantial research and development content. Excepting the aircraft industry, there is a strong correlation between the proportion of sales in different European industries accounted for by American firms and their research and development expenditure (Gruber, Mehta and Vernon 1967). These same industries also tend to be capital intensive and their market structure is oligopolistic (Watkins 1968).

Detailed facts of the industrial composition of foreign direct investment in Europe are still very limited. There are, in general, three main sources of data. First there are the official statistics of the investing countries. The US Department of Commerce publishes some information on the sales of foreign subsidiaries in Europe broken down by leading products. The classification used, however (shown in Table 10), is very broad and not always directly comparable

TABLE 10

Sales of US Manufacturing Affiliates in Europe, by Industry 1965

$m.

	Europe (total)	*EEC*	*UK*	*Other Europe*
Food products	1,500	670	730	100
Paper and allied products	166	62	102	2
Chemicals	2,743	1,302	1,241	200
Rubber products	537	232	219	86
Primary and fabricated metals	1,316	600	546	170
Non-electrical machinery	3,146	1,960	1,121	65
Electrical machinery	2,102	1,172	706	224
Transportation equipment	5,060	2,864	1,798	398
Other products	2,191	1,020	1,047	124
Manufacturing (total)	18,761	9,882	7,150	1,369

with that of the host countries. The British data are even more restricted; there is hardly any useful stratification of statistics of investment within manufacturing industry (Board of Trade 1968). Second, there are the official statistics of host countries. These are largely confined to the larger European countries, e.g. Italy, France, Germany and the UK although, in February 1969, the EFTA secretariat produced a comprehensive analysis of the structure of foreign investment in (and between) its member countries; otherwise the data are variable both in quality and coverage and rarely comparable with each other. Third, various estimates have been made by banks, other institutions and individual researchers on both the global pattern of US investment in Europe and on its distribution in particular sectors (Philips 1960, Johnstone 1965, Dunning and Rowan 1968, Layton 1966). The Chase Manhattan Bank, for example, regularly publishes information on the number of new subsidiaries or joint ventures set up by US firms in different European countries. The latest figures available are for the period from January 1958 to January 1966; these are set out in Table 11.

All these data confirm the fact that foreign (and particularly American capital is concentrated in the technologically dynamic sectors of European economies – and that, however small the *total* stake may be, in most of these industries it is very significant. Both Christopher Layton (1966) and Jack Behrman (1969) have listed some of the European industries in which there are substantial US interests. Table 12 reveals not only that these include some of the most rapidly expanding industries (which means that, even without any increase in the participation of foreign firms, their contribution to the total national output is bound to increase); but, that they are industries which, directly or indirectly, are 'catalysts' to the growth and prosperity elsewhere in the economy.

The word 'basic' as applied to a particular activity is taking on a new connotation in the second half of the twentieth century. At one time, the contribution of an industry to the national economy was largely assessed by the size of its labour force or the value of its output: in today's technological environment, a far more important ingredient of input is what we have referred to as *knowledge* capital, and that of the new materials, processes and products which such knowhow helps to create. This is, partly, because the success of many firms and industries is largely dependent upon the efficient acquisition and use of this particular input, and partly because, through their transmission to other firms and industries, e.g. customers, suppliers and competitors, etc., the *results* of knowledge and ideas can have a far-reaching impact on both the creation of future wealth and the maintenance of living standards.

Take the computer industry as an example. The value of this industry to a community may be expressed (and usually *is* expressed) in terms of its sales, or its sales minus purchases from other firms (i.e. its net output). But the real contribution of the computer industry is the difference between the national output generated when a certain quantity of resources are allocated to the production of computers,

TABLE 11

New Operations of US Companies in Europe January 1958/January 1966

	Bel.-Lux.	*Fr.*	*Ger.*	*Italy*	*Neth.*	*EEC*	*UK*	*Switz.*	*EFTA*	*Western Europe*
Chemicals and drugs	115	99	99	99	74	486	36	36	82	595
Petroleum and other fuels	26	25	38	26	18	133	17	5	31	167
Textiles and clothing	31	24	25	21	24	125	15	14	33	163
Non-electrical machinery	76	98	81	69	43	367	74	53	139	516
Food, beverages, and tobacco	22	34	34	29	23	142	19	17	39	187
Paper	15	24	16	13	5	73	9	11	28	104
Office machinery	8	15	18	5	7	53	10	15	29	85
Transportation equipment	22	45	15	24	12	118	17	17	37	157
Heavy equipment	16	22	11	9	7	65	13	5	19	87
Electronics and electrical machinery	56	96	73	79	42	346	54	42	101	455
Basic metals and metal products	47	35	51	37	21	191	20	12	38	239
Instruments and watches	11	21	36	18	22	108	19	20	41	150
Household appliances	5	20	14	11	4	54	9	10	20	76
Rubber	9	14	7	13	4	47	4	4	8	57
Glass	7	2	5	8	3	25	1	1	5	31
Research and engineering	18	29	13	11	16	87	10	12	23	112
Other industries	26	25	30	16	10	107	14	13	36	147
Services:	77	87	55	44	30	293	21	47	80	385
Finance	21	33	21	13	6	94	5	17	27	128
Retail and wholesale trade	4	7	3	4	1	19	3	1	6	26
Hotels	7	6	3	1	1	18	1	3	4	24
Marketing and publicity	17	17	10	12	10	66	6	11	20	87
Other services	28	24	18	14	12	96	6	15	23	120
Total	587	715	621	532	365	2,820	362	334	789	3,713

Source: Chase Manhattan Bank, *Report on Western Europe*, March/April, 1966.

TABLE 12

Indications of the US Share in Certain Industries in Europe

France 1963 (*Turnover*)	Percent	*Britain* 1964 (*Turnover*)	Percent	*West Germany* (*Percentage of Capital of Public Companies*)	Per cent
Petroleum refining	20	Refined petroleum products	over 40	Petroleum	38
Razor blades and safety razors	87	Computers	over 40	Machinery, vehicles, metal products	15
Cars	13	Cars	over 50	(of which cars t 40%)	
Tyres	over 30	Carbon black	over 75	Food industry	7
Carbon black	95	Refrigerators	$33\frac{1}{3}$–50	Chemicals, rubber, etc.	3
Refrigerators	25	Pharmaceuticals	over 20	Electrical, optics, toys, musical	10
Machine tools	20	Tractors and agricultural machinery	over 40	(of which computers 84%)	
Semi-conductors	25	Instruments	over 15		
Washing machines	27	Razor blades and safety razors	approx. 55	t = turnover of industry estimates	
Lifts and elevators	30				
Tractors and agricultural machinery	35				
Telegraphic and telephone equipment	42				
Electronic and statistical machines	43				
(of which computers 75%)					
Sewing machines	70				
Electric razors	60				
Accounting machines	75				

Source: Ministry of Industry (France), Dunning and Industry Estimates (Britain), Bundesbank (West Germany).

and that which would have been produced had these resources been used differently, and, possibly, the computers imported. Any cost-benefit analysis of the computer industry must obviously take these wider considerations into account – the repercussions of some of which may extend over several years (Mansfield 1968). The pharmaceutical industry is another area in which foreign capital often plays an important role and where the value of the output produced may be a very inadequate reflection of its true social worth (Teeling Smith 1966).

The type of products now being supplied by foreign enterprises in Europe are, then, in the van of technical and economic progress. The great majority of them were first commercially produced in the US and later exported to Western Europe – this constituting a form of 'technological gap' trade (Posner 1965). As European incomes and labour costs rose, and as the products became better known in European markets, US exporters gradually found it more profitable to set up local producing facilities (or to arrange for licensing agreements to be concluded with European firms) than to extend their domestic operations – a process accelerated by barriers to trade (including trade in knowledge), the possibility of imitative production by competitor firms and, more latterly, the formation of regional trade blocs (Johnson 1968). In some cases, once established, the European subsidiaries, benefiting from production in a lower wage economy, take over some of the export markets of their parent companies, and not infrequently export back to the US itself: hence the substitution of 'low-wage' trade for 'technological gap' trade (Hufbauer 1965). Nowadays the global strategy of the larger multi-national corporations fully recognizes the advantages of such an international division of labour. About one-sixth of all UK exports are accounted for by American firms; excluding Britain's traditional exports, this proportion rises to over one-third.

Foreign investment, then, not only opens up new markets to the investing country; it offers a technological short cut for the host country; it provides knowledge capital which stimulates secondary effects, the value of which may go well beyond the initial output generated. This is not to deny that, in some cases, it is possible for recipient countries to acquire knowledge capital by alternative, and possibly less expensive means than by direct capital inflows (Johnson 1968). Indeed, there is evidence that in developing countries at least, the multi-national corporation is not the most efficient vehicle of technological transplants (Baranson 1966), and is often seen by both Government and the private sector of the host economy as a disturbing force (Vernon 1968). But, assuming for this part of the chapter that inward investment is a desirable way to obtain external expertise and management skills, what evidence do we have that, in Europe's case, it has advanced economic growth and efficiency?

To answer this question, some assumption must be made about what would have happened in the absence of foreign investment. To what extent, for example, have the operations of UK and US firms added to the stock of European capital and to what extent have they replaced domestic activities? In particular industries, it is reasonable to suppose foreign investment has, in part, substituted for investment by native competitors. If Ford and Vauxhall had not grown as fast in the UK, B.M.C. and Rootes would almost certainly have grown faster. On the other hand, where foreign capital has been directed to completely new industrial sectors, e.g. computers, micro-electronics, it may be often acted as a catalyst to investment by competitor companies. Much depends here on the level of resource activity and the state of competition in the host countries, and the economic policies pursued by their Governments. In the lack of substantive evidence, one suspects that, in the situation of most European economies, up to around 1960, foreign investment complemented domestic capital formation. Since 1960, with the increasing demands made by foreign investment on local capital markets, it has probably substituted rather more for domestic investment – and, as we have seen, the proportion of capital formation in Europe accounted for by foreign firms is growing. In the UK, for example, US enterprises accounted on average for about 10 per cent of company capital formation between 1955 and 1965 (Dunning 1969a).

Much has been made by various writers, such as Brash (1966), Safarian (1967) and the Watkins Committee (1968), of the contribution foreign direct investment can make to improving industrial productivity in the host countries. This is achieved both by encouraging resources to move from where they are less productive to where they are more productive, and by raising the efficiency of resources in their present use. This, in turn, is made possible not only by the direct transplant technological and managerial expertise, but by the 'escalation of the competitive level' (Knoppers 1966), which the presence of non-resident companies sometimes affords. The generally superior performance of US subsidiaries in the UK, *vis-à-vis* their domestic competitors, has been documented elsewhere (Dunning and Rowan 1968); on average, over the period 1958/61, these firms recorded a productivity nearly one-fifth above that of their competitors.[1]

One of the most interesting examples of the impact of US investment in recent years has been the agricultural transformation of the Lower Rhône Valley following the establishment of the food-processing plants of Libby, McNeil and Libby in the region (Balassa 1966). In the early 1960s, Libby signed long-term contracts with the local farmers for supplying its processing plants with fruits and vegatables and, in turn, provided them with grains, as well as with advice for improving their methods of cultivation. Besides benefiting the suppliers, the improvements obtained in quality and yield have induced several French firms to follow Libby's example, as a result of which we see the beginnings of a transformation of the processing of fruits and vegetables from inefficient small-scale establishments into a modern industry in France. In the UK, US firms have made no less valuable contributions to the improvement of the industrial structure of the development areas of mid-Scotland, Northern Ireland, North East England and South Wales (Dunning 1969a).

In general, both US and UK investment in Europe has tended to make for a more oligopolistic market structure and has encouraged industrial rationalization and concentration. This has been both welcomed and feared by European Governments and competitive firms: welcomed because it has stimulated a type of competitive and industrial structure more suited to the economic needs of the 1960s – feared because of the possible influence these companies may be able to exert over domestic economic policies.

Foreign investment: a mixed blessing?

Let us summarize our argument so far. By their very nature, the foreign operations of multi-national companies tend to be both growth oriented, and growth stimulating to recipient countries. This is, partly, because they are most likely to be concentrated in those industries which are new and expanding, and, partly, because these industries often embody a high *knowledge* capital content. In addition, foreign firms usually enjoy certain advantages over their domestic competitors as a direct result of their being associated with their foreign parents, e.g. financial backing, the economies of integration, research and development facilities, use of famous trade names, access to managerial and marketing expertise, etc.,

[1] The argument of the previous two paragraphs has been elaborated in a later paper by the author (see Dunning, 1969b).

which are rarely charged for at full cost (Balassa 1966). For these reasons, foreign investors are increasing their stake and influence in European economies. As far as one can tell, the inflow of foreign capital has generally added to the total domestic capital stock, although recently both US and UK firms have relied increasingly on local capital markets for investment funds. This is not to deny that, in certain areas and industries, foreign firms have added to local inflationary pressures, by bidding up wages and creating labour shortages. The balance-of-payments effects of inward investment would appear to have been marginally beneficial to most host countries. Assuming, for example, that in the absence of US investment in Europe, local (including British) firms would have invested the same amount, then it has been estimated that, for every $100 increase in the assets of US manufacturing subsidiaries the net cost to the European balance of payments (*vis-à-vis* the US) works out at about $8 (Hufbauer and Adler 1968). But this figure excludes the impact of US firms on the export performance of their competitors and is, of course, net of capital inflows which in the period 1960/65 averaged a 6·1 per cent annual rate of growth (Hufbauer and Adler 1968).

In spite of their many and varied contributions, most host Governments in Europe maintain an ambivalent attitude to foreign capitalists; neither do investing countries see the European activities of their enterprises as an unqualified blessing (Kindleberger 1969). It is, for example, by no means certain that the social benefits of UK investment in Europe outweigh the opportunity costs of such investment – however favourable the private return on such investment may be (Dunning 1966). The loss of tax revenue to the investing country which could have been earned had the investment been made at home, and the adverse short-term balance-of-payments effect of an outflow of capital are two cases in point: neither concerns the individual business investor in his decisions whether or not to invest abroad. Two recent studies of the balance-of-payments effects of UK and US direct investment in Europe (Reddaway 1968 and Hufbauer and Adler 1968), cast considerable doubt on some popular notions of the benefits of foreign investment. This is not to deny that foreign investment may be welcome on other grounds; simply that, in an adverse balance-of-payments situation, there is some logic in a less liberal macro-economic policy towards outward investment.

To the host country, the problems are different and arise essentially out of a possible conflict of interests between the foreign investors and those of the host economy (Vernon 1967). The report of the task force on the structure of Canadian industry (Watkins 1968) summarizes the issues well. One paragraph of this report is particularly telling:

'The very inflows of inputs that come with foreign investment and create the benefits also tend simultaneously to generate costs or problems. The influx of senior personnel from the parent provides management skills of a higher quality; but the ease with which managerial and entrepreneurial skills can be imported may reduce incentives to improve these skills in the host country. Capital inflow increases aggregate saving and investment and the rate of capital growth; but the institutional development of a national capital market may be inhibited and the range of choice facing the investor reduced. The direct investment firm provides easy access for the subsidiary to the technology of the parent; but the latter is not necessarily the appropriate technology for the host country, and the potential to become a leader rather than a follower may be diminished. Foreign affiliation may provide an assured market for the subsidiary's output, particularly of raw materials and semi-processed goods; but, to the extent the taxation authorities do not ensure otherwise, the resulting 'prices' may not result in maximum benefit for the host country. In manufacturing, the subsidiary gains access to the trade mark for tested products and the residents of the host country to the latest consumer goods; but the subsidiary may become simply an appendage of the parent, copying products for the domestic market and, in the unlikely event it is efficient, restrained from exporting, while the absence of distinctive national products may limit national advertising and impede the development of national media in the host country.'[1]

More specifically, and in a European context, I would like to mention six causes for concern commonly expressed about the 'American Challenge' in Europe. As far as I know, no attempt has been made to quantify their importance and there is only scattered impressionistic evidence. Moreover, most reactions reflect potential rather than actual situations.

First, there is the fear that US investors, far from bringing new capital and technology into Europe, will simply use their presence to attract and absorb scarce domestic capital and skills, thereby depriving national firms of the use of those resources. This fear is not without foundation. Indeed, it is often the deliberate policy of

[1] Watkins (1968), pp. 38–9.

some multi-national corporations to minimize their cash investment abroad and borrow as much as possible from local capital markets (Behrman 1962). There have also been a number of cases of American firms buying, or trying to buy, into European companies to acquire the technical and/or managerial expertise of those companies for use in its world-wide operations.

Second, it is felt that decisions taken by the parent companies of foreign subsidiaries in Europe, which affect these subsidiaries, may not always be in harmony with those of the host countries. This is not really surprising, as the objectives of multi-national firms are clearly likely to differ – at least in emphasis – from those of host Governments. Every Government is aware that a multi-national corporate group which is able to provide export markets for the products of its country is also capable, by one means or another, of withholding such markets and cutting off jobs that depend on such exports. There is no real evidence that this has yet happened in Europe – although, implicity or explicity, export market-sharing agreements between US subsidiaries and their parent companies do exist. However, as long as multi-national companies have the *power* to pursue policies against the interests of host countries, Governments of these countries are bound to view their presence with some misgivings.

Then, too, policy in respect of the range of products manufactured by European subsidiaries of foreign parentage is likely to be taken more with the needs of the global strategy of the international investor and less with those of the subsidiaries (or the particular host countries) in mind. The case of the dismissal of 500 employees by General Motors at Gennevilliers and 800 workers of Remington Rand in Lyons in 1962, as part of rationalization plans of their European facilities, provoked very sharp responses from the French Government. The Ford deal of 1961 also resulted in some redundancies in the Doncaster plant. More recently the typewriter and shaver plants of Remington in Scotland have been closed down and their activities transferred to the Continent.

Allied to this second tension is a third – viz. the fear that the Government of the investing company might seek to promote extra-territorial policies through the medium of its overseas subsidiaries, which may operate to the disadvantage of the host country. Thus, although American enterprises in Europe are subject to European laws and policies, they are also part of the US industrial state, and, indirectly at least, can be used as instruments of US economic and potential policy. There are several areas in which this may cause conflicts of interest. In its pursuit of competition, for instance, the US has extended its anti-combine policy to firms resident abroad which are subsidiaries of American parents; such a policy, however, may not necessarily be in the best interests of host countries, who, for some reason or another, might find it desirable to encourage mergers between firms. Similarly, a host country which regards freedom of its enterprises to trade as an integral part of its foreign policy, will find any restrictions on this freedom imposed by foreign Governments an interference with this liberty.

Such impressions as we have on the tensions which might arise between the US Government and the various European economies, suggest that this is not, as yet, a serious area of conflict, although President Johnson's 1968 curbs on US investment to help improve the US balance of payments will tend to weaken rather than strengthen the external position of several European economies. But the fact that there has been no serious difference in interests in the past, does not mean that these might not arise in the future, and with US firms supplying a substantial share of Europe's newer exports, and being particularly strongly represented in fields where rationalization schemes are most likely to be prominent, important issues of policy are involved.

A fourth possible disharmony between investing firms and the host community arises out of the attempts of the former to minimize its international tax burden. This it may do by various devices, e.g. arbitrary transfer pricing, adjustments of royalties and service fees and the allocation of administration costs. Both Brash (1966) and Safarian (1966) cite cases of these devices being used against the interests of the host country. As far as US investment in Europe is concerned, our knowledge is very incomplete, but the fact that there are so few input/output transactions of *goods* between subsidiaries and their parent companies suggests that the opportunities for tax avoidance are very limited. These are rather more in the field of *services*, via the manipulation of royalties and fees, and it is here, particularly in the science-based industries, e.g. pharmaecuticals, where close vigilance on the part of the authorities of the host country is especially needed.

Fifthly, there is the belief that, where foreign subsidiaries are mainly manufacturing branch plants, relying on parent companies for research and development expertise, indigenous research and development may be curtailed or stifled – the implication being this is a bad thing. This was one of the arguments used by the Ministry of Health in its objection to the take-over of the Amalgamated

Dental Company (UK) by the Dental Supply Co. of New York in 1966.[1] Part of the cost of this may be a brain drain of technically skilled and professional personnel from the host country as employment opportunities become less.[2] There is the additional charge of foreign investors buying local companies and exporting knowledge and ideas back home, or engaging in unfair price competition, to limit or eliminate competition.

Such empirical data as we have on these issues are a little conflicting. On the other hand, a report of the Stanford Research Institute (1963) showed that while one-half of a sample of 200 US firms undertook research and development in Europe, most spent 4 per cent or less of their research and development budget there. The report went on to say that many US firms regarded their European research primarily as a means of monitoring European research and development, and of gaining entry into the European scientific community. On the other hand, as we have seen, US manufacturing firms in the UK tend to spend more on research and development than their UK competitors, and more often than not, it seems, where US firms take over UK enterprises, they increase rather than diminish UK research and development activities.

On balance, however, it is probably true that, but for the presence of US firms in some of the science-based industries, the European economy would be more, rather than less, dependent upon American technological and managerial expertise and manpower. For European firms would be forced to import much of the research and development they need, by way of licensing agreements, and this, far more than any monitoring of research and development by US companies in Europe, would encourage its polarization towards the US. The fact that this does not seem to have happened in the case of Japan is, however, worthy of further investigation.

Finally, there is the fear that if US firms gain control over key sectors of the UK economy, they can interfere with, thwart or sidestep national sovereignty and Government policy. This was at the root

[1] This was an interesting case in which two public bodies took opposing sides in the argument on where the public interest lay. The Ministry of Health feared that the take-over might result in production capacity being shifted abroad and that a conflict of interest might arise between the commercial interests of the new company and the socially oriented interests of the National Health Service, with respect to price, quality and exports. The Monopolies Commission dismissed these fears largely because, after investigation, it did not appear such a conflict of interests was likely to follow from the take over.

[2] This idea is explored more fully in Chapter 8.

of the French doubts some years ago and some of the German and UK scepticism to US investment today. It was most clearly seen in the cases of the Chrysler/Rootes deal in 1966 and the Litton/Imperial Typewriter take-over in 1967, where the Government asked for a number of specific assurances from the investing companies about the future of their UK operations. Up to now, there is little evidence that multi-national firms have seriously interfered with European economic policy, apart, perhaps, from their ability to circumvent certain financial controls. In the UK, for example, for good or bad, they are subject to precisely the same legislation as UK firms and, in several instances, notably colour films (1966), detergents (1967), petrol (1965), rubber tyres (1955) and pharmaceuticals (1967) have been subject to searching scrutiny by official enquiries.[1]

European policy towards US investment

Having outlined the main benefits and possible costs of foreign direct investment in Western Europe, we now turn to examine some of its policy implications. A simple projection of the growth of the US capital stake expressed as a percentage of the gross national product of various European countries in 1980, compared with the actual stake in 1965, assuming the trend of new investment follows that of the period 1950/65, shows that, in most cases, the American share will be twice or three times as important as it is today. Compared with a 1966 figure of 10 per cent, it is likely that between 20 and 25 per cent of the output of UK manufacturing industry will be supplied by US-controlled firms in 1981, compared with 10 per cent in 1966: the figures for European industry as a whole are 6 per cent and 12–15 per cent. Most of this projected growth in US participation arises because existing American firms are (i) represented most strongly in the faster-growing European industries and (ii) growing faster than their competitors in these industries. But these estimates may be on the generous side. There are, indeed, signs of some slowing down in the pace of US investment in Europe. Partly this is the result of the tighter controls on outward investment by the US Treasury, but it also reflects the overconfidence of American firms in their ability to operate profitably in European conditions (the rate of return on US capital in Europe has steadily declined since 1950 and is now less

[1] Mostly from the Monopolies and Restrictive Practices Commission. The Reports of this Commission provide some very useful insights into the operations of foreign-owned firms in the UK and their relationship with their parent companies.

than can be earned at home), and the improved efficiency of European enterprises in both their production and marketing operations (Dunning 1969a, Johnson 1968).

What, then, should Europe's attitude towards US investment be? Let me illustrate from the viewpoint of UK. Up to now, as we have seen, it has been generally welcoming. Applications by prospective investors have been considered on an *ad hoc* basis, but on the general

TABLE 13

Projections of US Capital Stake and Host Country GNP to 1980

	US Capital Stake	*GNP $m.*	*Projected US Capital Stake as a Percentage of Host Country GNP*	*Actual US Capital Stake as a Percentage of Host Country GNP*
	1980 $m.	1980	1980	1965
UK	37,550	273,400	13·73	5·19
France	10,970	382,900	2·86	1·71
Italy	15,840	263,200	6·02	1·73
Netherlands	3,933	69,980	5·62	3·60
Germany	40,590	502,100	8·08	2·17
Belgium and Lux.	3,351	42,670	7·85	3·43
EEC	112,234	1,534,250	7·32	2·11

presumption that, subject to the provision of certain safeguards, they should be approved. More recently, with some of the wider and longer-term implications of US investment in mind, the conditions of approval have been spelled out rather more specifically. This is an inevitable consequence of the growing influence of US-controlled firms. No longer can the effects of an individual investment be viewed in isolation from those which preceded it; nor can its economic repercussions be divorced from its political and cultural effects.

Apart from such safeguards, action so far taken to counter American investment has been aggressive rather than defensive. This is most clearly seen in the field of computers and micro-electronics where, for policy reasons, it has been decided that, if possible, Britain should retain a viable and independent domestic industry. To this end, financial backing was given by the Industrial Re-organization Corporation (IRC) in 1967 to the formation of International Computers Ltd. – a merger of three UK companies, English Electric, Plessey and ICT. This new company currently enjoys about the same share of the computer market as the American, owned I.B.M. The B.M.C./Leyland merger will similarly strengthen the UK position in the vehicles industry. There is also evidence of Government intention to rationalize and support the UK aircraft industry against any American takeover.

Such encouragement of 'countervailing power' is seen in other directions. Where possible, the Government uses its position as a powerful buyer in the pharmaceutical and telecommunications industry either to 'Buy British'[1] or to bargain effectively with US subsidiaries. Through the setting up of such institutions as the National Research and Development Corporation, which helps finance research in the science-based industries, and the National Computing Centre, which undertakes research into improved methods of programming and computer operations, as well as promoting computer usage, the Government is helping to strengthen the competitive position of UK firms and reduce the Anglo-American technological gap. This policy of countervailing power – which often involves the investment of public money; which some economists, at least, argue could be put to better use (Johnson 1968) – has certainly been more successfully exploited in the UK than on the Continent – partly because the reactions to American investment by individual European countries have differed so widely, and partly because of Britain's strong position in the industries in which US investment is concentrated.

Nevertheless, according to both Servan Schreiber (1968) and Christopher Layton (1969), the only way for Europe to escape from US economic domination is for European industry to be rationalized into larger units, for massive Government assistance to be given to the science-based industries and for much more money to be spent on higher education – particularly management education. This, Servan Schreiber argues, can only be done if individual European countries are prepared to accept a limited form of federal control over industrial and scientific policy and a 'transformation of the relationship between business, the university and the Government'. If Europeans want to control their economic growth, and hence their political and cultural destiny, they can no longer afford 'the luxury of economic nationalism'. A somewhat different approach is taken by Professor Harry Johnson, who believes that the most

[1] Of the computers bought by UK Government departments between 1958 and 1966, thirty-nine were from UK companies and sixteen from UK companies in Britain.

efficient way of advancing the economic power of European enterprises is to enlarge the market opportunities for profitable investment, and that this can only be done by negotiating freer world trade, rather than by introducing 'sophisticating protectionist measures' (Johnson 1968).

Where does Britain stand in this? If Servan Schreiber is right, then unless Britain joins the EEC, she will only be able to advance her living standard by a gradual surrender of her economic sovereignty to the United States. Except in certain very specialized fields, she is too small to compete with the United States of America or a United States of Europe. To obtain more markets, she would have to consider allying herself with a North Atlantic Free Trade Area. But, although this would probably result in a two-way increase in the trans-Atlantic flow of capital and knowledge, the UK's net dependence on the United States would almost certainly grow.

On the other hand, if Britain joined the EEC, it is likely she would be involved in more intra-European corporate alliances – particularly if the Community's merger rules and tax laws were rationalized. Her industries would be no less multi-national in character, but the pattern of ownership would almost certainly be diffused, and the balance of technological advantage would be more to her favour.[1] US investment in Britain would continue to increase – it may even be accelerated – but one suspects that the share of US participation in total UK growth would not be so marked.

Much of what has been written is, of course, little more than speculation, but in spite of her valiant attempts to build up independent science-based industries, it is doubtful whether Britain has got the resources to go it alone in the next twenty or more years. Though probably better placed than her French, German and Italian competitors, she is not in the favourable position of Sweden or Switzerland in having substantial qualities of unique products or services to sell. She is competing in a giant's world, producing and selling basically the same products as the giants, with the advantages growing in favour of the giants.

But this does not necessarily mean that Britain must surrender her economic dependence to the United States. There are two issues of importance here. First, what are the alternatives to inward direct investment – and all that this implies – as a means of acquiring the

[1] In 1964 the UK paid out £32·3m. in royalties and similar transactions to US firms and received £12·0m. from such firms. The corresponding figures in respect of Western European firms were £10·3m. and £16·1m.

technological and managerial expertise necessary to enable Britain to compete effectively in world markets? Japan has apparently managed to pull her economy up by its bootstraps without much foreign investment. What lessons are to be learnt from her experience? How far can unilateral tariff reductions achieve many of the benefits of inward investment and so on? More research is necessary here before we can accept Servan Schreiber's diagnosis of Europe's future.

Second, no assessment of the costs and benefits of foreign investment can be separated from its content and form. Basically this resolves itself into the question: 'What is the minimum amount of foreign particpation necessary for the host country to reap the maximum net benefits associated with it'?

To quite a large extent, the answer to this second question must depend on how successful the UK Government's economic policies are in (*a*) creating the kind of environment most likely to extract the maximum advantages from inward investment, and (*b*) ensuring that the actions of such firms, and, as far as possible, those of their parent companies as well, operate in the UK's best interests.

As regards the former, we consider that policy in both the UK and other countries in Europe should be directed to three main objectives. (These follow the lines proposed by the Watkins Committee to the Canadian Government in respect of US investment in Canada.)

(i) The strengthening of the competitiveness of the local economies, so that the various benefits of foreign investment are diffused throughout the economies and do not simply accrue, in the form of higher profits and dividends, to the investing companies. This competitiveness might be achieved in various ways, including the support of rationalization and other schemes to strengthen the countervailing power of native competitors, customers and suppliers of foreign firms.

(ii) The use of the local tax systems and local participation in the ownership of US-controlled firms as a means of increasing the European share of the benefits from US investment. This involves, *inter alia*, the tax authorities ensuring that the pricing procedures between US firms and their parent companies are (as far as possible) in the host countries' best interests, and exercising caution in the granting of special tax treatment (in the form of depreciation and investment allowances) or subsidiaries to US and other foreign firms.

(iii) The improvement of the quality of European factors of production, particularly management, by better education and training facilities and the encouragement of research and development, so that US firms operating in Europe will be challenged by high standards of performance of UK competitors.

Various measures already exist to ensure that, in particular areas of activity, at least, the actions of foreign-controlled firms do not operate against the interests of the various host countries. But with the increasing influence of US investment in Europe, a case might be made out for more specific guidance to be given on the principles of good corporate behaviour – similar to that published by the Canadian Government in March 1966. The following guiding principles, taken from the Watkins Committee's report, illustrate the Canadian case:

> Foreign firms are to strive for 'maximum competitiveness' and 'appropriate specialization' within the international firms. Market opportunities are to be exploited at home and abroad, natural resources processed in Canada where economic to do so, and Canadian procurement sources searched out and developed. A pricing policy fair to both the company and to Canadians is to be pursued, 'including sales to the parent company and other foreign affiliates.' Research and development capacity is to be developed. Sufficient earnings are to be retained to support the growth of the Canadian operations. Firms are to work toward a Canadian outlook within management and include 'a major proportion of Canadian citizens on its Board of Directors'. Firms are 'periodically to publish information on the financial position and operation of the company' and 'to have the objective of a financial structure which provides opportunity for equity participation in the Canadian enterprise by the Canadian public.' They are to 'recognize and share national objectives' and 'encourage and support Canadian institutions directed toward the intellectual, social and cultural advancement of the community.'[1]

One such policy, which we have not considered in this paper, is the introduction of measures to restrict the inflow of US investment. In general, we would consider this a defeatist measure, though we recognize that, for reasons of cultural independence or national security, it might be felt that certain industries should be excluded from foreign ownership. Like Servan Schreiber, we believe that this would only lead to a reduction in European living standards and it is by no means certain that the technological or economic dependence of

[1] Watkins (1968), pp. 231–2.

Europe on the US would be any less. If anything, we would support the adoption of more liberal policies, not only in respect of international investment but of international trade and migration as well.

Investment and growth at a macro-economic level

Looking now at growth at a macro-economic level, we ask ourselves two questions. First, to what extent do foreign capitalists appear to be attracted to host countries by their growth prospects? Second, is there any evidence that those countries which have attracted foreign investments in recent years have grown the fastest?

To answer the first question, we look at the growth of US manufacturing investment in the major European countries over two time periods – 1950/58 and 1959/65 – and relate this to two commonly suggested investment determinants – profitability and growth of output. Tables 14 and 15 present the rankings for the US and Table 16 for the UK. It can be seen that US investment has been mainly directed to the faster-growing economies: profitability would appear to be a secondary consideration. This conclusion is supported by other recent studies (Scaperlanda 1967), while a comparison between all US investment and sources of European economic growth (Denison 1967) reveals a correlation coefficient of +1 between the former variable and the rate of 'advance in knowledge' (Dunning 1969b). Our examination of the British data for the period 1958/65 reveals no such clear-cut relationship.

Other research has indicated that the influences of other variables on inward investment is less certain. Balassa (1965, 1967) and Scaperlanda (1967) have indicated that neither inter-industry nor inter-country tariff discrimination against US exports in the EEC appears to have affected the distribution of US investment in the period 1957/63. More important, Balassa suggests, is the incentive of larger national markets provided to foreign investors as a result of integration in the EEC. By allowing for the construction of larger plants and for increased intra-industry specialization, a wider market enables economies of scale and integration to be exploited and reductions in costs achieved. Plants set up in any one European country are able to cater for the whole of Europe, and producers may specialize in different varieties of a given commodity, or in its parts, components, and accessories, in factories located in the various member countries. In turn, the possibilities of increasing efficiency by applying US production and managerial methods in the larger market makes for rapid increases in consumer incomes and demand. Lastly, the

TABLE 14

US Investment in Manufacturing Industry in Europe, Profitability and Growth of Output 1950/58

(1) 1958 *Value of Index of Growth US Investment in Manufacturing Industry*	1950 = 100	(2) *Average Profitability of US Investment in Manufacturing Industry*	1950/58	(3) *Growth of Host Country Manufacturing Output*, 1958 *Index Value*	150 = 100
	Percent		*Percent*		*Percent*
Italy	547	Switzerland	36·6	Germany	217
Switzerland	373	Italy	21·0	Italy	183
Belgium and Luxembourg	368	Belgium and Luxembourg	18·1	France	173
Norway	340	UK	16·4	Netherlands	144
Germany	333	France	15·0	Norway	144
UK	251	Sweden	14·1	Belgium	130
France	245	Norway	13·9	Switzerland	128
Netherlands	209	Denmark	13·6	Sweden	125
Denmark	187	Germany	13·3	Denmark	123
Sweden	115	Netherlands	7·6	UK	116

TABLE 15

US Investment in Manufacturing Industry in Europe, Profitability and Growth of Output 1958/65

(1) 1965 *Value of Index of Growth US Investment in Manufacturing Industry*		(2) *Average Profitability of US Investment in Manufacturing Industry*		(3) *Growth of Host Country Manufacturing Output*, 1965 *Index Value*	
	1958 = 100		1959/65		1958 = 100
	Percent		*Percent*		*Percent*
		Denmark	20·0	Italy	183
Netherlands	562	Germany	18·7	Germany	162
Italy	434	Belgium and Luxembourg	17·2	Netherlands	159
Switzerland	431	Switzerland	16·7	Belgium	152
France	386	UK	12·5	Norway	150
Germany	379	Sweden	12·0	France	142
Belgium and Luxembourg	288			Sweden	141
Norway	253	Norway	11·0	UK	133
UK	243	Netherlands	9·7		
Denmark	213	Italy	8·9		
Sweden	200	France	6·8		

TABLE 16

UK Direct Investment in Europe, Profitability, and Growth of Output 1960/65

(1) 1965 *Value of Index of Growth of UK Direct Investment*		(2) *Average Profitability* of UK Direct Investment*		(3) 1965 *Value of Index of Growth o, Host Country Industrial Output*	
	1950 = 100		1960/65		1960 = 100
	Percent		*Percent*		*Percent*
Switzerland	577	Germany	16·2	Portugal	150
Sweden	282	Switzerland	11·9	Italy	138
Netherlands	272	Portugal	8·1	Netherlands	133
Germany	263	Netherlands	6·2	Norway	133
Denmark	209	France	3·6	Sweden	133†
France	173	Denmark	2·5	Belgium	132
Norway	161	Belgium and Luxembourg	1·8	Germany	130
Belgium and Luxembourg	133	Italy	−0·2	Denmark	129†
Portugal	133			Switzerland	128
Italy	111			France	125
				Luxembourg	108

* Average rate of return after overseas tax.
† 1964 value.

uncertainty associated with the establishment of plants for supplying markets of the partner countries is reduced by reason of the assumed irreversibility of the elimination of all trade impediments.

In an attempt to assess the extent to which foreign participation in European industry was motivated by market prospects, Messrs Bandera and White (1968) studied the relationship between US direct investment (D) and (i) the gross national product of various European countries (this was taken as a proxy for the size of the market (Y), (ii) the irinternational liquidity position (L) and (iii) the annual earnings of such investment (G) for the period 1953/62 viz:

1. $D = A_0 + A_1 Y$
2. $D = A_0 + A_1 Y + A_2 L$
3. $D = A_0 + A_1 Y + A_2 L + A_3 G$
4. $D = A_0 + A_1 Y + A_2 G$

They also introduced a second set of equations taking the annual increment of direct investment (dD) as the dependent variable, and correlating this with absolute levels of income (Y), changes in levels of income (Y) changes in liquidity (L) and annual earnings (G). Their results, as shown in Table 17, confirm, in general, the importance of the level of income as a factor influencing US investment. In manufacturing industry, the coefficient of determination (r^2) for equation (1) was significant at the 0·25 level for all countries with the exception of Sweden,[1] and was exceptionally high in the case of the UK and Italy. When L is added in equations (2) and (3) and G in equations (3) and (4), multiple r^2s remain high and the coefficients of Y statistically significant. However, the coefficients of L and G, although usually positive, as expected, are not statistically significant. Only in French manufacturing industry does L seem to be meaningful (Bandera and White 1968). Outside manufacturing L is seen to be important only in French and Belgian trade sectors and G only in German and Swedish petroleum.

By contrast, the second set of equations which tried to relate the variables stated as annual changes suggest far from conclusive results. Partly, however, this is due to statistical difficulties, and as Table 16 shows even here the GNP variable (both its level and rate of growth) provides a better explanation of US direct investments than either liquidity or annual earnings.

[1] The exceptionally low r^2 for Sweden can be attributed to a sharp decline in the value of US manufacturing investment in 1959 and 1960, when the assets of an established company in Sweden were sold out.

TABLE 17

Coefficient of Determination (R^2) between US Direct Investment in Europe and Other Variables

	Equation 1	2	3	4	5	6	7	8
Manufacturing								
Italy	0·99	0·98	0·98	0·98	0·70	0·67	0·83	0·67
Belgium and Luxembourg	0·86	0·88	0·94	0·94	0·14	0·30	0·31	0·48
France	0·75	0·88	0·91	0·75	0·74	0·74	0·77	0·83
Netherlands	0·92	0·92	0·86	0·88	0·71	0·80	0·85	0·83
West Germany	0·93	0·97	0·97	0·93	0·76	0·77	0·72	0·82
UK	0·97	0·88	0·98	0·97	0·46	0·62	0·69	0·66
Sweden	0·33	0·55	0·58	0·48	0·04	0·17	0·34	0·34
Petroleum								
Italy	0·98	0·98	0·98	0·98	0·02	0·08	0·26	0·08
Belgium and Luxembourg	0·81	0·81	0·84	0·84	0·08	0·09	0·84	0·33
France	0·84	0·87	0·87	0·85	0·01	0·09	0·17	0·12
Netherlands	0·92	0·92	0·94	0·94	0·09	0·11	0·21	0·16
West Germany	0·95	0·97	0·98	0·97	0·73	0·74	0·81	0·75
UK	0·98	0·98	0·98	0·98	0·30	0·40	0·54	0·40
Sweden	0·93	0·96	0·98	0·97	0·77	0·78	0·90	0·78
Trade Sector								
Italy	0·98	0·98			0·55	0·60		0·62
Belgium and Luxembourg	0·81	0·89			0·50	0·32		0·36
France	0·82	0·95			0·51	0·53		0·65
Netherlands	0·82	0·85			0·61	0·65		0·65
West Germany	0·97	0·98			0·01	0·30		0·31
UK	n.a.	n.a.			0·35	0·43		0·43
Sweden	0·85	0·87			0·17	0·24		0·35

Key to Equations

1. $D = A_0 + A_1 Y$
2. $D = A_0 + A_1 Y + A_2 L$
3. $D = A_0 + A_1 Y + A_2 L + A_3 G$
4. $D = A_0 + A_1 Y + A_2 G$
5. $dD = A_0 + A_1 Y$
6. $dD = A_0 + A_1 Y + A_2 dY$
7. $dD = A_0 + A_1 Y + A_2 dY + A_3 G$
8. $dD = A_0 + A_1 Y + A_2 dY + A_3 \mathrm{d}L$

where D = US direct investment
Y = gross national product
G = annual earnings of direct investment
L = gold and dollar reserves

There is also some evidence that foreign investors have preferred to invest in European countries in which the *rate of increase* in wage costs has risen the least and/or output per man hour has risen the most (Dunning 1963), but there is no correlation between the level of employee compensation and/or productivity and the distribution of the *stock* of US and UK investment in EEC or EFTA countries.

The second question concerning the *effects* of foreign investment on European growth is much more difficult to answer in quantitative terms. It is true Tables 14/16 have shown the association between investment and growth in output, but this tells us nothing about cause or effect. Outside Europe, Japan has been the fastest-growing nation in the world for some years now, but has relied hardly at all on foreign investment. The introduction of time lags yields no significant results. Time series data for individual countries are even less satisfactory, due to the extreme annual fluctuations of capital movements.

Part of the difficulty in calculating the impact of US direct investment on European economic development is that, in relation to domestic capital formation it is still quite small, and there are so many other determinants of growth. Table 18 shows that the proportion of gross domestic fixed-capital formation in various EEC countries and the UK accounted for by the expenditure of US subsidiaries on plant and equipment ranged in 1965, from 4·0 per cent in France to 10·0 per cent in the UK. If one could assume that this capital (and any local expenditure generated by it) represented a net addition to resource formation in the host countries, then the value of *sales* of US firms (less imports and remitted profits), might be said to represent their *direct* contribution to the growth of European output. The second part of Table 18 expresses the sales of US manufacturing subsidiaries in selected European countries to the gross national product of these countries in 1957 and 1965 and the income in sales to the increase in gross national product between these years. These calculations, however, ignore the *technological multiplier* effect of US investment on the output of competitors, suppliers, customers and so on (Quinn 1968).

If the alternative assumption of full employment in the host countries is made, then US investment must replace either other domestic expenditure or imports (unless capital imports rise by the same amount). If it replaces other investment, then its net effect on economic development is the difference between the level of output actually produced and that which would have otherwise been produced by domestic firms. If it replaces consumption, then

TABLE 18

Relative Significance of Plant and Equipment Expenditure and Sales of US Firms in Selected European Countries

	Plant and Equipment Expenditure by US Subsidiaries as Percentage of all Gross Domestic Fixed Capital Formation[1]					*Manufacturing Sales of US Subsidiaries as Percentage of GNP*			
	1957	1959	1961	1963	1965	1957	1963	1965	Δ *in Sales*/Δ *in gnp*, 1957/65
Belgium	2·2	2·6	3·3	3·8	4·5	(2)	(2)	(2)	(2)
France	1·8	1·9	2·1	3·0	4·0	1·4	2·5	2·8	4·7
West Germany	1·8	2·9	4·2	3·9	4·1	2·2	3·3	3·9	5·3
Italy	2·0	1·3	2·9	4·1	5·0	0·9	1·8	2·2	3·4
Netherlands	2·6	1·2	3·2	5·4	4·8	2·3	3·4	4·4	6·5
EEC	2·2	2·6	3·3	3·8	4·5	1·7	2·8	3·5	4·6
United Kingdom	7·8	5·7	7·4	7·9	10·0	5·9	6·9	7·5	9·7

[1] In machinery and equipment.
[2] Included in Netherlands.

Source: *Economic Bulletin for Europe*, Vol. 19, Nov. 1967, p. 67. US Department of Commerce, *Survey of Current Business*, Nov. 1966, p. 8, and OECD *Main Economic Indicators*, various issues.

TABLE 19

Sales of US Affiliates in Europe and all-European Firms

	All-European Firms				*US Affiliates*		
	(1) 1957	(2) 1964	(3) 1957/64 1957 = 100	(4) 1957	(5) 1964	(6) 1957/64 1957 = 100	(7) Column 4 × Column 3
Food products	34,183	44,796	131·1	734	1,308	178·2	962
Paper and allied products	7,188	10,846	150·9	34	148	435·2	51
Chemicals	18,310	34,039	185·9	822	2,273	276·5	1,533
Rubber products	2,451	3,697	150·8	262	517	197·3	395
Non-electrical machinery	19,420	26,807	138·0	1,009	2,735	271·1	1,392
Electrical machinery	10,802	16,958	157·0	678	1,968	290·2	1,064
Metal products	32,868	42,634	129·7	435	1,115	256·3	564
Transportation equipment	20,506	31,956	155·8	1,700	4,700	276·5	2,649
Total	145,728	211,733	145·3	5,674	14,764	260·2	8,610

Source: All-European firms: G. C. Hufbauer and F. M. Adler, *Overseas manufacturing investment and the balance of payments*, US Treasury Department, Tax Policy Research Study No. 1, 1968. US firms: US Department of Commerce, *Survey of Current Business*, November 1966, and *US business investments in foreign countries*, 1960.

because the savings ratio has been raised, the long-term benefits will be equal to the investment/*net* output ratio.

One other glimpse of the relative significance of the US firms to European growth may be obtained by the use of *shift* and *share* analysis. (Thirlwall 1967, Dunning 1969b.) Let us illustrate from the data in Table 19. Between 1957 and 1964, the total manufacturing sales of US subsidiaries in Europe rose by 160·2 per cent compared with an increase of 45·3 per cent for all European firms. To calculate what part of this differential growth is due to difference in structure, or industrial mix, of US investment and what part to the faster rate of growth of US affiliates *within* particular industries, one can first estimate what the average rate of growth would have been in US affiliates had their rate of growth in each group of products been that of European firms. This works out at 51·7 per cent (column 7/ column 4). The difference between this and their actual rate of growth (108·5 per cent) measures the *differential sector* growth component and that between the adjusted rate of growth and the actual rate of growth of European firms (7·6 per cent) the *structural* and *composition shift* effect. In the present example, it can be seen that almost all of the faster growth of the output of US firms is explained by the former effect. What part of this, in turn, reflects differences in the *efficiency* of US affiliates and European firms cannot be adduced without further data on the inputs of the two groups of firms.

REFERENCES

B. Balassa (1965). 'Tariff protection in industrial countries: and evaluation,' *Journal of Political Economy*, Vol. LXXIII, December 1965.

B. Balassa (1965). 'American investment in the Common Market,' *Banco Nazionale del Lavoro, Quarterly Review*, June 1966.

B. Balassa. *Trade Liberalization among Industrial Countries*, New York, McGraw-Hill, 1967.

V. N. Bandera and J. T. White. 'U.S. direct investments and domestic markets in Europe,' *Economia Internationale*, August 1968.

J. Baranson. 'Transfer of technical knowledge by international corporations to developing economies,' *American Economic Review*, Papers and Proceedings, May 1966.

R. S. Basi. *Determinants of United States Direct Investments in Foreign Countries*, Bureau of Economic and Business Research, Series No. 3, Kent State University, Ohio, 1963.

J. N. Behrman. 'Foreign associates and their financing,' in R. Mikesell (ed.), *U.S. Private and Government Investment Abroad*, Oregon, 1962.

K. Berrill. 'Foreign capital and take-off,' in W. W. Rostow (ed.), *The Economics of Take-off into Sustained Growth*, 1963, Macmillan.

Board of Trade. 'Book values of overseas investments,' *Board of Trade Journal*, January 26, 1968.

D. T. Brash. *American Investment in Australian Industry*, Australian National University Press, 1966.

M. Brown. *On the Theory and Measurement of Technological Change*, Cambridge University Press, 1966.

N. K. Bruck and F. A. Lees. 'Foreign content of U.S. corporate activities,' *Financial Analysts' Journal*, September/October 1966.

R. d'Arge. 'Note on Customs unions and direct foreign investment,' *Economic Journal*, Vol. LXXIX, June 1969.

M. J. Desai. *Costs and Returns of Overseas Investment from the Viewpoint of the Host Country*, unpublished paper given at an International Conference on Overseas Investment in Development (Bellagio, 1967).

J. H. Dunning (1958). *American Investment in British Manufacturing Industry*, Allen & Unwin, 1958.

J. H. Dunning (1963). 'American investment in Europe,' *Aspect*, December 1963.

J. H. Dunning (1966). 'US subsidiaries in Britain and their UK competitors,' *Business Ratios*, No. 1, Autumn 1966.

J. H. Dunning and D. C. Rowan. 'Inter-firm efficiency comparisons: US and UK manufacturing enterprises in Britain,' *Banco Nazionale del Lavoro, Quarterly Review*, June 1968.

J. H. Dunning (1969a). *American Investment in the British Economy*, Political and Economic Planning, Broadsheet No. 507, February 1969.

J. H. Dunning (1969b). *Technology, U.S. Investment and European Economic Growth*, paper given to Seminar on the International Corporation at the Sloane School of Management, Boston, Spring 1969.

European Free Trade Association. *Foreign Direct Investment in E.F.T.A. Countries*, Geneva, 1969.

C. Freeman and A. Young. *The Research and Development Effort in Western Europe, North America and the Soviet Union*, Paris, O.E.C.D., 1965.

J. Gervais. *La France face aux investissements Etrangers*, Editions de l'Enterprise Moderne, Paris, 1963.

Z. Grilliches and D. Jorgenson. 'Sources of measured productivity change,' *American Economic Review*, Papers and Proceedings, Vol. LVI, May 1966.

W. Gruber, D. Mehta and R. Vernon. 'The R and D factor in international trade and international investment of United States industries,' *Journal of Political Economy*, Vol. LXXV, February 1967.

G. C. Hufbauer (1965). *Synthetic Materials and the Theory of International Trade*, Duckworth, 1965.

G. C. Hufbauer and F. M. Adler. *Overseas Manufacturing Investment and the Balance of Payments*, Tax Policy Research Study No. 1, US Treasury Department, 1968.

S. Hymer. *Direct Foreign Investment and International Oligopoly*, June 1965 (mimeo).

H. Johnson. *Comparative Cost and Commercial Policy Theory for a Developing World Economy*, The Wicksell Lectures, 1968.

A. W. Johnstone. *U.S. Direct Investment in France*, Harvard University Press, 1965.

D. Keesing. 'Labour skills and comparative advantage,' *American Economic Review*, Papers and Proceedings, Vol. LVI, May 1966.

J. Kendrick. *Productivity Trends in the United States*, National Bureau of Economic Research, General Series No. 71, 1960.

P. Kenen. 'Nature, capital and trade,' *Journal of Political Economy*, Vol. LXXII, October 1965.

C. Kindleberger (1968). *International Economics*, Kenneth Irwin, 1968.

C. Kindleberger (1969). *American Business Abroad*, Yale University Press, 1969.

A. T. Knoppers. *The Role of Science and Technology in Atlantic Economic Relationships*, The Atlantic Institute, 1966.

S. Kuznets. *Capital in the American Economy: its Formation and Financing*, Princeton, 1961.

C. Layton. *Trans-Atlantic Investments*, The Atlantic Institute, 1966.

C. Layton. *European Advanced Technology. A Programme for Integration*, Allen & Unwin, 1969.

A. Maddison. 'How fast can Britain grow?,' *Lloyds Bank Review*, January 1966.

Management Today. *The March of the Multi-nationals*, March 1968.

Management Today. *American Firms in Britain*, February 1969.

R. Mikesell. Decisive factors in the flow of American investment in Europe,' *Economica Internationale*, August 1967.

R. Nurkse. 'The problem of international investment today in the light of nineteenth century experience,' *Economic Journal*, Vol. LXIV, December 1954.

E. A. Philipps. 'American direct investment in West Germany manufacturing industries,' *Current Economic Comment*, No. 22, May 1960.

J. Polk, I. Meister and L. Veit. *US Production and the Balance of Payments*, National Industrial Conference Board, 1966.

M. V. Posner. 'International trade and technical change,' *Oxford Economic Papers*, Vol. XXII, 1961.

W. B. Reddaway, S. J. Potter and C. T. Taylor. *Effects of UK Direct Investment Overseas*, Cambridge University Press, 1967 and 1968.

H. J. Robinson. *The Motivation and Flow of Private Foreign Investment*, Stanford, 1961.

F. R. Root. 'The role of international business in the diffusion of technological innovation,' *Economics and Business Bulletin*, Summer 1968.

W. W. Rostow. *The Stages of Economic Growth*, Cambridge University Press, 1961.

E. Russell Eggers. 'The pattern of American investment in Europe,' in *The Changing World*. Proceedings of Second International Investment Syposium, London, 1965.

W. E. G. Salter. *Productivity and Technical Change*, Cambridge, 1960.

A. Scaperlanda. 'The EEC and US foreign investment: Some empirical evidence,' *Economic Journal*, Vol. LXXVII, March 1967.

A. Safarian. *Foreign Ownership of Canadian Industry*, McGraw-Hill, 1966.

J. J. Servan-Schreiber. *The American Challenge*, Hamish Hamilton, 1968.

G. Teeling-Smith (ed.). *Science, Industry and the State*, Pergamon, 1966.

B. Thomas. 'The historical record of international capital movements to 1913,' in J. H. Adler, *Capital Movements and Economic Development*, Macmillan, 1967.

R. Vernon (1966). 'International investment and international trade in the production cycle,' *Quarterly Journal of Economics*, Vol. LXXX, May 1966.

R. Vernon (1967). 'Multi-national enterprise and national sovereignty,' *Harvard Business Review*, March/April 1967.

R. Vernon (1968). 'Economic sovereignty at bay,' *Foreign Affairs*, October 1968.

M. Watkins. *Foreign Ownership and the Structure of Canadian Industry*. (Report of the task force on the structure of Canadian industry), Queen's Printer, Ottawa, 1968.

B. R. Williams. *Technology, Investment and Growth*, Chapman Hall, 1967.

8

THE EFFECTS OF UNITED STATES DIRECT INVESTMENT ON BRITISH TECHNOLOGY[1]

Introduction

Next to Canada, the United Kingdom claims a larger share of the foreign direct investments of United States companies than any other country in the world. At the end of 1967, there were more than 1,600 American subsidiaries and Anglo-American-financed firms operating in Britain with a cumulative investment stake of \$6,101 million.[2] While recent years have seen some deflection of new US investment in Europe towards the Common Market countries and Switzerland, the United Kingdom remains the single most important European host. During the past decade, American subsidiaries and Anglo-American-financed firms have financed between 6 and 7 per cent of corporate capital formation in Britain and earned 8 to 9 per cent of the profits. In 1965 they employed 6 per cent of the labour force in manufacturing industry, supplied 10 per cent of the total goods made in UK factories and accounted for 17½ per cent of British visible exports (Dunning 1969a). Further details of the growing participation of US companies in the UK economy since 1950 are given in Table 1.

Some 85 per cent of American investment in the UK is concentrated in manufacturing industry and petroleum refining and distribution, but US firms are also active in the British film industry and in such diverse fields as vending machines, bowling alleys, book publishing, exploration for gas in the North Sea and supermarkets. A broad industrial classification of the US *ownership* of net assets in the UK at the end of 1965 is given in Table 2. This is compared with the

[1] This chapter is based partly on a broadsheet prepared by the author for Political and Economic Planning (Dunning 1969a) and partly on a paper published by Max Steuer and the author in Moorgate and Wall Street, Autumn 1969.

[2] *Survey of Current Business*, September 1968.

TABLE 1

US Subsidiaries and their Significance in the UK Economy 1950/66

	1950	1957	1958	1959	1960	1961	1962	1963	1964	1965	1966
1. US cumulative investments as a percentage of UK gross national product (GNP)	2·6	3·6	3·8	4·2	5·1	5·2	5·3	5·5	5·6	5·9	6·2
2. US cumulative investments as a percentage of net capital stock of companies	n.a.	4·5	4·7	5·3	6·4	6·5	6·5	6·8	6·9	7·1	7·2
3. New US investment as a percentage of net fixed capital formation of companies	n.a.	18·3	17·9	14·0	12·9	15·7	15·5	19·2	16·7	20·2	n.a.
4. Expenditure on plant and equipment by US firms in manufacturing and petroleum as a percentage of gross fixed capital formation in UK industry	n.a.	10·0	9·5	7·4	7·3	9·1	8·5	9·9	9·6	11·5	n.a.
5. Sales of US firms in UK manufacturing industry as a percentage of UK manufacturing output	n.a.	5·7	6·3	6·2	6·7	7·2	7·4	8·3	8·9	9·6	10·5*
6. Income earned by US firms in UK as a percentage of net trading profits of UK companies	3·0	7·3	7·4	8·1	7·8	9·9	8·8	9·0	10·5	10·7	n.a.
7. Income earned by US firms in UK manufacturing industry as a percentage of net trading profits of UK companies in UK manufacturing industry	3·2	5·6	6·4	7·7	7·7	10·8	10·2	11·4	12·4	13·7	n.a.

* Author's estimate.
Source: *National Income Blue Book* (various issues). US Department of Commerce, *Survey of Current Business* (various issues).

TABLE 2

Industrial Distribution of US Subsidiaries and Leading UK Public Companies 1965

	Leading UK Companies Net Assets		*Leading US Subsidiaries US Share of Net Assets*		*Column 3/1*	*Column 4/2*
	(1)	(2)	(3)	(4)		
	£m.	*Percentage*	*£m.*	*Percentage*		
(*a*) *Research-intensive industries*						
Chemicals and allied products	2,458	16·0	524·5	35·0	21·3	2·19
Mechanical engineering	1,340	9·5	285·5	19·1	21·3	2·01
Electrical engineering	1,460	8·7	112·9	7·5	7·7	0·86
Motor vehicles	894	5·8	271·3	18·1	30·0	3·12
Rubber products	300[1]	1·9	40·7	2·7	13·6	1·42
	6,452	41·9	1,234·9	82·4	19·1	2·19
(*b*) *Other industries*						
Food, drink and tobacco	2,860	18·6	78·2	5·2	2·7	0·28
Metal manufacture	1,548	10·0	60·2	4·0	3·9	0·40
Textiles, clothing and footwear	1,537	10·0	28·7	1·9	1·9	0·19
Paper and paper products	1,179	7·7	14·9	1·0	1·3	0·12
Other	1,816	11·8	80·3	5·4	4·4	0·37
	8,940	58·1	262·3	17·5	2·9	0·30
Total manufacturing	15,392	100·0	1,492·2	100·0	9·7	1·00

[1] Author's estimate.

Source: US data – *Board of Trade Journal* and *Survey of Current Business Statistics on Income, Prices, Employment and Production.* UK data – *Ministry of Labour*.

distribution of the assets of the leading UK public companies, and in Column 5 a US concentration quotient is derived which shows the relative importance of the US stake in particular industries. It can be seen that not only is US investment strongly concentrated in research-intensive industries, but that its share of the assets of the leading UK public companies in these industries is three times that elsewhere.

Table 3 sets out a more detailed industrial breakdown of the net assets *controlled* by the one hundred leading US manufacturing firms in Britain, compiled from their balance sheets and ranked by their research and development content. The interesting feature of this table is that 57·5 per cent of US capital is concentrated in industries accounting for 86·7 per cent of US research and development (*r* and *d*) expenditure in 1961/66, and only 9·3 per cent is within industries where the proportion of *r* and *d* expenditure to sales is less than 1 per cent.

In certain British industries, American companies play a dominating role. They supply more than one half of the cars, office machinery, sewing machines, earth-moving equipment, domestic boilers, shoe-making machinery, breakfast cereals, cosmetics and toilet preparations, vacuum cleaners, pens and pencils, razor blades, foundation garments and films produced in the UK and nearly half the petrol and drugs sold to the National Health Service. I.B.M., the second largest computer firm in Britain, supplies nearly two-fifths of the market. About the same proportion of detergents, telephones, refrigerators, rubber tyres, watches and clocks are manufactured by US companies. Outside manufacturing industry, 15 per cent of the bank deposits in Britain are with American firms (Kenney 1968) and 50 per cent of the films shown in British cinemas are distributed by US companies. Many of the leading advertising agencies are American controlled, as is the largest credit and financial reporting enterprise, together with several important market research and management consultancy firms (MacMillan and Harris 1968).

Much of the recent growth of American investment has been self-financed. Something like 45 per cent of the $4,500m. invested in Britain since 1950 has represented profits reinvested by established US ventures. According to the Board of Trade (1968), 67·5 per cent of the American assets in UK industry in 1965 belonged to firms which were set up before 1946, although these are well under one half the total number. In addition, US companies have obtained many hundreds of millions of pounds of debt capital and trade credit from UK sources. At the end of 1965, US firms *controlled*

TABLE 3

Classification of 100 Leading US Financed Firms in UK Industry by Research and Development Content

	US Subsidiaries (1967) Net Assets £m.	US Subsidiaries (1967) Percentage to all Assets	US Research Intensity (1961/66)	Percentage of Total US Research[1]
(*a*) *High research-intensive products*				
Office machinery	47·6	3·0	24·3	(2)
Plastics and synthetics	45·2	2·8	14·4	(3)
Electronic and communication equipment	99·8	6·2	12·8	22·4
Other electrical machinery	61·2	3·9	7·1	14·3
Instruments	69·0	4·3	5·8	4·2
Pharmaceuticals	60·9	3·8	5·3	(3)
Other machinery	147·5	9·1	4·2	12·9
Other chemicals	53·6	3·3	4·1	16·0
	584·8	36·4	6·2	72·6
(*b*) *Medium research-intensive products*				
Vehicles	338·8	21·0	3·3	14·1
Rubber products	46·8	2·9	2·1	1·9
Metal goods	50·2	3·1	1·5	4·5
Bricks, pottery and glass	20·2	1·3	1·6	1·3
Petroleum	421·1	26·1	1·1	4·6
	877·1	54·4	2·1	21·9
(*c*) *Low research-intensive products*				
Food products	122·2	7·6	0·4	1·7
Other	28·2	1·7	0·5	2·1
	150·4	9·3	0·5	3·2
Total	1,612·3	100·0	3·6	100·0

[1] Excluding aircraft.
[2] Included in other machinery.
[3] Included in other chemicals.

Source: US subsidiaries, *Company Balance Sheets*. US Research Intensity (total *r* and *d* expenditure as a percentage of net sales). National Science Foundation, *Research and Development in Industry* (various years).

assets in British industry worth at least $9,000m. Of *all* new investment by these firms since 1955, only about a third has been financed directly from the US – and this includes the $350m. involved in the Ford deal of 1961.[1]

Most of the 1,660 or so US firms in Britain – and these include all enterprises, big and small, in all fields of activity – are fully owned subsidiaries. Of the 541 largest manufacturing and service companies in 1965 (excluding those in oil, banking and insurance), 366 (with 77 per cent of the net assets of all US firms) were 100 per cent subsidiaries and 52 (with 14 per cent of the net assets) were 51–99 per cent owned by American capital. The remainder were either branches or mainly UK financed. The importance of joint ventures has been increasing in recent years – particularly in the engineering and metal manufacturing industries.

There are some very sizeable American investments in Britain.[2] The five biggest are Esso (10th largest company in the UK), Ford (24th largest), Woolworth (33rd), Vauxhall Motors (43rd) and Gallahers (46th). These companies now account for about two-fifths of the total US capital stake, while the next largest twenty-four companies, which include such household names as Hoover, Heinz, Kodak, Goodyear, Hedley's and I.B.M., account for another two-fifths. In 1965, some thirty-seven US-controlled firms owned net assets worth £5m. or more and eighty-three owned assets of £2·5m. This means that, contrary to popular impressions, the great majority of American subsidiaries in Britain are of small to medium size.

This paper sets out to examine the impact of US investment in Britain on the host country's technological position. While recognizing that there are alternative ways of acquiring knowledge than by inward direct investment[3] (Bonin 1967, Johnson 1968), it does not attempt to deal with these in any substantive way. The paper starts from the premise, which it does not attempt to defend, that direct investment is an important means of the international transmission of technology, and that improved technology is vital to the UK's

[1] The dependence on local funds appears to be increasing. In 1966–67 American subsidiaries operating in Europe financed 45 per cent of their capital expenditure from local funds and 15 per cent from the US. These ratios compare with 32 per cent and 26 per cent, respectively, in 1960–63.

[2] For further details see J. H. Dunning and the Economists Advisory Group (1969).

[3] Some of these are set out in H. A. Johnson's *Comparative Cost and Commercial Policy Theory for a Developing World Economy*, The Wicksell Lectures, 1968.

economic development. Inadequate technology is a major explanation of past set-backs: improved technology is a major hope for future advances (Denison 1967).

There is a rapidly growing literature of the effects of foreign investment on the economy of developed host countries.[1] Our purpose here is to concentrate on one aspect of the problem, taking the United Kingdom as a case study. There is no implication, of course, that the technological effects of inward investment are the only, or even the overriding ones. But they are significant. In serious studies, and in popular discussion, reference is made to a number of alleged advantages and disadvantages from the technological point of view. The third and fourth sections of this paper attempt some *a priori* clarification of these arguments. Use will be made of stylized facts, familiar economic reasoning, and the few statistics which have been published. To our knowledge, no formal models have been devised to explain these relations, although there is a good deal of thinking around the subject – particularly from the viewpoint of the less-developed countries (Baranson 1966, Root 1968, Quinn 1969). Perhaps, some aspects of our analysis will serve as forerunners to these. A final section of the chapter hazards some policy conclusions.

The word technology has been variously defined. For our purposes, we propose to define technology as 'the body of knowledge that is applicable to the production of goods and the creation of new goods' (Root 1968) – or even more simply 'the way in which resources are converted into commodities' (Jones 1968). All forms of the 'how' of corporate activity are included in this definition, not only those involving 'product design, production and techniques and industrial systems to plan, organize and carry out a production plan' (Baranson 1966), but skills relating to the managerial decision-taking process as well. Sometimes, this new knowledge will be embodied in tools, machinery, or other items of capital equipment; sometimes in production or marketing processes, or in 'rights' to these, e.g. specifications, drawings, blueprints, patents, etc.; some times in specialized skills, e.g. organization and management, and personal contact. Similarly technology may be proprietary or non-proprietary (Quinn 1968); it may be 'general,' 'system specific' or 'enterprise specific' (Hall and Johnson 1968). The question to be discussed is how far, and in what ways, do the operation of US companies in the UK affect this transference of technology? What are its net costs and benefits to the host

[1] Recent studies include Deane (1967), Johnstone (1965), Layton (1966), Brash (1966), Safarian (1966), Watkins (1968), Stonehill (1967), Litvak and Maule (1969).

country, compared with obtaining knowledge in different ways, or not obtaining it at all?

The relationship between direct investment and technological change

The complementarity between the export of capital and knowledge is of comparatively recent origin, and is almost entirely a reflection of the growth of the multi-national company. For most of the nineteenth century, Britain poured out capital to the Americas and the Commonwealth. But by far the greater part of this took the form of portfolio investment; in 1913, for example, fixed-interest-bearing securities accounted for 85 per cent of the UK capital stake overseas and 70 per cent of these were directed to Government or railroad ventures (Feis 1930). Side by side, but largely independent of this flow of capital, was a migration of labour and entrepreneurship. The US railroads were built with English capital and Irish labour, but UK management or technology were rarely directly involved; by contrast, the American cotton textile industry owed much of its early development to UK skills and technology but was almost entirely domestically financed (Coram 1967).

The subsequent evolution of the joint stock company, accompanied by the growing complexity of production and managerial technology, brought together, as a package deal, the export of capital and knowledge, while international market forces have tended to stimulate the flow of these inputs relative to the output of goods they create. As a world phenomenon, international direct investment is growing at the rate of 10 per cent per annum – about twice that of world gross national product. In 1966, US foreign subsidiaries and associated companies produced abroad four times the value of US exports, and the income earned on US direct foreign investments is increasing at twice the rate of her visible exports (Behrman 1969).

It is not the purpose of this chapter to trace the reasons for these developments. But the extent to which they involve the international diffusion of technology will depend on (*a*) the 'knowledge' content of the investment *vis-à-vis* that which is already available in the host country; this is self-evident and need not be enlarged upon here, save to point out that there is a close correlation between the industrial composition of US foreign investment in Europe and US expenditure on research and development,[1] (*b*) the age and form of the foreign

[1] For further details see Chapter 7.

investment, (*c*) the policy of the investing company towards its overseas operations, and (*d*) the competitive environment in which the investment firm is operating.

In the past, most kinds of foreign manufacturing operations have begun by the establishment of sales and distributing ventures. These have been followed by investment in the simpler types of manufacturing processes, involving transmission of formulae, specifications, plant layout diagrams, etc., but embodying only a small technological content. As the subsidiary undertakes more complex manufacturing operations, and adaptations have to be made to processes or products to meet local requirements, its need to understand, as well as to use, the technology of its parent company increases. The value of knowledge input continues to grow as the subsidiary widens its operations laterally and vertically, and reaches its peak with the setting up of its own research and development operations. When a foreign company takes over an existing domestic concern, the technological impact is more dramatically revealed. The subsidiary company then becomes immediately linked to the investing country's techno-economic environment.

The extent to which international companies disseminate technological expertise will also depend on their organizational structure and the relations between the parent company and its subsidiaries. Professor M. V. Perlmutter has distinguished three stages of management evolution of the multi-national company (Perlmutter 1969). The *ethnocentric* organization is one where the minimum of autonomy is allowed to subsidiaries; all top decisions are taken by the parent company in the belief that they have a monopoly of such knowledge. Knowledge is transmitted but without the appreciation of such knowledge that managers of a *polycentric* organization will have. Such an organization recognizes that local situations are different from those faced by the parent company and in other subsidiaries. Rather more autonomy of decision taking is allowed – advice is offered rather than commands given. The subsidiary's management is better integrated with that of the rest of the group, and particularly with that of the parent company, and there are frequent exchanges of ideas and visits. All the same, in this federation of loosely connected subsidiaries, it remains rare for foreigners to reach top executive positions, and organizational problems arise, due to the lack of overall co-ordination of activities.

In Perlmutter's view, the most desirable pattern of activities is that which he classifies as *geocentric*. A geocentric company is characterized by two features. First, the top management in all its operations is truly international – the best man is chosen for the job in particular countries irrespective of nationality: second, all activities are closely co-ordinated, and there is the fullest possible interchange of knowledge throughout the world. In such cases, innovations and ideas flow not only from parent to subsidiary, but subsidiary to parent and between subsidiaries.

Finally, the international transmission of knowledge will be influenced by the structure of competition facing the investing firm both in the investing and in the host countries. Several writers (Hymer 1960, Kindleberger 1969a) have emphasized that the modern multi-national company is primarily a vehicle for the transfer of entrepreneurial talent rather than financial resources, and that the impetus to foreign direct investment arises largely from the desire to exploit an economic advantage which a firm has over its competitors – or, in the case of a following, rather than a leading firm, from the need to protect its market position. Furthermore, one would expect the transmission of knowledge to be greater where it would otherwise be the most impeded, e.g. in industries operating in imperfectly competitive markets.

How do these general considerations apply to the UK? First, as in other parts of Europe, the participation of US firms in Britain is most concentrated in the science-based industries. In 1965, 69·3 per cent of the total output of such enterprises were supplied by industries responsible for 73·3 per cent of company-financed research and development expenditures in the United States in 1962 (Gruber, Mehta and Vernon 1967). US-owned enterprises also contribute significantly to the output of UK consumer goods which satisfy high-income or labour-substituting wants, and involve fairly standardized production techniques, e.g. washing machines, cameras, pack foods, cosmetics. More often than not, both types of product were first commercially produced in the US and later exported to the UK, prior to the establishment of local manufacturing facilities and the accompanying transmission of technological expertise.

Second, most US subsidiaries in Britain are fully developed and integrated manufacturing units. The import of components and semi-manufactured goods from the United States is, generally, quite small; most firms take fully into account the difference in input prices and local market needs in their process and product policies; and the average US subsidiary spends at least the same amount on research and development as its UK competitors (Dunning 1966). In a growing number of cases, there is some product or process specialization between the US parent and its UK subsidiary, or between different manufacturing subsidiaries in Europe. The potential need for technological knowledge is therefore very great, although, not always does it follow that such knowledge will be used.

Third, most US offshoots in Britain are parts of polycentric organizations (Dunning 1969a). Their degree of autonomy in managerial decision-taking varies a good deal with circumstances, but the kind of decisions which most have to take involves the type and degree of expertise and judgement which can stand to benefit from advanced managerial technology. On the whole, the skill of the top management of US subsidiaries compares favourably with their UK counterparts; a higher proportion of executives are likely to have degrees or the equivalent; their average age is younger; they are keenly receptive to new ideas (Thomas 1969).

Finally, US (and other foreign) firms in Britain are strongly concentrated in oligopolistic industries. At least four-fifths of all American investment in manufacturing industry (including oil refining) is within the industries with high concentration ratios – motor vehicles, rubber tyres, office machinery are well-known examples (Dunning 1969b). Several of these industries have been subject to searching official enquiries, the reports of which give substantial support to the claim frequently voiced by the chief decision-takers of American subsidiaries that the most significant advantage they enjoy over their competitors is their access to superior technological and managerial techniques.

We conclude, then, that, for a variety of reasons, the UK economic environment is potentially a fertile one for the reception of knowledge and ideas from the US transmitted through the medium of direct investment.

In the next section of this paper, we shall consider some costs and benefits to the British economy arising from the technological impact made by US subsidiaries in Britain. We shall not, however, attempt to analyse the wider macro-economic implications of these costs and benefits, nor examine the environmental conditions which may affect the balance between them. We shall touch upon this latter question in the final section of this paper.

The technological problems arising from US investment

Popular thinking on this topic has two simple themes, an optimistic one and a pessimistic one. Up to fairly recently, the emphasis has been very much on the advantages of US investment. The incoming American firm is seen to be beneficial to the British economy in three ways.

1. It introduces new products. These benefit the consumer directly, promote other innovations through competition, and, in the case of intermediate goods, raise productivity.
2. By drawing on the research and development efforts of its parent company, it greatly expands the flow of new ideas and knowledge available to the United Kingdom.
3. American management techniques mean that British factor inputs are employed more efficiently than they otherwise would be, particularly if these techniques are imitated by domestic firms as well.

In a sentence, inward investment is seen as a vehicle which brings advanced American technology and ideas to this country.

Of course, the United Kingdom, while being among the more self-effacing economies, is not, on any criteria, an under-developed economy. British investment in, and contributions to, modern technology are both substantial. Few observers would regard the United States as the only source for innovations in the British economy. Indeed, in some ways, American firms are seen more as competitors, even as dangerous rivals to UK firms. And this gives rise to a number of negative views about US investment in Britain. Basically, there are four of these.[1]

1. Where US enterprises take over British firms, which have made significant research contributions, the benefits of these contributions (and all future contributions) accrue to the United States rather than to the United Kingdom.
2. The take-overs may reduce or eliminate research efforts in the United Kingdom, transferring such activities to the parent enterprise. The firm is still operating in the UK, but it is doing less research than a comparable domestic firm.
3. As a result of (1) and (2), the British economy is becoming technologically more dependent on the United States. This argument often has a national security aspect.
4. American exports to the United Kingdom are based on superior technology. When these become quantitatively large, they are replaced by manufacturing operations in the UK, using basically similar techniques. Meanwhile, the parent company introduces a new generation of products and processes. The implication, in which direct investment plays a critical part, is that the UK is always using outdated methods.

[1] See also Chapter 7, and Kindleberger 1969b.

Again, in one sentence, American investment, far from aiding UK technological progress, is holding it back.

In fact, US investment in Britain is unlikely to be unequivocably good or bad for the host economy. The effects range over every aspect of economic life; balance of payments, industrial relations, regional development, national income, income distribution, and so on. And even one area, such as the technological impact, may have its positive and negative sides. Probably, some persuasive evidence could be found in support of each of the three favourable arguments and each of the four unfavourable arguments. It seems reasonable not to assert that the truth lies entirely with one group or the other. On the other hand, one can attempt to evaluate the significance of the various claims and make a judgement about where the balance of advantage lies and, from the point of view of policy, point to the optimum amount of inward investment – if indeed there is such a thing. Alternatively, since some investing firms are likely to be better for United Kingdom technology than others, one can try to set out the criteria for good and bad.

At the same time, even if a conceptually meaningful distinction could be drawn between foreign subsidiaries which, in general, are helpful to Britain's technology and those which are harmful, in practice, it may not be possible to determine this with hindsight. This last point is not always appreciated in popular discussion, and even by official decision takers. We turn now to the individual arguments against US investment in the UK.

1. *The take-over case*

The most striking alleged damaging effects from US (and other) direct investment arise in the case of a domestic firm which has a productive research programme and, also, a stock of unexploited innovations. Not only do the benefits of research advances now accrue to the overseas parent; there is, at least, the possibility that the research effort in the United Kingdom will be disbanded or markedly reduced. In the United Kingdom, the cases of the take-over of Cossor by Raytheon in 1962 and Solatron by Schlumberger in 1961 are frequently quoted as unfortunate examples of this type of inward investment. What is rarely mentioned is the obvious point that there must be some take-over price which would adequately compensate the host country for the sale of its asset. To argue that any take-over is disadvantageous to the nation implies that the sale price is always below the assets' social worth and we may ask why? How does this come about?

(a) The effect on the stock of unexploited innovations

Let us consider separately, first the question of the stock of unexploited innovations, and second that of the reduced research effort. If the stock of unexploited innovations is acquired by an American company at an economic rate, i.e. something like the present discounted expected value, there is no loss. A simple point, but one which is often overlooked, is that foreign investment need not reduce or displace domestic investment. In the case of a take-over of this kind, the former owners can, and often do, invest the proceeds elsewhere.[1] What matters is that they sell at the right price, regardless of the innovation potential in the sale. What is the likelihood of their doing this?

A classic British view, or mental worry image, is of a creative domestic firm arriving at an important research breakthrough and near bankruptcy at roughly the same time. The American investor appears like a Victorian villain and buys the ideas for a song. Certainly, there are imperfections in capital markets. An individual firm may be under-financed and not be able to save itself. But might not other British interests seize this opportunity? There are, at least, three reasons why this might not be possible. First, there may be an overall shortage of capital, second, mistakes may be made in the investment decision, and third, either the investment opportunities or the expected profitability of a particular investment may be viewed differently from US than from UK eyes.

We doubt if anyone would want to argue that US firms take over UK firms because of any *general* lack of capital in the UK economy. The whole cast of the discussion is that certain special, and significant, opportunities are being lost to foreign interests. That other domestic factors could be better employed if combined with more capital is, of course, true. This is a fundamental feature of inward direct investment. However, if the 'wrong' firms are yielding to American take-over bids, we have to look for more specific causes. The issue of a general deficiency of investment funds is a different one.

A more powerful suggestion is that US firms are better at appraising the economic potential of new ideas than their British counterparts. In the UK, domestic firms may not foresee as accurately as foreigners

[1] There are few writers who entertain a notion of a fixed stock of profitable investments. Without going into this issue, we may say that we find it implausible. Two points can be noted: (i) the new investment can, in principle, be abroad rather than at home; (ii) the alternative profitability should be taken into account in determining the sale price of the take-over.

which are the more profitable prospects. Like the firm that knew that half its advertising was wasted, but did not know which half, UK firms may not be very good at identifying research value. All research is expensive, and many new developments prove to be economic disasters. But even if the UK has a comparative disadvantage in research recognition (and this is by no means proven), the answer does not lie in holding active ownership in the entire stock of British innovations. The theory of current maximizing would suggest that if the UK has a comparative disadvantage in one direction, it should pursue its comparative advantage in another. Doubt arises because of the possibility of a conflict between current and long-term maximizing. This point, often suggested, but not convincingly argued, will be touched on in later sections.

Even with equal ability to appraise a stock of innovations, however, there still are reasons why US take-overs could occur at uneconomically low prices. The arguments fall into two categories. One turns on the distribution of risks; the other, on the economies of size. Let us suppose that each stock of ideas, or patents, is like a portfolio to which it is possible to assign a probability to each pay-off, positive and negative. The distribution, as a whole, has an expected value, which is the average pay-off on a large number of repeated trials. It also has a variance. In general, greater variance reduces the attractiveness of an investor of given expected value.

When an investor buys shares in a single company, the variance and expected value per unit are not affected by the number of units purchased. This is because the behaviour of each unit is perfectly correlated with every other unit: they are completely dependent. But suppose that we have two assets of equal expected value and equal variance, but which are completely independent. Obviously they are not shares in a single company. Instead, we are thinking of two totally distinct assets whose distribution of pay-offs happen to be described by the same relevant parameters. An investor who has purchased both assets has the same per unit expected value, but a reduced per unit variance. In the limit, if enough of such assets can be purchased, the variance falls to zero. The point is that the more similar but independent assets a single interest can acquire, the less relevant is the variance of each asset and the more relevant is the expected value of each. This simple proposition is analogous to the law of large numbers. Multiple purchases of independent assets reduces risk.

It seems reasonable to assume that large firms can undertake more take-overs than small firms. There are more large American firms than British firms. If we assume that the Americans have the same subjective trade-off between risk and expected value as the British, then, on the argument of the previous paragraph, they will tend to acquire the assets with higher expected value. Suppose there are two types of research-oriented firms with stocks of unexploited innovations. The first offers high risks and high pay-offs; the second low risks and low pay-offs. The Americans, by each making many purchases in the former category, will reduce their risks. The British firms, restricted by size to making one or two take-overs, will have to invest in the lower risk, lower pay-off category.

In essence, this point is a scale argument leading to a divergence between social and private interests. Risk variance matters a lot to the single firm contemplating a single or small number of take-overs. For the United Kingdom as a whole, the independent variances somewhat cancel themselves out. The United States firms, through sheer size, tend to become self-insuring. They can pay more for the high-risk, high-reward assets. And so the British firms place a lower price on these stocks of technology, and one below the social value. This is a delicate argument, and one that may be unimportant empirically. But it makes logical sense.

So far, no account has been taken of competition between potential American buyers. We are looking for rational reasons why British interests may allow foreign take-overs of innovating firms at uneconomic prices. Yet, even if we find such reasons, why should American firms allow one of their number to buy at a low price? Competitive theory suggests that they would not. This leads to two new considerations, the relationships between monopoly and technology and the fact that ideas may be worth more to some people than to others. Before tackling these points we should consider the possibility that the trade-off between risk and return may differ between countries.

The previous argument dealt with the possibility of foreign take-overs at low price (setting aside the question of competition between American firms) given equal ability between British and American businessmen and an equal trade-off between return and risk. A further possibility is that evaluation of risk may be a function of income. A high variance may be less off-putting to Americans. The important thing is the distinction between the individual firms and the economy as a whole. A firm may be small and relatively poor in an economy which is large and rich. If the economy is small and poor, individual risk avoidance will be in the social interest. For the United Kingdom as a whole, individual risk avoidance may be inappropriate.

Finally, there is the argument that certain innovations may be worth more to United States firms than to the United Kingdom firms because their marketing opportunities differ. It is often suggested that the successful exploitation of ideas can rest critically on large-scale marketing facilities. If the United Kingdom interests are behaving rationally, they will sell out if the price is higher than the present value of the stock of discoveries to them. The fact that the Americans can do even better with the stock seems immaterial. The take-over is still advantageous to the host country.[1] If certain research, in fact, cannot be optimally exploited by British interest, it is foolish to want to retain these results.

Why then do United Kingdom firms invest in research activities, the results of which cannot be profitably retained? Certainly the productivity of research is not very predictable. Perhaps, quite often, ideas come up which cannot be profitably exploited by the discoverer. Or it could be that chance is not the only factor, and poor research decisions are made. There is a great tendency for European firms to copy their American counterparts in the research-intensive industries. Some firms may operate research programmes which are inappropriate given their marketing potentials and simply reflect current United States practices. In that case it would not be surprising that the ideas when they develop are worth more to American interests. Nor would it be against the United Kingdom interests to sell.

(*b*) *The possible disruption of research activities*

Having discussed the stock of ideas and their role in a foreign take-over, we turn now to the question of disruption of research activities. This is the other major alleged loss. A research organization takes time to develop, requires fruitful interaction between its members, and so is really more than the sum of its component parts. The first question to ask is why might the new American owners want to disband or reduce the activities of such an intricate and complex machine? The research organization is not a saleable commodity, so they are giving it up for nothing.

The most obvious explanation is that the parent organization can do the same work more efficiently. If this is the case, then the economic benefit to the United Kingdom of its research activities was probably illusory in the first place. They would never be in a

[1] An exception is the possibility of external effects, which we will take up later.

position to market a product ahead of their American competitors. A more likely explanation is the belief, on the part of the parent enterprise, that there are advantages to be achieved by centralizing its research effort. If the local organization could contribute more to the firm by remaining intact, the parent would be inclined to leave it, or even augment it. Centralization means here that either the investing company hires more research inputs in its own country to support the newly acquired subsidiary, or transfers some of the British researchers to the United States. The latter leads into 'brain drain' type issues, and contains others as well.

If an American firm pays the salary of a British researcher and owns the ideas he produces, it is not easy to see how it matters to the UK economy whether that researcher is located in the UK working for the subsidiary or in the States working for the parent. There is, of course, the question of the tax on his income. This is, however, a matter of the economics of immigration and is not especially relevant to his work as a researcher. Digressing slightly, this point should be borne in mind in any discussion of the brain drain. The loss of property in ideas can happen to a country without its scientists moving. Take-overs, when research departments are not disbanded, or new foreign establishments which hire host-country researchers, are probably quantitatively far more important than actual emigration of scientists.

Part of the loss to the United Kingdom of redundant research workers having to seek new employment depends on the view that one takes of the demand for and the mobility of this kind of labour. Our impressions are that both are quite high. If the scientists and technicians are readily absorbed elsewhere in the economy, the social costs on the UK technology are not very serious due to a foreign take-over. Were the particular combination of research inputs to be especially valuable, then one must explain why the Americans disbanded them. It appears that any loss to the United Kingdom economy will arise largely through the take-over itself, not through what is done with the research organization afterwards. The question of the proper sale price for the research department is the same as that of the proper price for the existing stock of ideas, and requires no special treatment here.

2. *The new establishment case*

Next, we turn to the question of the establishment of a new enterprise, as opposed to the take-over of one already in existence. We consider two possibilities – the new establishment either sets up a substantial research effort in the UK or none at all. In the former case the labour inputs may be hired locally, again raising the brain drain issue. If research workers are imported from the US, which seems unlikely, then these will add to the total number of research workers in the UK.

Typically, however, a research effort on the part of a subsidiary will be largely manned by United Kingdom citizens. According to a survey carried out by the American Chamber of Commerce (1967), only 421 of the 404,000 people employed by 161 leading US subsidiaries in Britain were American nationals, of whom 229 occupied positions of management. Other research suggests that where UK firms and US affiliates compete side by side the latter spend at least as much on research and development as the former (Dunning 1966). It is also the case that American subsidiaries frequently contract-out research to other United Kingdom firms. At first sight this would seem all to the good. The UK needs inward investment which will lead to sizeable research efforts. Why? If the brain drain is bad, why is it good for British scientists to work for American subsidiaries? Only if this creates substantial technological and competitive spillover effects (Quinn 1968) will this be the case.

These arguments should be set in the context of the general state of United Kingdom technology. A recent study (Peck 1968) produces interesting statistical evidence of the salient, and widely agreed, generalization in this area. First, the UK economy has a very large commitment in research-dependent activity, more so even than the United States. The proportion of the manufacturing labour force concentrated in the research-intensive sectors of the UK economy, e.g. electronics, chemicals, aircraft, and the proportion of exports accounted for by these products (Dunning 1969c) is markedly higher than most other European countries. Secondly, the ratio of engineers to scientists among the technical labour force is low by international comparison and is sub-optimal on certain direct evidence. Thirdly, the overall supply of technically trained people is inadequate on similar grounds. Less qualified people are used to a greater extent than elsewhere, with probably damaging results. Finally, with the educational emphasis on scientists, which implies purer research, and the overall shortage, it is not surprising that few technically qualified people are to be found in management and such fields as sales. Peck concludes that the fundamental problem is the shortage of qualified people and only a substantial increase in educational inputs will help. Meanwhile, he recommends concentrating *r* and *d* resources and making appropriate commitments in a limited number of areas.

If these observations are broadly correct, the newly established foreign subsidiary which does not undertake research in the UK *may* be doing the economy a service. Even the take-over case, which results in reduced or terminated research, may counteract the prevailing tendency to spread local research efforts too widely. Whether or not this is so, will depend on the comparative research productivity of US and other firms, the ease at which the research workers laid off can find appropriate employment elsewhere in the UK economy, and their inclination to emigrate abroad.

3. *Technological dependence*

We next consider the very broad and loose argument that the inflow of US capital leads to a situation where the United Kingdom is becoming technologically dependent on the United States. The presumption is that something should be done, either selectively, or across the board, to reduce the inflow and this would lead to greater British economic independence.[1] Why this should happen is not quite clear, as it is very likely, if direct investment were curtailed, that British firms would conclude more licensing agreements with US firms, and imports from the US would increase. This might affect the *form* of the dependence but not necessarily its amount.

Most economists agree that the rate of growth of the national output of an advanced industrial country is closely linked to its pace of innovation (Denison 1967). Whether or not a substantial proportion of this innovation originates from foreign subsidiaries is not really relevant – except in so far as it affects the efficiency of research and development activities. A more sophisticated counter-argument might hold that the proportion matters *because* it affects the quantity and success of the host country's effort.[2] Yet it is by no means certain which way this association runs, positively or negatively. As long as international patent rights are respected, a United States innovation cannot be duplicated by British researchers. And on a variety of general grounds, one could maintain that, in many cases, ideas, and their diffusion throughout the economy, stimulate more ideas. So the association may well be positive.

Other writers have asserted that closer examination of a large number of British achievements reveals close ties with American (or other foreign) ideas, and that it is hard to distinguish the purely British contributions. But this is a really silly worry. Only those

[1] We abstract from the military, or national security, aspects of this argument in this paper. See Kindleberger (1969b).

[2] This is an argument which has sometimes been used against the very substantial participation of US investment in the Canadian economy.

concerned with the most naïve nationalism would worry about the purity of British innovations. Indeed, it is hard to think of another area where the cost of autonomy is likely to be as high as in the production of ideas. The characteristic of the successful researcher is that he draws on the maximum of relevant material, irrespective of its nationality, or other characteristics of origin. Autonomy means that researchers must develop all stages of a process, not just those where they have particular ability.

Economic analysis suggests that one of the economic advantages of innovation arises from the monopoly power it affords. Naturally, income anticipated from innovation must support the cost of research, including the cost of the inevitable failures. But implied in much of the current concern about the profits earned by foreign firms in some science-based industries in the UK is that the monopoly rewards of innovation are considerably more than enough to compensate the research costs involved. We see no evidence to accept this proposition as a general rule (Dunning 1969a) although, where this is shown to be the case, the benefit to the United Kingdom of research by US (or other foreign) subsidiaries in the UK will be much less than it may appear. On broader grounds, some support for scepticism with respect to the economic pay-off of research can be found in the substantial amount of Government subsidy for research. Particularly for the United States, it is often pointed out that a very large proportion of the total research activity in that country is Government supported (Peck 1968).

So much for our analysis of a number of arguments relating to the adverse impact of American investment to British technology. In general, the various propositions seem much less clear and the alleged problems more illusive in effect than when first stated. A similar outcome occurs when we turn to the three major benefits. After considering these we can attempt a tentative synthesis.

The advantages for UK technology

The argument that direct investment introduces new products into the United Kingdom is complicated by the fact that, in many cases, trade could have done the same. The products, however, may well be cheaper to the user. This is partly for tariff reasons, and partly because production costs are generally lower in the UK than in the US (Gates and Linden 1960, Dunning 1969a). However, our concern in the present paper is not with the gains from trade, but with those which may arise from technological reasons. We assume that, on balance, one effect of direct investment is to speed the pace of new product diffusion throughout the economy – and that this is all to the good.

Only two points against this proposition have occurred to us. One is an E. J. Mishan type argument, with horror at modern times and a Tati-like nostalgia for the past (Mishan 1966). This is clearly outside the scope of the present paper. The other point is analogous to the infant-industry thesis. With Americans leading the UK in many fields, we fail to develop as we could do under a breathing spell. Of course, any gain in time may well be accompanied with a reduced incentive to change. Those antagonistic to direct investment usually list foreign products, particularly familiar household names, as a *prima-facie* case for the dangers of the American penetration. But all such lists can genuinely show is that more familiar products are produced by foreign subsidiaries than is generally recognized.

(*a*) *Research benefits*

The primary technological benefit most frequently quoted for inward investment is the size of the research effort undertaken by American parents of UK subsidiaries. The implication is that the British economy, through the presence of such subsidiaries, can draw on a research effort several times the size of our own domestic effort and usually at well below market cost. This is true – up to a point. Potentially, a very great deal of research is made available to the UK economy in this way and, generally speaking, there would appear to be few constraints on its transmittance across the Atlantic. However, US affiliates in Britain rarely produce the same range of products as their parent companies, or use identical production processes or serve the same markets. This means that *some* of the output of US research laboratories will be irrelevant for the UK. We do not know what the proportion or 'relevant' research is, but it clearly differs between industries and individual firms. A survey of US subsidiaries in the pharmaceutical industry, published earlier in 1969 (Dunning 1969a), revealed that, in the opinion of the research or technical directors of the larger subsidiaries, between 75 per cent and 100 per cent of the research findings of their parent companies was of direct relevance for their UK operations, while in the case of smaller firms this was as low as 10–15 per cent. In the electronics industry, the proportions ranged equally widely, but were generally in the 25 per cent to 50 per cent bracket.

Some idea of the relative contribution of American research effort to the UK economy is to multiply the sales of US manufacturing

TABLE 4

Estimated Contribution of US Research and Development Transferred to UK by US Subsidiaries

	Sales of Sub-sidiaries 1965	*US r and d Percentage of Sales*	*Column* 1 × *Column* 2	*UK r and d*	*Column* 2/3 × 100
	$m.			$m.	
Research-intensive products					
Chemicals[1]	1,241	4·3	53·3	166·6	32·0
Rubber products	219	2·1	4·6	14·3	32·2
Non-electrical machinery	1,121	4·2	47·1	143·4	32·8
Electrical machinery	706	9·8	69·2	299·3	23·1
Transportation equipment	1,798	3·3[2]	59·3	96·3[2]	61·6
	5,085	4·6	233·5	719·9	32·4
Other products					
Food products	730	0·5	3·7	42·0	8·8
Paper and other products	102	0·7	0·8	9·8	8·2
Metals	546	1·0	5·5	66·9	8·2
Other products	1,047	0·5	5·2	89·9	5·8
	2,425	0·6	15·2	214·4	7·1
All products[3]	7,510	3·7	248·7	928·5	26·8

[1] Excluding petroleum refining.
[2] Motor vehicle only.
[3] Excludes petroleum refining and aircraft.

Source: US Department of Commerce, *Survey of Current Business*, Nov. 1966; National Science Foundation, *Research and Development in Industry* (various years); *Annual Abstract of (U.K.) Statistics*, 1967, Table 158.

subsidiaries in Britain in various lines of activity (see Table 2), by the percentage of American sales accounted for by *r* and *d* expenditure. The results are given in Table 4. While the US contribution is almost certainly an underestimate, it is nowhere near as great as is sometimes supposed. Of course, part of the UK research effort is itself accounted for by US subsidiaries. Here the evidence would suggest that, in most UK industries, the *amount* of research undertaken by US subsidiaries compares very favourably with that of UK companies, although its accent is slanted rather more to applied or development research. To some extent this latter tendency is being counteracted by the setting up of specialized research departments of multi-national firms in various locations throughout the world. But, perhaps most important of all is the question of the allocation of the *benefits* of research and development between the US subsidiary and its parent company, and the rest of the UK economy. Much will depend here on the structure of competition and the efficiency of Government policy (Watkins 1968). The benefits of cost-reducing innovations could, in principle, be captured entirely by the parent company in higher profits. But, normally, part of these reduced costs would be passed on to the British consumer. Subsidiary profits will naturally be taxed, and that makes it much harder for the foreign company to retain an overriding proportion of the benefit. On the other hand, by appropriate manipulation of intra-company prices, the subsidiary may avoid considerable taxation.

We conclude, then. The idea that the presence of US subsidiaries enables the UK to benefit from the great bulk of US research is considerably exaggerated. Not only is only part of this research of any use to the UK economy, but, because of market imperfections, such knowledge as is received may extend beyond the subsidiaries to their competitors or other firms generally. And in some cases, there is the problem of perpetual monopoly. The firm with a patented advantage and an established market has the incentive to go on to the next innovation, and in this way is able to maintain its monopoly position indefinitely.

(*b*) *Managerial advantages*

A second widely held view of the value of US direct investment is the one which emphasizes the advantages of American managerial and organizational skill. J. J. Servan-Schreiber (1968) is among the many who point out that capital transfer, while large, is not the whole story. Much of the capital for the activities of US firms abroad is raised in host countries. American technology, in the sense of production of basic scientific innovation, is met by many European contributions. If it was just a matter of technical knowledge about products and processes, the 'American Challenge' would be much less formidable. What really counts is the American comparative advantage in managerial technology. The United States, so the argument runs, is primarily exporting this rather than capital.

Our reading of the discussion of the alleged superiority of American managers suggests three aspects. One is that they are better at selecting, supervising, training and motivating labour inputs. More resources and attention go into this than is common in European industry. Second, they have a clearer grasp of the goal of profit-making and/or growth maximization, and are less easily distracted by side considerations. Third, they give more attention to, and place more emphasis on, marketing and sales than their host-country competitors (*Management Today* 1969). It seems reasonable to take these generalizations as being broadly true, and try to examine some of their more important implications.

If American management technology is superior, and this extends to their foreign operations, how does this benefit the British economy? Two arguments are usually advanced. One is that resources are more efficiently deployed than they would be under domestic management, and this output is higher than it otherwise would be. Again, some, but not all, of this extra output will accrue to the UK economy. The rest will result ultimately in repatriated profit. But that part which is retained either as higher wages, or other factor payments, or lower product prices, or through tax revenue, is a clear gain to the UK. Further details of the extent of this gain are given in Chapter 9 and in Dunning (1969a).

When a foreign firm raises all its capital in the UK and imports only its name, a few American managers and the skills of its parent company, this is really an example of the 'brain drain' in reverse, as the UK is gaining particularly scarce and much-needed entrepreneurial skill. For some reason, those most antagonistic to inward investment seem to find this apparently beneficial case among the most insidious, though they do not present any reasons for that view.

The other alleged gain of American management, in technological terms, is the spill-over effect. Better management inspires competitive firms to improve. In practice, it is difficult to tell how important this gain has been. In general, mobility of top management between subsidiaries and domestic firms has been fairly limited. It may also be argued that, if a British firm wishes to move in the direction of United States management practices, there are plenty of avenues open for it to do so, e.g. through the employment of consultants, access to US technical literature, recruitment and training of personnel, etc., in the States. Moreover, unlike process or product technology, most managerial technology is non-proprietary and general, rather than firm specific in character. On the other hand, there is some evidence that, in industries in which US subsidiaries and UK firms compete side by side, the latter have improved their productivity and profitability relative to the former in recent years (Dunning 1969a). It would not seem unreasonable to suppose that part of this improvement is due to the spill-over effect of US management technology. One can also take a larger number of cases of US firms passing on both general and system-specific technology to their suppliers of components and parts in the UK (Dunning 1958).

Similarly, the characteristics of better management are rarely so specific that they are likely to be of use only to firms which are directly competitive. The principles underlying many new managerial and organizational techniques are of fairly general applicability – capital budgeting, economic forecasting and linear programming are three examples. Through the normal course of labour mobility, contacts with trade and research associations, and with customers and suppliers, the transmission of this kind of knowledge – and the philosophy behind it – can be very considerable. And, even if the benefits of better management are retained in the initiating firm, there is plenty of evidence, in the case of US investment in the UK at least, that the productivity of factor inputs within these firms has been advanced. It is also noteworthy that the decision-takers in US subsidiaries, who are UK nationals, are generally better trained and likely to reach senior executive positions at an earlier age than their counterparts in domestic firms, and about one half of them received at least part of their training in the US (Dunning 1969a).

We admit that such fragmentary evidence is by no means conclusive. We also accept that part of the competitive stimulus arising from US firms in Britain could be achieved in other ways. Some of the recent increase in the efficiency of domestic firms in industries in which US firms participate is undoubtedly due to the easing of UK import restrictions – particularly on consumer goods. Import competition is, in part, a substitute for direct investment, but it cannot, of itself, bring about the same income or technological expansionary effect, which may be quite marked.[1] Moreover, in the context of the external economic policy, which recent UK Governments have pursued, US firms have almost certainly benefited the UK balance of payments (Dunning 1969a). In 1965 they accounted for 17½ per cent of all UK manufacturing exports (although only 9 per cent of manufacturing sales) and, between 1957 and 1965, one-third of the increase in exports. In general, where they compete side by side with UK companies, they export a higher proportion of their output.

[1] Put quite crudely the presence of US firms enables UK firms to see *how* certain particular things might be done which trade could never do.

In a Canadian context, the argument has been advanced that the presence of foreign subsidiaries actually inhibits the development of top-level managerial skills on the part of host-country managers. This is because ultimate decision-taking rests with the parent company managers, and also the top jobs in the subsidiaries may be held, in part, by foreign nationals. This argument would appear to have little relevance for the United Kingdom. For one thing, the proportion of foreign-owned firms is not as high as, and the use of host-country nationals greater than, in Canada. If inward investment were less, some managers would be in more important positions in smaller firms. But this is unlikely to raise either their earning powers or abilities. While sceptical of the extent of some of the alleged benefits to managerial technology from inward investment, we are very doubtful about this harmful effect.

Some statistical evidence: US investment and UK export performance

We have seen that US investment in the UK is strongly concentrated in the research-intensive industries. This helps explain why between 1957 and 1965 the sales of US subsidiaries of research-intensive products rose by 131·7 per cent compared with those of other products of 118·9 per cent (113·7 per cent excluding paper). It has also helped to advance UK exports of research-intensive products. There is, in fact, a reasonably close statistical association between the growth of US investment in different UK industries and their export performance in recent years. As a proportion of the total US and European exports, Britain's share of the exports of research-intensive products fell from 18·5 per cent in 1957 to 15·7 per cent in 1965. Over this same period, the contribution of US affiliates to all UK exports rose from 12·1 per cent to 17·4 per cent. This would suggest that without the contribution of US companies, the UK's performance in technological products would have been even less impressive – a hypothesis which is supported by the much faster rate of growth of exports from those European countries which have attracted the largest share of new US investment since 1955 (Dunning 1969c).[1]

[1] These data are confirmed by other statistics on the export performance of US subsidiaries in the UK. According to the Board of Trade (Board of Trade, 1968), US manufacturing subsidiaries accounted for 18·7 per cent of the exports of the leading UK companies in 1966. Their contribution to the exports of research-intensive products was, however, considerably higher – 28·0 per cent – while they supplied only 4·6 per cent of other exports.

Contribution of US Subsidiaries in UK to Export of Selected Manufactured Products

	Sales of US Affiliates			*Exports of US Affiliates*			*Exports of all UK Firms*			*Percentage of UK Exports to all European and US Exports*	
	1957 $m.	1965 $m.	*Growth* 1957 = 100	1957	1965	*Growth* 1957 = 100	1957 $m.	1965 $m.	*Growth* 1957 = 100	(*a*) *All UK Exports* (1965)	(*b*) *Of which US Affiliates* (1965)
Research-intensive products											
Chemicals and allied[1] products	517	1,241	240·0	n.a.	172	n.a.	749	1,230	164·2	13·0	1·8
Rubber products	139	219	157·6	n.a.	43	n.a.	109	131	120·2	16·0	5·3
Non-electrical machinery	480	1,121	233·5	n.a.	461	n.a.	1,615	2,806	173·9	15·9	2·6
Electrical machinery	270	706	261·5	n.a.	149	n.a.	636	927	145·8	13·9	2·2
Transportation equipment	789	1,798	227·9	n.a.	799	n.a.	864	1,585	183·4	19·7	9·9
Total	2,195	5,085	231·7	n.a.	1,621	n.a.	3,973	6,679	168·1	15·7	3·8
Other products											
Food products	491	730	148·7	n.a.	27	n.a.	326	567	173·9	16·4	0·8
Paper and allied products	21	102	485·7	n.a.	18	n.a.	109	142	130·2	8·5	1·1
Metals	230	546	237·4	n.a.	13	n.a.	1,221	1,562	127·9	13·3	0·1
Other products	366	1,047	286·0	n.a.	112	n.a.	1,221	1,326	108·6	13·4	1·0
Total	1,108	2,425	218·9	n.a.	170	n.a.	2,877	3,597	125·0	13·5	0·6
All products[2]	3,303	7,510	227·4	829	1,791	216·0	6,850	10,276	150·0	14·4	2·6

[1] Excluding petroleum products. [2] Excluding petroleum, including instrument products and aircraft.

Source: Sales of US subsidiaries, US Department of Commerce *Survey of Current Business* November, 1966. Exports of US subsidiaries, *Board of Trade Journal*, 16/8/68, Table 8, p. 5. Exports of all UK firms, United Nations, *Commodity Trade Statistics* 1957 and 1965.

One other piece of evidence worth mentioning is illustrated in Table 6. Here we have compared the rate of growth of capital in 100 of the largest US affiliates in Britain between 1955 and 1966 compared with that of the leading public companies. Once again, the US firms show up particularly well in the research-intensive

TABLE 6

Growth of Net Assets of Leading US and UK Manufacturing Firms 1955/67

	US Subsidiaries 1955/67 1955 = 100	*UK Firms* 1955/66 1955 = 100	*Column* 1/2
Research-intensive industries			
Chemicals	257·1	113·6	2·26
Non-electrical machinery	195·4	152·7	1·28
Electrical machinery	470·2	184·2	3·92
Vehicles	142·1	104·0	1·37
	216·5	130·2	1·66
Other industries			
Food and drink	227·5	156·7	1·45
Metal manufacture	136·6	119·9	1·14
Other products	187·9	163·5	1·15
	193·5	148·8	1·30
All industries	212·7	140·7	1·51

Source: Balance sheet of 100 leading US manufacturing subsidiaries, 1967. Ministry of Labour, *Statistics on Income, Prices, Employment and Production*, December 1967.

industries, which suggests that their share of the output of these same industries is growing faster than their share elsewhere in the manufacturing sector.

Policy conclusions

The staggering success of the multi-national corporation as a means of organizing production and distribution shows little sign of slowing down. In part, this success rests on economies of scale which appear to be related to research and innovation. It seems reasonable to assume that the multi-national firm will remain an important source of the transmission of new technology across national boundaries.

In previous sections of this chapter we have attempted to outline the economic implications of a number of arguments which have been raised in connection with the affects on British technology of United States subsidiaries coming here. This discussion suggests a number of conclusions.

In the case of take-over, there are various answers to a problem of lack of ability of a particular kind, namely, the ability to value a firm's research property correctly. In the short run, scientific and entrepreneurial expertise can be hired, from the United States and elsewhere, and in the long run, more resources can be devoted to education, including business education. UK Government support of many kinds could be extended. But it is doubtful whether a specialist ministry could make more profitable decisions in this area than private investors. However, there is nothing to stop the Government from trying, along with private investors – nothing that is, but the necessity of defending the inevitable crop of costly ventures which fail.

The most important conclusion of this chapter is that none of the arguments relating to the technological impact of US investment appear to have any *a priori* claim to plausible generality. While the alleged dangers to the United Kingdom technology cannot be ruled out on theoretical grounds, there are no general reasons to suppose action should be taken on the basis of them. Closer examination also suggests that the kind of detailed information required to discriminate between desirable and undesirable inward investment is not likely to be obtained. Nor is the ability to forecast which sensible discrimination would imply.

In certain cases, the arguments about alleged dangers appear to be contradictory. This is particularly so of the view that the inward investing firm, if a take-over, should, in the interests of the United Kingdom, maintain or augment its research efforts here. And in the case of a new establishment, it is also contradictory to hold that research efforts in the UK are essential to aiding United Kingdom technology.

In their report on the effects of foreign direct investment on the structure of Canadian industry, the Watkins Committee argued most persuasively that the nature and extent of the benefits which any host country might derive from the operation of foreign-owned firms is crucially dependent on (*a*) its competitive environment, and (*b*) the effects of its public policies on the organization of production and distribution (Watkins, p. 69). The Committee emphasize that if technology superior to that already existing is introduced by foreign firms, the extent to which this is advantageous to the host economy, rather than the investing country, will depend on 'whether the improvements get outside the firm and thus raise [Canadian] income generally, or remain in the firm and simply raise profits accruing to the parent' (p. 70). To the extent that competition is imperfect, and resources immobile, and that these impediments to the diffusion of technological advances are not mitigated by public policy, the benefits of direct investment will be emasculated. However, this argument could be generalized to cover all firms, irrespective of nationality. It is essentially a debate about the distribution of the gains of technology (which admittedly may well affect the future rate of technological change), and involves complex relations between private and social gains.

If real economic advantages lie with the multi-national firm, at least in certain sectors, it is far more important to engage in activities which will allow participation in this form of economic organization than to attempt to discriminate or generally restrict the inflow. For the United Kingdom the main constraint on such participation is the balance of payments. This constraint seriously inhibits both the development of United Kingdom-based multi-national firms and UK portfolio investment in the successful foreign-based international companies.[1]

REFERENCES

American Chamber of Commerce. 'American manufacturers in the United Kingdom,' *Anglo-American News*, September 1967.

J. Baranson. 'Transfer of Technical Knowledge by International Corporations to Developing Economics,' *American Economic Review*, Papers and Proceedings, Vol. LVI, May 1966, pp. 260–61.

J. Behrman. *Some Patterns in the Rise of the Multi-national Enterprise*, Research Paper No. 18, University of North Carolina Press, 1969.

G. Bertin. *L'investissement des firms étrangères en France*, Paris, 1963.

Board of Trade. 'Book values of overseas investment,' *Board of Trade Journal*, 26/1/68.

Board of Trade. 'Overseas transactions in 1966 – trade credit and exports,' *Board of Trade Journal*, 16/8/68.

[1] For a much fuller discussion of the welfare complications of foreign direct investment to host countries see Johnson (1969), Kindleberger (1969b) and Rolfe (1969).

B. Bonin. *Licensing and joint ventures as alternatives to direct investment*, 1967 (an unpublished paper prepared for the Task Force on the Structure of Canadian Industry [the Watkins Committee]).

D. Brash. *American Investment in Australian Industry*, Australian National University Press, Canberra, 1966.

T. Coram. *The Role of British Capital in the Development of the United States*, M.Sc. (Econ.) thesis, University of Southampton, 1967.

E. Denison. *Why Growth Rates Differ*, The Brookings Institution, 1967.

J. H. Dunning. *American Investment in British Manufacturing Industry*, Allen & Unwin, 1958.

J. H. Dunning. 'US subsidiaries and their UK competitors,' A case study in business ratios, *Business Ratios*, Autumn 1966.

J. H. Dunning (1969a). *American Investment in the British Economy*, P.E.P. Broadsheet, No. 507, February 1969.

J. H. Dunning (1969b). 'Foreign direct investment in the United Kingdom economy,' in I. A. Litvak and C. J. Maule, *Foreign investment: the experience of host countries*. Praeger, New York, 1969.

J. H. Dunning (1969c). 'European and US trade patterns, US foreign investment and the technological gap,' Paper given to Conference of International Economic Association on *The Mutual Repercussions of North American and Western European Economic Policies*, Algarve, Portugal, September 1969.

H. Feis. *Europe, the World's Banker*, 1870/1914, Yale University Press, 1930.

T. Gates and R. Linden. *Cost and Competition Abroad*, National Industrial Conference Board, New York, 1960.

W. Gruber, D. Mehta and R. Vernon. 'The *R* and *D* factor in international trade and international investment of United States industries,' *Journal of Political Economy*, Vol. LXXV, February 1967.

G. R. Hall and R. E. Johnson. 'Transfers of United States aero space technology to Japan,' paper given to Conference on technology and competition in international trade, sponsored by Universities – National Committee for Economic Research, New York, October 1968.

S. Hymer. *Direct Foreign Investment and International Oligopoly*, June 1965 (Mimeo).

R. Jones. *The Role of Technology in the Theory of International Trade*, paper given to Conference on technology and competition in international trade, sponsored by Universities – National Bureau Committee for Economic Research, New York, October 1968.

H. Johnson. *Comparative Costs and Commercial Policy Theory for a Developing Economy*, The Wicksell Lectures, 1968.

H. Johnson. *The Efficiency and Welfare Implications of the International Corporation*, paper given to Seminar on the International Corporation for Sloan School of Management, M.I.T., Spring 1969.

A. Johnstone. *United States Direct Investment in France*, Cambridge (Mass.), 1965.

J. E. Kenney. 'American enterprise in Western Europe: the case of Great Britain,' *Review of Social Economy*, Vol. XXVI, No. 2, September 1968.
C. Kindleberger (1969a). *American Business Abroad*, Yale University Press, 1969.
C. Kindleberger (1969b). *Restrictions on Direct Investment in Host Countries*, a discussion paper for the University of Chicago Workshop on International Bureau, March 1969.
C. Layton. *Trans-Atlantic Investment*, The Atlantic Institute, 1966.
J. MacMillan and B. Harris. *The American Take-over of Britain*, Leslie Frewin, 1968.
E. J. Mishan. *The Cost of Economic Growth*, Staples Press, 1966.
O.E.C.D. 'Technological Gaps: Their Nature, Cause and Effects,' *The O.E.C.D. Observer*, April 1968, pp. 18–29.
M. J. Peck. 'Science and technology,' in R. E. Caves and associates, *Britain's Economic Prospects*, Brookings Institution, 1968.
H. V. Perlmutter. 'The tortuous evolution of the multi-national corporation,' *Columbia Journal of World Business*, Vol. IV, No. 1, January/February 1969.
J. B. Quinn. 'Scientific and technical strategy at the national and major enterprise level,' paper prepared for UNESCO Symposium on *The Role of Science and Technology in Economic Development*, Paris, 1968.
S. Rolfe. *The International Corporation*, background papers for conference of International Chamber of Commerce at Istanbul, May 1969.
A. Safarian (1966). *Foreign Investment in Canadian Industry*, McGraw-Hill, 1966.
J. J. Servan-Schreiber. *The American Challenge*, Hamish Hamilton, 1968.
A. Stonehill. *Foreign Ownership in Norwegian Enterprises*, Oslo Central Bureau of Statistics, 1965.
D. Thomas. 'The Anglo-American Manager,' *Management Today*, February 1969.
US Department of Commerce. *Technological Innovation: Its Environment and Management*, Washington, D.C. US Government Printing Office, January 1967, p. 9.

9

INTER-FIRM EFFICIENCY COMPARISONS: US AND UK MANUFACTURING ENTERPRISES IN BRITAIN*

Introduction

Our purpose here is to suggest a method of evaluating the efficiency of firms, with a view to comparing the performance of British and US firms operating in the United Kingdom. In later sections of this Chapter we shall:

(*a*) define the efficiency of the firm;
(*b*) propose an operational measure of efficiency as defined;
(*c*) carry out a number of tests of the proposed measure, and
(*d*) draw certain tentative conclusions regarding the relative efficiency of British and US firms operating in the United Kingdom.

Before embarking on the analysis, as a whole, we give a brief preliminary account of the origins and aims of the research study for which a means of undertaking inter-firm efficiency comparisons was required.

The origins and aims of the research

As a result of official enquiries and earlier research undertaken at Southampton, evidence has accumulated regarding:

(*a*) the rates of return on capital (at book values) obtained by British manufacturing enterprises operating overseas;
(*b*) the rates of return on capital (at book values) obtained by British manufacturing enterprises operating in the United Kingdom;

* The authors are indebted to Miss H. Gibbs and Mrs A. Harris of the University of Southampton and Mr M. Barron of the University of Reading for their help in the preparation of the statistics for this paper. First published (with Professor D. C. Rowan) in *Banca Nazionale del Lavoro Quarterly Review*, No. 85, June 1968. We have also drawn on parts of an article, US subsidiaries and their UK competitors: a case study in business ratios, *Business Ratios*, Autumn 1966.

(*c*) the rates of return on capital (at book values) obtained by US enterprises operating:

(i) in overseas countries in which UK enterprises also operate, and
(ii) in the UK, and

(*d*) in some cases, the rates of return on capital obtained by domestic enterprises in overseas countries in which both US and UK enterprises operate.

Given this data, which were aggregative in nature, it became possible to compare the rates of return obtained by UK firms with those obtained:

(*a*) by US firms operating in the same economy, and
(*b*) by domestic firms.

The results of these comparisons, which have been set out elsewhere in this volume,[1] suggested two main conclusions:

(*a*) UK firms (in aggregate) were consistently less profitable than US firms:

(i) in the United Kingdom;
(ii) overseas, and

(*b*) UK firms operating in overseas markets were (in aggregate) frequently less profitable than *all* firms, both domestic and foreign, operating in the same country.

From this evidence, on the assumption that the rate of return on capital employed was a plausible index of economic 'efficiency', the obvious inferences were that:

(i) UK firms were less efficient than a surprisingly wide range of their competitors, and
(ii) that this lesser 'efficiency' must, in some measure, be due to shortcomings (avoidable and unavoidable) of UK management.

These inferences, though appealing, could not, however, be drawn with any great confidence from the data available. For this there were a number of reasons, the most compelling being that the industrial distribution of UK firms operating in overseas countries was known to differ very considerably from the US firms and firms of other nationalities, while attempts to correct for this factor

[1] See, especially, Appendix to Chapter 6.

could not be other than crude. Accordingly, an attempt was made to check the impression created by the aggregative figures by comparing:

(*a*) the rates of return on capital earned by a selective sample of US firms engaged in manufacturing in the UK, and

(*b*) the rates of return earned by UK firms over the same period which:

(i) operated in the same industry;
(ii) were of approximately the same size, and
(iii) produced broadly similar products.

These results of these 'paired' comparisons are shown in Table 1. Clearly, they support the aggregative data rather than the reverse. Unfortunately the 'paired' comparisons were open to serious objections for, although the 'pairs' were selected as carefully as possible,

TABLE 1

Rates of Return on Capital Earned by US Subsidiaries and 'Paired' UK Competitors in the UK, 1958/61[1]

	1958–59		1959–60		1960–61		1958–61	
	US	UK	US	UK	US	UK	US	UK
Food	15·9	12·7	13·4	9·9	17·8	9·4	15·6	11·1
Chemicals	26·2	15·6	19·4	16·0	13·8	16·4	19·0	16·0
Engineering:								
(*a*) Motor vehicles	29·8	14·7	25·1	16·6	17·3	8·3	24·0	13·2
(*b*) Electrical equipment	21·2	16·8	20·1	19·0	19·3	11·4	21·3	17·0
(*c*) Instruments and watches	21·5	13·3	17·9	13·8	15·4	14·5	17·7	14·2
(*d*) Other	17·8	12·3	17·2	14·5	18·4	13·2	18·0	14·7
All engineering	26·8	15·1	18·8	15·3	17·8	12·8	19·2	15·1
Other manufacturing	21·2	12·9	20·5	15·5	19·0	11·1	20·6	13·5
All firms	20·9	14·5	18·7	15·4	17·3	12·9	19·0	14·5

[1] Unweighted average of Gross Operating Profit ÷ Total Assets.
Source: Published Company Accounts.
Firms paired included those producing abrasives, photographic equipment, office machinery, pharmaceuticals, refined oil, canned foods, rubber tyres, cork products, domestic appliances, boilers, machine tools, toys, printing machinery, plastics, pens, telephones and watches.

problems of product heterogeneity and spread could not be entirely resolved. Hence Table 1, though suggestive, was very far from being conclusive.

At this stage, all that could be said with any confidence was that a problem of relative efficiency might well exist. The evidence was considered by the National Economic Development Office (NEDO) to be sufficient to initiate a more systematic enquiry. The aims of this enquiry, which was carried out at the University of Southampton, were to discover whether:

(i) the apparent differences in rates of return on capital earned by US and UK firms operating in the United Kingdom reflected a real difference in economic efficiency rather than conceptual and statistical differences, and

(ii) if differences in efficiency could be shown to exist, a significant part of them could be attributed to identifiable weaknesses in UK management.

Because of the difficulties, already mentioned, with aggregative data, statistical information was sought directly from firms by means of a questionnaire. The questionnaire was sent to:

(*a*) all US firms known to be manufacturing in the UK, and

(*b*) those UK firms designated by US firms as their 'closest' competitors.

In this way it was hoped to undertake 'paired' comparisons in which the method of defining the 'pairs' was itself defined and in which the resultant 'pairs' would have a relatively unambiguous and acceptable meaning.

Depending on the response of firms to these requests for data, it was planned to send questionnaires to a sample of UK firms structured, on the basis of industrial classifications, in the same way as US firms which returned usable data. In the event, though the response rate from US firms (some 45 per cent) was acceptable, if rather disappointing[1], the response rate of UK firms (roughly 8 per cent) was not only disappointing but entirely unacceptable. In view of this it seemed futile to proceed with the structured sample.

The practical upshot, therefore, is that our enquiry failed to provide the data necessary for a comprehensive comparison of UK and US firms manufacturing in the UK. Nevertheless, a considerable

[1] Though the firms which did reply accounted for more than 75 per cent of the total US investment in UK manufacturing industry in 1960.

amount of useful information regarding US firms in the UK was obtained, and some of these data can be fruitfully compared with the information already available regarding UK firms. In addition, we found it possible to make fairly detailed comparisons between the performance of seventeen US and UK firms.

Inter-firm efficiency comparisons: preliminary problems

Few words in the English language (and probably in most others) can be more loaded than 'efficiency'. Since its employment in this context cannot be avoided, the essential first step of our analysis must be to define it as precisely and as unprovocatively as possible. To begin with we must distinguish two general senses in which it can be employed: the first of these is *private* efficiency; the second is *social* efficiency.

If we examine, even rather superficially, the private efficiency of a firm, it is clearly capable of at least two definitions. These arise from the interests of the owners of the enterprise on the one hand and its controllers or managers upon the other.

From the point of view of the owners of the firm (that is, the shareholders) it is a plausible first approximation to think of efficiency as a function of two variables:

(i) the rate of return on shareholders' funds;
(ii) the risk factor.

Taking the argument one stage further we can argue that:

(*a*) the rate of return on shareholders' funds is itself determined by:

- (i) the rate of return on total assets;
- (ii) the debt/equity ratio (the gearing) of the firm, while

(*b*) the risk element is a function of:

- (i) the variance of the rate of return on total assets, and
- (ii) the debt/equity ratio.

Proceeding one stage further again (*b*) (i) – the variance of the rate of return on total assets – may be thought of as depending on two groups of factors:

(*a*) those arising out of the characteristics of the industry concerned, and
(*b*) those arising out of the characteristics of the firm's managers.

This would give, as a first approximation, an efficiency index of shareholders (including potential shareholders) for the ith firm in the jth industry as:

$$_{S}E_{ij} = f\left[\frac{P_i}{TA_i}, \frac{D_i}{TA_i}, \sigma_j, \sigma_i\right] \tag{3.1}$$

where:

$_{S}E_{ij} \equiv$ the efficiency index of shareholders

$\frac{P_i}{TA_i} \equiv$ rate of return on total assets

$\frac{D_i}{TA_i} \equiv$ debt/total assets ratio

$\sigma_j \equiv$ 'cyclical' variance of $\frac{P_j}{TA_j}$ about its mean when $\frac{P_j}{TA_j}$ is the average rate of return for the industry

$\sigma_i \equiv$ variance of $\frac{P_i}{TA_i}$ about the industry mean.

This index is, of course, extremely crude. Its definition implies that in valuing the shares of the firm, and thus in determining the flow of new equity capital, the relevant variables are those appearing in (3.1). This immediately invites the objection that some investigators have found that share values are differentially influenced by distributed and undistributed profits. On this argument, the more relevant variable is not $\frac{P_i}{TA_i}$ but that part of $\frac{P_i}{TA_i}$ which, after tax and depreciation, is, in fact, distributed. Against this finding, it can be argued that the proportion of the net rate of return which is distributed is based on management's assessment of the long-run rate of return net of tax and depreciation. Hence, if tax and depreciation policies are relatively stable, the dividend rate is, given the debt/equity ratio, simply a proxy for the long-run expected $\frac{P_i}{TA_i}$ while allocations to reserves are residual.[1]

These problems, though of considerable interest, are not of major importance in this context. Our index, though crude, is simply

[1] The literature on this question is extensive, cf. Modigliani and Miller (1958).

concerned to suggest that, in valuing firms, shareholders and potential shareholders might well think along the lines it implies. Moreover, an index of this form, or a modification of it, is testable.

The index defined in (3.1) is derived from a very general and probably rather naïve hypothesis about the utility functions of shareholders and potential shareholders. Our second index of private efficiency relates not to shareholders but to managers. In general there is no reason to suppose, other than their need (which may be relatively infrequent) to raise funds in the equity market, that the managerial efficiency index should be related to (3.1). The divorce of ownership from control in modern enterprise is too familiar to need extended comment. To define a managerial index we need to know, or at least formulate plausible hypotheses about, the form of the managerial utility function.

Unfortunately, not much is known about the specification of managerial utility functions.[1] An attempt to obtain further information on this point was made in the questionnaire. The results are tabulated in Table 2. From this it seems that managers attach primary

TABLE 2

Managerial Efficiency Indicators, Ranking of Importance (% of Firms)

	1st	2nd	3rd	4th	5th	Not Listed	Total
Rate of return on total assets	52·8	22·0	10·2	12·6	—	2·4	100·0
Growth of total assets	3·1	7·1	18·1	27·6	33·9	10·4	100·0
Rate of return on shareholders' funds	16·5	22·8	18·1	20·5	11·8	10·2	100·0
Growth of sales	25·2	30·7	26·0	15·7	—	2·4	100·0
Growth of market share	6·3	15·0	20·5	11·8	18·9	27·6	100·0

Source: *Southampton Enquiry*.

importance to the rate of return on total assets. After this appears the growth in sales; and only after this comes the rate of return on shareholders' funds.

This information, though interesting, must nevertheless be treated

[1] For a summary of the work done in this field see Williamson (1963), Baldwin (1964), Marris (1964), Howe (1964) and Cohen and Cyert (1965).

with a good degree of caution.[1] The sample from which it is derived consists in only 130 US and UK enterprises operating in Britain. Moreover, the data is subjective in that it relates to what managers *say* guides their actions not what can, in practice, be shown to guide them. However, these results do accord quite well with those of previous enquiries. Hence as a tentative first approximation it seems reasonable to define the efficiency index of managers as a function of:

(*a*) the rate of return on total assets $\frac{P_i}{TA_i}$

(*b*) the rate of growth of sales $\dot{S}_i \equiv \frac{dS}{dt}$

(*c*) the rate of return on shareholders' funds, and write:

$$_mE_{ij} = f\left[\frac{P_i}{TA_i}, \dot{S}_i, \frac{D_i}{TA_i}, \sigma_i\right] \tag{3.2}$$

We have called these two indexes 'private' simply because they are derived from the assumed utility functions of two distinct groups of persons identified by both legal and functional relationships with the firm. There is no obvious reason why, if we look at the efficiency of a firm from the social point of view, we should be concerned with either index. This does not, of course, mean that (3.1) and (3.2), assuming they (broadly) reflect the behaviour of the two groups for whom they are defined, have no social relevance. On the contrary (3.1), or some refinement of it, may well influence the flow of capital to firms (and thus the industrial pattern of growth). Similarly (3.2) will influence managerial decisions and thus the rate of innovation. From the social point of view, the forms of (3.1) and (3.2) are of great significance. Nevertheless, in assessing the social efficiency of an enterprise, neither the rate of return on total assets nor the rate of return on shareholders' funds is *necessarily* an adequate index. Nor, by the same token, is the rate of growth of sales.

Strictly speaking, any attempt to define an index of the social efficiency of an individual firm must involve a detailed assessment,

[1] As regards inter-firm comparisons the point is sometimes made that British and American managers possess significantly different utility functions and that the differences between these is an important factor in determining the relative profitability of the firms they manage. Our information is not adequate to throw any light on the question.

in terms of cost-benefit analysis, of the firm's performance. To put matters formally, define:

$O_{ijm} \equiv$ the quantity of the mth output of the ith firm in the jth industry

$P_{ijm} \equiv$ the price of the mth output

so that:

$$\sum_{m=1}^{m=s} O_{ijm} P_{ijm} \equiv \text{value added of the firm:} \qquad m = 1, 2 \ldots s$$

Next define:

$X_{ijk} \equiv$ quantity of the kth input of the ith firm in the jth industry: $\quad k = 1, 2 \ldots r$

and

$\bar{P}_{ijk} \equiv$ the price of a unit of the kth input of the ith firm in the jth industry: $\quad k = 1, 2 \ldots r$

so that

$$\sum_{k=1}^{k=r} X_{ijk} \bar{P}_{ijk} \equiv \text{total cost of the firm's inputs}$$

Lastly define:

$\hat{S}_{ijb} \equiv$ value of the social benefits generated per period by the firm

$\hat{S}_{ijc} \equiv$ value of the social costs generated per period by the firm.

Then our index of social efficiency $_{\hat{S}}E_{ij}$ is given by:

$$_{\hat{S}}E_{ij} = \frac{\sum_{k=1}^{k=r} X_{ijk}\bar{P}_{ijk} + \hat{S}_{jic}}{\sum_{m=1}^{m=s} O_{ijm}P_{ijm} + \hat{S}_{jib}} \qquad (3.3)$$

and measures the social cost, on a number of assumptions which we have not yet examined, of producing a unit of social value output.

Since the purpose of the index is precisely inter-firm comparisons we need to assume that:

(i) all the P_m and $\bar{P}_m$ are the same for each firm within the jth industry, and
(ii) the O_m and X_k are homogeneous for each firm within the same industry.

Provided these assumptions are satisfied, then (3.3) defines an acceptable index of the social efficiency, in any given period, of the firm under observation.

The index (3.3) is, of course, static. It tells us nothing about the direction or rate of change of the firm's social efficiency. A simple dynamic index to meet these requirements can, however, readily be defined in terms of (3.3) as:

$$_{\hat{S}}E_{ij'} \equiv \frac{_{\hat{S}}E_{ij}{}^{(t)} = {}_{\hat{S}}E_{ij}{}^{(t-1)}}{_{\hat{S}}E_{ij}{}^{(t-1)}} \qquad (3.4)$$

which gives the relative rate of change of social efficiency for the firm between periods t and $t - 1$.[1]

Logically (3.3) and its dynamic variant (3.4) are acceptable indexes, given the assumptions set out earlier, of the social efficiency of the firm and its rate of change. They raise, however, three important difficulties. The first of these arises because, granting their acceptability, they may, as a matter of fact, be only very loosely related to the indexes of private efficiency defined in (3.1) and (3.2). Since these are assumed to influence the behaviour of managers and investors, this would mean that maximizing behaviour on the part of these two groups, even if successfully conducted, would not necessarily increase social efficiency.

The second and third difficulties are essentially ones of measurement. In the first place social costs and social benefits are not readily given operational definitions. In the second, there are, even given the definition, considerable problems of measurement. Hence, though social costs and benefits may well differ significantly between firms in the same industry, it is necessary to exclude them and work with a truncated index.

We can thus argue that, if the truncated version of (3.3) namely:

$$_{\hat{S}}E_{ij} = \frac{\sum_{k=1}^{K=r} X_{ijk}\bar{p}_{ijk}}{\sum_{m=1}^{m=s} O_{ijm}p_{ijm}} \qquad (3.3^*)$$

[1] A method similar to this has been applied to industry data by Reddaway and Smith (1960) and Dunning and Utton (1967).

is to be useful we need to show that, in practice, low values of (3.3*) are associated with high values of (3.1) and (3.2) or their principal components. If it can be shown that such an association exists, then two conclusions follow:

(i) our index has a behaviouristic significance consistent with the *modus operandi* of the market mechanism, and
(ii) where measurement of (3.3*) is not possible it can be replaced by some more readily measurable variable which is a principal component in (3.1) and (3.2).

Inter-firm efficiency: some alternative measures

Now that we have defined our index (3.3*), it is worth while to give a very brief account of its relationship to other commonly used indexes of social efficiency. The discussion which follows is not meant to be exhaustive and, in theoretical terms, is elementary. Nevertheless, a short illustrative account may be beneficial.

Suppose, for each of the firms (call them A, B) producing homogeneous products ($O_1, O_2 \ldots O_m$) and employing only two factors of production, homogeneous capital (K) and homogeneous labour (L) in the process, we have observations (which are known to be correct) of the following variables:

$$\sum_{m=1}^{m=n} O_m p_m \equiv \text{gross value added} \equiv Op$$

$$K\bar{p}_k \equiv \text{gross value of the capital stock}$$

$$L \equiv \text{labour input}$$

$$w \equiv \text{money wage rate of labour}$$

We can then define the following familiar ratios:

(i) labour productivity index $\equiv \dfrac{Op}{wL} \equiv \gamma \equiv$ value added per unit of labour . (4.1);

(ii) capital productivity index $\equiv \dfrac{Op}{Kp_k} \equiv \phi \equiv$ value added per unit of capital . . . (4.2);

(iii) profitability index $\equiv \dfrac{Op - wL}{Kp_k} \equiv \Pi \equiv$ rate of profit per unit of capital . . . (4.3).

Our index (3.3*) becomes, in this notation,

$$\alpha \equiv {}_{S}E \equiv \frac{wL + q^*Kp_k}{Op} \tag{4.4}$$

where q^* is the social 'cost,' in a sense to be defined, of employing a unit value of capital over the accounting period for which we have data.[1] Assume also that q^* is measurable and known. We can now, by means of a simple diagram, depict the relationship between the indexes defined in (4.1) . . . (4.4).

In Fig. 1, for unit value output, we have plotted assumed value of:

$$Kp_k \quad \text{and} \quad wL \text{ for firms } A \text{ and } B$$

these values define the points A and B on the diagram.

Suppose also, as is perfectly possible, that for the period of observation,

$$\Pi_A = \Pi_B$$

that is both firms have an identical observed rate of profit. Then,

since $\dfrac{Op_A}{wL_A} > \dfrac{Op_B}{wL_B}$ by (4.1) firm A is more efficient

$\dfrac{Op_B}{K_{Bpk}} > \dfrac{Op_A}{K_{Apk}}$ by (4.2) firm B is more efficient

since $\Pi_A = \Pi_B$ by (4.3) both firms are equally efficient.

On this basis, none of the ratios (4.1) to (4.3) is very helpful individually. Together, they simply confuse. Observing all three does not help us, in the least, to rank the firms ordinally or cardinally.

The point at issue is, of course, extremely simple and familiar. Until the relative cost of the two inputs is known it is impossible to say, ordinally or cardinally, which firm is the more efficient unless the following pairs of inequalities holds:

$$\frac{Op_A}{wL_A} > \frac{Op_B}{wL_B} \quad \text{and} \quad \frac{Op_A}{K_{Apk}} \geqslant \frac{Op_B}{K_{Bpk}} \tag{4.4}$$

If this holds then A is more efficient than B. In addition, Π_A will then be greater than Π_B. Two, or if both (4.4) are inequalities, all three criteria will rank A above B. However, there need not be, and, in general, will not be, any common cardinal ranking.

[1] In a later article we also impute an opportunity cost of w. This is notated as w^*. See Dunning and Barron (1967) and Dunning (1969b).

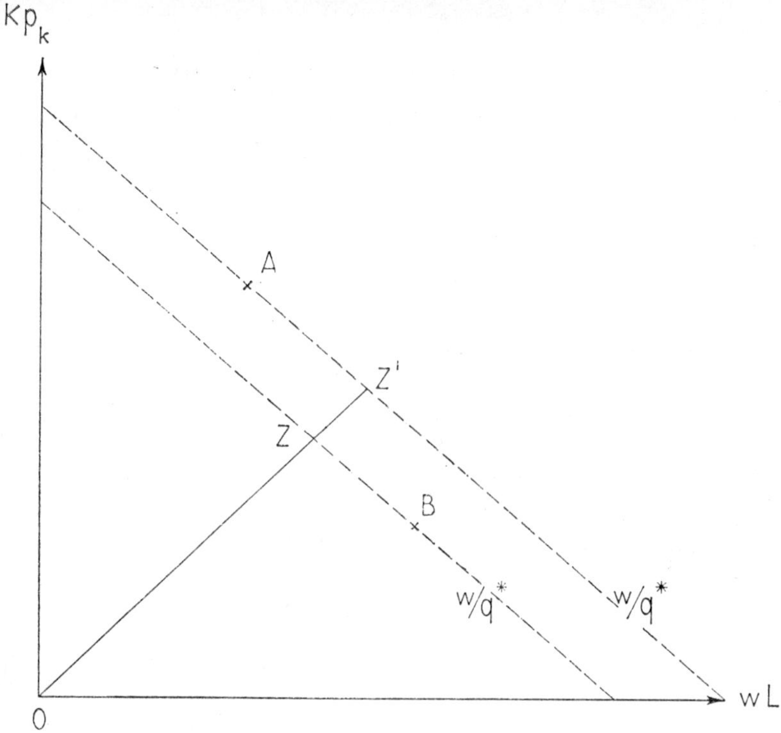

Fig. 1

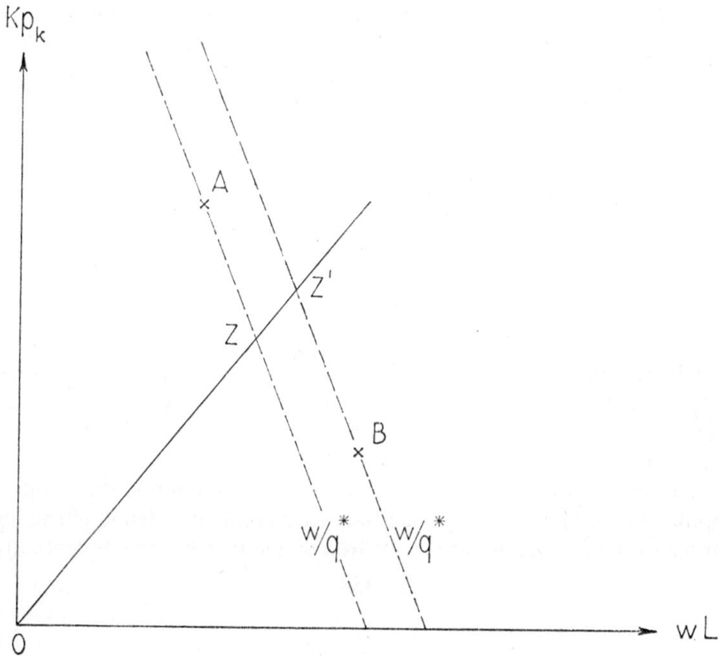

Fig. 2

Consider now the meaning of our own index. In Fig. 2 we have simply added to Fig. 1 two lines constructed with slope w/q^*. One of these lines passes through *A*, the other through *B*. Each line defines the total social cost of unit value production by *A* and *B*. Two points are now clear:

(i) firm *A* is more efficient than firm *B* (although, by assumption $\Pi_A = \Pi_B$), and
(ii) the ratio OZ/OZ' provides a cardinal ranking of the two firms.

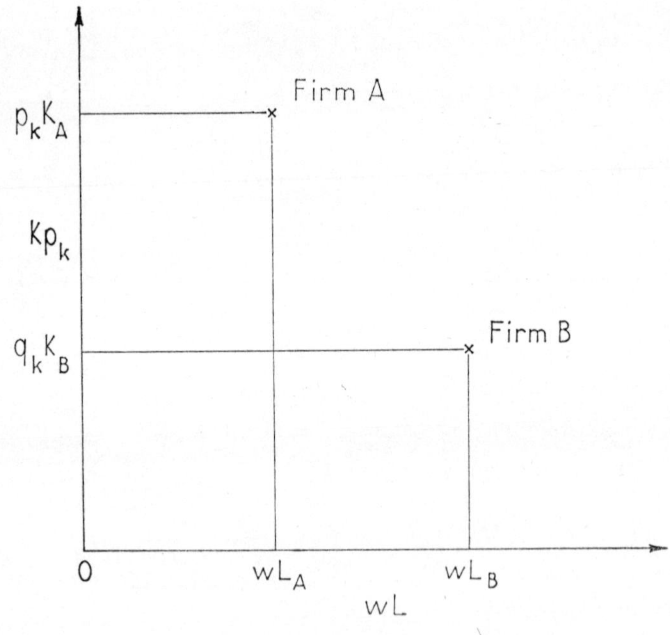

Fig. 3

Clearly, as we have done in Fig. 3, had we chosen a different slope w/q^*, it would have been firm *B* which was the more efficient. Equally clearly if $q^* = \Pi_A = \Pi_B$ then both firms would have been equally efficient.

This discussion, of course, does no more than reiterate the familiar point that (4.1) and (4.2), since they each implicitly define efficiency in terms of minimizing the input of a single factor, are conceptually inadequate. The use of the profitability criterion (4.3) is free from criticism on this score. Nevertheless, the observed rate of profit, as we have seen, is not necessarily a good indicator, either ordinally or cardinally, of the relative efficiency of firms. By contrast α, as defined in (3.3*) and (4.4) is an acceptable index of static efficiency. However, since α is defined in terms of q^* – a non-observable variable – it remains to be seen whether it can be made operational.

From this discussion, the rationale of our approach becomes clear. Our procedure is:

(*a*) to regard α (a simple approximation to (3.3*)) as an appropriate index of efficiency, and
(*b*) after estimating α for each firm, to compare it with:

(i) $\dfrac{Op}{wL} \equiv \gamma$ (the index of labour productivity)

(ii) $\dfrac{Op}{Kp_k} \equiv \phi$ (the index of capital productivity), and

(iii) $\dfrac{Op - wL}{Kp_k} \equiv \Pi$ (the index of profitability)

in order to examine how far, if at all, each of these variables is correlated with α and thus capable, where data do not permit the measurement of α, as acting a proxy for it.

Before carrying out this exercise, however, it seems desirable to undertake a short digression setting out some possible alternative approaches to measuring the economic efficiency of the firm.

Alternative approaches to measuring efficiency

Economic theory implies that we should distinguish three elements in determining the relative efficiency of two firms in the same industry. These are:

(*a*) relative *technical* efficiency, which arises because one firm possesses a production function which, for all possible ratios of factor prices, requires less inputs to generate a unit of output;
(*b*) relative *allocative* efficiency, which arises because one firm selects its minimum cost combination of factor inputs for a given set of factor prices while the other does not;

(*c*) relative scale efficiency, where one firm selects the optimal (least cost) scale of production and the other does not.

Where constant returns to scale is the rule and the most efficient production function is known (or computed from the data) it is possible, as M. J. Farrell (1957) has shown, to provide precise indexes

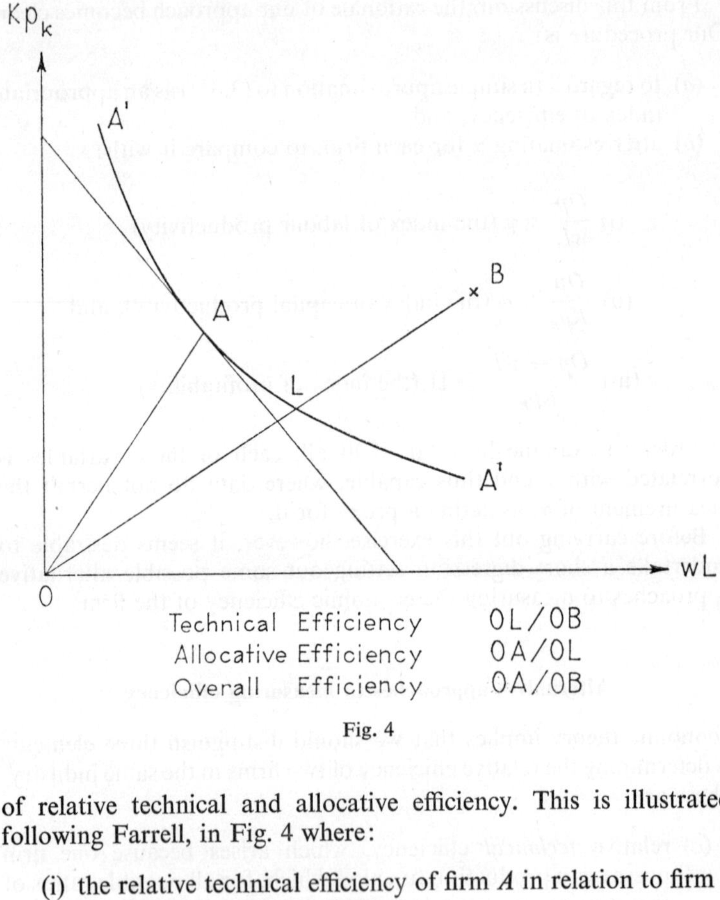

Fig. 4

of relative technical and allocative efficiency. This is illustrated, following Farrell, in Fig. 4 where:

(i) the relative technical efficiency of firm *A* in relation to firm *B* is given by the ratio *OL*/*OB*.
(ii) the relative allocative efficiency is given by *OA*/*OL*, and
(iii) the relative overall efficiency is given by the product of these *OA*/*OB*.

There are two types of difficulty inherent in this approach. The first is the amount of information required. This is illustrated in Fig. 4 where it is clear that, to give a precise meaning to technical and allocative efficiency, we need to know:

(*a*) the ratio q^*/w, and
(*b*) the production function of the more efficient firm $'A'$ in order to construct the isoquant $A'A'$.

Beyond this, if comparisons are to be made over a group of firms constituting an industry, we need:

(*c*) to establish one firm as the most efficient in the industry, and
(*d*) to postulate that there is a single most efficient production function within the industry.

These difficulties are illustrated in Fig. 5. Suppose, assuming constant returns to scale, that for each firm in industry *K*, we observe for all *i* firms:

(i) $\dfrac{K_i p_k}{Op_i} \equiv$ capital stock associated with unit value output

(ii) $\dfrac{wL_i}{Op_i} \equiv$ labour cost associated with unit value output.

These observations define, for each firm, a point in the plane $\dfrac{K_i p_k}{Op_i}$ and $\dfrac{wL_i}{Op_i}$. They thus generate a scatter diagram of the form of Fig. 5.

Now, along any line drawn from the origin, the ratio $K_i p_k/wL_i$ is constant. For this given ratio, the most efficient firm is that located nearest the origin. A line joining the observations of all such firms, for all observed $\dfrac{K_i p_k}{wL_i}$ can be regarded as the 'efficiency frontier' of the industry. This frontier is shown by the dotted line. Given this frontier, it is possible to compare the efficiency of any two firms with the same $\dfrac{K_i p_k}{wL_i}$ ratio – that is to obtain an index of technical efficiency.

As between firms *on* the frontier, no comparison is possible unless the ratio q^*/w is known. Even if it is known, it is entirely possible that two firms on the frontier may display identical efficiency either because the superior allocative efficiency of one offsets the superior technical efficiency of the other, or because two (or more) firms have a minimum cost combination, given q^*/w, which differs because their production functions differ. Unambiguously to interpret the comparative efficiency of a group of firms, we must know the specification of their production functions and not simply be able to identify a point (or points) upon them.

If we know the production functions of all firms, then, assuming constant returns to scale, we can, for any given value of q^*/w, calculate

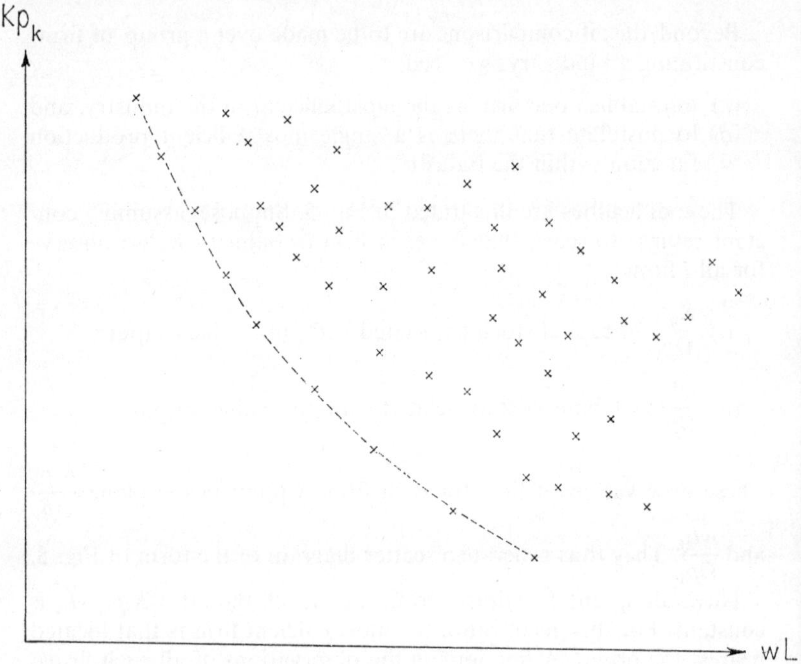

Fig. 5

for each firm, the minimum social cost of producing unit value output. We can then define the relative technical efficiency of firms *A* and *B* as:

(*a*) the ratio of the minimum total costs of *A* to the minimum total costs of *B* for unit value output given q^*/w; and measure the allocative efficiency of any firm by

(*b*) comparing its observed $\frac{K_i p_k}{wL_i}$ ratio with the optimal ratio, given q^*/w, defined by its production function.

It should be noted that, even if the production function of each firm is known, the most efficient firm is defined only for a given q^*/w, or more probably for a given range of values of q^*/w. For the production contours of different firms for unit value output may easily cut. If they do, then, beyond certain critical values of q^*/w, the efficiency ranking may be reversed. Logically, therefore, this approach, to be helpful, requires us to:

(*a*) have knowledge of the production functions of all firms, and
(*b*) set (or calculate) a value for q^*/w.

In principle, it should be possible to estimate the production functions of each firm within an industry. However, in order to be able to discriminate between various plausible forms of the production function and obtain worthwhile estimates of its parameters, there must be an adequate number of observations of both output and factor inputs.

In practice we have far too few observations, commonly 3 or 4, to permit us to undertake an exercise of this kind. Moreover, price indexes for the inputs and outputs of individual industries are not always available. Thus, shortage of data (and its shortcomings) make it impossible to estimate firms' production functions even if, as we would be loth to do, we restricted ourselves, for convenience, to production functions of a given type (say the familiar Cobb-Douglas) and reduced the number of parameters to be estimated by assuming that labour was always paid its marginal product. Indeed, even if we accept a number of special assumptions of this kind, each of which has its cost, our data are still too scanty to make estimation along these lines worth while.

On the other hand, our proposed index of efficiency (α) is defined in such a way that it is:

(*a*) independent of assumptions about the form of the production function of any firm;
(*b*) independent of assumptions regarding managerial behaviour;
(*c*) independent of the assumption that the firm is in complete equilibrium (marginal products of both factors equal to their marginal real costs) or partial equilibrium (marginal product of labour equal to the real wage rate).

Admittedly α, to be measurable, requires an assumed value of q^*. But, as we have seen, this is also true for cardinal inter-firm efficiency comparisons which employ either a modification of the Farrell technique or depend upon the estimation of a production function for each.

We, therefore, conclude that the employment of α as an index of the static social efficiency of the firm has a great deal to recommend it on the grounds of:

(*a*) its simplicity;
(*b*) its small information requirements, and
(*c*) its independence of special or even general assumptions.

Methods of relating α to alternative indexes of efficiency

Our index of social efficiency is defined as:

$$\alpha = \frac{wL + q^* Kp_k}{Op}$$

Our problem is to examine the relationship between this and three alternative indexes namely:

(i) $\Pi \equiv \dfrac{Op - wL}{Kp_k}$

(ii) $\gamma \equiv \dfrac{Op}{wL}$

(iii) $\phi \equiv \dfrac{Op}{Kp_k}$

Of these, we would prefer the relationship between α and Π to be the closest for, as we have seen, there is some reason to suppose that Π influences the behaviour of both shareholders and managers and thus the dynamic social process of increasing industrial efficiency.

Within the limitations imposed by our data Π, the exact value of which will depend on the definitions of Kp_k[1], γ and ϕ are generally observable. α, which depends upon the value of q^*, is not. We need, therefore, to give careful consideration to the value or values we propose to assign to q^*.

Notionally q^* is the social cost of employing a value unit of capital in one use rather than in another over the accounting period of a year. It is thus the social opportunity cost of capital.

One way of defining q^* is therefore to equate it to be the minimum rate at which an enterprise can borrow. This is probably, for enterprises in general, commonly the rate charged on bank advances.

[1] For a discussion of four variants of Π see p. 370ff.

This rate, of course, varies over time. In recent years it has rarely, if ever, been below 5 per cent. We can thus define a minimum value of q^* as:

$$q^*\text{min} = 5 \text{ per cent}$$

The justification for setting the minimum value of q^* at this low level is twofold:

(*a*) enterprises can often borrow at rates close to this figure but rarely at rates significantly below it, and
(*b*) where risk factors are negligible, then a management seeking to maximize profits would clearly tend to employ capital until its marginal yield was equal to the minimum rate at which it could borrow.

Let us now look at the other end of the spectrum. Since it is the social opportunity cost of capital which we are attempting to value, there are clearly good reasons for arguing that this is correctly estimated by the highest gross operating profit which can be earned on total assets in any use. Rates of return of over 50 per cent are not unknown. Hence even if a very substantial discount is made for the excess of private over social risks, this suggests a social opportunity cost of the order of 30–40 per cent.

At first sight, this argument is persuasive. On the other hand, our definition of α requires a social opportunity cost for capital which is of *general* applicability. Rates of return of the order just described are uncommon, and in general, occur only in disequilibrium situations or where there are peculiar social or institutional constraints on the mobility of capital. To permit them to provide a numerical estimate of q^* would imply that those rates were of general applicability. This is not the case.

If we look at published data on the profits earned (gross of tax and depreciation) on total assets (at book value) by the leading public companies in UK industry in recent years,[1] these seem to lie, in the main, between 15–19 per cent. These rates are, of course, the averages for industries. In any industry, the rates for individual firms are distributed about the mean. If the rate earned by firms in the upper quartile is taken and a rough allowance made for the excess of private over social risk, this would give us a social opportunity cost of capital on total assets at book value of the order of 15–20 per cent.

[1] Viz. 1950/65. See Ministry of Labour (1962 and 1966).

It thus seems not unreasonable to put the upper value of q^* ($\equiv q$ max) at 20 per cent and the most plausible value at 15 per cent. We thus arrive at three possible values for q^*:

$$q^* \text{ min} = 5 \text{ per cent}$$
$$q^* \text{ min} = 15 \text{ per cent}$$
$$q^* \text{ max} = 20 \text{ per cent}$$

Hence, for each firm, there are three values of α which can be calculated.

The value of α depends not only on q^* but also upon the value placed on capital. Data obtained in the enquiry enable us to compute various estimates of the value of capital employed by an enterprise. We have chosen to examine two in detail. The first is:

$$Kp_k \equiv \text{net fixed assets (book value)} + \text{current assets (book value)}$$

The second attempts to correct for the well-known shortcomings of book valuations by making use of the insurance valuations of both fixed assets and inventories. Data on insurance valuations were obtained in the questionnaire. We thus obtain an estimate of the revised value of capital as:

$$\begin{aligned} Kp_{kr} \equiv\ & \text{net fixed assets (insurance valuation)} \\ & + \text{current assets} + \text{inventories (insurance valuation)} \\ & - \text{inventories (book value)} \end{aligned}$$

Since each estimate of α can be constructed on the basis of either Kp_k or Kp_{kr}, we now have six possible values of α.

By their definition, both Π and α can be calculated on the basis of either capital estimate.

We now consider the problems of calculating – or more strictly – interpreting γ, the labour productivity index.

The data obtained from our questionnaire gives information not only on wL ($\equiv$employee compensation) for each firm but also on L ($\equiv$the number of employees). For any two firms in the same industry, since our method is essentially a cross-sectional rather than a time series approach, unless there are strong reasons for thinking that the firms face demand schedules of significantly differing elasticities, we can then calculate either γ as we have defined it or the more familiar index:

$$\left.\frac{Op}{L} \equiv \frac{\text{value added}}{\text{number of employees}}\right\} \equiv \gamma^*$$

These indexes will give the same result only if w is invariant between firms.

In practice, w is not invariant between firms in the same industry. We need, therefore, to make some assumption which justifies our selection of γ rather than γ^*.

The simplest assumption, which we have not tested, is that firms, in general, tend to pay each employee his or her marginal value product. If this assumption is made, then, where two firms have different values of wL but identical numbers of employees, the inference is that this is to be explained by the firm with the higher wage bill choosing to employ a more productive labour force and paying the same rate as its rivals, not for labour measured by the number of employees, but for labour measured in efficiency units. In this case wL is an index of some notional variable $L^* \equiv$ labour input measured in efficiency units.

It is not, of course, difficult to think of objections to this assumption. One firm may pay an average wage per 'efficiency employee' greater than another for a variety of reasons of which managerial inefficiency may be one. Nevertheless, the assumption seems acceptable as a first approximation.[1]

Given this assumption it is clearly necessary to use γ and not γ^* as our index of labour productivity.

The relationship between α and Π

Before summarizing the relationship between these variables revealed in our data, it may be worth while to recall briefly what we are attempting to test.

We have argued that α is a theoretically acceptable index of the static social efficiency of an enterprise. If this is so and can, in fact, be shown to be closely related to Π we can accept, provisionally, that:

(i) Π is related to social efficiency, and
(ii) where α is not calculable Π may be used as a proxy for it.

From (ii) it further follows that if two firms exhibit differing rates of profit on capital (Π) we may infer that the probability is that the

[1] Tests were made imputing the average earnings per employee in the *industry* in which the competing firms were operative. They did not materially affect the rankings of α.

firm with the higher rate of profit is the firm with the higher social efficiency – though not necessarily in the same proportion.

Finally (i) implies that the market processes, provided shareholders' and managers' utility functions are of the types assumed earlier, do in fact tend to both static and dynamic social efficiency.

By definition, α and Π should be negatively related since the former is an index of the social cost of producing unit value output and the latter is the rate of profit. In general, however, in the absence of any assumptions regarding the forms of firms' production functions, we cannot put forward any *a priori* expectation regarding the value of the relationship.[1]

Since α is the social cost of producing unit value output, we can, on the assumption that Kp_{kr} is a superior measure of the real capital employed by a firm to Kp_k, confine our attention to values of α based upon it. Our first task is therefore to test the relationship between:

$$\left.\begin{matrix}\alpha_r(q^* = 0{\cdot}05)\\ \alpha_r(q^* = 0{\cdot}15)\\ \alpha_r(q^* = 0{\cdot}20)\end{matrix}\right\} \text{ and } \Pi \text{ and } \Pi_r$$

where the suffix r indicates that Kp_k has been replaced by Kp_{kr}.

A scatter diagram of observations of α_r (0·15) and Π_r for the two years 1960/61 suggests that the relationship between the two is well approximated by either of the following forms:

$$\Pi_r = a \log \alpha_r$$

$$\Pi_r = a^1 + \frac{b}{\alpha_r}$$

[1] The specification of this relationship is given by the formula:

$$\frac{1}{\alpha} = \frac{\dfrac{\Pi}{\Pi^*} + \dfrac{wL}{w^*L}\left(\dfrac{w^*L}{q^*K_{pk}}\right)}{1 + \dfrac{w^*L}{q^*K_{pk}}}$$

where $w = w^*$ this expression simplifies to

$$\frac{1}{\alpha} = \frac{\dfrac{\Pi}{\Pi^*} + \dfrac{wL}{q^*K_{pk}}}{1 + \dfrac{wL}{q^*K_{pk}}}$$

These observations, which are for all industries, also suggest that to either of these forms the fit will be close.

In the table below we set out the correlation coefficients between α_r and Π_r for each of the years 1958/61 for all the firms, British and American, for which we have usable data.

TABLE 3

Correlation Between α_r and Π_r 1958/61

	$\Pi_r = a^1 + \frac{b}{\alpha_r}$				$\Pi_r = a \log \alpha_r$			
	1958	1959	1960	1961	1958	1959	1960	1961
$\alpha_r(0{\cdot}05)$	0·909	0·897	0·945	0·955	−0·915	−0·748	−0·879	−0·910
$\alpha_r(0{\cdot}15)$	0·967	0·924	0·981	0·979	−0·942	−0·746	−0·895	−0·894
$\alpha_r(0{\cdot}20)$	0·968	0·925	0·985	0·979	−0·922	−0·733	−0·885	−0·874
Number of observations	78	79	86	90	78	79	86	90

From this table two provisional inferences may be drawn:

(i) the linear relationship between Π and $1/\alpha$ provides a better fit than the semi-logarithmic relationship between Π and x, and

(ii) for each of the four years for which we have data α_r is closely related to Π, particularly when q^* is given the value of 0·15 or 0·20.[1]

It is also clear that a comparison of firms by profit rates tends to overstate relative social efficiency. For example, a fall in α_r from 1·0 and 0·5, which is a doubling of efficiency, will, in general, be associated with an increase in the rate of profit Π_r from 10 per cent to close to 35 per cent.

On the basis of Table 3, it seems that, with some reservations, we may regard Π_r as an acceptable proxy for α_r. Unfortunately Π_r is not always measurable since the insurance valuation of fixed assets and inventories is not in general available. We therefore need to

[1] It is worth noticing that the values of α are not very sensitive to estimates selected for q^*.

see how close a relationship exists between α_r – the efficiency index – and alternative measures of Π which can be derived from published data. These alternative definitions of Π are:

$\Pi_1 \equiv$ Profits/Total Assets (net of depreciation)
$\Pi_2 \equiv$ Profits/Total Assets (gross of depreciation)
$\Pi_3 \equiv$ Profits/Net Assets
$\Pi_4 \equiv$ Profits/Net Assets (gross of depreciation)

Of these four definitions, Π_2 and Π_4 require a word of comment. It is a commonplace that depreciation policies differ between enterprises. It follows that where any estimate of the capital stock net of depreciation is employed to calculate a variant of Π the results may be seriously distorted by the cumulative effect of differing depreciation policies. Where figures for accumulated depreciation are available some attempt to eliminate this possible source of bias can be made by adding accumulated depreciation to the net capital stock estimates. Admittedly, since Π_1–Π_4 all depend on book values, other important sources of bias may still be present in the figures. But this, though unavoidable, is not a good reason for failing to attempt some correction for variation in depreciation policies.

In the table below we give the correlation between α_r (0·15) and Π_1–Π_4 as well as the correlation between Π_r and Π_1–Π_4.

The first comment on this table is that all of the Π variants, particularly the two total assets concepts – Π_1 and Π_2 – are very closely related to Π_r. This is helpful and, at the same time, a little

TABLE 4

	Correlation Coefficients of α_r with $q^* = 0{\cdot}15$ and $\Pi_i = a'i + bi/\alpha_r$				Correlation Coefficients of Π_r and $\Pi_1 - \Pi_4$			
Year	Π_1	Π_2	Π_3	Π_4	Π_1	Π_2	Π_3	Π_4
1958	0·907	0·936	0·788	0·823	0·941	0·967	0·866	0·890
1959	0·951	0·969	0·907	0·924	0·975	0·987	0·922	0·928
1960	0·939	0·971	0·838	0·950	0·957	0·984	0·857	0·957
1961	0·963	0·973	0·931	0·948	0·979	0·988	0·954	0·966

surprising since only in the case of one firm was the book value and insurance value of capital the same while only 10 firms in our sample had revalued their assets.

The second point which emerges is that all the Π variants, despite their being based upon book values, are about as closely related to α_r as Π_r. This implies that if Π_r is an acceptable proxy for α_r so too are Π_r and Π_2. This is an important point since one or the other of these concepts can be fairly readily calculated for many firms from published data.

On the basis of these calculations we can reach the following provisional conclusions:

(i) a close relationship between α_r and Π_r exists for each year for which we have data;
(ii) the relationship is least close for 1958;
(iii) in each year, the relationship is significant at the 1 per cent level or below;
(iv) the form of the relationship is probably best expressed by the function:

$$\Pi_r = a' + \frac{b}{\alpha_r}. \text{ where } a' < 0;$$

(v) hence, in comparing the social efficiency of firms on the basis of profit rates, the relative efficiency of those with the greater profit tends to be overestimated;
(vi) provided we use profit rates based upon total assets (defined either gross or net of accumulated depreciation) the relationship between rates of profit on book values of assets and α_r seems to be about as close as that for Π_r;
(vii) if the relationship between α_r and Π_r is taken to be sufficiently close to justify the use of Π_r as a proxy for α_r, then little distortion of results is likely if any of the Π variants are used instead of Π_r.

The calculations which we have reported above compared α_r and Π for a sample of approximately 90 firms operating in different industries. As a test of the relationship between α and Π this is unobjectionable. Unfortunately, when comparisons are made across industries it is not possible to accept α_r as an index of efficiency. This is so because if, in two industries, the degree of monopoly possessed by firms differs – as it may – α will reflect this since its denominator is value added which is a function of price and which, as a result, for any given social cost per unit of real output, will be lower per unit value output in the more monopolistic industry. Since Π will be correspondingly higher this will not weaken the α, Π relationship. It does, however, invalidate the use of α as an index of social efficiency across industries.

Accordingly, we need to show that, in addition to the relationship between α and Π which exists *across* industries, a similar relationship exists between firms in the same industry. To this end, the data has been re-examined on the basis of the following industrial groups for which a sufficient number of observations exist to permit the calculation of correlation coefficients:

(i) food, drink and tobacco;
(ii) chemicals;
(iii) non-electrical engineering.

The results of this further investigation are set out in the tables below.

Extensive comment on these results is probably not necessary. It is clear, however, that the relationship between α and Π_r remains a very close one. On the other hand, the relationship between α and a measure of profit rates, related to unadjusted valuations of the capital stock, is a good deal less close – particularly in the case of food, drink and tobacco.

In this case, with only six observations, the results are of very dubious value. It is thus not unreasonable to conclude that, such as they are, the results for the three identifiable industry groups do not seriously weaken our two main conclusions that:

(i) Π_r and α are sufficiently closely related for the former to be regarded as a useful proxy for the latter, and
(ii) where estimates of Π_r cannot be obtained any of the variants of Π, and particularly Π_1 or Π_2 may be provisionally accepted as a proxy.

One point remains to be established in this section – namely that α and Π exhibit significant variation: that is that there is considerable variation in social efficiency. A statistic which can, with reservations, be used to establish this is the coefficient of variation. This statistic is defined as:

$$V \equiv \frac{\text{standard deviation}}{\text{mean}} \equiv \frac{\sigma}{M}$$

TABLE 5

	1. FOOD, DRINK AND TOBACCO							
	$\Pi_r = a_i + b_i/\alpha$				$\Pi_I = a_{Ii} + b_{Ii}/\alpha$			
	1958	1959	1960	1961	1958	1959	1960	1961
$q^* = 0{\cdot}05$	0·949	0·953	0·937	0·996	0·819	0·818	0·736	0·939
$q^* = 0{\cdot}15$	0·999	0·998	0·943	1·000	0·676	0·655	0·686	0·932
$q^* = 0{\cdot}20$	0·999	0·996	0·941	0·999	0·628	0·605	0·671	0·929
N	6	6	6	6	6	6	6	6
	2. CHEMICALS							
	$\Pi_r = a_j + b_j/\alpha_r$				$\Pi_I = a_{Ij} + b_{Ij}/\alpha$			
	1958	1959	1960	1961	1958	1959	1960	1961
$q^* = 0{\cdot}05$	0·950	0·965	0·971	0·982	0·921	0·953	0·969	0·978
$q^* = 0{\cdot}15$	0·986	0·989	0·989	0·994	0·964	0·979	0·986	0·988
$q^* = 0{\cdot}20$	0·992	0·993	0·993	0·996	0·972	0·984	0·989	0·990
N	14	15	16	17	14	15	16	17
	3. NON-ELECTRICAL ENGINEERING							
	$\Pi_r = a_k + b_k/\alpha$				$\Pi_I = a_{Ik} + b_{Ik}/\alpha$			
	1958	1959	1960	1961	1958	1959	1960	1961
$q^* = 0{\cdot}05$	0·849	0·818	0·777	0·774	0·813	0·701	0·602	0·699
$q^* = 0{\cdot}15$	0·954	0·963	0·955	0·874	0·883	0·877	0·745	0·842
$q^* = 0{\cdot}20$	0·944	0·956	0·966	0·876	0·868	0·885	0·753	0·857
N	29	29	29	36	29	29	32	36

and it obviously needs to be interpreted with caution where the mean of any series is close to zero.

TABLE 6

Coefficient of Variation

(All Firms)

	Variable	1958	1959	1960	1961
$1/\alpha$	$q^* = 0{\cdot}20$	0·424	0·613	0·686	1·130
$1/\alpha$	$q^* = 0{\cdot}15$	0·439	0·639	0·680	1·110
Π_r	—	0·834	1·021	0·998	2·558
Π_2	—	0·932	0·941	0·943	2·425

Finally, it is worth asking whether, in view of the high correlation of α and Π both across industry and within industry, the index α often yields an index of efficiency substantially different from that which would be inferred from Π or, more precisely, whether the use of α would seriously change the efficiency ranking of a firm which would be inferred from its observed Π. Clearly, since the correlation between α and Π is high, such cases could not be plentiful. Nevertheless, examination of the data readily reveals a number of such cases. It is equally simple to find cases in which, though earning identical observed rates of profit, firms are of considerably different social efficiency according to our index.

These points are not without interest. In the first place, they remind us that α and Π, though related by definition, are not necessarily closely correlated. A firm can raise its profit rate while reducing its efficiency, and increase its efficiency while reducing its profit rate. But precisely because this can and does happen, the use of observed profit rates as indexes of social efficiency between pairs of firms is a dangerous proceeding. For comparisons between the two or more reasonably large groups of firms, Π in one of its variants may be an acceptable proxy for α. But for comparisons between small groups – or at the limit between pairs of firms – the use of Π is far more hazardous. Wherever possible comparisons of this kind should be supplemented by comparisons using α_r. If this cannot be done they need to be treated with very considerable reserve.

Alternative measures of efficiency

So far this study has set out to establish that, on the assumption that α is an acceptable approximation to a theoretically correct measure of static efficiency, then where α cannot be measured it may plausibly be approximated by either Π_r or one of the Π variants. This enables us to argue that if two firms record different Π_r there is a probability that the firm with the higher value of Π_r is the more efficient.

We now turn to a second issue – the relative performance of alternative measures of efficiency noted in an earlier section namely:

$$\gamma \equiv \frac{Op}{wL} \equiv \text{value added per efficiency unit of labour}$$

$$\phi \equiv \frac{Op}{Kp_k} \equiv \text{value added per unit of capital}$$

and, or rather weaker assumptions,

$$\gamma^* \equiv \frac{Op}{L} \equiv \text{value added per worker employed.}$$

The theoretical inadequacy of these measures has already been discussed briefly. It remains, however, to investigate empirically whether they are, in practice, related to α or Π_r. The information bearing on these matters is set out below. Because of lack of observations, information relating to the food, drink and tobacco industry has not been used.

Examination of the results for all firms makes it clear that two measures, namely:

$$\gamma^* \equiv \frac{Op}{L}$$

and

$$\phi \equiv \frac{Op}{Kp_k}$$

perform relatively poorly. On the other hand the remaining two measures:

$$\gamma \equiv \frac{Op}{wL}$$

and

$$\phi_r \equiv \frac{Op}{Kp_{kr}}$$

display a useful degree of correlation with both $\frac{1}{\alpha}$ and Π_r though these correlations are less high than that of $\frac{1}{\alpha}$ with Π_r.

This impression is confirmed by the data for the chemical industry for which even ϕ (value added as a percentage of the book value of capital) shows a useful correlation. Data for the non-electrical engineering industry, on the contrary, show that all four measures perform extremely poorly, though, as before, γ and ϕ_r provide a higher measure of correlation than γ^* and ϕ.

The conclusions which can be drawn from this brief examination are these:

(i) none of the four alternative measures of 'efficiency' performs as well $\left(\text{in terms of correlation with } \frac{1}{\alpha}\right)$ as Π_r;

(ii) their performance is unreliable;

(iii) the two measures which give the most useful performance (γ and ϕ_r) depend upon:

(*a*) the availability of data on the wage bill, and

(*b*) data on the insurance value of fixed capital and stocks;

(iv) hence where ϕ_r is calculable Π_r will usually also be calculable and is to be preferred both on theoretical and empirical grounds;

TABLE 7

Alternative Measures of Efficiency

(All Firms: British and American)

	Correlations with $\frac{1}{\alpha}$ $q^* = 0{\cdot}15$				Correlations with Π_r			
	1958	1959	1960	1961	1958	1959	1960	1961
γ^*	0·672	0·789	0·730	0·736	0·670	0·778	0·710	0·642
γ	0·803	0·935	0·926	0·894	0·789	0·890	0·875	0·812
ø	0·396	0·537	0·492	0·566	0·308	0·544	0·503	0·510
ø*r*	0·726	0·815	0·786	0·794	0·650	0·829	0·819	0·767
N	78	79	86	90	78	79	86	40

TABLE 7 (*continued*)

Alternative Measures of Efficiency
(Chemical Industry)

	Correlations with $\frac{1}{\alpha}$ $q^* = 0{\cdot}15$				Correlations with Π_r			
	1958	1959	1960	1961	1958	1959	1960	1961
γ^*	0·699	0·799	0·777	0·864	0·736	0·787	0·787	0·881
γ	0·950	0·971	0·982	0·987	0·893	0·928	0·948	0·967
ø	0·882	0·943	0·949	0·960	0·918	0·973	0·977	0·976
ø*r*	0·943	0·957	0·954	0·968	0·977	0·987	0·936	0·987
N	14	15	16	17	14	15	16	17

Alternative Measures of Efficiency
(Non-electrical Engineering)

	Correlations with $\frac{1}{\alpha}$ $q^* = 0{\cdot}15$				Correlations with Π_r			
	1958	1959	1960	1961	1958	1959	1960	1961
γ^*	0·511	0·418	0·637	0·705	0·482	0·366	0·488	0·589
γ	0·702	0·589	0·713	0·608	0·646	0·536	0·560	0·550
ø	0·310	0·326	0·227	0·396	0·213	0·258	0·210	0·334
ø*r*	0·582	0·668	0·538	0·615	0·520	0·634	0·602	0·650
N	29	29	32	36	29	29	32	36

Note: $N \equiv$ Number of observations.

(v) similarly when γ is calculable, providing information regarding the book value of the capital stock is available, so too will be the variants of Π. Hence the value of γ, in practice, depends very much on its ability relative to that of Π_1–Π_4.

TABLE 8

Relative Performance: Efficiency Proxies
(γ and Π)

	Correlations of $\frac{1}{\alpha}$ with $q^* = 0{\cdot}15$ with								
	γ			Π_1			Π_2		
	All Firms	Non-Elect. Eng.	Chemicals	All Firms	Non-Elect. Eng.	Chemicals	All Firms	Non-Elect. Eng.	Chemicals
1958	0·803	0·702	0·930	0·907	0·883	0·964	0·936	0·923	0·968
1959	0·935	0·589	0·971	0·951	0·877	0·979	0·969	0·939	0·981
1960	0·826	0·713	0·982	0·939	0·745	0·986	0·971	0·893	0·989
1961	0·984	0·608	0·987	0·861	0·861	0·988	0·900	0·900	0·991

We illustrate by comparing the relative performance of γ, Π_1 and Π_2. These are set out in Table 8. Two points emerge immediately:

(*a*) both Π_1 and Π_2 exhibit a closer relation with $\frac{1}{\alpha}$ than ϕ whether the data are that for all firms or either of the industry sub-groups, while

(*b*) the correlation coefficients of Π_2 in particular show not only higher values but considerably greater stability.

It thus seems not unreasonable to conclude that none of the four alternative proxies (γ, γ^*, ϕ and ϕ_r) is comparable in performance to Π_r, or the various variants of Π_1 as an indicator of efficiency provided that $\frac{1}{\alpha}$ is regarded as an appropriate measure of efficiency.

The relative efficiency of US and UK firms

The argument of this paper so far has been directed to establishing that:

(*a*) the static $\frac{1}{\alpha}\left(\equiv \frac{Op}{wL + q^*Kp_k}\right)$ is a theoretically valid approximation to an index of social efficiency, and (*b*) where this statistic cannot be measured, the rate of profit on capital (appropriately defined) may usefully be employed as a proxy.

If we accept these propositions it follows that meaningful comparisons of the relative efficiency of groups of firms can be undertaken. However, due to the very poor response rate of UK firms to the Southampton questionnaire the best we have been able to do with the data available is to make broad comparisons between $\frac{1}{\alpha}$ for US firms and UK industry in general. In this connection, two exercises were attempted.

First, we compared $\frac{1}{\alpha}$ for the US firms in our sample with that of all UK manufacturing industry for each year 1958/61 by taking as q^* the *average* rate of profit (Π) actually earned by the leading UL public companies.[1] The results are set out in Table 9. These tell us, *inter alia*, that (i) the average social efficiency of US firms for the period 1958/61 was 20 per cent higher than it would have been had US firms been earning the average rate of profit in UK industry and

TABLE 9

Comparative Overall Performance of US Firms and UK Industry, 1958/61

	1958	1959	1960	1961	1958/61
1. Average Π for all firms	12·00	15·00	15·00	15·00	13·50
2. $\frac{1}{\alpha}$ for US firms assuming Π in 1 as q^*	1·20	1·20	1·20	1·18	1·19
3. Number of US firms with $\frac{1}{\alpha} > 1$	50	45	50	51	50
4. Number of US firms with $\frac{1}{\alpha} < 1$	20	25	28	29	27

Source: UK data: Ministry of Labour – *Statistics on Incomes, Prices, Employment and Production.* US data – *Southampton Enquiry.*

[1] In this instance, gross income ÷ by gross assets (Π_r on p. 364). See Ministry of Labour (1962 and 1966).

(ii) that three-quarters of US firms operated at a higher level of social efficiency than the average during this period.

The second exercise was to compare the average $\frac{1}{\alpha}$ for US firms *in particular* industries with that of their competitors by taking as q^* the average rate of profit (Π) earned by UK public companies *in those industries*. In Table 10 we present these results for the year 1961.

TABLE 10

Productivity ($Op/wL + q^*K_{pk}$) of American Firms in UK Industry, 1961

Industry	UK Average Π	$\frac{1}{\alpha}$ US Firms	Number of US Firms with $\frac{1}{\alpha}$ >1·00	<1·00
Chemicals, etc.	13·7	1·58	14	3
Metal manufacturing	13·2	1·25	3	1
Non-electrical engineering	13·7	1·03	11	12
Vehicles	12·2	1·37	6	1
Electrical engineering	12·1	1·08	3	3
Metal goods n.e.s.*	15·9	0·95	2	2
Textiles and clothing	13·2	1·07	1	1
Food, drink, tobacco	15·5	1·25	6	0
Other manufacturing	15·2	1·09	8	3
All manufacturing	13·8	1·18	51	29

* n.e.s.: not elsewhere specified.

Source: UK data: Ministry of Labour – *Statistics on Incomes, Prices, Employment and Production.* US data – *Southampton Enquiry.*

Note: The Total Manufacturing line was calculated separately. Hence, the industry data will not add or average to it.

Again we see in all industries except metal goods (not elsewhere specified), US firms recording a higher social efficiency, with the comparative advantage being most clearly marked in the chemicals, vehicles, metal manufacturing and food, drink and tobacco industries.

The remaining comparisons of inter-firm efficiency in this section of the paper are based upon evidence that Π – of one variant or another – is an acceptable proxy to $\frac{1}{\alpha}$. It needs, however, to be emphasized that differences in Π tend to overstate differences in efficiency as measured by $\frac{1}{\alpha}$.

Using Π as the appropriate proxy, we can proceed by classifying US firms into broad industrial groups and comparing their average Π to:

(i) the average for UK industry as a whole;
(ii) the average for the 'best' (i.e. most profitable) UK companies.

These comparisons, which are summarized in Tables 11 and 12, use:

(*a*) Questionnaire responses for US firms;
(*b*) data from *Company Assets and Income* for UK firms.

TABLE 11

Profit/Capital Ratios for Selected US Firms and UK Public Quoted Companies, 1958–61

Industry	1958		1959		1960		1961		Overall 1958/61	
	UK	US	UK	US	UK	US	UK	US	UK	US
Chemicals	13·7	17·1	16·5	27·2	16·5	28·6	13·7	22·5	15·1	24·0
Metal engineering	15·1	26·7	14·6	26·2	16·0	17·2	13·2	15·5	14·7	19·3
Non-electrical engineering	15·9	19·5	15·1	20·5	14·7	23·5	13·7	19·6	14·8	20·8
Vehicles	17·7	19·3	19·1	24·5	18·6	22·3	12·2	14·7	16·7	20·0
Electrical engineering	15·7	30·9	15·7	39·1	13·6	23·4	12·1	15·5	14·1	26·8
Metal goods n.e.s.	18·3	23·8	18·6	25·6	18·8	26·2	15·9	19·8	17·8	23·7
Textile and clothing	10·5	13·2	13·7	5·3	13·8	4·6	13·2	4·6	12·9	6·8
Food, drink and tobacco	16·4	25·6	16·0	22·8	15·8	21·7	15·5	20·6	15·9	22·5
Other manufacturing	14·7	14·4	15·4	19·2	16·0	21·0	15·2	17·1	15·4	18·0
All manufacturing	15·0	20·4	15·7	24·8	15·7	22·9	13·8	17·0	15·0	21·1

n.e.s. – Not elsewhere specified.
Source: US firms – *Southampton Enquiry*. UK firms – Ministry of Labour *Statistics on Incomes, Prices, Employment and Production*, April 1962 and March 1964.

These tables require no very extensive comment. Essentially, Table 11 does no more than confirm the hypothesis from which the enquiry began. Table 12 is, however, rather more interesting and its findings may be more conveniently examined by reference to a chart.

Consider Fig. 6, which gives a cumulative distribution of Π for all firms. If (returning to our earlier convention that $q^* = 0{\cdot}15$) we take 15 per cent as the social (gross) opportunity cost of capital,

TABLE 12

Frequency Distribution of UK and US Companies by Profitability 1958/60*
(Percentage of all Companies in Group)

Π (Percentage)	Food		Chemical		Metal and Engineering		Other		All Industry	
	US Firms	UK Firms	US Firms	UK Firms	US Firms	UK Firms	US Firms	UK Firms	US Firms	UK Firms
0–4	—	7	—	3	2	29	2	50	4	89
5–9	1	36	2	11	8	82	2	136	13	265
10–14	—	78	1	26	7	195	6	229	14	528
15–19	2	61	2	29	12	194	3	166	19	450
20–24	4	25	3	16	11	130	7	87	25	258
25–29	—	5	5	11	6	49	8	23	19	88
30–34	2	2	3	1	3	22	2	13	10	38
35–39	—	1	—	2	1	13	1	11	2	27
40 and over	2	—	7	1	4	14	2	6	15	21
Total	11	215	23	100	54	728	33	721	121	1,764

(Percentage)										
0–4	—	3	—	3	4	4	6	7	3	5
5–9	9	17	9	11	15	11	6	19	11	15
10–14	—	36	4	26	13	27	18	32	12	30
15–19	18	28	9	29	22	26	9	23	16	26
20–24	37	12	13	16	20	18	21	12	20	15
25–29	—	2	22	11	11	7	25	3	16	5
30–34	18	1	13	1	6	3	6	2	8	2
35–39	—	1	—	2	2	2	3	1	2	1
40 and over	18	—	30	1	7	2	6	1	12	1
Total	100	100	100	100	100	100	100	100	100	100

* UK companies exclude US firms.
Source: UK firms – *Company Assets, Income and Finance in* 1960. H.M.S.O. 1962. US firms – *Southampton Enquiry*.

then almost exactly 50 per cent of UK firms exceed this figure. By contrast the figure is exceeded by 76 per cent of US firms. The same information is presented in Fig. 7 in the form of a frequency polygon. This shows that the modal Π for UK firms is 12 per cent; for US firms it is 22 per cent. Charts drawn up for the main industrial sub-groups broadly confirm this particular picture.

Since the data for UK firms are derived from that of the 1,912 largest British public companies, it seems likely that it overstates,

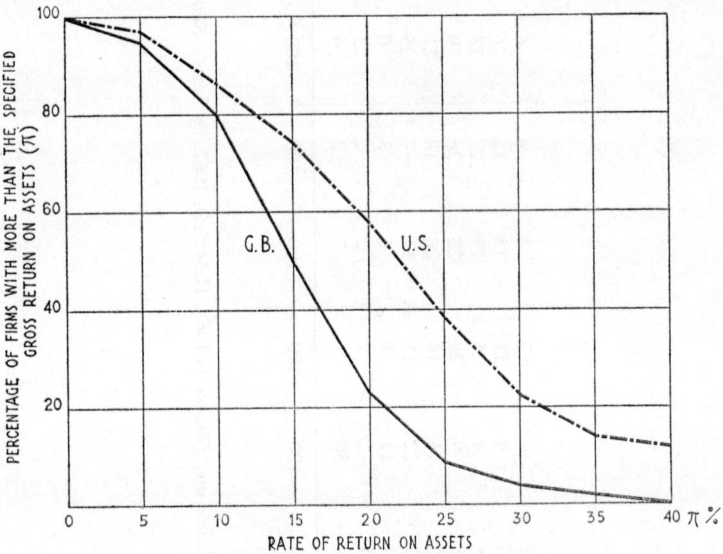

Fig. 6. Cumulative Distribution of Gross Rate of Return on Assets (Π) for Firms in all Industries 1958/60. Average 1958/60.

rather than understates, the rate of profit of British industry as a whole. If this is so, and Π is an acceptable proxy for $\frac{1}{\alpha}$, there seems to be good reason for arguing that a *prima-facie* case exists for the view that, in general, British firms operating in Britain are less efficient than US firms.

There remains the possibility that the particular years of the comparison (1958/60) overstate the relative profitability of US firms and thus their relative efficiency. This can be tested rather crudely by examining a time series of relative profitability in manufacturing. The time series is reproduced in Table 13.

TABLE 13

Rates of Return on Capital of British and American Financed Firms in Manufacturing Industry, 1950/64

Year	UK Public Companies	US Capital in UK	US/UK Percentage
1950	11·1	20·3	183
1951	10·8	20·5	190
1952	7·9	15·2	192
1953	8·1	16·3	201
1954	9·6	19·1	199
1955	9·8	18·4	188
1956	8·7	13·9	160
1957	8·3	14·7	177
1958	8·1	16·9	209
1959	9·1	17·0	187
1960	8·9	13·3	149
1961	7·5	11·3	151
1962	6·8	9·4	138
1963	7·4	11·5	155
1964	7·8	12·5	160
1965	11·2	12·7	113
1966	7·2	9·7	135
1950–66	8·7	14·9	171

Rate of return on capital is defined as trading profits − taxation − depreciation ÷ total assets − accumulated depreciation − current liabilities.

Source: UK data – Ministry of Labour *Statistics on Incomes, Prices, Employment and Production*. Taxation data derived from *Economic Trends* for comparability with tax deducted from earnings of US Cos. in UK. US data – *Survey of Current Business*, US Dept. of Commerce.

Examination of this series shows that for 1958/60 the relative profitability index defined as:

$$\frac{\Pi_{US}}{\Pi_{UK}} \times 100$$

averaged 181·67, while for the whole period (1950/66) it averaged 171. On the other hand this series suggests that the relative profitability index has been declining. It is thus possible, even if some allowance is made for the apparent tendency of the index to rise in cyclical upswings, that the comparisons made possible by the questionnaire do somewhat overstate the relative profitability advantage of US firms and thus their apparent relative efficiency. Nevertheless the qualitative case must remain.

Deficiencies in the data

It is obvious that the comparisons of the previous paragraphs establish a *prima-facie* case for arguing that US firms in Britain are, in general, more efficient than their British counterparts only to the

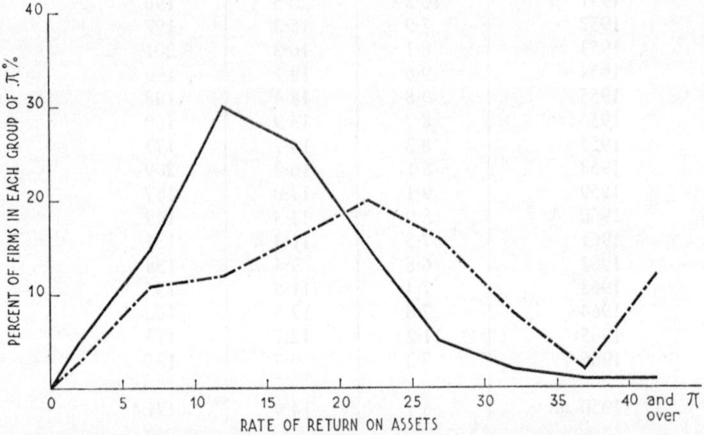

Fig. 7. Frequency Polygon of Gross Rate of Return on Assets (Π) for Firms in all Industries 1958/60. Average 1958/60.

extent that the data are not biased in the direction of this conclusion. We may distinguish the following possible sources of bias:

1. *Accounting conventions*

If accounting conventions differed systematically between the two groups of firms this might have the result of overstating (or understating) the relative profitability of US firms. Since US firms are essentially subsidiaries (in effect branches) of parent US enterprises it is possible that US tax laws might encourage US firms to 'shift' profits to their UK subsidiaries by charging, for example, low prices for products or services purchased from the US parent (Shulman, 1966).

2. *Concealed subsidies*

Undercharging for products or services purchased from the US parent provides a concealed subsidy. A particular form of this is the access which US subsidiaries have to the benefits of research, development, design and, in some cases, marketing expenditures undertaken by the US parent. In so far as this access is not charged as a cost at the appropriate rate, US subsidiaries operating in the UK will enjoy higher profits than they otherwise would. Accordingly they will appear to be more efficient than they in fact are. It is indeed entirely possible that an 'appropriate' (which is difficult both to define and measure) adjustment for these elements would reduce the profitability of US firms below that of their British counterparts.

3. *The industrial choice*

The data for UK firms used in our comparisons refer to the largest British public companies. The industrial distribution of these is not the same as the industrial distribution of the US firms replying to the Southampton enquiry. Since this is so it is obviously possible that the aggregate figures (all firms) of relative profits might be influenced by a relatively greater concentration of US firms in the higher-profit industries. This objection does not, of course, apply to the comparisons for industrial sub-groups provided the product mix for firms in these sub-groups is comparable and provided profitability is not correlated with variations in the product mix within any sub-group.

Accounting conventions

The evidence available from the Southampton enquiry suggests that US firms operating in the UK follow British accounting practices as regards such items as depreciation. There is thus, on this count, little reason to suspect overstatement of profits. By the same token, since Britain is a high-tax country, there is small advantage in shifting profits to the UK by undercharging. Finally, of the purchases made by US firms operating in the UK it seems that only about 5 per cent come from the US and not all of this was purchased from US parent companies. Hence the scope, as well as the incentive, for profit shifting by undercharging was, in general, rather small. There seems therefore, little reason to expect the profit figure to be significantly distorted by accounting practices.

The basis of our comparison is, however, the rate of profit per unit of capital measured at book values. Clearly book values may reflect replacement costs differentially between the two groups. This possibility cannot be excluded. However, US firms have, in recent years, expanded at a much faster rate than British industry as a whole. As a consequence, it seems likely that the book values of their assets correspond more closely to current replacement values than those of their UK counterparts. If this is correct, accounting distortions seem likely to decrease rather than increase the apparent relative advantage of US firms so that an appropriate adjustment, if it could be made, would increase the apparent relatively greater efficiency of US firms.

Concealed subsidies

In this field there is certainly a bias in favour of US firms, particularly those in the pharmaceutical, electronic and industrial instrument industries. In the first of these cases the extent of the bias has been estimated to be very considerable, amounting to about half of the recorded rate of profit on capital.[1] Unfortunately, *it is not possible* to give any worthwhile estimate of the extent of the general bias. It is therefore not possible to adjust the profit figures for US firms appropriately. It is, perhaps, worth recording that, though US firms certainly enjoy a measure of subsidy from the research and development expenditure of their US parents, their own research expenditure in the UK generally exceeds, as a percentage of value added, the average of British firms in the same industry. Hence, though the concealed research subsidy undoubtedly tends to raise the apparent profitability (and hence efficiency) of US firms, it does not seem to inhibit research by US firms operating in the UK.

Industrial choice

A test of the influence of the differing industrial distribution of US and UK firms on the profit comparisons can in principle be carried out as follows.

Let:

$\Pi_{US} \equiv$ recorded rate of profit for US firms;

$\Pi_{UK} \equiv$ recorded rate of profit for UK firms;

$\Pi_{US}^* \equiv$ calculated rate of profit which would have been recorded by US firms if their industrial distribution of sales had been that of UK firms.

[1] Committee of Public Accounts (1959/60).

Then:

$$\begin{aligned}\Pi_{US} - \Pi_{UK} &\equiv \text{apparent profit advantage}\\ &\equiv (\Pi_{US} - \Pi_{US}^*) + (\Pi_{US}^* - \Pi_{UK})\\ &\equiv \text{distribution effect} + \text{apparent efficiency effect.}\end{aligned}$$

Such evidence as we have suggests that, for US firms engaged in manufacturing, the distribution effect was *negative* for the years 1958 and 1961. Hence the measured profit advantage tends to *understate* rather than overstate the apparent efficiency advantage of US firms. In 1958 this understatement was very considerable: the profit advantage of US firms was 27 per cent, while the distribution effect was −15 per cent. In 1965 it was small. Compared with a profit advantage of 30·4 per cent, the distribution effect was −3 per cent in 1965 and only slightly positive for the year 1961.[1] It seems, however, not unreasonable to conclude that for the period covered by the Southampton enquiry, the apparent profit advantage is probably understated.

It appears then that the profit rate comparisons of the previous section are likely to involve:

(i) understatement of the relative US advantages on two counts;
(ii) overstatement on one count.

Where the balance lies must be a matter of 'guesswork' or 'judgement' since no quantitative calculation is possible. For what it is worth we believe that the apparent profit advantage of US firms is not overstated – except in the pharmaceutical industry. It is, indeed, more likely that the reverse is true.

Performance ratios of US and UK firms

The index of efficiency employed in this paper is essentially static. Though, as we know, a dynamic index of efficiency change can be derived from it, the data available do not permit us to make comparisons of the rate of change of efficiency achieved by US and UK firms. Indeed, even if the response of British firms to the questionnaire had been more acceptable, the time span covered by the enquiry (1958/61) would have been rather too short, and probably too strongly influenced by the cycle, to permit worthwhile comparisons to be made. However, if the arguments of this paper are accepted,

[1] Dunning (1966).

TABLE 14

Classification of Performance

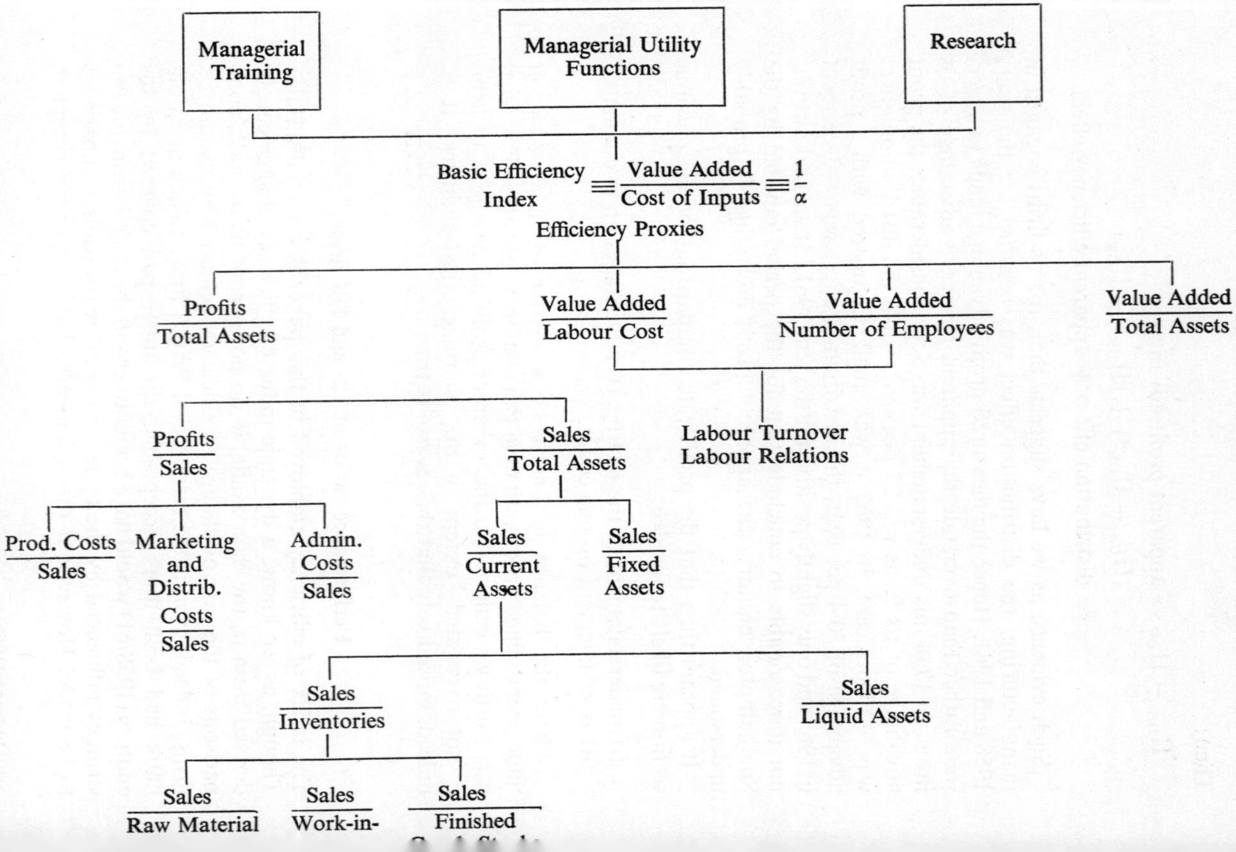

it seems that US firms' static efficiency is greater than that of UK firms. This inevitably raises the question as to how far the (apparent) lesser efficiency of UK firms is to be explained by avoidable managerial shortcoming.

Before considering this difficult and controversial issue let us make a short digression to explain the approach to the analysis of differences in efficiency which we had hoped to follow at the start of the Southampton enquiry. In planning our questionnaire, we aimed to obtain data which would make it possible to compare not only the efficiency index $\frac{1}{\alpha}$ for US and UK firms, but also certain *secondary* and *tertiary* ratios which, for US and UK firms operating in the same industry over the same period of time, would have permitted a potentially useful classification of comparative performance. To exemplify, the aim of the questionnaire was to obtain data which would make it possible, for each firm participating in the enquiry, to construct the following schematic classification of performance.

As it happened, we obtained the necessary data to make such detailed comparisons from only seventeen 'pairs' of UK and US firms — hardly a sufficient number on which to make any generalizations about comparative Anglo-American performance. An analysis of the secondary and tertiary ratios of these groups of firms has been presented elsewhere,[1] so we will do no more than summarize our conclusions in this paper.

The main reason why US firms record a higher rate of return on their capital than their UK competitors is that they are able to earn a higher profit/sales (P/S) ratio rather than to achieve a speedier turnover of capital (S/C).[2] In turn these secondary ratios are influenced by a variety of tertiary ratios, the most important of which are:

(i) a higher labour/productivity and/or a more intensive capital/labour ratio;

(ii) a lower administrative cost to sales and/or a more intensive marketing and distribution to other departmental costs ratio. There is no reason to think that US firms record a lower manufacturing costs to sales ratio than UK firms.

(iii) a broadly comparable sales/fixed assets ratio but a lower sales/liquid assets ratio.

[1] Dunning (1966).

[2] In the period 1957/63 the P/S ratio for US manufacturing firms averaged 5·8 per cent and for UK manufacturing establishments 3·6 per cent.

It would, of course, be relatively easy to move farther down the 'pyramid' of ratios and narrow down the differences more specifically. For example, a low output to labour input (O/wL) may be due, *inter alia*, to high labour turnover or poor labour relations. Productivity (α) might be high because of a greater utilization and more efficient application of skill and knowledge, as might be assessed by the proportion of research and development costs to total costs or the proportion of senior executives possessing University degrees or equivalent formal training. To test some of these propositions and also the extent to which profitability of US-financed firms is related to the degree of influence exerted on techniques and decision-taking by the American parent or associated company, we draw once again on the data of the large sample of US firms, and the information supplied by their UK competitors.

First, we look at the extent to which variations in labour productivity (Op/wL) seem to be related to (*a*) the rate of labour turnover, and (*b*) the quality of labour relations. The results are given in Table 15, the assessment of relations being those given by the firms in question. Here, there is no direct evidence that low labour turnover

TABLE 15

Labour Productivity of Sample of UK and US Firms by (1) Rate of Labour Turnover, (2) Quality of Labour Relations, 1961

	Number of Firms in Sample	$\frac{Op}{wL} \times 100$
(1) *Annual rate of labour turnover*		
under 5 per cent	11	173
5–15 per cent	18	172
15–25 per cent	11	195
25–40 per cent	14	189
over 40 per cent	11	145
(2) *Quality of labour relations**		
Good	52	181
Not good	25	148

Source: *Southampton Enquiry*.

* Presumed to be good in all cases except where (*a*) firms considered their labour relations average rather than good (none considered them bad); (*b*) some days had been lost in disputes.

is associated with high productivity, though there is a suggestion that the quality of labour relations may be an important variable.

Second, there is some reason to suppose that profitability is linked with the amount of research undertaken. This relationship is portrayed in Table 16, which also reveals quite decisively that US and UK firms in which executives possess degrees or equivalent formal qualifications, earn considerably higher profits than those who do not. It is noteworthy too that, while this relationship is broadly the same for both the US and UK firms in the sample, a much higher percentage of executives in US firms possessed University degrees or equivalent formal qualifications.

TABLE 16

Profitability of Selected US and UK Firms by (1) Expenditure on Research, (2) Qualifications of Executives, 1961

	Number of Firms in Sample	*Average P/TA*
(1) *Percentage of research costs to manufacturing costs*		
under 1	22	10·6
1–5	32	18·6
5–10	10	20·3
over 10	12	21·2
(2) *Proportion of executives having university degrees or equivalent formal qualifications*		
0–24 per cent	26	13·5
24–49 per cent	31	17·9
50–74 per cent	29	19·5
75 per cent and over	18	23·8

Source: *Southampton Enquiry.*

Finally, we turn to test the hypothesis that the profitability of American-financed firms in the UK is directly related to the degree of US influence on decision-taking and control. We have sought to assess such influence by relating the *P/TA* ratio of these firms to five main indexes of 'Americanization'.

(i) the proportion of their equity capital owned by their American parent or associate companies.

(ii) the proportion of their non-US executives who at any time have received training in the US.

(iii) the nationality of their Managing Director and Board of Directors;

(iv) the extent to which their overall and departmental management techniques are strongly or negligibly based on current US practice, and

(v) the extent to which control over their decision-taking lies in the hands of the US parent or associate company.

TABLE 17

Profitability of US Firms by (1) Ownership Pattern, (2) Proportion of Executives having Received Training in US, 1961

	Number of Firms in Sample	*Average P/TA*
(1) *Percentage of equity held by US company*		
100	76	19·5
51–99	12	16·0
50 and under	10	16·5
(2) *Proportion of executives having received training in US*		
Nil	44	23·2
under 25 per cent	20	15·5
25 per cent and over	25	15·2

Source: *Southampton Enquiry.*

If it is true, as is commonly suggested, that the superior quality of US management is one of the main factors responsible for the high rates of return earned by American firms in British industry, one might reasonably expect those subsidiaries which are closely controlled in decision-taking or decisively influencing in techniques by their US associates to earn higher profits than subsidiaries autonomous of American control or expertise.

The results of these relationships are presented in Table 17, 18 and 19. Though not completely conclusive either way, they do reveal a number of interesting features. First, on average, wholly owned US subsidiaries record higher profits than jointly financed companies, and US firms with American managing directors seem to do considerably better than those with UK managing directors.

Second, there is no evidence that firms who send their executives for training in the US earn higher profits than those who do not: if anything the reverse seems to be true. Neither is a substantial US representation on the UK firms' Board of Directors associated with profitability. Third, the importance of a close relationship with the US parent or associate company seems to be shown far more in the techniques of management utilized than in the control exercised

TABLE 18

Profitability of US Firms in UK by Nationality of Managing Director and the Board of Directors, 1961

	Number of Firms	*Average P/TA*
Nationality of managing director		
UK	78	16·5
US	21	26·4
Composition of board of directors		
One half or more US	38	17·5
More than one half UK	56	19·8

Source: *Southampton Enquiry.*

over the actual decision taken. US subsidiaries whose methods are negligibly influenced – apart (rather surprisingly) from marketing policy. Fourth, it is clear that the optimum degree of American control both over method and decision-taking varies according to department. In certain directions, e.g. marketing policy, a modified application of US principles and methods yields the best results. In others, e.g. budgetary control, and, to a lesser extent, product innovation and development, a strong reliance on US techniques and policies appears desirable: by contrast, in the fields of capital expenditure and industrial relations, firms which claim the greater local autonomy also record the higher profits.

Static efficiency and managerial efficiency

The ratios just described – or any others of a similar kind – do not, and by their nature, cannot tell us *why* differences in efficiency between firms exist, still less how far such differences reflect *avoidable*

TABLE 19

Profitability of US Firms in UK by Control Exercised by Parent Company

Managerial Function	*Number of Firms*	*Average P/TA*	*Number of Firms*	*Average P/TA*	*Number of Firms*	*Average P/TA*
			Degree of Influence by US			
	Decisive		*Moderate*		*Negligible*	
					%	
Overall managerial policy	29	19·8	52	18·4	17	19·0
			Methods Influenced by US			
	Strongly		*Moderately*		*Negligibly*	
Capital expenditure	31	19·1	42	18·2	25	19·1
Product innovation and development	37	22·2	40	16·2	21	17·8
Production planning	8	23·7	31	15·7	59	19·8
Research expenditure	23	23·3	44	16·8	31	18·3
Budgetary control	31	21·8	27	14·5	40	19·4
Marketing policy	16	13·8	38	22·4	44	17·6
Wage and labour policy	4	23·6	19	18·2	75	18·7
			Decisions Influenced by US			
	Strongly		*Moderately*		*Negligibly*	
Capital expenditure	50	18·6	38	17·3	10	24·3
Product innovation and development	42	19·4	43	17·9	13	19·7
Production planning	8	19·4	27	17·5	63	19·3
Research expenditure	27	21·9	44	14·4	27	22·9
Budgetary control	25	21·6	21	16·7	42	18·7
Marketing policy	17	14·2	40	22·2	41	17·3
Wage and labour policy	3	16·7	20	17·0	75	19·4

Source: *Southampton Enquiry*. Average return on capital 18·8 per cent.

Definitions:

(*a*) *Regarding influence on overall managerial policy:*
Decisive: the final decision usually rests with the US parent.
Negligible: the final decision is usually independent of any views expressed by the US parent.

(*b*) *Regarding managerial methods:*
Strongly: implies that the company's techniques are virtually identical with those of its US parent and have been adapted from it.
Negligibly: implies that the company's techniques have been developed almost entirely independently of the practices of the US parent.

(*c*) *Regarding managerial decisions:*
Strongly: decisions **dominated** by the views of the US parent.
Negligibly: decisions **unaffected** by the views of the US parent.

Where none of these is applicable the appropriate classification is **moderately**.

managerial shortcomings. Their function is simply to show in a fairly systematic manner in which area of a firm's operations its performance differs from that of other firms.[1]

If one tries to trace the *reasons* for the superior profitability of US firms, the most common explanation advanced is that such firms have access to more, and sometimes better, research and managerial and marketing methods than are available to their UK competitors. This, so it is argued, gives them an unavoidable managerial advantage, or alternatively puts the UK firms at an unavoidable managerial disadvantage. What are the formal implications of this statement?

Consider the problem of comparing two firms, one US and one British, where both belong to the same industrial group and have an identical product mix. Assume that $\frac{1}{\alpha}$ of the US firm is higher than that of the UK firm. The problem is to say how much of its relative inefficiency is attributable to 'avoidable managerial shortcomings'. The simplest approach is to argue that the UK firm could have made use of the production function of the US firm (that is that the same technical opportunities were open to it) and also could have used the same techniques for maximizing the same objective function. On these assumptions the UK firm could have been at the position shown for the US firm. Since it was not, this could only have been because of the avoidable ignorance, sloth or perversity of its management. This is substantially the approach of elementary economic theory. There is assumed to be a production function for the industry which defines, for a given range of relative input prices, 'best practice' technique. This production function is generally available. Firms that are not on the optimal profit maximizing point (as the hypothetical US firm may be assumed to be) simply exhibit avoidable technical and allocative inefficiency. In the long run they either mend their ways or cease operations. In short a dynamic adjustment process operating through competition *eventually* ensures an equilibrium in which all firms arrive at the US position and all firms earn the normal rate of profit (= opportunity cost of capital *plus* the risk premium attributable to the industry).

However, the long run may be very long indeed – certainly far too long for an analysis of this kind to have any diagnostic value or policy implications. For in practice the production function of the US firm may *not* be generally available either because:

[1] For a discussion of the limitations of ratio analysis see Dunning (1969(b)).

(i) the technical knowledge it embodies is not generally accessible, or
(ii) because the extent to which the UK firm can reconstruct its operations is constrained by the period of time allowed for the reconstruction process itself.

There is, unfortunately, even if the reconstruction period is arbitrarily defined, no way of giving clear-cut meaning to the alternative positions open to any given management without detailed knowledge of the situation existing in each firm. It is thus impossible to give any precise quantitative assessment of the extent to which (apparent) differences in efficiency are due to avoidable managerial shortcomings. On the other hand it is arguable that the classificatory scheme illustrated in Table 14 may, on rather weak assumptions, suggest areas in which avoidable managerial shortcomings exist. For example if US arms showed, on average, relatively high sales/inventory ratios it might be argued that, simply because of the nature of inventory, adjustment to this ratio (in whole or in part) by British competitors could be accomplished fairly quickly. In short, a general tendency for UK firms to record significantly higher inventory/sales ratios might be regarded as qualitative evidence of an 'avoidable managerial shortcoming'.

The implication of this discussion is clear. 'Avoidable managerial shortcomings' can be defined only with reference to the alternative positions open to management. Since the range of alternative positions is a function of the length of the reconstruction (or adjustment) period, the problem of assigning a meaning to them is explicitly dynamic. It is thus hardly surprising – though at first sight possibly disappointing – that the essentially static approach of the paper can provide only very limited and qualitative suggestions concerning it.

Suppose, however, we had sufficient data to permit us to construct, for each firm, an index of dynamic efficiency:

$$\alpha'_{ij(t)} = \frac{\dfrac{1}{\alpha_{ij(t)}}}{\dfrac{1}{\alpha_{ij(t-1)}}} \times 100$$

This would provide a measure of the rate at which, in any period, the social efficiency of the firm was changing.[1]

Using α' it would be possible to compare the dynamic performance

[1] The idea of α' and other measures of changes in productivity and efficiency is worked out more fully in J. H. Dunning and M. Utton (1967).

of US and UK firms. On the not very strong assumption that the significant range of choice confronting a management within any period was the same for other firms in the same industry, it would then be possible to compare the managerial efficiency of UK and US firms at the margin of managerial decision.

This information would not, of course, enable us to say how far managerial shortcomings (as revealed by the static approach) were avoidable: it would, however, enable us to say how far existing differences in efficiency were being increased or diminished by managerial decisions at the margin. This is, of itself, useful information since the fact that the gap between the ratio of profit of US and UK firms has recently been diminishing in the UK (and indeed, in Australia also) suggests that investigation along these lines might show that α' for UK firms was greater than that for US firms.

The dynamic index would permit us to make crude tests of other hypotheses. For individual industries, we might expect the rate of change of efficiency of UK firms to be a function of the gap between their efficiency and that of US firms in the same industry. This could fairly readily be noted. We could also test how far the rate of change in the efficiency in UK firms in a particular industry depends upon the presence of US competitors – an hypothesis of some interest since it is commonly argued that one result of extensive US investment in a country is to improve the efficiency of domestic producers through competition.

At this stage, since data which would enable us to measure α' are not available, it is not worth while to elaborate the tests which could be based upon it. It seems clear, however, that in order to form any worthwhile judgement upon such matters as:

(*a*) how far relative managerial shortcomings are being reduced (and are therefore avoidable);
(*b*) how far UK firms exhibit managerial efficiency at the margin as great or greater than their US competitors, and
(*c*) how far the presence of US firms in an industry stimulates technical advance,

an index of the form of α' is required.

Our suggestion, therefore, is that further research should be directed towards obtaining data which could be analysed in terms of the classificatory scheme of Table 14 and the index α_{ij}. The main contribution of our static approach is probably to show that the *prima facie* evidence of differing efficiency is sufficiently strong to point to the need for such research.

REFERENCES

W. L. Baldwin. 'The motives of managers' environmental constraints and the theory of managerial enterprise,' *Quarterly Journal of Economics*, Vol. LXXVIII, May 1964.

Board of Trade. 'Various articles on direct overseas investment of UK companies,' published in the *Board of Trade Journal*. See particularly issues of November 14, 1962, August 7, 1964, and January 26, 1968.

K. J. Cohen and R. M. Cyert. *Theory of the Firm. Resource Allocation in a Market Economy*, Prentice Hall, 1965.

Committee for Public Accounts. 'First and Second Reports,' Session 1959/60, p. 217.

R. M. Cyert and J. G. March. *A Behavioral Theory of the Firm*, Prentice Hall, 1963.

J. H. Dunning (1966). 'US subsidiaries in Britain and their UK competitors,' *Business Ratios*, Autumn 1966.

J. H. Dunning and M. Utton. 'Measuring changes in UK industrial productivity and efficiency, 1954/63,' *Business Ratios*, Summer 1967.

J. H. Dunning and M. J. Barron. 'A productivity measure of business performance,' *Business Ratios*, Autumn 1967.

J. H. Dunning (1969(a)). *American Investment in the British Economy*, P.E.P. Broadsheet No. 507, February 1969.

J. H. Dunning (1969(b)). 'Profitability, productivity and other measures of business performance,' *Investment Analyst*, No. 23, June 1969.

M. J. Farrell. 'The measurement of productive efficiency,' *Journal of the Royal Statistical Society*, Series A, Vol. 112, Part III, 1957.

G. R. Fisher. 'Some factors influencing share prices,' *Economic Journal*, Vol. LXXI, March 1961.

M. Howe. 'Variations on the full cost theme,' *Manchester School of Economic and Social Studies*, Vol. 32, January 1964.

R. Marris. *The Theory of Managerial Capitalism*, Macmillan, 1964.

Ministry of Labour. *Statistics on Incomes, Prices, Employment and Production*, April 1962 and March 1966.

F. Modigliani and M. H. Miller. 'The cost of capital, corporation finance and the theory of investment,' *American Economic Review*, Vol. XLVIII, June 1958.

W. B. Reddaway and A. D. Smith. 'Progress in British manufacturing industries in the period 1948/54,' *Economic Journal*, Vol. LXX, March 1960.

J. S. Shulman. *Transfer pricing in multi-national business*. Ph.D. thesis, Harvard University, 1966.

O. E. Williamson. *The Economics of Discretionary Behaviour: Managerial Objectives in the Theory of the Firm*, Prentice Hall, 1963.